THE COMPLETE IDIOT'S GUIDE® TO

Chess

Third Edition

by Patrick Wolff

ALPHA

A member of Penguin Group (USA) Inc.

ALPHA BOOKS

Published by the Penguin Group

Penguin Group (USA) Inc., 375 Hudson Street, New York, New York 10014, U.S.A.

Penguin Group (Canada), 10 Alcorn Avenue, Toronto, Ontario, Canada M4V 3B2 (a division of Pearson Penguin Canada Inc.)

Penguin Books Ltd, 80 Strand, London WC2R 0RL, England

Penguin Ireland, 25 St Stephen's Green, Dublin 2, Ireland (a division of Penguin Books Ltd)

Penguin Group (Australia), 250 Camberwell Road, Camberwell, Victoria 3124, Australia (a division of Pearson Australia Group Pty Ltd)

Penguin Books India Pvt Ltd, 11 Community Centre, Panchsheel Park, New Delhi—110 017, India

Penguin Group (NZ), cnr Airborne and Rosedale Roads, Albany, Auckland 1310, New Zealand (a division of Pearson New Zealand Ltd)

Penguin Books (South Africa) (Pty) Ltd, 24 Sturdee Avenue, Rosebank, Johannesburg 2196, South Africa

Penguin Books Ltd, Registered Offices: 80 Strand, London WC2R 0RL, England

International Standard Book Number: 1-59257-316-9
Library of Congress Catalog Card Number: 2005920503

07   06   8   7   6   5   4   3

Interpretation of the printing code: The rightmost number of the first series of numbers is the year of the book's printing; the rightmost number of the second series of numbers is the number of the book's printing. For example, a printing code of 05-1 shows that the first printing occurred in 2005.

Printed in the United States of America

Note: This publication contains the opinions and ideas of its author. It is intended to provide helpful and informative material on the subject matter covered. It is sold with the understanding that the author and publisher are not engaged in rendering professional services in the book. If the reader requires personal assistance or advice, a competent professional should be consulted.

The author and publisher specifically disclaim any responsibility for any liability, loss, or risk, personal or otherwise, which is incurred as a consequence, directly or indirectly, of the use and application of any of the contents of this book.

Most Alpha books are available at special quantity discounts for bulk purchases for sales promotions, premiums, fundraising, or educational use. Special books, or book excerpts, can also be created to fit specific needs.

For details, write: Special Markets, Alpha Books, 375 Hudson Street, New York, NY 10014.

Publisher: *Marie Butler-Knight*
Product Manager: *Phil Kitchel*
Senior Managing Editor: *Jennifer Bowles*
Senior Acquisitions Editor: *Paul Dinas*
Development Editor: *Ginny Bess Munroe*
Senior Production Editor: *Billy Fields*

Copy Editor: *Michael Dietsch*
Cartoonist: *Shannon Wheeler*
Cover/Book Designer: *Trina Wurst*
Indexer: *Angie Bess*
Layout: *Becky Harmon*
Proofreading: *Mary Hunt*

Contents at a Glance

Contents

Foreword

Chess will challenge and reward you for a lifetime. Every chess player has felt the thrill of victory and the satisfaction of a game well played. Yet at the same time everyone—yes, even grandmasters—has felt like an idiot at the chess board. With this book you will be well equipped for the challenges of chess so you can reap its rewards.

I know how much joy chess can bring. I also know that to play and enjoy it to the fullest you need a guide. There is no better guide than Patrick Wolff. He won this nation's highest title twice, the first time at age 24. Now, more than a dozen years later, he writes about chess with the same skill as he plays it, imparting his wisdom to a new generation of players.

This book will guide you step by step along the path of chess mastery. Patrick starts from scratch by explaining the rules and how the pieces move. Then, chapter by chapter, he teaches you the basic tactics and strategies of good chess. Of all the lessons he teaches, the most important one is this: Think ahead!

Countless books have been written to help us lesser mortals learn this simple advice, but Patrick's is one of the best I have ever seen. He teaches you not just to look at what you threaten, but to look at what threatens you. In other words, don't drop your guard. Curb your desire to play the first move that pops into your head and always pay attention to what your opponent is doing before making a decision.

I also recommend it because unlike most primers, it is chock full of diagrams and visual aids. This means you can follow it even when you travel and don't have a chess set with you. In addition, Patrick set aside the last seven chapters to open up the entire world of chess that lies beyond the 64 squares. You will learn about the World Champions, how computers play chess (plus how to beat your computer!), how to find other people to play with online or in your local chess club, and much more.

I wish this book had been around when I first learned chess. I'm glad it's here for you.

Larry Evans is a five-time U.S. chess champion and nationally syndicated chess columnist. Often called the "Dean of Chess," he represented America on 8 Olympic teams and has written more than 20 books on chess. He served as Bobby Fischer's second and is an inductee into the Chess Hall of Fame.

Introduction

You've never played chess, but it seems fascinating, and you'd like to learn the rules. Or maybe you know how to play, but you've never understood how to tell whether a move was good or bad. Or maybe you've even picked up a few pointers somewhere, but you'd really like to be able to play a decent game. (Maybe there's even someone you'd like to beat!) In any case, you want some way to find out more about chess: how to find an opponent, how to read the chess column in your newspaper, where to get chess books and other chess materials, what organizations to join and how to contact them (maybe not just for you but also for your son or daughter), how computers play chess (and maybe how to beat your own computer!), and who are the chess superstars.

This is the book for you.

I've been playing in national and international chess competitions for almost 20 years. In that time, I've become one of the best chess players in the country and the world, including being the U.S. champion twice, in 1992 and 1995. So I have the expertise to explain it all to you.

But more important, I have years of experience teaching people of all levels how to play chess. I know lots of people think chess is for high-brows, but I also know that's nonsense. Chess is an incredibly fun game. It offers a lifetime of excitement, beauty, and challenge to anyone who takes it up. Sure chess exercises your brain: That's what makes it so great! But it's absolutely not just for intellectuals. Anyone can learn chess and learn to play it well, and just about everyone who does so loves it forever after. I bet you'll love chess, too.

I wrote the first edition of this book more than four years ago to provide people with a guide to learning and playing chess. Since then, I've been gratified by the wonderful feedback I received. I wanted to write this third edition to see whether I could take the best suggestions I received during that time and make this book even better. I hope you'll find it a fun and helpful introduction to the best game in the world.

How to Use This Book

I've divided this book into four parts. Each part is self-contained, so you can jump around at your convenience. However, I think you'll get more out of Parts 1–3 if you read them from beginning to end in order. Part 4 is more for reference and amusement, so you can skip around there as much as you like.

Part 1, "Let's Play Chess," gets you started. Chapter 1 gives you some background, and it's mostly for fun, while Chapters 2 and 3 teach you the rules, and how to read and write chess moves. If you've never played chess before, start here! Even if you have played chess, you might want to check these chapters out to make sure you've got everything straight. In particular, the rest of the book uses chess notation, so if you're not sure how to read and write chess moves, make sure you read Chapters 2 and 3! Chapter 4 teaches you how to checkmate a lone king with just a queen or a rook and a king. Not only is it good to know how to do this just for itself, learning how to do this is an excellent way to learn other things, such as the power of the queen and the rook, and how to make plans in chess. Even if you have some experience playing chess, I strongly advise you to read through Chapter 4.

Part 2, "Tactics," teaches you the importance of capturing your opponent's pieces while holding onto your own, explains how to do so, and shows you some very important and typical ways to use your chess army to capture your opponent's forces. The last chapter in Part 2 then shifts the focus from capturing the rest of your opponent's army to capturing his king. (You do know that the aim of chess is to capture the king, right? If not, make sure you read Chapter 2 in Part 1!)

Part 3, "Strategy," gets into some subtler stuff than Part 2. You have to learn how to strengthen your position even when there's no move that will capture one of your opponent's pieces, or menace your opponent's king. This part explains how to tell which moves are good or bad, and why. By the time you've finished reading this part, you'll be able to choose the right strategies to set up the winning tactics. Your opponent won't know what hit him!

Part 4, "Beyond the Basics," takes you far into all corners of the world of chess. If there's anything you want to find out about chess that doesn't have to do with learning the rules, learning how to read and write chess moves, or learning the basic tactics and strategies, this is the section to read.

Diagrams

A diagram is a picture of a chess position. A lot of this book, especially Parts 1–3, require you to follow the progress of a chess game as each player makes moves. This presents a dilemma. Even experienced chess players find it difficult to do this without setting up the position on a chess set, and I'm sure you would, too. But that means you would have to have a chess set with you whenever you wanted to read this book, and that would be extremely inconvenient, which is certainly something I want to avoid.

The solution: diagrams, and lots of them. In the first half of the book you'll find that every single position and almost every single move from each position gets a separate diagram. As the book progresses, I've assumed that you're becoming more comfortable with following one or two moves from a chess position, but you'll still see lots and lots of diagrams. My goal has been to make it easy for you to read this book anywhere you want, and not to force you to have a chess set with you to do so. I still recommend that you have a chess set handy for when you want to look at certain positions or moves carefully, but for the most part you can read this book without a chess set if you want.

Exercises

When you learn to play chess well, you're learning a skill. And as with any skill, you can't learn it without practice. Therefore, at the end of Chapters 2–14 I've included a number of exercises. I strongly recommend that you do each set of exercises after reading each chapter.

The exercises vary in difficulty. Some are relatively easy, and some are quite hard. Don't expect to be able to answer all of the exercises perfectly. I have constructed the exercises so that some of them reinforce what you've already learned, while some of them take you beyond what was covered in the chapter. Try your best to do the exercises, and then compare your work with the answers in the back of the book. (You may want to try to do them just from looking at the accompanying diagram, or you may want to set the position up on a chess set and move the pieces as you think. Either way you do the exercises is fine.) The purpose of the exercises is *not* to test yourself. Rather, the purpose is to help you learn the material even better. Although the harder exercises will force you to work more, I think you'll find them especially instructive and rewarding.

Website: www.wolffchess.com

I have also created a website specifically designed to complement this book and improve your chess even further. I explain more about this website in Chapters 15 and 18. Also, the website itself explains how to use it for your maximum benefit.

The website address is www.wolffchess.com.

If you have never played chess before, or if you have trouble remembering how to play, don't go to the website yet. Read the book first. The website is designed for someone who feels comfortable with the material in Chapters 2–14. So if that material is totally new to you, you should finish those chapters first.

After you finish those chapters, or if as you read them you feel comfortable with them, the website will enable you to practice and refine your chess game so you can take it to the next level. As much as I love books (you should see how many chess books I have in my home!), I think the computer has a lot of unique advantages for learning chess. My hope is that the website can be at least as valuable and convenient as any book (except this one, of course!) could be for improving your chess game.

Extras

To make the learning experience as easy and fun as possible, I've highlighted lots of tips and facts along the way. Look for the following elements in the book to guide you along.

Chess Lore

I needed some way to tell you all sorts of interesting things about chess. This is the box for it. You might find anything here, but whatever you find, I hope you'll enjoy it.

Chess Talk

Chess has lots of funny words and phrases. This box tells you what they mean so you won't get confused.

Blunders

This box tells you what not to do. After all, one of the best ways to learn how to play better is to learn what to avoid.

Patrick's Pointers

This box gives you advice for how to play better chess. Here I've boiled it down to the essentials!

Special Note to the Reader

In later chapters of this book, I will be using positions from real games between grandmasters. Chess players have a standard way of referring to those games. For example, if Smith played White against Jones playing Black, in Walla Walla, Washington, in 1997, that game would be referred to by writing "Smith–Jones, Walla Walla, WA, 1997."

Acknowledgments

Experience with the first edition of this book taught me that writing a book is a collaborative effort. Writing this third edition has driven that lesson home. One person may be the author, but many people make such a project possible, and make it (hopefully) a success. I owe many people thanks for their involvement with this book.

Thanks to Allen Kaufman, executive director of Chess-in-the-Schools, for suggesting that I would be a good person to write the first edition of this book. I hope he continues to believe his judgment was correct with this third edition.

Thanks to my editors at Alpha Books: Paul Dinas, Ginny Bess, Billy Fields, and Michael Dietsch. You've all been wonderful. Many thanks also to Macon Shibut, who did a wonderful job reviewing the manuscript for this third edition and who contributed much new material to Part 4, especially regarding Chapter 21.

Many people helped out by finding the odd fact, by making suggestions, or by providing materials. They are too numerous to mention, but I owe each of them many thanks. One person who stands out among them is Hanon Russell, who provided most of the photographs for the first edition of this book from his truly impressive private collection of chess materials, and who helped me add some additional photos for this third edition. Thank you for opening up your library to me!

Many thanks to the people who have helped me in the earlier editions. Christopher Chabris, my friend and colleague, helped me enormously in writing the first edition of this book through his editing, research, and writing contributions. Frisco Del Rosario did a wonderful job reviewing the manuscript for the second edition and made many helpful suggestions along the way.

Most of all, thanks to my wife, Diana Schneider. I have so much to thank you for, and I intend to spend the rest of my life doing so. You bring me joy every day and I hope I do the same for you.

Illustration credits:

p. 5 Photograph by Jerome Bibuld, Courtesy of the Russell Collection.

p. 17 House of Staunton, Courtesy of the Russell Collection.

p. 288 Courtesy of the Russell Collection.

p. 293 Courtesy of the Russell Collection.

p. 296 Courtesy of the Russell Collection.

p. 299 Courtesy of the Russell Collection.

p. 300 Courtesy of the Russell Collection.

p. 305 Courtesy of New In Chess.

p. 307 Courtesy of New In Chess.

p. 333 Mindscape.

Special Thanks to the Technical Reviewer

The Complete Idiot's Guide to Chess, Third Edition, was reviewed by an expert who double-checked the accuracy of what you'll learn here, to help us ensure that this book gives you everything you need to know about chess. Special thanks are extended to Macon Shibut.

Trademarks

All terms mentioned in this book that are known to be or are suspected of being trademarks or service marks have been appropriately capitalized. Alpha Books and Penguin Group (USA) Inc. cannot attest to the accuracy of this information. Use of a term in this book should not be regarded as affecting the validity of any trademark or service mark.

Part 1

Let's Play Chess

If you've never played chess before, this part gets you started. First you get a little history, and find out what makes chess such a wonderful game. Next you learn the rules for playing chess, as well as reading and writing chess moves. Finally, I show you how to give checkmate with just the queen or the rook (with the help of your king).

Some people think it must be hard to learn the rules, and feel intimidated. I promise you that with a little patience, you'll find it's easy to learn. By the end of this part, you'll even start learning the skills you need to win!

Why Play Chess?

In This Chapter

- Chess: easy to learn and a lifetime of fun
- The history of chess
- The popularity of chess today

Many people feel intimidated by chess. People often think that chess is just for intellectuals, or that chess is too hard to learn unless you can do calculus in your head. And if you have to be so smart to play chess, how could it be much fun?

But chess is some of the most fun there is! And get that idea out of your head that you have to be some kind of genius to learn how to play chess. Could millions of people in the United States alone play and *enjoy* chess if they had to be some kind of genius to learn it? The truth is, hundreds of millions of people around the world play chess, and more people are learning the game every day, because chess is the most fascinating, most exciting, and most enjoyable game in the world!

But tons of people are still intimidated by chess. Many people find chess intriguing, but they don't think that they could learn it. And you know, I totally understand why people think that. I mean, look at the chess column in your newspaper (if it has one); see those weird-looking symbols, letters, and numbers that don't make any sense? Who wouldn't be intimidated? Or maybe you know an eight-year-old who plays chess, and you think to yourself, "I'm not going to be shown up by someone who's still in the second grade!"

Well, if you think chess is kind of interesting, but also maybe a bit intimidating, this book is written for you. I teach you the rules, show you how to play, and even tell you how you can find an opponent to play with. And it's not going to hurt.

Are We Having Fun Yet?

I remember how it feels not to understand the basics. I'll take you through them slowly and explain everything step by step. Because I really understand the ins and outs of chess, I can teach you quite a lot without getting you confused. Before you even finish, I bet you'll find you can beat that eight-year-old! (And I even have a special chapter on how to beat your computer, in case that's been giving you a headache.)

But just as important, I want to make sure you enjoy learning chess as much as I know you'll enjoy playing it. After all, chess is a game. What's the point of playing a game if you don't enjoy it?

Part of the reason I'm so sure you'll enjoy chess is that I know from my own experience how wonderful a game it is. After all …

- Chess is easy to play anywhere. For just a few dollars, you can buy a set that fits in your pocket. Or you can play against one of the many computer programs on the market. Or you can even find an opponent on the Internet and get a game literally 24 hours a day!

- Chess is the fairest game I know. No dice spoil good play by a bad roll; no umpire robs one side of a deserved victory. All that matters is how well you play.

- No matter how big or small you are, no matter how old or young you are, you can learn to play as well as anyone.

- The rules of chess are easy to learn. Trust me: once you read the next few chapters, you'll have the rules down cold.

- Once you learn the rules, there's always more strategy to learn to play better; you can never be bored by chess. Every game has the potential for the tension of battle, the beauty of new ideas, and the excitement of conquest!

People have been enjoying chess for more than 1,000 years, and chess has never been more popular than it is today. Let me tell you some more about the amazing history of chess, and then I'll tell you how popular it is today.

Once the Game of Kings ...

Chess is so old that nobody knows for sure when or where it began. People have been playing games with pieces on some kind of board for thousands of years, and the earliest version that has definitely been linked to chess is a game called *chaturanga*, played in India almost 1,400 years ago. Yet there is controversy about whether this really is the oldest version of chess: Artifacts that seem to be chess pieces have been excavated in Italy, and some people claim they should be dated at the second century C.E. Because it's so hard to draw definite conclusions from such scanty evidence, we may never know for sure where chess really came from.

Chaturanga moved east before it came to the West. Buddhists who traveled to spread their religion brought the game with them to China, Korea, and Japan. And in fact, both China and Japan have their own versions of chess (called Chinese chess and *shogi*). But very little else is known about the eastward movement of chaturanga.

We know much more about the journey of chaturanga through the West. It reached Persia, where it was called *chatrang*. When Persia was conquered by Arabs in the middle of the seventh century, the game was again renamed, this time to *shatranj*. And this is the game that was brought to Western Europe in the eighth and ninth centuries by the early invasions of Spain and Sicily. The following figure shows an example of an ancient chess piece.

An ancient chess piece, discovered in 1831.

By about the year 1000, shatranj was widely known throughout Europe. It was popular among religious orders, in the courts of kings, and among some soldiers. But although this was definitely the ancestor of chess, it was not the same game! Shatranj was probably played on the same board, but some of the pieces were different, and some of the rules that governed the same pieces in both shatranj and modern-day chess were different.

Sometime in the late fifteenth century, the game was radically changed. Before, there had not been a queen; now it was added. Also, the bishop replaced another piece. And some of the rules were changed to make the game more exciting. In particular, the lowly pawn was allowed to promote to any piece it wanted when it reached the other side of the board. (You will learn about these rules and more in Chapters 2 and 3.) And the game was renamed, so that it was called *chess*.

Chess must have been a huge improvement on shatranj, because it spread like wildfire throughout Europe, replacing the old game completely. Suddenly, the game was played by more people: Some masters even started writing and selling books on how to play chess well (see the following illustration). (But no *Complete Idiot's Guide*, to the best of my knowledge!) There was even a period of time during the seventeenth century in Italy when the leading chess players were sponsored by royal patrons! (Ah, that was the time to be a grandmaster!)

Chess Lore

The word "grandmaster" refers to the highest international title one can receive in chess. The word had been used throughout the nineteenth and early twentieth centuries to refer to a very strong player, but it wasn't until 1950 that the specific title was created. In order to earn the title, you must prove your abilities in tournaments against other grandmasters, but once you've earned the title, it can't be taken away. There are currently around 650 active (that is, who still regularly compete in chess tournaments) grandmasters in the world.

Unfortunately, the royal subsidies for chess died out. But the game was still very popular. During the eighteenth century, chess was played in popular coffeehouses throughout Europe. And a few professionals could make a living by playing against the regular patrons of whichever coffeehouse they inhabited. Eventually, this gave rise to clubs devoted to chess, which sprang up in the big European cities.

An illustration from Game and Playe of the Chesse, the first printed book on chess in Europe.

And they weren't just playing chess in Europe! Over here in America, people began to play chess more and more. For example, both Thomas Jefferson and Benjamin Franklin not only played chess, but even wrote about it. But whereas chess had once been the game of the aristocracy (why else would it have kings, queens, and knights?), by the start of the 1800s it was becoming more popular with ordinary folks like us, both in Europe and America.

Well, with all those people playing chess in coffeehouses, it was only a matter of time before actual chess tournaments were organized. One of the people who did the most to popularize chess in the middle of the 1800s was Howard Staunton, one of England's greatest chess players. Staunton advocated standards for laws, notation, and the timing of moves. Until then, there had been slightly different variants of chess played in different regions. No standard system had been worked out for recording the moves. And sometimes a game would have to be aborted because one player would take so long to move the other would fall asleep! So a time limit had to be imposed on how long you could think on a move. After Staunton standardized the rules, he organized the first international chess tournament in 1851, in which the best players from around the world competed. (Of course, the tournament was held in London, where Staunton lived.)

From that point on, chess blossomed into the most popular game in the world. Tournaments were held everywhere, adopting the standard rules. Newspapers started printing columns devoted to chess. One by one, countries organized national federations to coordinate chess activity. (You can learn how to contact the United States national federation—as well as other national federations—in Chapter 17 and Appendix A.) Matches between the strongest players were held to determine the world champion. Eventually, a federation to govern all the national federations and also to run the world championship title evolved, and exists to this day. The game that had started as chaturanga, a lowly pawn among games, had grown to become chess: king of all games!

Chess Lore

You probably have heard of Bobby Fischer, but few people know about the other great American chess genius, Paul Morphy (see his picture). This remarkable man was born in New Orleans in 1837. By the age of 20, he was recognized as clearly the strongest chess player in America. But the strongest chess players in the world all lived in Europe, so in 1858 Morphy voyaged overseas to challenge them.

What happened in those matches cannot be understood, it can only be admired. Morphy didn't just win, he crushed his opponents mercilessly! His victories showed that he was clearly the best player in the world. How did he become so good when all the major chess activity was still in Europe? Nobody can say. But for this feat, Morphy is recognized as the greatest natural chess talent in the history of chess.

Morphy returned to America in 1859 to find that he had become a national hero. Here was the first American to defeat the Europeans at one of their own games! But Morphy didn't want the life of a professional chess player. As it was, he had only been marking time until he could be admitted to the bar in Louisiana. (He had to wait until he was 21 years old.) So, after his extraordinary triumph, he retired from chess and returned to New Orleans.

Sadly, his law career was unsuccessful and his personal life was tragic. As he grew older, he suffered from delusions of persecution. He never married and was cared for by his sister and mother. Paul Morphy died soon after turning 51, but his brief chess career was so marvelous that he will be remembered always as one of the great geniuses of chess.

Paul Morphy.

Now the King of Games

Today, hundreds of millions of people play chess, making it the most popular game in the world. You can find players matching wits in parks, in schools, or simply across the kitchen table at home. Of course, there are also thousands of chess clubs. Formal tournaments allow for even more serious competition. (Later in this book, I'll tell you how you can find clubs and tournaments that are near where you live.)

The explosive growth of the Internet has opened vast, exciting new opportunities to enjoy the King of Games. Literally thousands of websites are devoted to chess. Go to a popular web portal like Yahoo! and you will find more people playing chess than almost any other game. There also are online chess clubs where you can find opponents 24 hours a day: players of every level strength, from all around the globe. And although a big part of the fun of chess is in the opportunity it gives you for meeting interesting people, in a pinch you don't even need a real live opponent. Millions of chess-playing computer programs are sold every year for the PC. You can even get a chess-playing game for your Palm Pilot!

Believe it or not, chess is a spectator sport, too! That might sound funny if you're conditioned to the fast-paced action of televised sports. *"Two guys playing chess—isn't that a bit like watching grass grow?"* In fact, when you think about it, chess has special qualities that make it one of the very best spectator sports. Chess spectators actually get to *play alongside* their superstars. When you follow a live game in progress, you evaluate positions, speculate about each side's plan, weigh possible moves … In other words, you do exactly the same things as the actual players are doing! It's as if you were allowed to get down on the court to play with Shaq and Kobe.

Here again, technology has added to the ways chess enthusiasts enjoy their favorite pastime. In big international tournaments, games are played using special boards and sets with embedded electronic sensors that display the current position on video screens for spectators to follow. At the same time, wireless headsets deliver expert commentary to chess tournament audiences. Online, things get even better! Major tournaments set up websites that stream the games, live and in real time, to tens of thousands of spectators worldwide. Here, too, there will be running commentary, of course—both expert and not-so-expert, because the fans can post their own observations on the unfolding battle.

Chess Goes To Hollywood

With so many people playing, it's no surprise that chess shows its face in popular culture more and more. Most of these appearances are in a "supporting role," of course, in advertising, movies, or television shows. However, sometimes chess even takes center stage for itself.

For example, the Oscar-nominated film *Searching for Bobby Fischer* was all about the (mostly) true story of a talented young player, Josh Waitzkin. More recently, Vladimir Nabokov's novel *The Luzhin Defense* was made into a chess movie, starring John Turturro. There was even a major musical titled, simply, *Chess*. Its creator, Tim Rice, had previously written such hit shows as *Evita* and *Jesus Christ Superstar*. His plot loosely adapted personalities and events from the real 1972, 1978, and 1981 World Championship matches.

Even Harry Potter plays chess! One of the pivotal scenes in the movie *Harry Potter and the Sorcerer's Stone* was a chess battle. Pursuing the forces of darkness, Harry, Ron, and Hermione must somehow traverse a chessboard battlefield where behemoth stone pieces are crushing captured rivals to rubble. The heroes themselves become pieces in this deadly game. At its climax, Ron sacrifices himself so that Harry can deliver checkmate and proceed safely.

The opening scene in the 1963 James Bond classic *From Russia With Love* presented a glamorous fantasy vision of how top-level matches are staged. (Alas, I'm afraid that tuxedoed waiters and audiences all in evening clothes are more typical of James Bond's world than that of real chess professionals!) The scene introduced a villain, Kronsteen, as a chess player—intimating the calculating nature of his evil genius, I suppose. Kronsteen receives a summons from SPECTRE (Special Executive for Crime, Terror, Revenge and Extortion) headquarters just as he stands to win a prestigious international tournament. Rather than obey immediately, he risks the wrath of his SPECTRE bosses by staying at the board until the victory was sealed. The filmmakers used a position based on an actual game from the 1960 USSR Championship.

Mr. Spock played a futuristic three-dimensional version of chess in the old *Star Trek* television series. One episode turned on Spock's deduction that someone must have tampered with the Enterprise's computer. Otherwise, by Spock's logic, it should not have been possible for him to win against a chess program that he himself had coded. (Chapter 19 reveals the flaw in this reasoning.)

Chess Lore

The popular TV game show *Jeopardy!* has used chess as a topic on more than one occasion. Here are a few examples, all of which appeared on actual *Jeopardy!* broadcasts. If you can't solve them now, I guarantee you will be able to by the time you finish this book! Until then, you can look up the solutions in Appendix C. Don't forget to phrase your responses as a question, Jeopardy-style!

Chess for $100:

Before becoming a legend, this star of *The Maltese Falcon* hustled strangers at chess in NYC.

Chess for $200:

The only chess move in which a player may move two of his own pieces at the same time.

Chess for $300:

In 1997, at the age of 14 years 2 months, France's Etienne Bacrot became the youngest one of these.

Chess for $400:

A special way a pawn may capture—it's French for "in passing."

Chess for $500:

Bobby Fischer beat this man in Iceland in 1972 to take the World Chess title.

Of course, a chess set fit right into the Huxtable home from the beloved TV series, *The Cosby Show*. (And Bill Cosby is himself a chess player in real life, by the way!) Whether it was Theo gamely trying to beat his dad, or little Rudy smacking the chess clock and gathering the pieces into a heap, chess made regular cameos in the series. The list of other popular television icons who revealed themselves as occasional chess players includes everyone from Thomas Magnum (Tom Selleck's character in *Magnum, P.I.*) to Alex Keaton (Michael J. Fox, in *Family Ties*); from stylish detectives Tubbs and Crockett (Philip Michael Thomas and Don Johnson, in *Miami Vice*) to Bart Simpson (*The Simpsons*). An episode of *The West Wing* was centered on chess games between President Bartlet (Martin Sheen) and two of his staffers (Rob Lowe and Richard Schiff). The course of the games mirrored a simultaneous diplomatic "chess match" that was playing out between the president and China.

One of the most remarkable technology stories of the last decade was the defeat of then World Chess Champion Garry Kasparov by IBM's computer Deep Blue in a six-game match. Literally millions of onlookers swamped the IBM server that was providing live coverage of the play, making this match perhaps the biggest online event in history. Kasparov's loss was much more than just a chess story—it made newspaper and TV headlines around the world! Pundits of all sorts weighed in about "what it all meant" for the relationship between computers and humans. (I've got my own point of view, which you can read in Chapter 19.) Yet, although it must have pained Kasparov to lose that match, at least he got a partial "revenge," beating a machine in a 2001 Super Bowl Pepsi commercial. Chess has truly come into its own when it is the star of a Super Bowl TV spot!

Austin Powers (Mike Myers) plays for mate in Austin Powers: The Spy Who Shagged Me.

(Austin Powers: The Spy Who Shagged Me *(c) MCMXCIX, New Line Productions, Inc. All rights reserved. Photo by Kim Wright. Photo appears courtesy of New Line Productions, Inc.)*

As we begin the twenty-first century, we are more and more becoming a society of people who depend upon and celebrate the products of our intellect. What better game for us than chess? Computers have given us the possibility of a partner that is always ready to play chess, and the Internet has made it possible to find a new partner any time we want. There's never been a better time to start playing the world's greatest game.

The Least You Need to Know

- ◆ Chess has a long history, extending back more than 1,400 years.

- ◆ Chess has become one of the most popular games in the world, and its popularity continues to grow.

- ◆ Anyone can easily learn how to play chess, and this book teaches you how.

Chapter 2

Drawing the Battle Lines

In This Chapter

- ◆ Becoming familiar with the chessboard and the pieces
- ◆ Beginning a chess game
- ◆ How to move each chess piece
- ◆ Reading and writing chess moves

You are about to learn how to play the world's greatest game of war, strategy, and conquest. A chess game pits two armies, evenly matched, across a simple terrain. Only pure skill decides who is victorious and who is defeated. The aim of the game is simple: Capture and kill your opponent's king, while protecting your own. But you will accomplish that goal only by using strategy and tactical foresight.

Meet the Chessboard

The chessboard (yes, it's a chessboard, not a "checkerboard") has 64 squares arranged in eight vertical rows and eight horizontal rows. The squares alternate between one color and another, usually white and black. Sometimes other colors are used—such as tan and green, or yellow and brown—but the squares are always referred to as "white" and "black." (In other books, they are sometimes referred to as "light" and "dark," but in this book, to keep it simple, we'll just use white and black.)

To begin a game, the board must be placed so that the right corner square nearest each player is white. Throughout this book, we will refer to pictures of the board, called "diagrams," that look like Diagram 1. Notice that the bottom-right corner in this and every diagram is white!

Diagram 1: A typical example of the chessboard diagram.

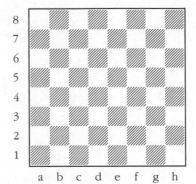

Diagram 2: Letters and numbers of the files and ranks.

Naming the Squares

Now that we've oriented the board, we can give each square a specific name. This is absolutely essential so that we can refer quickly and easily to where each piece is placed at any moment in a game. It will also allow us to say quickly and easily where each piece has moved, is moving, or can move.

The way we name the squares is simple and efficient. Look again at the chessboard diagram with the white corner in the bottom right. The vertical column of squares (which we will call a *file*) at the very left is called the "a-file." The file to its right is called the "b-file," and so on to the rightmost file, which is called the "h-file" (because "h" is the eighth letter of the alphabet). Meanwhile, the horizontal row of squares (which we will call a *rank*) at the bottom of the diagram is numbered 1, and called the "first rank." The one just above it is numbered 2, and called the "second rank," and so on to the topmost rank, which is numbered 8 and called the "eighth rank."

Chess Talk

A **file** is a column of eight squares going from top to bottom. A **rank** is a row of eight squares going from left to right. Notice that a chessboard has eight files and eight ranks.

Each square is named by putting the letter of its file next to the number of its rank. So for example, the bottom-right corner square is called "the h1 square," or simply "h1" for short. To help you remember the letters and numbers of the files and ranks, every chess diagram in this book will be lettered and numbered like Diagram 2.

Meet the Pieces

A "chess set" is a collection of all the chess pieces you need to play a game of chess (see Diagram 3). A game of chess is played between two sides. One side is called "White," and the other side is called "Black." Just as in the case of the chessboard, other colors are sometimes used; but the two sides are always referred to as "White" and "Black." Each side gets exactly the same number and kinds of pieces.

Diagram 3: An example of the White side of a typical chess set. Left to right, the pieces are king, queen, bishop, knight, rook, pawn.

You'll soon learn how each piece moves. But first, you must learn these simple rules:

- The aim of the game is to capture your opponent's king while keeping your own king from being captured.

- White always makes the first move of the game.

- The players move alternately. That is, first White moves, then Black moves, then White moves, then Black moves ....

Patrick's Pointers

Squares whose corners connect to make a straight line are called "diagonals." For example, the squares b1 and a2 form one of the shortest diagonals on the chessboard; and the squares h1, g2, f3, e4, d5, c6, b7, and a8 form one of the longest diagonals on the chessboard.

◆ Only one move can be made at a time. The way to make a move is to take one of your pieces and put it onto another square. When you have done that, your turn is over, and it's your opponent's turn.

◆ Only one piece can ever occupy a square at one time. If one of your own pieces occupies a square, you cannot move another one of your pieces there.

◆ If one of your opponent's pieces occupies a square that you could move one of your pieces to, then you can move your piece to that square and take your opponent's piece off the board at the same time. This is called *capturing a piece.* After a piece is captured, it can't come back into the game. You don't have to move a piece to a square that is occupied by your opponent's piece, but if you do, capturing it is mandatory, not optional.

◆ You must move when it is your turn, even when there are no good moves to be made.

Now let's meet the pieces.

Chess Talk

When you **capture a piece** or simply **capture**, you move one of your pieces to a square occupied by one of your opponent's pieces, thereby removing his piece from the game. After a piece is captured, it's gone for the rest of the game. And by the way, to **take** a piece means the same thing as to **capture** a piece—either way the piece is gone!

The Pawn

The pawn is the "grunt," the foot soldier in your army. In a game of kings, queens, and knights, the pawn is a lowly peasant, drafted to fight for his monarch. But don't let that fool you into thinking he is unimportant! The great eighteenth-century chess player Andre Philidor said, "The pawn is the soul of chess," and with good reason! The strategy of most chess games is largely determined by the placement of these humble fellows, and every grandmaster knows that the difference of one pawn is often the difference between victory and defeat.

Each side gets eight pawns. The pawn in this book is represented by Diagram 4. At the start of the game, White puts the pawns along the second rank, and Black puts the pawns along the seventh rank, as illustrated in Diagram 5. Remembering the names of the squares, we can say that White puts the pawns on a2, b2, c2, d2, e2, f2, g2, and h2 at the start of the game, while Black puts the pawns on a7, b7, c7, d7, e7, f7, g7, and h7 at the start of the game.

Diagram 4: What a pawn looks like for reference in this book.

Here's how the pawn moves:

◆ Pawns never move sideways, backward, or diagonally backward.

◆ Pawns always capture one square ahead diagonally to the left or right.

◆ On its first move—and only on its first move—each pawn may move either one or two squares forward. After it has made its first move, it can only move one square ahead forward in a turn.

Patrick's Pointers

Some people find it confusing that the pawn captures differently than it moves. Fortunately, it is the only piece that does so. Just remember, it captures one square diagonally in front to the left or right, and it moves one square straight ahead—except that when it's on its original starting square, it can move either one or two squares straight ahead. (But it still captures the same way!)

◆ The pawn is the only piece that captures differently than it moves!

◆ If there is a piece (*friend* or *foe*) on the square in front of it, the pawn is blocked and cannot move to (or beyond) the square the piece is on. However, being blocked does not affect the pawn's ability to capture.

In Diagram 6, the pawn on h4 cannot move because it is blocked, but the pawn on f2 can move to either f3 or f4. Black's pawn on h5 cannot move because it is blocked, but the pawn on c5 can move to c4.

In Diagram 7, White's pawn on g4 can capture any Black piece on f5 or h5, and Black's pawn on g5 can capture any White piece on f4 or h4. Notice that either pawn may make a capture even though it is blocked by an opposing pawn.

The pawn is the least powerful of all the pieces, but is never to be taken for granted.

Chess Talk

When referring to a piece as **friend** or **foe** I mean that if it's a **friend** it's one of your pieces, and if it's a **foe** it's one of your opponent's pieces.

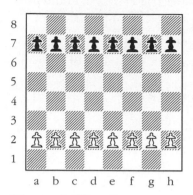

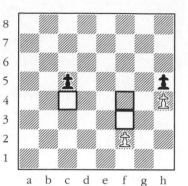

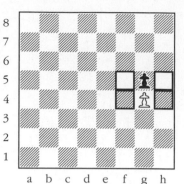

Diagram 5: Where the pawns start the game.

Diagram 6: Each pawn can move to any of the squares highlighted in front of it.

Diagram 7: Each pawn can capture any enemy piece on either of the highlighted squares diagonally in front of it.

The Knight

The knight is usually depicted as a horse or a horse's head. As you'll see, there is good reason for this, because the knight literally moves as though it were leaping over the other pieces, whether friend or foe.

Each side gets two knights. The knight in this book is represented by Diagram 8. At the start of the game, White puts the knights on b1 and g1, and Black puts the knights on b8 and g8, as illustrated in Diagram 9.

Diagram 8: What a knight looks like for reference in this book.

Here's how the knight moves:

- ◆ The knight moves like an "L": two squares up and one square to the left or the right; or two squares to either side and one square up or down; or two squares back and one square to the left or right.

◆ It does not matter whether there are any pieces, either friend or foe, in the path of the "L": the knight can still move to the square at the end of the "L" path.

◆ If one of the opponent's pieces is at the end of the "L" path, the knight may land on that square and capture the piece at the same time. But if a piece of the same color as the knight is on a square at the end of the "L" path, the knight cannot move to that square.

In Diagram 10, the knight on d5 may move to e3, c3, b4, b6, c7, e7, f6, or f4. According to Diagram 11, the knight on e5 may move to g6, g4, f3, d3, or c6, or it may capture the black pawn on c4 or d7. However, it may not move to f7. The knight is more powerful than the pawn and about as powerful as the bishop—which you're going to learn about next.

> ### Patrick's Pointers
>
> The knight is the only piece that doesn't move in a straight line. Don't worry if you find the knight a little confusing: Everyone does at first. With a little practice, it'll become second nature. And after you've learned how the pawn and the knight move, you've learned the two trickiest pieces by far!

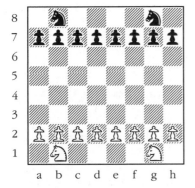

Diagram 9: Where the knights start the game.

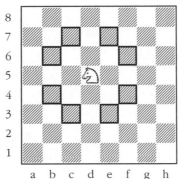

Diagram 10: The knight can move to any of the highlighted squares.

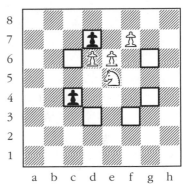

Diagram 11: The knight can move to any of the highlighted squares.

The Bishop

It may seem strange for a representative of the Catholic Church or another denomination to be fighting for the king, but we must remember that things were different in bygone times. When chess arrived in England, the shape of the piece was thought to resemble a bishop's miter. That seemed to fit somehow, and so it was christened "bishop" in English.

Chess Lore _____

The bishop is not thought of as a cleric in every language. In Italian, he is *alfiere*, which means "standard-bearer," in German he is *laufer*, which means "runner," and in French he is the *fou*, or the "fool (which was a reference to the court jester)." Apparently, the piece got its English name from the time many hundreds of years ago when the game was just becoming popular in Europe.

Each side gets two bishops. The bishop in this book is represented by Diagram 12. At the start of the game, White puts the bishops on c1 and f1, while Black puts the bishops on c8 and f8, as illustrated in Diagram 13.

Diagram 12: What a bishop looks like for reference in this book.

Here's how the bishop moves:

♦ The bishop moves only along the diagonals.

♦ It can move as far as it wants along any diagonal, forward or backward, until it encounters an edge or a piece.

♦ If there is a piece of the same color along a diagonal, the bishop cannot move to that square, nor can it move beyond that square.

♦ If there is an opposing piece along a diagonal, the bishop can't move beyond it. However, it can move to the square occupied by the enemy piece, thereby capturing it, whereupon the move ends.

♦ Notice that the bishop only moves on the squares of the same color as it starts on.

According to Diagram 14, the bishop can move to a2, b3, c4, e6, f7, g8, h1, g2, f3, e4, c6, b7, or a8. In Diagram 15, the white bishop can't move to a6, but it can capture the black knight on f1.

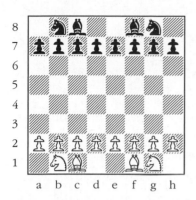

Diagram 13: Where the bishops start the game.

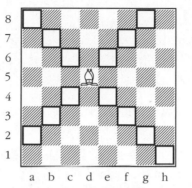

Diagram 14: The bishop can move to any of the highlighted squares.

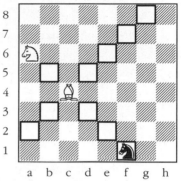

Diagram 15: The bishop can move to any of the highlighted squares.

The bishop is about as powerful as the knight (maybe just a smidgen more), but less powerful than the rook—which we'll talk about next.

The Rook

Please don't call the rook a "castle," because that misses the point. The rook did not originally symbolize a castle's tower, but rather a warrior's chariot, as it was in the ancient Indian version of the game. As chess became popular in Europe, the piece evolved to look like something that was more familiar to the Europeans.

Each side gets two rooks. The rook in this book is represented by Diagram 16. At the start of the game, White puts the rooks on h1 and a1, while Black puts them on h8 and a8, as illustrated by Diagram 17.

Diagram 16: What a rook looks like for reference in this book.

Here's how the rook moves:

♦ The rook moves only along the files and the ranks.

♦ It can move as far as it wants along a file or a rank, forward or backward, left or right, until it encounters an edge or a piece.

♦ If there is a piece of the same color along a rank or a file, the rook cannot move to that square, nor can it move beyond it.

♦ If there is an opposing piece along a rank or file, the rook can't move beyond it. However, it can move to the square occupied by the enemy piece, thereby capturing it, whereupon the move ends.

In Diagram 18, the rook can move anywhere along the d-file or anywhere along the fourth rank. The rook in Diagram 19 can capture the pawn on d6, but it can't move to d7 or d8. The rook also can't move to g4 or h4.

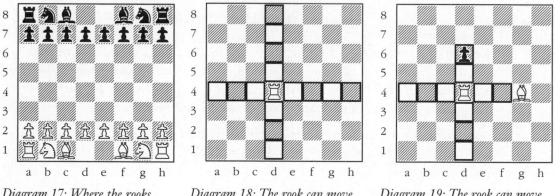

Diagram 17: *Where the rooks start the game.*

Diagram 18: *The rook can move to any of the highlighted squares.*

Diagram 19: *The rook can move to any of the highlighted squares.*

The rook is heavy-duty artillery, but even it pales before her royal highness—the queen.

The Queen

Chess is a game of royalty, so it should be no surprise that the royal couple reigns supreme. The queen's supremacy is her power: she is the most powerful piece of all. Actually, the queen used to be one of the weakest pieces, but this did not fit the European mentality, which wanted each member of the royalty to be special. How fortunate for us, because the queen's supreme power makes chess all the more exciting!

Patrick's Pointers
Sometimes people get confused about whether the white queen starts on d1 or e1, and whether the black queen starts on d8 or e8. It is easy to remember if you keep in mind that chess was played when chivalry was still very much alive, so as a sign of respect to the queen it always starts the game on the same color square as she is.

Each side gets only one queen. The queen is represented in this book by Diagram 20. At the start of the game, White puts the queen on d1, and Black puts the queen on d8, as illustrated by Diagram 21.

Diagram 20: What a queen looks like for reference in this book.

Here's how the queen moves:

♦ The queen moves along the diagonals and the ranks and the files. (In other words, it moves like both a rook and a bishop.)

♦ It can move as far as it wants along a diagonal or rank or file, backward or forward, left or right, until it encounters an edge or a piece.

♦ If there is a piece of the same color along a diagonal, rank, or file, the queen cannot move to that square, nor can it move beyond it.

♦ If there is an opposing piece along a diagonal, rank, or file, the queen can't move beyond it. However, it can move to the square occupied by the enemy piece, thereby capturing it, whereupon the move ends.

According to the location of the queen in Diagram 22, it can move anywhere along the d-file or the fifth rank, as well as anywhere along the diagonals that the d5 square is on.

In Diagram 23, the queen on d5 can capture the bishop on d2, but it can't move to d1; it can also capture the pawn on b7, but it cannot move to a8; and the queen cannot move to g5 or h5.

Bobby Fischer once wrote, "The queen is boss!" It moves like a rook and bishop put together, and it's even more powerful. But it's not the most important piece. That honor is reserved for the king.

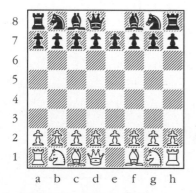

Diagram 21: Where the queens start the game.

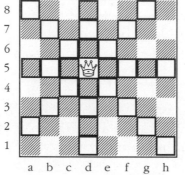

Diagram 22: The queen can move to any of the highlighted squares.

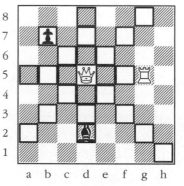

Diagram 23: The queen can move to any of the highlighted squares.

The King

Every version of chess, going back to ancient times, has had the king, a male monarch whose capture was the object of the game. Some things just never change.

Each side gets only one king. The king is represented in this book by Diagram 24. At the start of the game, White puts the king on e1, and Black puts the king on e8, as illustrated by Diagram 25. Diagram 25 also shows how to set up the board at the beginning of a chess game!

Diagram 24: What a king looks like for reference in this book.

Patrick's Pointers

Earlier in this chapter I said that the object is to capture the opponent's king, but that's not quite right. Actually, the aim is to put it in a position where the king can't escape capture on the very next move. (When that happens, it's called checkmate, which you learn about in Chapter 3.) In fact, because the king can never move into check, and because you must always get the king out of check when it's in check (if you can), the king is never actually captured in a normal chess game.

Here's how the king moves:

♦ The king moves one and only one square along a rank, file, or diagonal, forward or backward, left or right.

♦ If there is a piece of the same color on one of the squares next to the king, the king can't move to that square.

♦ If there is an opposing piece on one of the squares next to the king, the king can move to that square, thereby capturing the piece, whereupon the move ends.

♦ When an opposing piece threatens to capture the king, we say the king is "in check." When your king is in check, you must get it out of check in the very next move.

♦ The king can never move onto a square that will put it into check.

Patrick's Pointers

Notice how the starting positions of each side's pieces are completely symmetrical—see Diagram 25—except for the king and the queen. Because of this, there is a useful shorthand way to refer to each "half" of the board. The a-file to the d-file is called the "queenside," because that is the side with the queens; and the e-file to the h-file is called the "kingside," because that is the side with the kings.

In Diagram 26, the white king can move to c5, c4, c3, d3, e3, e4, e5, or d5.

Remember that the king can never move into check. So in Diagram 27 the white king can move to c5 or e5, or it can capture the pawn on d5. The black king can move to a1, b1, c1, c2, b3, a3, or a2.

Diagram 25: Where the kings start the game.

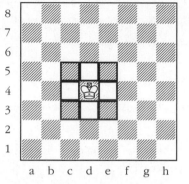

Diagram 26: Each king can move to any of the highlighted squares immediately next to it.

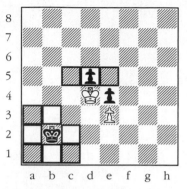

Diagram 27: Each king can move to any of the highlighted squares immediately next to it.

The Two R's: Reading and 'Riting Chess Moves

One of the most wonderful things about chess is that we can save every game ever played, and we don't need a VCR to do it. All you have to do is write down the moves as you play them, and you can re-create the game whenever you want. Likewise, I can tell you to set up any particular chess position I want, and then tell you what moves to play over. But before you can read or write these moves, you need to learn how.

People who do not already know how to read the notation for chess moves often freak out when they see or hear it. I once brought a chess book to read while waiting for an acquaintance who doesn't play chess. When he arrived, he saw my book and said, "Oh, I didn't know you read ancient Greek!" Chess notation really was Greek to him.

Actually, after you know the names of the squares and the pieces, it's very easy to learn and it completely makes sense. I think the best way to explain chess notation is to divide it into separate parts: how to read and write pawn moves with or without capture, and how to read and write all *other* moves with or without capture. So let's break it down and take it step by step.

Pawn Moves Without Capture

The way to express where a pawn moves if it does not capture a piece is simply to name the square to which it moves. Consider Diagram 28, which is identical to Diagram 25, the starting position.

If I want to write that White's first move is to move his e-pawn from e2 to e4, I simply write: "1.e4" (see Diagram 29). The "1" indicates that it is the first move of the game. (If it were, say, the forty-second move, it would be written as: "42.e4".) The "." after the "1" is written to make it easier to read—it is not spoken. And of course "e4" expresses what square the pawn moved to.

The exact same system is used for black moves as well as white moves, with one very small difference. When a Black move is written by itself, it is written in the same way, except that instead of one period separating the number from the name of the square, there are three. Suppose that White's first move is to move his pawn from e2 to e4 and Black responds by pushing his c-pawn one square forward. If Black's move is written alone, it is written as: "1...c6" (see Diagram 30). If both moves are written together, they are written as "1.e4 c6", which means, "White's first move was to push his e-pawn two squares forward, and Black's first move was to push his c-pawn one square forward." (Notice that if two moves are written after a number, the first move is always White's move and the second move is always Black's move.)

> ### Patrick's Pointers
>
> If you want to emphasize that a particular move is good, you can put "!" after it. Or to say that it is really good, you can put "!!" after it. If you want to say it is bad put "?" after it, and to say that it is really bad put "??" after it.

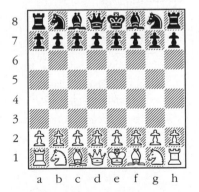

Diagram 28: *Starting position of the chessboard and pieces.*

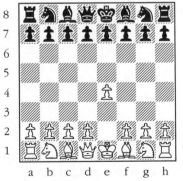

Diagram 29: *White's move is written "1.e4".*

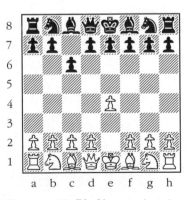

Diagram 30: *Black's move is written "1...c6".*

Pawn Moves With Capture

When a pawn captures another piece, the way to express it is to …

1. Write the letter of the file the pawn is on.

2. Write an "x" which indicates a capture.

3. Write the name of the square the captured piece was on (which is now the name of the square to which the pawn has moved).

For example, suppose the first two moves (for both sides) of a game are: 1.e4 c6 2.d4 d5, as shown in Diagram 31. Now suppose that for his third move White captures the pawn on d5 with his pawn on e4. The way to write this is "3.exd5", which is spoken as "three e takes d5". See Diagram 32 for an illustration of this move.

If Black responds by capturing the pawn with his pawn on c6, the move is written, "3...cxd5". If Black's move is written in conjunction with White's move, it is written "3.exd5 cxd5". See Diagram 33 for an illustration of this. Notice that once again the exact same system is used for Black moves as well as White moves, with the small difference that when a Black move is written alone, three periods separate it instead of only one.

Diagram 31: The position after 1.e4 c6 2.d4 d5.

Diagram 32: White's move is written "3.exd5".

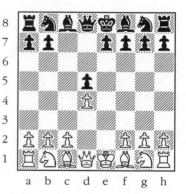

Diagram 33: Black's move is written "3... cxd5". White's and Black's moves together are written "3.exd5 cxd5".

All Other Moves Without Capture

The way to express how a piece other than a pawn moves if it does not capture a piece is simply to name the piece and then name the square it moves to. Because it would be awkward to write the whole name for the piece on every move, the pieces are abbreviated as follows:

K=King   Q=Queen   B=Bishop   R=Rook   N=Knight

"N" is used for "knight" because "K" is already taken for the king. (When the moves are spoken aloud, you say the name of the piece, not the letter that is used as its abbreviation. The letters are used only in reading and writing the moves.)

Suppose in the starting position you (playing White) want to move your knight on g1 to f3. (Remember you can do this because the knight can't be blocked the way other pieces can—it "jumps" over other pieces!) How do you write this? Easy: "1.Nf3" which is pronounced "one knight f3," or just "knight f3" if nobody is interested in which number move it is.

And if Black wants to respond by moving his knight from g8 to f6, the move is written "1...Nf6" if the move is written alone, and "1.Nf3 Nf6" if it is written next to White's move. See Diagrams 34 and 35 for an illustration of this.

Sometimes two pieces of the same color can move to the same square, and we need to make it clear which piece actually moved there. When this happens, we write the name of the file after the piece that moved, for example, "32.Nde6", to make clear that it was the knight on the d-file that moved to the e6 square on the thirty-second move. If naming the file doesn't work (for example, if there are knights on d4 and d8), we write the name of the rank after the piece that moved, "32.N4e6", to make clear that it was the knight on the fourth rank that moved to the e6 square on the thirty-second move. These moves are spoken as "thirty-two knight d e six" and "thirty-two knight eight e six," respectively. Diagrams 36 and 37 illustrate this.

Diagram 34: White's first move is written "1.Nf3".

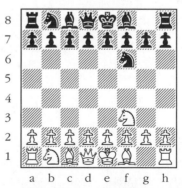

Diagram 35: Black's response is written "1...Nf6". White's and Black's moves together are written "1.Nf3 Nf6".

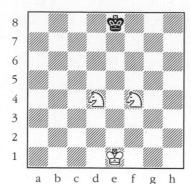

Diagram 36: If White's thirty-second move is to move the knight from d4 to e6, it's written "32.Nde6".

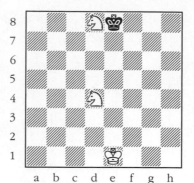

Diagram 37: If White's thirty-second move is to move the knight from d4 to e6, it's written "32.N4e6".

Patrick's Pointers

If you have a computer you can play chess with, here's a good way to practice reading and writing chess moves: Play a game against the computer, and have it list the moves of the game. While you are playing, you should write down both your moves and its moves without looking at the computer's list of the moves. When the game is finished, compare your record of the moves with the computer's.

All Other Moves With Capture

The way to express where a piece other than a pawn moves, if it captures a piece, is to …

1. Name the piece that moves.

2. Write an "x" which (just like with pawns) indicates a capture.

3. Name the square it moves to. (This should be sounding pretty familiar by now.)

Suppose the first three moves (for both sides) of a game are as follows: 1.e4 c5 2.Nf3 d6 3.d4 cxd4. (See Diagram 38.) If White's fourth move is to capture the pawn on d4 with his knight, the move is written "4.Nxd4". (See Diagram 39.) As you can probably guess by now, the "x" is pronounced as "takes" or "captures," so the move, "4.Nxd4" is pronounced "four knight takes d four," or just "knight takes d four" if nobody cares what number move it was.

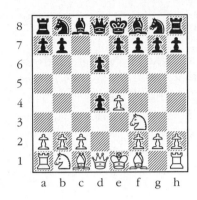

Diagram 38: The position after 1.e4 c5 2.Nf3 d6 3.c4 cxd4.

Once again, it's possible for two pieces of the same color to be able to capture the same piece (thereby moving to the same square). The system for making clear which piece did the capturing is the same as for moves without capture: The file of the piece is distinguished, and if that doesn't work, the rank is distinguished. For example, suppose that on his twenty-sixth move Black has rooks on a8 and e8, and he wants to capture a piece on d8 with his rook. We would write, "26...Raxd8" to make clear that it was the rook on the a-file that made the move. Sometimes distinguishing the file doesn't work. If, for example, Black wanted to capture a piece on a7, and Black had rooks on a6 and a8, we would write, "26...R8xa7" to make clear that it was the rook on a8 that captured the piece on a7. Diagrams 40 and 41 illustrate this.

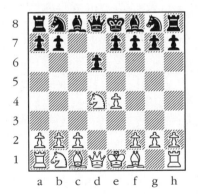

Diagram 39: White's move is written "4.Nxd4".

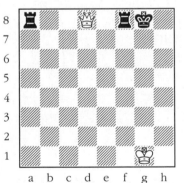

Diagram 40: If Black's twenty-sixth move is to capture the queen with his rook on a8, it's written "26...Raxd8".

Diagram 41: If Black's twenty-sixth move is to capture the queen with his rook on a8, it's written "26...R8xa7".

Now Take a Deep Breath

You've learned a lot already! You've learned the names of the squares, how to set up the board and the pieces, most of the rules of play, how the pieces move, and how to read and write chess notation. In fact, you're just about ready to start playing chess. You only have to learn a few more rules, which are covered in Chapter 3. But before you start that chapter, you may want to do the exercises at the end of this chapter to test your mastery of what you've learned here. If you have any trouble, don't get flustered; simply look at the answer in Appendix C and refer back to the relevant section in the chapter.

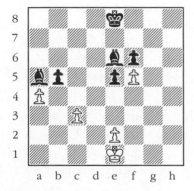

Exercise 1: *List all the squares to which White can move each pawn. Write each move each pawn can make in correct chess notation.*

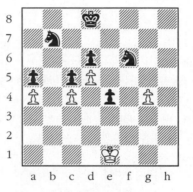

Exercise 2: *Can Black move either of his knights? If so, say where each one can go. Write each move either knight can make in correct chess notation.*

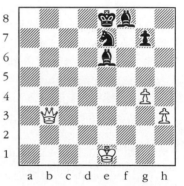

Exercise 3: *List all the squares to which Black can move either bishop. Write each move either bishop can make in correct chess notation.*

Exercise 4: *List all the squares to which White can move the rook. Write each move it can make in correct chess notation.*

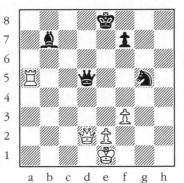

Exercise 5: *List all the squares to which Black can move the queen. Write each move it can make in correct chess notation.*

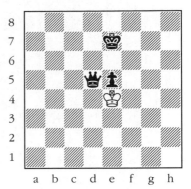

Exercise 6: *List all the squares to which White can move the king. Can it capture the queen on d5? Can it capture the pawn on e5? Write each move it can make in correct chess notation.*

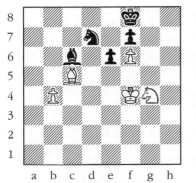

Exercise 7: *Whose turn is it? List all the legal moves in the position. Write each move in correct chess notation.*

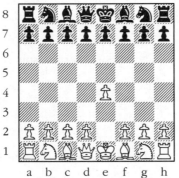

Exercise 8: *List all of Black's legal moves in the position. Write each move in correct chess notation.*

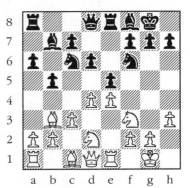

Exercise 9: *It is White's move. List all the legal moves White can make with each pawn. Then list all the legal moves White can make with either bishop. Write each move in correct chess notation*

Exercise 10: *It is Black's move. List all the legal moves Black can make with either knight. Then list all the legal moves Black can make with either rook. Write each move in correct chess notation.*

Exercise 11: *What moves can Black play? Write each move in correct chess notation. What do you think is Black's best move?*

Exercise 12: *It is White's move. List all of White's legal moves, and then write each one in correct chess notation. What do you think is White's best move?*

The Least You Need to Know

◆ The vertical rows of squares are files (a, b, … h) and the horizontal rows of squares are ranks (1, 2, … 8); together the square names become a1, b2, … h8.

◆ The correct way to position the pieces at the beginning of the game. (See Diagram 25.)

◆ The king can never move to a square where it could be captured.

◆ You should learn how to read and write chess moves so you can more easily follow the instructions in the rest of the book.

3

Rules of Engagement

In This Chapter

◆ How to capture "en passant"

◆ What it means to "promote" a pawn

◆ The rules for how to "castle"

◆ How the game is won or lost

◆ How sometimes no one wins

You're almost ready to start playing chess. After you finish this chapter, you'll know all the rules. You only have two things more to learn. First, you'll learn the three special moves that aren't like all the others. Then you'll learn all the ways a game of chess can be won, lost, or declared a tie. Then you'll be ready to play a game with anyone!

Three Special Moves

In Chapter 2, you learned how each piece moves. But there are three special moves that need a little more explanation. More specifically, the pawn has two special moves, and the king has one special move. What makes these moves "special" is that they are only possible under certain circumstances. You might think of them as particular "powers" the king and pawn have that go beyond their normal movements. After you learn these three special moves, you'll know everything there is to know about how the pieces move.

You might find each special move a little confusing at first, especially the last special move, the one the king can do. That's normal. Almost everyone finds these three moves a little strange when they first learn them. That's why I've devoted half of this chapter just to explaining them. I'm sure that if you read through the explanations carefully, and take the time to do the exercises, you'll soon find these moves come naturally. As you get more experience playing chess, you'll come to appreciate each of these three special moves: Each one greatly enriches the game!

Pawn Capturing a Pawn *En Passant*

The pawn has two special moves. The first one is a special way for it to capture another pawn, called capturing *en passant*, which is French for "in passing." The idea is that under certain circumstances, a pawn can capture another pawn that passes by it.

Consider Diagrams 1, 2, and 3. As I'm sure you remember from Chapter 2, pawns normally move only one square at a time, but when a pawn is on its starting square, it has the option of moving either one or two squares forward. In Diagram 1, if the

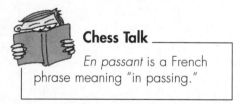

Chess Talk

En passant is a French phrase meaning "in passing."

white pawn were to move only one square forward, it would be on the d3 square, where the black pawn could capture it. But what if it moves two squares forward? Then it lands on the d4 square, where the black pawn normally can't capture it. The white pawn has passed right by the black pawn.

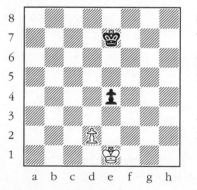

Diagram 1: White to move.

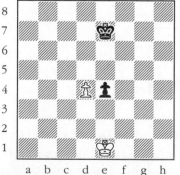

Diagram 2: White plays 1.d4.

Diagram 3: Black plays 1...exd3, capturing the white pawn en passant.

But here is where the pawn's first special move applies. In such a situation, when a pawn moves two squares forward and by doing so lands a square immediately to the left or right of an opposing pawn, then on the very next move, *and only on the very next move*, the pawn may be captured by the opposing pawn *as if it had only moved one square forward*.

The best way to remember this rule is to understand its point. The idea is to not let a pawn sneak by an opposing pawn without giving the opposing pawn one chance to capture it. In Diagrams 1 and 2, by moving two squares forward the white pawn was able to pass by the d3 square, which the black pawn controls, and get to safety on d4. In doing so, it "passed by" the opposing pawn's control of the square in front of it. The *en passant* rule gives the opposing pawn one chance to capture the pawn as if it had moved only one square; that is, to capture it as it passes by the square it controls. But the opposing pawn only gets one chance! If it doesn't capture the pawn on the very next move, the *en passant* capture is no longer possible.

Notice from the caption to Diagram 3 that an *en passant* capture is written just like a normal pawn capture, as though the captured pawn had moved only one square instead of two. In some books, you may see "e.p." written after such a capture to indicate that it's an *en passant* capture, but strictly speaking that isn't necessary, and we won't write "e.p." after an *en passant* capture in this book.

Promoting the Pawn

The pawn's second special move is truly amazing. Many chess games are won or lost because of this special move. I like to imagine that this special move is an answer to a complaint I would make if I were a pawn.

What's the complaint? Well, remember that unlike all the other pieces, the pawn can't move backward. This means that as the pawn marches forward, it's on a one-way trip. Consider the plight of the pawn in Diagram 4.

Diagram 4: White's pawn nears the opposite end of the board.

This pawn has almost managed to arrive at the opposite end of the board. Suppose he advances one more square. Is that it for the poor little guy? Does he have to sit uselessly on the edge of the board for the rest of the game?

In fact, the pawn has an exciting future ahead of it! When the pawn reaches the edge of the board, it is "promoted." That means the pawn can be transformed into any piece (of the same color) that you want, except the king. Actually, it *must* be transformed. Once the pawn reaches the edge of the board, promoting it is mandatory, not optional. But then, nobody ever complains, because it's such an advantage to be able to turn what would be a useless pawn into a knight, a bishop, a rook, or especially the most powerful piece of all: a queen. The transformation happens in the same turn as moving the pawn to the edge of the board, and the turn ends once the pawn has been replaced by the piece you choose.

> **Patrick's Pointers**
>
> Each pawn can be promoted only once, but there is no limit to the number of pawns you may promote—except, of course, that the most pawns you can possibly promote is eight!

Even if none of your pieces of a certain kind has been captured, you may still promote the pawn into another one of that piece. So, for example, even if you still have your queen, you may promote your pawn to a queen; even if you still have both your knights, you may promote your pawn to a knight, and so on.

Writing the move for a pawn promotion is easy. You simply write the pawn's move in the normal way, and then put "=" followed by the abbreviation for whatever piece to which the pawn was promoted. If the pawn is promoted to a queen, for example, you write the pawn's move in the normal way, plus "=Q" after it.

Consider Diagram 5, where it's White's turn and he has two pawns that he can push to the eighth rank and promote. If the pawn on f7 moves forward one square and becomes a knight (see Diagram 6), the move is written "1.f8=N". If the pawn on a7 moves forward one square to become a queen (see Diagram 7), the move is written "1.a8=Q".

Diagram 5: *It's White's turn to move, and he can promote either the pawn on f7 or the pawn on a7.*

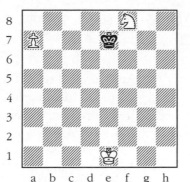

Diagram 6: *Pawn being promoted to knight, written "1.f8=N".*

Diagram 7: *Pawn being promoted to queen, written "1.a8=Q".*

Chess Lore

Even grandmasters get confused sometimes about the rules. One of America's strongest grandmasters is Yasser Seirawan. Yasser loves to try to reach a position where he can promote one of his pawns. Commenting on this aspect of his play, another one of America's strongest grandmasters, Joel Benjamin, joked to me, "Yasser keeps pushing his pawns even after he's checkmated!"

A few days later, I told Yasser about this joke. "That's not fair," he said, "it only happened once!"

"You mean, it actually happened?"

"Well, many years ago, when I was a kid playing in my first tournament, I played a master. And just when I was about to promote my pawn, he checkmated me. But before he could say anything, I promoted my pawn to a king."

"Did he tell you that was against the rules?"

"Nah. He just checkmated my other king too, and that was that."

King's Special Privilege

There's only one more move for you to learn: the king's special move. On its very first move, so long as certain conditions are met, the king has the privilege of *castling*. When the king "castles," it moves either two squares to the right or two squares to the left, and then the rook the king has moved closer to jumps over the king to land on the square immediately on the other side of the king.

Sound confusing? Don't worry: everybody finds this move hard to understand at first. I will list the rules for castling, but first let me show you what castling looks like. Look at Diagram 8.

Chess Talk

Castling is the king's special move. If your king has not yet moved, if at least one of your rooks has also not yet moved, and if other conditions hold, you may be able to castle.

Let's suppose it's White's turn to move, and he decides to castle. In fact, White can castle to either the kingside or the queenside, so let's consider each case in turn.

If White castles kingside, he moves his king two squares to the right, to g1, and then he moves the rook on h1 to f1. This is all done in one turn. Notice that the *only* time you can ever move two of your pieces in a single turn is when you castle. Diagram 9 shows White castling in this way.

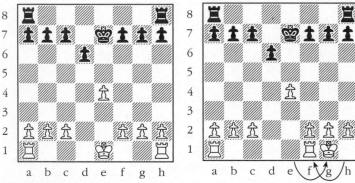
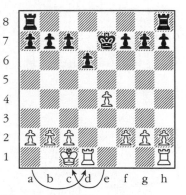

Diagram 8: White can castle king-side or queenside.

Diagram 9: White castling king-side.

Diagram 10: White castling queenside.

If White castles queenside, he moves his king two squares to the left, to c1, and then he moves the rook on a1 to d1. Once again, this is all done in one turn. Diagram 10 shows White castling in this way.

Here are the rules for how to castle:

♦ The move of castling takes place in one turn, and it involves moving two pieces. First, the king moves two squares to the right or to the left, and then the rook it has moved closer to moves to the square immediately on the other side of the king.

♦ There must be no pieces, *either friend or foe*, on any square between the king and the rook being used for castling. (You may not capture a piece while castling!)

♦ Castling must be the first move of the king. After the king has moved, it may not castle for the rest of the game. (Because castling is a move of the king, this means that each player may castle only once at most per game.)

♦ The rook being used to castle must also not have moved yet. But the fact that one rook has moved doesn't disqualify you from using the other rook to castle.

♦ The king can't castle out of check. This does not mean that once the king has been in check, it can't castle. As long as the check is removed in some way other than by moving the king, it may still castle **on another move** (as long as the other requirements are met). But when the king is actually in check, it may not castle to escape check.

> ### Patrick's Pointers
>
> If the king is in check, castling is not permitted. But nothing stops you from castling with a rook that is attacked! The only requirement that applies to the rook is that it must not have made a move. Whether it's actually being attacked doesn't matter.

♦ The king can't castle into check. (Naturally, because the king can never move into check anyway.)

♦ If one of your opponent's pieces controls the square the king must "jump over" to castle, castling is prohibited. That means that if White wants to castle kingside, but the f1 square is controlled by an enemy piece, White can't castle kingside while that square is controlled. And if White wants to castle queenside, but the d1 square is controlled by an enemy piece, White can't castle queenside while that square is controlled. Similarly, Black can't castle kingside while the f8 square is controlled by an enemy piece, nor can he castle queenside while the d8 square is controlled by an enemy piece. But once there is no longer any enemy piece that controls the crucial square next to the king, the prohibition is lifted.

♦ There is a special way to write the move of castling. Kingside castling is written as "O-O", and queenside castling is written as "O-O-O". If, for example, White's twelfth move is to castle kingside, it is written "12.O-O"; and if, for example, Black's ninth move is to castle queenside, it's written "9...O-O-O".

Let me show you another illustration of castling for both sides, plus how it's written, in the next three diagrams.

Notice that in Diagram 11, White can't castle kingside, because the bishop on f1 is in the way. It's White's turn to make his eighth move, and he decides to castle queenside. This is written "8.O-O-O".

Notice in Diagram 12 that Black can castle kingside, but he can't castle queenside, because the queen on d8 and the bishop on c8 are in the way. Black decides he wants to castle in response (see Diagram 13). This is written "8...O-O".

Don't worry if you find castling confusing. Everybody does at first. Take a careful look at the rules of castling and the exercises at the end of the chapter to test your understanding of this rule.

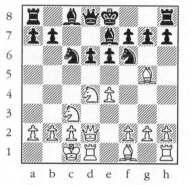

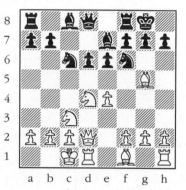

Diagram 11: The bishop on f1 prevents White from castling kingside, but he can castle queenside.

Diagram 12: White has played 8.O-O-O, and now it's Black's turn. Black can't castle queenside because of the queen on d8 and the bishop on c8, but he can castle kingside.

Diagram 13: Black has played 8...O-O.

Win, Lose, or Draw: How Does That Happen?

When you play a game of chess, it can end in one of three ways: you can win, you can lose, or you can *draw*. Let's first learn how a game is won or lost, and then we'll learn how a game can be a draw.

Chess Talk _____

A **draw** is a tie—that is, nobody wins. When a game ends in a draw, it means that both players fought to a standstill. This is reflected in how a win, a loss, and a draw are rewarded in a chess tournament. A win is worth one point to the winner, a loss is worth zero to the loser, and a draw is worth half a point to each player.

Checkmate—the Aim of the Game!

Remember from Chapter 2 that the aim of the game is to put your opponent's king in a position where it can't escape being captured on the next move. When the king is in check (it's threatened with capture) and there is no move that can prevent it from being captured in the very next move, we say the king is "checkmated." Checkmate ends the game. When you checkmate your opponent, you win; when your opponent checkmates you, you lose. It's that simple.

Sometimes someone who's just starting to play chess will try to answer checkmate with a check. Nice try, but no dice. Checkmate is immediate and final. In fact, it doesn't even matter if you could checkmate your opponent in the very next move! Checkmate is checkmate, and it ends the game. Period.

It takes a little time to be able to recognize checkmate when it happens. Just remember that it's checkmate when all of the following are true:

- ◆ The king is in check.

- ◆ The king can't move to a square where it's not in check.

- ◆ The piece giving check can't be captured.

- ◆ There is no piece to put in the way between the king and the piece giving check.

Chess Lore _____

Do you wonder where the words *check* and *checkmate* come from? You may remember from Chapter 1 that an early version of chess was played in Persia. In that game, the king was called "shah." Furthermore, the word *mat* meant "helpless" in Persian. *Shah* became *check* in English, and *mat* became *mate*.

Patrick's Pointers

If a move puts the opponent's king into check, a "+" is put after the move. So for example, if Black's fortieth move is to move the rook to f3, and this move puts White into check, the move is written "40...Rf3+".

An Example of Checkmate

It's White's turn to move (see Diagram 14), and he decides to move his rook from d1 to d7 where it will attack two of Black's pawns, on b7 and f7 (see Diagram 15). But White's aggression is misplaced here, because he has left his own king very vulnerable. Black takes advantage of White's mistake by playing 1...Re1# (see Diagram 16). There is no move White can play to remove the king from check in the next move, so he is in checkmate, and Black wins the game.

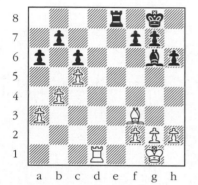

Diagram 14: White to move.

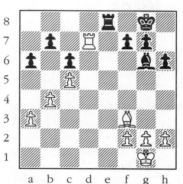

Diagram 15: White plays 1.Rd7??, leaving his own king vulnerable.

Diagram 16: Black plays 1...Re1#.

Throwing in the Towel

There is one other way to win. A player may give up at any time during a game, just like a boxer may throw in the towel at any time during a fight. Giving up is called *resigning*. If you're just starting to play chess, my advice is never to resign. Play every game to the end! As you get better, however, you'll start to recognize when your position has deteriorated to the point that—even though you can't see exactly how it'll happen—you will inevitably be checkmated. If your game has reached such a dreadful state, it may make sense to resign rather than to continue a hopeless struggle. By far the most common way for a grandmaster to lose a chess game is to resign before the inevitable checkmate.

> ### Patrick's Pointers
>
> When a move gives checkmate, this is indicated by putting "#" after the move. So, for example, if you see the move, "28.Be6#", you know that this move is checkmate, and you pronounce it "twenty-eight bishop e six checkmate."

Chess Talk _____

When you concede defeat to your opponent, it's called **resigning**. It's never easy to admit defeat, but if you must do so, always be gracious. The polite way to resign is to say, "I resign," compliment your opponent on a game well played, and shake his or her hand.

Sometimes Nobody Wins

A game of chess doesn't always have a winner and a loser. When no one wins and no one loses, both players draw. In fact, games between grandmasters end in draws just as often as one side wins or loses. There are four ways that a game can end in a draw, so let's go through them one at a time.

Insufficient Material to Deliver Checkmate

Sometimes so many pieces have been captured on both sides that it's simply no longer possible to put the enemy king into checkmate. Because the only way to win the game is through checkmate, if it isn't possible to give checkmate, the game is a draw. This is pretty rare, however, because it has to be absolutely impossible for checkmate to happen.

In Chapter 4 you will learn how to force checkmate with just a lone queen or a lone rook against a king. So if one side has at least a rook or a queen, there can't be *insufficient material* to draw. And if one side has a pawn, remember that it could always promote to a rook or a queen. And furthermore, two knights, a knight and a bishop, and two bishops can all give checkmate against a lone king.

The bottom line? Insufficient material is basically just king versus king, or where, aside from the kings, one side only has a knight or a bishop—so don't worry too much about it. Just keep in mind that if it is absolutely impossible for either player to checkmate the other, the game is drawn.

There are also some positions where even though there are more pieces on the board, it turns out to be impossible to construct a checkmate, usually because of the way the pawns block each other and also block the other pieces. Don't worry about this: it's extremely rare! But if you like playing with puzzles, you might try to figure out what such a position could be.

Chess Talk _____

Insufficient material is when neither side has enough pieces to put the other king into checkmate. When this happens, the game is drawn.

Friendly Agreement

Just as either side can at any time resign the game, both players can at any time simply agree to a draw. Sometimes it can be polite to agree to a draw. For example, if it's absolutely clear that neither side has any realistic chance to win, the gracious thing to do is to offer a draw. Or if you are playing a friendly game and your opponent suddenly has to leave, and you don't think you have an obviously better position, again the gracious thing to do is to agree to a draw.

When grandmasters play against one another, it's common for them to agree to a draw even in fairly complicated positions. Sometimes this is because the position only seems complicated, and both players realize the game really should be a draw. Sometimes grandmasters agree to a draw because each player is afraid of losing! (I myself have been a party to both kinds of "grandmaster draws.") Because you are just starting to learn chess, I strongly urge you to play out every position to the end. Losing a game here or there is not nearly so bad as losing a chance to learn more and so improve your game.

Maybe these first two ways for a game to end in a draw seem a little obvious or boring to you. But pay attention! The next two ways are not so obvious at all.

> **Patrick's Pointers**
>
> In this chapter, I explain the four basic ways a chess game can end in a draw. However, if you play in a chess tournament, you should know that there are other ways a game can end in a draw.

Perpetual Check

Remember that whenever your king is in check, you must remove it from check on the very next move. And remember also that the king is in checkmate when it is in check and there is no way to remove the check on the very next move. But suppose your king is in check, and you remove it from check, and then it's in check again, and then you remove it from check, and then it's in check again, and so on.

When one side continually checks the other side, it's called *perpetual check*. If one side announces that he'll give perpetual check, and there's no way to escape from it, the game is drawn.

> **Chess Talk**
>
> When your opponent can keep checking your king forever, you are in **perpetual check**. If your opponent announces he will give perpetual check, the game is a draw. Just make sure it's really true that you have no way out of the checks!

It's important to remember that perpetual check is different from simply giving a lot of checks. Perpetual check occurs only when one side can put the other side in check forever. That's why, if one player announces he will give perpetual check, the game is drawn. What would be the point of continuing the game?

So often in chess, a picture is worth a thousand words. See the adjoining diagrams for some examples of positions that are, and are not, cases of perpetual check.

In Diagram 17, Black is in check. Can White give perpetual check? The answer is no, it isn't perpetual check because after 1...Kc7 (Diagram 18), White has only one more check with the rook (2.Rc8+ or 2.Rd7+), whereupon Black will capture the rook. Then there certainly won't be any more checks!

In Diagram 19, Black is in check. Can White give perpetual check? Black has no move other than 1...Ka7 (see Diagram 20). When White plays 2.Rd7+ (see Diagram 21), Black must move the king to either b8 or a8. White will play 3.Rd8+, then 4.Rd7+, then 5.Rd8+, and so on. If White demonstrates this and announces that he will give perpetual check, he can claim a draw.

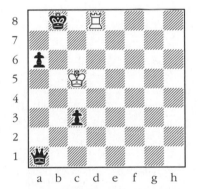

Diagram 17: Black is in check.

Diagram 18: Black plays 1...Kc7, and now it's clear that White can't give perpetual check.

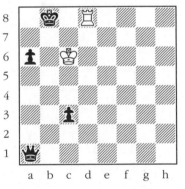

Diagram 19: Black is in check.

Diagram 20: Black plays 1...Ka7.

Diagram 21: White plays 2.Rd7+. He can give perpetual check by playing Rd8+ and Rd7+ forever.

Stalemate

Suppose there is literally no move you can make. This means that it's your turn to move, but there is simply no square to which you can move any piece. (This isn't common, but it happens more often than you might think.) What do you think happens in that case?

Many people who are just learning the rules assume that if one side can't make any legal move, that side loses the game. But in fact, what happens is the game is a draw. Often when I explain this rule to people, they think it doesn't make sense. After all, if someone can't make a single move, doesn't that mean he's helpless? And if he's helpless, why should the game be a draw? Shouldn't he lose instead?

I understand that thought. But on the other hand, remember that the object of the game is to capture the enemy king. The whole point of *stalemate* is that it is "stale"—you haven't attacked the king at all. And you can't win without attacking the king. See the diagrams for some examples:

Chess Talk

When it's one player's turn to move, and his king is not in check, but he has no legal move, he is in **stalemate**. When one player is in stalemate, the game is drawn.

- In Diagram 22, it's White's turn to move. This position is not stalemate, because White has one legal move: 1.g4.

- In Diagram 23, it's White's turn to move. This position is stalemate, because White has no legal moves at all, so the game is a draw.

◆ In Diagram 24, it's Black's turn to move. This position is stalemate, because Black has no legal moves at all, so the game is a draw.

◆ In Diagram 25, it's Black's turn to move. This position is not stalemate, because Black has two legal moves: 1...h6 and 1...h5.

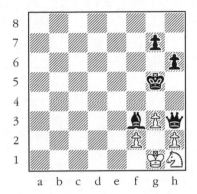

Diagram 22: It's White's turn, but it's not stalemate.

Diagram 23: It's White's turn, but he has no legal move, so he's in stalemate.

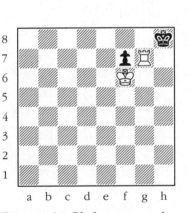

Diagram 24: Black to move: stalemate.

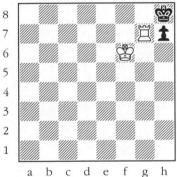

Diagram 25: Black to move: not stalemate.

Okay, One More Deep Breath and You're Ready to Play!

Don't worry if you're still a little unsure about a few of the rules. It may take a little time before you've got them down cold. Use the exercises to train your knowledge and understanding, and if you have trouble with any of the exercises, simply reread the appropriate section and study the illustrative diagrams.

Exercise 1: If Black plays 1...f5+, can White respond with 2.exf6?

Exercise 2: It's White's turn. If he wants to promote his pawn on c7 to a queen, what is the only move he can make to do this? Write the move down.

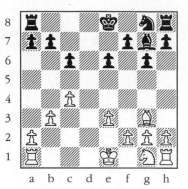

Exercise 3: It's White's turn, and he wants to castle queenside. Write that move down. If White castles queenside, can Black respond by immediately castling queenside himself?

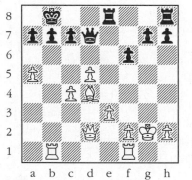

Exercise 4: How can Black give White perpetual check?

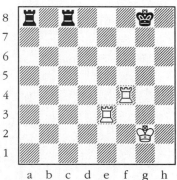

Exercise 5: Do you see how White can force checkmate in two moves? (To force checkmate in two moves means to make one move, and then whatever move the opponent makes in response, the next move you make is checkmate.)

Exercise 6: It's Black's turn to move. Is he in stalemate?

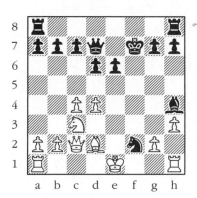

Exercise 7: *Can White castle, either kingside or queenside? If castling on either side (or both sides) is legal, write down the move in correct chess notation.*

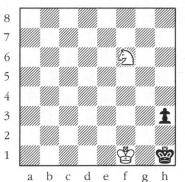

Exercise 8: *It is White's turn. Should this position be declared a draw? Does it matter what move White plays?*

Exercise 9: *It is Black's turn. This position is very similar to Exercise 8. Black has two legal moves; one of them loses, the other draws. Which is the right move, and why?*

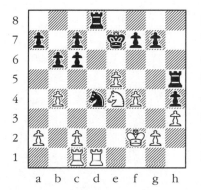

Exercise 10: *White to move (Kasparov–Kramnik, Holland, 2001). If White plays 1.g4, can Black capture en passant?*

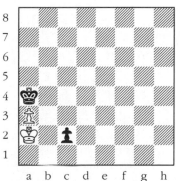

Exercise 11: *It is Black's turn. Black can and should promote his pawn. What should he promote it to? Why?*

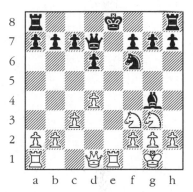

Exercise 12: *It is Black's turn. (How could you know even if I didn't tell you?) Can he castle kingside? Can he castle queenside?*

The Least You Need to Know

◆ A special move for a pawn to capture another pawn that has passed by it is called *"en passant."*

◆ Promoting a pawn is mandatory, not optional.

◆ The king can only castle on its very first move.

◆ You win the game if you checkmate your opponent or if he gives up.

◆ Four ways for the game to end in a draw are: insufficient mating material, friendly agreement, perpetual check, and stalemate.

Chapter 4

How to Win with Just One Piece

In This Chapter

- ◆ How to formulate a winning strategy
- ◆ Learning the power of the queen and rook
- ◆ Cornering the king
- ◆ Going in for the kill

In this chapter, I show you how to force a lone king into checkmate with a queen and how to force a lone king into checkmate with a rook. What's the point of learning how to do this? Well, to begin with, it's a useful skill to have in its own right. After you study this chapter, you can be confident about winning a position where you have only a queen or only a rook left.

But there are two even more important reasons to learn this skill. First, there's no better way to get a feel for the power of the queen and the rook than by learning how to force checkmate against the lone king with each.

But more importantly, learning how to force a lone king into checkmate is an excellent way to learn how to plan. Chess is a war between two evenly matched armies. Such a war can be won only if you lead your army more effectively than your opponent leads his. The essence of leading your army effectively is to lead it in accordance with a plan that correctly fits the needs of your position at any moment. In subsequent chapters, you'll learn how to recognize what those needs are, and how to achieve them. But even before you start to learn what strategies your plan should adopt, and what tactics your plan must take into account, you should get a sense for what I mean by forming a plan in the first place. This chapter will help you do just that.

I strongly recommend that you read this chapter with a chessboard and chess set by your side, so you can play out all the moves in this chapter. It's okay if you don't have a set and board—I have put in enough diagrams for you to follow all the moves just reading the book. But I do think the chapter is even more useful if you can play over the moves on a board.

One final thing: I explain this mainly from the point of view of the player with the extra queen or rook. For every position, I tell you how to play for the win. There is no way I can possibly examine every legal move Black might play in response. Focus on the ideas behind White's moves. After you think you've understood it, you might want to practice playing these positions with a friend, or computer, so you can practice giving checkmate against all possible king moves.

Checkmate with Queen and King Versus King

Consider the position in the adjoining Diagram 1. Suppose you're playing White. Obviously you have the advantage, because your opponent has only his king, and you have a king and a queen! In fact, you're already winning. How should you play?

Diagram 1: White's advantage is big enough to win. But how?

Making a Plan

Let's not make any moves right away. Let's think about this first. What should your plan be? Well, it's hard to imagine aiming for anything else except checkmate. After all, Black just doesn't have anything else on the board except his king, so there isn't anything to attack in Black's position except his king. If there was ever a time to go for checkmate, this is it!

"But wait a minute," you might ask, "isn't checkmate always the goal? What's different about saying I should go for checkmate now?"

That's a good question, and it brings up a mistake that many beginning players make. It's certainly right that the *ultimate* goal is always to checkmate your opponent's king. But it's not always right to have that as your *immediate* goal. Many times, the right thing to do is to try to improve your position (or attack your opponent's position) in ways that don't directly involve checkmate. In fact, if you try to attack the king before you're ready to do so, you may accomplish nothing but to make your own position worse! This will become clearer to you as you learn more about chess strategy.

At any rate, it's clear that in this position checkmate is the thing to aim for. That's the goal. What plan should you make to achieve it?

Here are two very important hints:

Blunders

Don't make a move without having some kind of plan behind it. A plan doesn't have to be anything fancy: just a clear idea of what you want to accomplish based on an assessment of the strengths and weaknesses of your position and your opponent's position.

- ◆ The queen can't checkmate a lone king on an open board by herself—the queen needs the help of the king.

- ◆ The queen and king can't checkmate the opposing king unless it's on the edge or the corner of the board.

If it's not clear to you why either of these is true, use your board to try and construct a checkmate with just a queen and king against a lone king that violates one of the two hints above. You'll see that it can't be done.

Now then, what plan should you make to give checkmate? Taking your cue from the two hints above, it should be clear that you must use your own king, and you must drive the enemy king to the edge or the corner. And in fact, the winning plan is to do just that. Let's see how to do it.

Diagram 2: White to move.

Constricting the King

In case you've forgotten what position we're starting from, Diagram 2 gives the same position as Diagram 1. Step one is to constrict the king's movements as much as possible. This will make it easier to drive the king back to the edge or corner of the board. To accomplish this end, the best first move is 1.Qd5 (see Diagram 3). Why is this such a good move? Look how much the black king is constricted by the queen in Diagram 4. The queen blocks the king from crossing either the d-file or the fifth rank. So this first move helps enormously in the plan of driving the king to the edge (or corner) of the board.

Many beginning chess players, when they first try to give checkmate with a queen and a king, instinctively give check, and then give check again, and again, and again, and again. But how would that help drive the king to the edge of the board? It doesn't. In fact, the best way to force checkmate doesn't involve giving check even once before it's time to give checkmate!

Diagram 3: White plays 1.Qd5! to constrict the king's movement as much as possible.

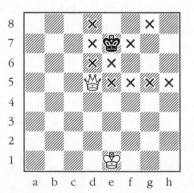

Diagram 4: The Xs show all the squares Black's king can't move to.

Bringing Your King Up to Help

Let's go back to the position after 1.Qd5. How will Black respond? Black realizes that the king is in greatest danger on the edge of the board, so he should try to keep the king away from the edge. Keeping this in mind, let's suppose he plays 1...Kf6 (see Diagram 5). Is there any queen move you can make that will constrict the king even further? You might think 2.Qe4, but I think this move gives up just about as much as it gains: If you play 2.Qe4, you take the e-file away from the king, but you give up the fifth rank. Because for the moment, there is no better square for the queen than d5, let's use this move to bring your king up to help the queen by playing 2.Kf2 (see Diagram 6). This is a very good move, because it helps accomplish the other thing we decided we needed to achieve to give checkmate: it brings the king closer to the queen.

Suppose Black responds by moving his king back to where it was before and plays 2...Ke7, as in Diagram 7.

Now what should White do? Actually, White has two very good moves. If you were thinking to keep bringing the king up to help the queen by playing 3.Ke3, 3.Kf3, or 3.Kg3, give yourself a pat on the back, because those are all very good moves. However, I'm going to show you a different way to proceed. Before bringing the king up, we're going to use the queen to drive Black's king into the corner.

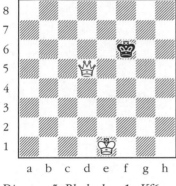

Diagram 5: Black plays 1...Kf6.

Diagram 6: White plays 2.Kf2 because further constriction of the king is not possible at the moment.

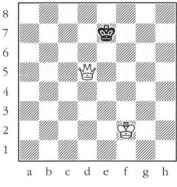

Diagram 7: Black plays 2...Ke7.

Driving the King to the Corner

Diagram 7 shows the white queen at d5. The plan is to drive the king back to the corner using just the queen. The black king will then be helpless, so you can bring your own king up for the final kill. My suggestion is for White to drive the king farther back by playing 3.Qc6 (see Diagram 8).

By the way, do you notice how the queen is always played a knight's move away from the king? Doing this enables the queen to take the maximum number of squares away from the king. In fact, the next several moves are all going to put the queen a knight's move away from the king.

What can Black do now? All he can do is move the king. Wherever he moves it, White can keep driving the king back by placing the queen on the right square—always a knight's move away! Suppose Black plays 3...Kf7; now you should play 4.Qd6, as in Diagram 9.

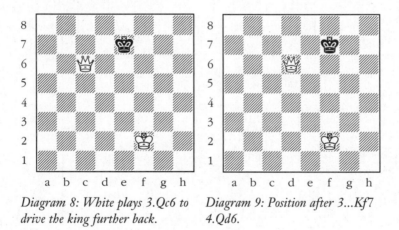

Diagram 8: White plays 3.Qc6 to drive the king further back.

Diagram 9: Position after 3...Kf7 4.Qd6.

The next several moves are all going to follow the same pattern. So if Black plays 4...Ke8, White plays 5.Qc7, as in Diagram 10.

Now keep pushing the king into the corner, i.e., 5...Kf8 6.Qd7 Kg8 7.Qe7 Kh8, as Diagram 11 shows.

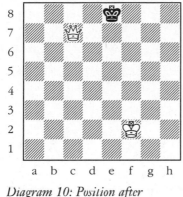 

Diagram 10: Position after 4...Ke8 5.Qc7.

Diagram 11: Black keeps running, and White keeps chasing.

Beware of Giving Stalemate!

What should you play now? Look at Diagram 12. If your first instinct was to play 8.Qf7?, then slap yourself on the wrist. **You've just put Black in stalemate!** (You remember stalemate, right? If not, refresh your memory in Chapter 3.)

Time to Bring Up the King

Let's go back to Diagram 11, with the queen still on e7. There's no way you can improve the position of the queen because the black king has been driven as far back as possible. Now it's time for White to bring the king up for the kill, so let's play 8.Kg3, as shown in Diagram 13.

Black has nothing to do but to move his king back and forth. While he's doing that, you bring your king up, and when you're ready, you give checkmate. The game might finish: 8...Kg8 9.Kg4 Kh8 10.Kg5 Kg8 11.Kg6 Kh8 12.Qh7#. The final checkmate is shown in Diagram 14. It took only 12 moves and a good plan to force checkmate!

Is it clear to you how White forced checkmate? If not, go back over the section. Don't worry too much about particular moves, and focus on understanding what the main ideas were and how White realized them: driving the king into the corner, avoiding stalemate, and bringing up his own king to deliver the checkmate. Notice how much more effective following a logical plan is than merely giving check after check with the queen would have been!

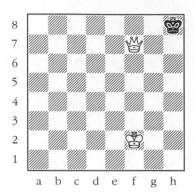

Diagram 12: If White plays
8.Qf7?, Black is in stalemate.

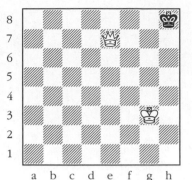

Diagram 13: White plays 8.Kg3.

Diagram 14: White brings the
king to g6, and then plays the
queen to h7, giving checkmate.

Chess Lore

Sometimes even world champions give stalemate by mistake! In 1988, a chess tournament was held in Canada where the strongest grandmasters in the world competed in "blitz" chess. In chess competitions, a special timer is used, called a "chess clock." Every time a player makes a move, he presses a button that stops his own clock and starts the clock of his opponent. In blitz chess, each player gets only five minutes to play all his moves!

Players met in elimination matches of six games. Whoever won more games (draws not counting) out of six defeated his opponent and moved on to play the next opponent. In the second round, World Champion Garry Kasparov played a grandmaster from Bulgaria, Kiril Georgiev. Kasparov was winning the first game, but running out of time. Quickly he reached an endgame where he had queen and bishop against Georgiev's lone king. Then, suddenly, the game was over. The audience was stunned: Kasparov had accidentally stalemated Georgiev's king! The game was drawn, and Kasparov, flustered by his carelessness, actually lost the match and was eliminated from the tournament.

Checkmate with Rook and King Versus King

In many ways, the procedure for giving checkmate with the rook is similar to doing it with the queen. Once again, you must drive the king back to the edge or a corner; and once again, you must use your own king to help. But because the rook is a weaker piece than the queen, you need to use your king more actively in the procedure. In particular, you need to use your king in the process of driving the opposing king to the edge of the board, because the rook (unlike the queen) can't do it alone.

Constricting the King

Consider the position in Diagram 15. How can you best constrict the king with the rook? The best move is 1.Ra6!, which prevents the king from crossing the sixth rank, as in Diagram 16.

Why is this the best move? Well, the goal is to force the king to the edge of the board; after this move, the king can't go beyond the seventh rank. That's a lot of progress for one move!

> **CAUTION**
>
> **Blunders** _____
>
> Always be careful not to give stalemate when you're trying to force checkmate!

Diagram 15: White to move.

Diagram 16: White plays 1.Ra6!.

Bringing the King Up to Help

White has just moved 1.Ra6, and it's Black's move. How will Black respond? Suppose Black plays 1...Kd7. There is no way the rook can do anything more to restrict the king, so it's time for White to bring up his own king by playing 2.Kd2. Look at Diagram 17 to see the position after these moves.

Black moves the king over to attack the rook by playing 2...Kc7 3.Kc3 Kb7, reaching Diagram 18. Notice that the black king is now attacking the white rook. This is a perfect illustration of one way the rook is weaker than the queen. The king can never move next to the queen, but it can move diagonally next to the rook. So the plan of staying a knight's move away from the king isn't going to work with the rook!

Patrick's Pointers

If Black had played 1...Kf8, White could have played 2.Ra7!, restricting the king even further by controlling the seventh rank. But after 1...Kd7, it's not a good idea to play 2.Ra7+?, because after 2...Kd6 it's harder to restrict Black's king.

There's no reason for concern, however, just because the black king is attacking the rook. You can simply move the rook to another square along the sixth rank where the king isn't attacking it, for example, 4.Re6 (see Diagram 19). This will keep the black king constricted, and give you time to bring up the white king to participate in the hunt.

Diagram 17: Black plays 1...Kd7, and White responds with 2.Kd2.

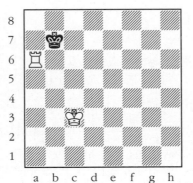

Diagram 18: Position after 2...Kc7 3.Kc3 Kb7.

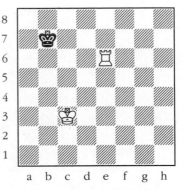

Diagram 19: Position after 4.Re6. Notice that the black king is still prevented from crossing the sixth rank.

Black may try to move the king over to attack the rook again by playing 4...Kc7, as in Diagram 20.

White brings up the king to join the fight: 5.Kc4 Kd7 6.Kd5! (see Diagram 21). Now the rook on e6 is protected by the white king. Black's plan was to attack the rook to try to free his king, but here the active white king foils Black's plan by coming to the aid of the rook. The black king can't capture the rook because it's protected by the white king.

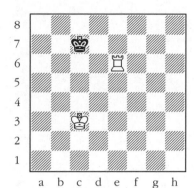

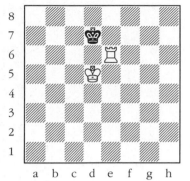

Diagram 20: Black plays 4...Kc7 to attack the rook next move with 5...Kd7.

Diagram 21: Position after 5.Kc4 Kd7 6.Kd5. Now the rook on e6 is protected and can't be captured.

Driving the King Back

Notice that the black king is now badly constricted in Diagram 21. Not only can it not cross the sixth rank, it also can't cross the e-file. The next step in White's plan is to keep taking more squares away from the black king, thereby driving him back to the edge or the corner. This is just like what we did with the queen; the big difference is that with the rook, you need more help from the king.

Let's continue playing the game out. The black king runs, and the white rook chases: 6...Kc7 7.Rd6 Kb7 8.Rc6 (see Diagram 22). Now the black king is confined to a tiny box of four squares: b7, b8, a7, and a8!

On the next move, as shown in Diagram 23, Black plays 8...Kb8. How should White progress from here? Once again, White needs to use the king. Because Black's king is confined to the squares b8, b7, a8, and a7, it makes sense for White to bring the king over so it is closer to those squares.

Diagram 22: Position after 6...Kc7 7.Rd6 Kb7 8.Rc6. Black's king is now severely restricted.

Diagram 23: Position after 8...Kb8.

In Diagram 24, White brings his king closer to the action: 9.Kc5 Kb7 10.Kb5. The black king is confined to the same 4 squares, but now the white king is nearby, ready to help the rook drive the black king even further back.

Suppose Black plays 10...Ka7 as shown in Diagram 25. Now we can see just how useful it is to have the king nearby. White responds by playing 11.Rb6 as shown in Diagram 26, and now the black king is really being driven into the corner! But whenever the king starts getting close to running out of moves, you have to be careful not to give stalemate.

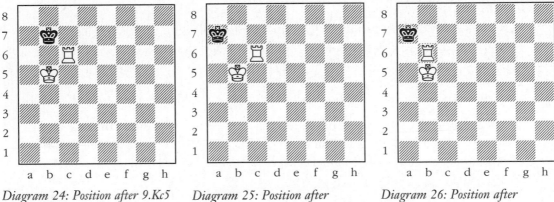

Diagram 24: Position after 9.Kc5 Kb7 10.Kb5.

Diagram 25: Position after 10...Ka7.

Diagram 26: Position after 11.Rb6.

Beware of Giving Stalemate!

Consider Diagram 27, which shows the position after Black plays 11...Ka8. White can't improve the location of his rook, so it's time to move the king. Should the white king move to a6 or c6?

If you thought White should play 12.Ka6? (see Diagram 28), give yourself another slap on the wrist! That move puts Black into stalemate and the game would be drawn. Just as with the queen, you must always be careful not to take away all the squares from the king while you are hunting it down with the rook.

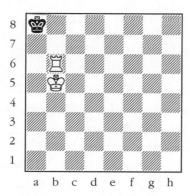

Diagram 27: Position after 11...Ka8.

Diagram 28: Position after 12.Ka6?. The game is a draw.

Going In for the Kill

The right way for White to play is 12.Kc6 as shown in Diagram 29. This move brings the king closer, without giving checkmate. Now play continues: 12...Ka7 13.Kc7 Ka8. Do you see in Diagram 30 how White can give checkmate now?

White can now give checkmate with 14.Ra6#. The hunt is a success.

Did you notice that you never once gave check with the rook until you gave checkmate? There was never any reason to give check, so it was never part of our plan. The only check that really counts is checkmate (see Diagram 31)!

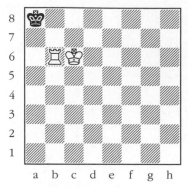

Diagram 29: Bring the king closer without giving stalemate.

Diagram 30: Position after 12...Ka7 13.Kc7 Ka8.

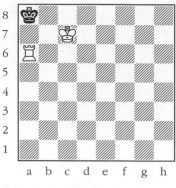

Diagram 31: Checkmate!

Could You Do It Again?

Do you feel comfortable about giving checkmate with a queen or a rook against a king? If you have a friend who's also learning how to play chess, you may want to practice with him or her. Take turns forcing checkmate with the rook or the queen against each other. If you're learning on your own, go over the chapter carefully. Imagine how you would have played if, at various points, Black had moved his king to a different square than we considered in the chapter. Use the exercises to test your mastery of this chapter.

Finally, use this chapter to think about the importance of playing moves according to some kind of plan. Don't think that such a plan has to be as detailed and thorough as the plan we were able to use in this chapter. Most chess positions are too complicated for anyone—even a grandmaster—to make a plan that goes much beyond a few moves. The important thing is to make your moves in accordance with an idea, a goal that you want to achieve that meets the needs of the position.

Exercise 1: *White can force check-mate in two moves. How can that be achieved? Is 1.Qe6 a good move or a bad move?*

Exercise 2: *White can force check-mate in two moves. How can that be achieved?*

Exercise 3: *Name all the squares on which Black could put a queen to give checkmate.*

Exercise 4: *This one is tricky! Although White has only a lowly pawn, he still has a winning plan. What is the plan, and how can it be achieved?*

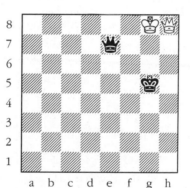

Exercise 5: *It's Black's turn. What is his best move? Can he win?*

Exercise 6: *How should Black capture the queen?*

Exercise 7: How can White force checkmate in two moves?

Exercise 8: This is the same position as Exercise 11 in Chapter 3. Again, it's Black's move. How can Black win? Suggest a reasonable series of moves leading to Black checkmating White. (Hint: It shouldn't take you more than 25 moves, and if you're really good you can do it in 10.)

The Least You Need to Know

♦ The key to checkmating the king with a queen or a rook is to force the king to the edge or the corner, and to use your own king.

♦ Always watch out for stalemate when going for the kill!

♦ Don't just make moves, have a plan!

♦ The plan you make must be based on the goal you should set and the best way to achieve it.

Part 2

Tactics

Now that you're ready to play chess, it's time to learn how to play better! This part and the next one teach you how to play chess well. Chess thinking is divided into two areas: tactics and strategy. This part teaches you tactics, and the next part teaches you strategy.

A tactic is a move or sequence of moves designed to achieve a goal. The most common goals are to capture your opponent's pieces and to give checkmate. I teach you the tactics you need to make sure you capture more of your opponent's pieces than he captures of yours. I also show you some tactics to apply directly to the attack against the king, and you get to see some examples of successful attacks against the king. Let's get ready to rumble!

5

It's a Material World

In This Chapter

◆ The relative value of each piece

◆ What material is and why it's good to have more material than your opponent

◆ How to win material

◆ How to avoid losing material

When you read Chapter 4, you probably noticed something: it's pretty useful to have an extra rook or queen at the end of the game! In fact, if you did Exercise 4 in Chapter 4, you saw that even a single extra pawn at the end of a game can make the difference between winning and losing. And as you will see in later chapters, having more pieces or pawns than your opponent is useful throughout the game in many other ways.

If you want to improve at chess, the first things you must do is learn to avoid losing your pieces and pawns, and to capture your opponent's pieces and pawns when you can do so.

In this chapter, you'll learn why this is so important and how to do it. You'll learn the relative value of each piece, how to avoid losing your pieces and pawns, and how to capture those of your opponent.

The Concept of Material

Always remember that chess is a game of war. And in chess, as in war, all other things being equal, the bigger army will win. Why? Well, if you have more to attack with than your opponent has to defend with, your attack will overwhelm the defense. If you have more to defend with than your opponent has to attack with, your defense will turn away the attack. When you have more to attack and defend with than your opponent does, you have more power, which chess players call more *material*. A *material advantage*, as chess players call it, is an advantage in power. When you have a material advantage over your opponent, you have a more powerful army than your opponent.

Chess Talk

The word **material** is a general word referring to the number and strength of one's pieces. A **material advantage** is an advantage in that regard.

When Fewer Pieces = More Material

Most people probably agree that the United States has the most powerful military in the world. So even if the United States went to war with a country that had four times the population, the United States would still win, right? But wait a minute, the other country has almost four times as many people than the United States, so it could potentially field an army that was four times bigger. So why wouldn't the other country win?

Without getting bogged down in military science, I think one thing at least is pretty clear: Four times the population might mean they have more soldiers, but we have extremely sophisticated weapons. (Our soldiers are probably better trained as well.) They might have more soldiers and maybe even more weapons, but our soldiers with our weapons are worth more. Even with less, we have more power.

Well, imagine that the pawn is a foot soldier and the rook is a tank, and you begin to see how this applies to chess.

Sometimes a material advantage means having more than your opponent. But sometimes a material advantage means that what you have is worth more.

The Relative Worth of the Pieces

So just how powerful is each piece, relative to every other piece? There is a standard scale that answers this question. This is a very useful scale to know, and you should commit it to memory. Do keep in mind that it's only an approximation, but it's a heck of a good approximation! The relative power of the pieces are as follows:

Pawn	1 point
Knight	3 points
Bishop	3 points (plus a teensy bit more)
Rook	5 points
Queen	9 points

There are two words chess players use to talk about capturing one piece for another: *trade* and *exchange*. To trade a piece for another is to capture one of your opponent's pieces in return for allowing one of your pieces to be captured. To trade bishops, for example, is to capture your opponent's bishop in return for allowing your bishop to be captured. But a trade doesn't have to be one piece for its counterpart: you can trade a knight for a bishop, trade two rooks for a queen, and so on.

The word *exchange* is used similarly: You can exchange knights, or exchange two pawns and a bishop for a rook. But the word *exchange* also has a very specific meaning: To have the advantage of the exchange means to have a rook more than your opponent, when your opponent has only an extra knight or bishop to compensate. For example, if you have an exchange for a pawn, it means you have a rook more than your opponent, while your opponent has either an extra knight or bishop, and also an extra pawn. (You have the advantage of the exchange, while your opponent has an extra pawn in return for that disadvantage.)

> **Patrick's Pointers**
>
> Aim for the bishop in positions where it can find long diagonals, and where it can move around a lot. Aim for the knight in positions with lots of pawns, especially when you can find a secure square for the knight, where the pawns block the diagonals of your opponent's bishops.

Should you trade a bishop for a knight? Although the bishop and the knight are worth about the same, they are very different pieces, and each thrives in different kinds of positions. The bishop can zoom across the board, so it likes positions where the pawns do not get in the way of its diagonals. The knight likes to find a secure square it can sit on in the middle of the action; its leaping ability means it's not hampered by the presence of other pieces.

In the long run, pawns tend to get exchanged, so it's not a bad bet that the bishop will become more powerful toward the end of the game. That is why I have said that the bishop is a teensy bit more powerful than the knight. But whether the bishop or the knight is really the better piece in any particular position is much more important than the long-term tendency for the bishop to become the stronger piece.

You learn more about the relative value of the knight and the bishop in Chapter 10. For now, consider them of about equal worth.

What About the King?

Notice that the king isn't on the scale. Why not? Well, the loss of the king means the loss of the game, so you aren't about to give up your king for another piece! In that sense, the king has an infinite value.

But it still makes sense to ask how powerful it is. After all, just because you dare not lose the king doesn't mean that you can't use it to attack and defend. The scale tries to give a relative weight to the power of each piece. Even though we can't exchange the king for another piece, wouldn't it be nice to know how powerful it is in relation to the other pieces?

Here's the answer: it's worth about three points, which is to say it's about as powerful as the knight or the bishop. Just be careful when you use the king, though, because its importance goes far beyond its power!

How Do You Use This Scale?

Basically, you always want to trade up when you can. If you can grab a pawn, do so. If you can give two pawns to get a bishop, that's a good trade. If you can get a rook for three pawns, that's an even better trade. And so on.

This is only a rough scale. It is not a perfect indication of the relative value of each piece. There are particular piece combinations that work well together and particular piece combinations that don't work so well together. There are also certain situations where some pieces' values increase, while some other pieces' values decrease. You will learn some of these situations in later chapters, and experience will teach you other situations. (See Chapter 16 for how to learn more once you finish this book.)

But although it is only a rough scale, it works very well. Grandmasters use it regularly. So should you.

Because the scale of the relative worth of the pieces is so useful, chess players sometimes use it to distinguish between three different kinds of pieces:

1. The pawn is not even called a piece at all! It is so low down on the scale that it does not deserve to be called a "piece," so it is just called a pawn.

2. The bishop and the knight are called "minor pieces," because they are not so powerful.

3. The rook and queen are called "major pieces," because they are the most powerful pieces of all.

How to Win Material and Avoid Losing Material

It's simple: Capture your opponent's pieces, and don't let your own pieces get captured. If you capture one of your opponent's pieces, and one of yours can be captured, make sure the piece you take is worth more than the one your opponent takes.

I can imagine what you're thinking, "Okay, it sounds simple, but how do I make sure that I capture pieces when I can, that I don't let my own pieces be captured, and if there is a trade of pieces how can I make sure that I trade up?"

"How Do You Get to Carnegie Hall?"

The answer: practice, practice, practice. Hey, you didn't think you were going to be able to get better without practice, did you? But don't despair! I will explain how you should practice, and I will give you a lot of exercises to practice with. Are you ready to go to work? Let's start with Diagram 1.

It's White's turn to move. Study this position, and before you continue reading, list (or just think to yourself) every single capture White can make. Then try to decide which one (if any) he should make.

Diagram 1: White to move and find the best capture.

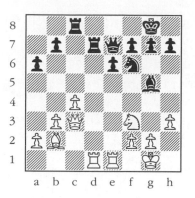

There are four captures White can make:

- ◆ White can capture the pawn on e6 with his rook on e1 (1.Rxe6).

- ◆ White can capture the knight on f6 with his queen on c3 (1.Qxf6).

- ◆ White can capture the rook on d7 with his rook on d1 (1.Rxd7).

- ◆ White can capture the bishop on g5 with his knight on f3 (1.Nxg5).

Which capture (if any) should White make? Using our scale of the relative value of the pieces, we can see that there are two captures White should definitely not make, one capture that is neutral, and one capture White should definitely make. See Diagrams 2 and 3 for an illustration of the first capture White shouldn't make.

White should not play 1.Rxe6??, because Black will then recapture the rook with either his queen on e7 or his pawn on f7, and White will lose a rook for a pawn—a very bad trade. (By the way, Black has another way to win a rook other than by capturing the one on e6 with either the pawn or the queen. Do you see what it is?) Next see Diagrams 4 and 5 for an illustration of the second capture White shouldn't make.

White also should not play 1.Qxf6??, because Black will then recapture the queen with either his pawn on g7 or his bishop on g5, and White will lose a queen for a knight: another *very* bad trade. Now see Diagrams 6 and 7 for an illustration of the third capture, the one that is basically neutral.

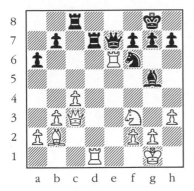

Diagram 2: White plays 1.Rxe6??, a very bad move.

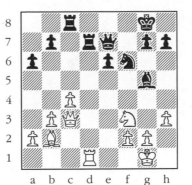

Diagram 3: Black plays 1...fxe6, and wins a rook for a pawn.

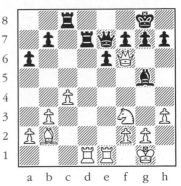

Diagram 4: White plays 1.Qxf6??, a very bad move.

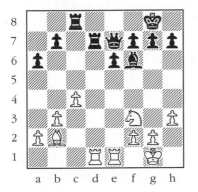

Diagram 5: Black plays 1...Bxf6 and wins a queen for a knight.

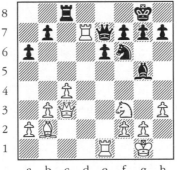

Diagram 6: White plays 1.Rxd7, capturing the rook on d7 with his rook on d1.

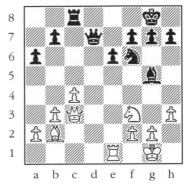

Diagram 7: Black recaptures the rook by playing 1...Qxd7, and material is still even.

It is neither good nor bad for White to play 1.Rxd7, because Black will recapture the rook with his queen, and White will simply have made an even trade: rook for rook. Now look at Diagram 8 for the fourth possible White capture, the one White should play.

The capture of the bishop, 1.Nxg5!, is excellent because there is no way Black can recapture the knight that takes this bishop. White gains a whole bishop for nothing!

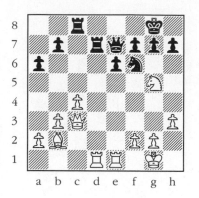

Diagram 8: White plays 1.Nxg5! and wins a bishop for nothing!

Here's another position for you to study (see Diagram 9). It's White's turn to move. Once again, either make a list or tell yourself mentally what are all the captures White can make, and then decide which one (if any) White should choose.

There are three captures White can make:

♦ White can capture the pawn on b5 with his knight on c3 (1.Nxb5).

♦ White can capture the pawn on d5 with his rook on d2 (1.Rxd5).

♦ White can capture the pawn on d5 with his knight on c3 (1.Nxd5).

Try to decide for each capture whether White should play it or not, and then read what I say about it. See Diagrams 10 and 11 for an illustration of the first capture White can make.

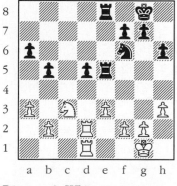

Diagram 9: White to move.

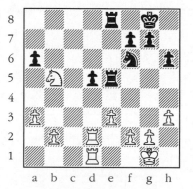

Diagram 10: White plays 1.Nxb5??, a very bad move.

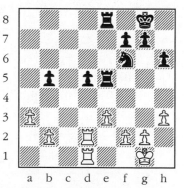

Diagram 11: Black recaptures the knight with 1...axb5.

If White plays 1.Nxb5??, Black will respond 1...axb5 and gain a knight for a pawn. White should not do this! Now for an illustration of the second capture White can make, see Diagrams 12, 13, and 14.

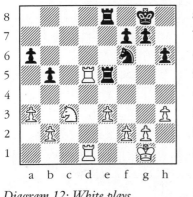
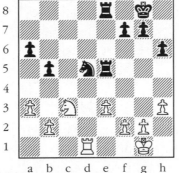
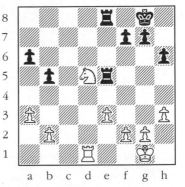

Diagram 12: White plays 1.Rxd5?, a bad move.

Diagram 13: Black recaptures the rook with 1...Nxd5.

Diagram 14: White recaptures the knight with 2.Nxd5.

If White plays 1.Rxd5?, Black will respond 1...Nxd5 (see Diagram 13), and gain a rook for a pawn. But we can't stop here, because White can make another capture: he can capture the knight on d5 with 2.Nxd5 or 2.Rxd5 (see Diagram 14). Still, White will only get a knight and a pawn, and Black will get a rook. That still gives Black a material advantage, so 1.Rxd5?, although not as bad as it looks at first, is still a mistake.

The best move is the third possible capture: 1.Nxd5! (see Diagram 15). Now suppose that Black responds with 1...Nxd5 (see Diagram 16). Then White can play 2.Rxd5 (see Diagram 17), and if Black plays 2...Rxd5 (see Diagram 18), White responds with 3.Rxd5. White begins by capturing a pawn, and then every capture and recapture is just an even trade, which still leaves White with a material advantage of one pawn.

How can you be sure that a series of captures will come out in your favor? One thing you must do is count the number of pieces (or pawns) attacking and defending whatever you want to capture. If you attack it one more time than it is defended, the last man standing will be one of yours.

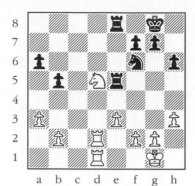

Diagram 15: White plays
1.Nxd5!, the best move, which
wins a pawn.

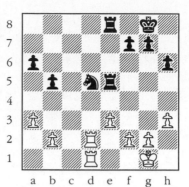

Diagram 16: Black recaptures the
knight with 1...Nxd5.

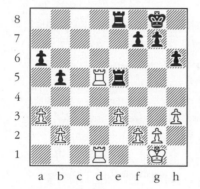

Diagram 17: White recaptures the
knight with 2.Rxd5.

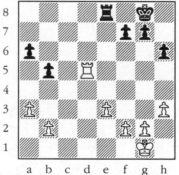

Diagram 18: Black recaptured the
rook with 2...Rxd5, and White
recaptured again with 3.Rxd5,
reaching this position.

But that doesn't mean you should automatically capture something if you attack it
one more time than your opponent defends it! You must also make sure that you do
not lose a more valuable piece for a less valuable piece. (Think about Diagrams 12
and 13. White got a knight and a pawn, but it cost him a rook. Even though he was
the last man standing, he came out behind.)

The only way to make sure things work out for you is to calculate the consequences
of each capture. A good rule of thumb is to start a series of captures with your least
valuable piece (or a pawn).

"Do I Really Need All of This Practice?"

There have been a lot of diagrams for you to study in the last few pages. It may feel somewhat overwhelming. Don't worry if you feel you can't work through it all at once. Take your time and read at the pace that feels most comfortable for you. However, I strongly recommend that you think about all the positions. (In fact, in some positions some other captures are possible that I didn't explain. You should try to figure out the consequences of those captures for yourself!) You will find a lot of exercises at the end of the chapter, and I recommend that you do many—if not all—of these as well.

Why do I recommend all this work? The answer is simple. Learning how to capture your opponent's pieces and how not to let your own pieces be captured is all about learning certain skills. It's not hard to get the idea that it's good to have more material than your opponent and bad to have less material than your opponent. The hard part is actually being able to recognize when you can win material and when you're in danger of losing material. There is no other way to develop these skills than by practicing.

What skills do you need to develop in order to win material and avoid losing material? There are really just three:

♦ You need to develop the ability to see in any position which pieces (and pawns) are attacking other pieces (and pawns) and which are being attacked.

♦ You need to be able to calculate what the result of a capture will be.

♦ You need to be able to assess whether the result of a capture will give you a material advantage or not. (Always remember the scale of relative worth!)

The way to develop these abilities is to train yourself by looking at many different positions and seeing which pieces attack which pieces, what will happen in each case if you capture a piece, and whether the resulting position would give you a material advantage. The exercises at the end of this chapter are there for you to do just this kind of training.

How to Defend Against a Threat to One of Your Pieces

In the next two chapters, you learn how to use and to be aware of your opponent using many tricks of the trade—ways to win material. But before we close this chapter we should consider one more thing: Just how do you defend against a threat to one of your pieces? After all, we've been looking at all the ways to capture material. But what about when you are the one who is being threatened with capture? What should you do?

There are five ways to meet a threat to one of your pieces:

♦ Move the piece that is being attacked.

♦ Defend the piece that is being attacked.

♦ Block the attack on the piece.

♦ Capture the piece that is attacking you.

♦ Attack something else in your opponent's position.

Let's illustrate each one of the ways to meet a threat to one of your pieces with an example.

Moving the Piece That Is Being Attacked

Look at Diagram 19. Suppose you are Black, and you notice that your queen on b6 is being attacked by the bishop on e3. It's your move. What do you do? Well, the simplest thing to do is to move it away to where it's no longer being attacked, right? Diagram 20 shows the position after Black has done just that. It is White's turn again, and the Black queen can't be captured because it has moved away.

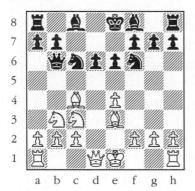
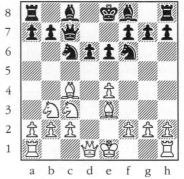

Diagram 19: Black to move: The queen is attacked by the White bishop on e3.

Diagram 20: Black plays 1...Qc7, moving the queen out of the attack.

Defending the Piece That Is Being Attacked

This works well so long as the piece of yours that is being attacked is not more valuable than whichever one of your opponent's pieces is attacking it. But if your piece is more valuable, this is not a good way to meet the threat.

Suppose you are White in Diagrams 21 and 22. In Diagram 21, Black is attacking the rook on c1 with his queen on f4. White defends that rook with his other rook, as shown in Diagram 22. Now it would be a mistake for Black to capture the rook on c1, because White would recapture the queen with the rook on d1 and White would win a queen for a rook—a very good trade for White!

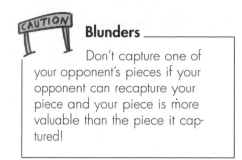

Blunders

Don't capture one of your opponent's pieces if your opponent can recapture your piece and your piece is more valuable than the piece it captured!

But in Diagram 23, Black is attacking the rook on c1 with his bishop on f4. Now it would be a bad idea for White to defend this rook, because if Black takes the rook with his bishop, then even if White recaptures the bishop, Black has won "the exchange" (a rook for a bishop), which is a good trade for Black and a bad trade for White.

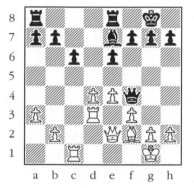
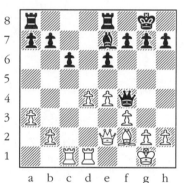
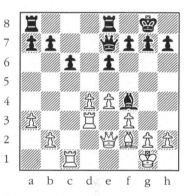

Diagram 21: White to move: The rook on c1 is attacked by Black's queen.

Diagram 22: White defends the rook on c1 by playing 1.Rdd1.

Diagram 23: White to move: The rook on c1 is attacked by the bishop on f4.

Blocking the Attack on the Piece

You must keep two things in mind if you want to do this. First, if a knight attacks a piece, there is no way to block it. (Remember, knights jump over pieces!) Second, the piece that blocks the attack must be defended, and it must be of lower or equal value to the piece that is attacking. Diagrams 24 and 25 illustrate this second point. In the first diagram, White attacks the queen on c7 with his bishop on g3. In the second diagram, Black defends the attack by moving his bishop to d6. White can capture the bishop, but then Black will recapture the bishop with his queen, and the result will simply be an even trade.

Capturing the Piece That Is Attacking You

Again, whether this is a good idea depends on whether the piece you are thinking about capturing is protected, and what the relative value of the pieces is. Look again at Diagram 24. It would be a very bad idea for the black queen to capture the bishop on g3, because White would recapture with either the h-pawn or the f-pawn, and Black would lose a queen for a bishop.

But Black has another piece that can capture the bishop.

Certainly it is a bad idea for Black to take the bishop with his queen, but what about taking it with his knight on h5? In Diagram 26, Black captures the bishop with the knight. White will recapture the knight with one of his pawns, and the result will be an even trade—this time knight for bishop, rather than bishop for bishop as in Diagram 25.

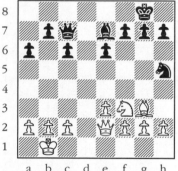
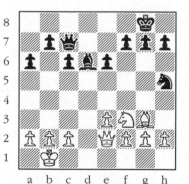
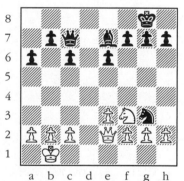

Diagram 24: Black to move: the black queen is attacked by the bishop on g3.

Diagram 25: Black plays 1...Bd6, blocking the attack to the queen.

Diagram 26: Black plays 1...Nxg3, and after 2.hxg3 or 2.fxg3 material will still be even.

Attacking Something Else in Your Opponent's Position

The final way to meet an attack on one of your pieces is just to ignore it altogether and do something else. In that case, just make sure that whatever you do is important enough to be to your advantage if you both carry out your threats! Also, be sure that your threat can't be parried in such a way that you leave yourself vulnerable to the original threat.

Consider Diagram 27. Black attacks the knight on c3 with his rook on c8. White decides to parry this threat by attacking the queen on f8 with his bishop. In Diagram 28, White has attacked the queen. Now it would be a very bad idea for Black to capture the knight, because White would capture the queen, and even after Black recaptured the bishop with his king, White would have won a queen for a knight and a bishop—an excellent trade (see Diagram 29).

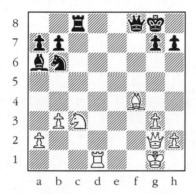

Diagram 27: White to move: the knight on c3 is attacked by the rook on c8.

Diagram 28: White attacks Black's queen by playing 1.Bd6.

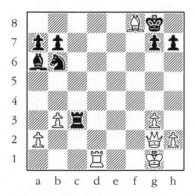

Diagram 29: Position after 1...Rxc3?? 2.Bxf8: White has won a queen for a knight. Even after 2...Kxf8, White will have a material advantage.

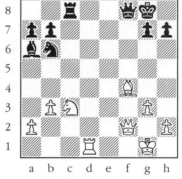

Diagram 30: White to move: the knight on c3 is attacked by the rook on c8.

But just a small change in the position can make all the difference! Consider Diagram 30. Once again the knight on c3 is attacked, and once again White decides to meet the threat by attacking the queen on f8 with his bishop on d6. Diagram 31 shows the position after White does this. But this time the white queen is on a slightly different square—f2 instead of g2—so now Black can capture the queen with his own queen, and with check! White has to meet the check, so he recaptures the queen, but then the threat to Black's queen is gone, and Black can capture the knight on c3 with his rook. See Diagrams 32 and 33.

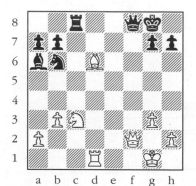

*Diagram 31: White plays
1.Bd6??, attacking the queen.*

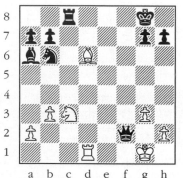

*Diagram 32: Black plays
1...Qxf2+!.*

*Diagram 33: White plays 2.Kxf2,
but now Black will win a knight
for nothing with 2...Rxc3.*

Practice, Practice, Practice!

It is *so* important to develop the skills of winning material (and not losing material) that the next two chapters are devoted entirely to teaching you the most common tricks for winning (and losing) material. Before you start the next chapter, I recommend that you do the exercises at the end of this chapter. Yes, I know there are a lot of them, but they are there for your benefit! Don't worry if you have some trouble with them. You can always turn back to the relevant section of the chapter if you are unclear about something. By trying to solve the exercises, and studying the answers if they give you trouble, you will develop the skills you need to win at chess. And believe me, chess is always more fun when you win!

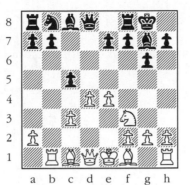

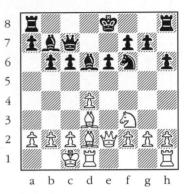

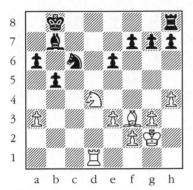

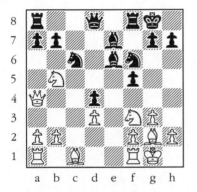

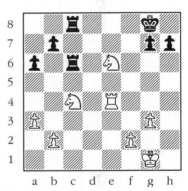

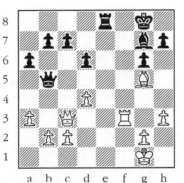

Exercise 1: *It's White's turn. List all the pieces and pawns the knight on d4 attacks. Should White capture any of them?*

Exercise 2: *It's White's turn. Do either 1.Rxb7 or 1.dxc5 win a pawn?*

Exercise 3: *It's White's turn. What two pawns does he attack? Should he capture either of them?*

Exercise 4: *It's White's turn. Do either 1.Nfxd4 or 1.Nbxd4 win a pawn? Does 1.Qxd4 win a pawn?*

Exercise 5: *It's Black's turn. What is his best move?*

Exercise 6: *It's Black's turn. Which knight should he capture?*

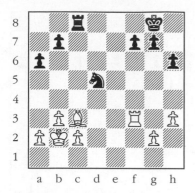

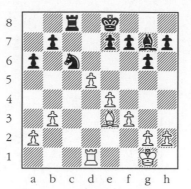

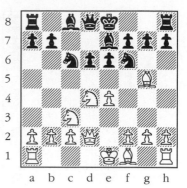

Exercise 7: It's Black's turn. Can he win material by capturing the bishop on c3 with either the rook or the knight?

Exercise 8: It's White's turn. Will White have a material advantage after the sequence 1.dxc6 Rxc6, and if not is 1.dxc6 still the best move?

Exercise 9: It's White's turn. List all of the captures White can make. Do any of them give White a material advantage?

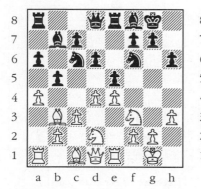

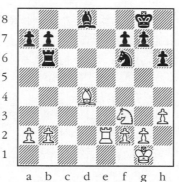

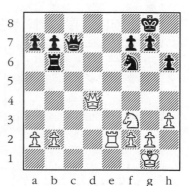

Exercise 10: It's White's turn. List all of the captures White can make. Do any of them give White a material advantage?

Exercise 11: It's White's turn, and he attacks both the knight on f6 and the rook on b6. Should White capture either of them?

Exercise 12: It's White's turn. Should he capture any of Black's pieces?

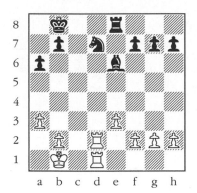

Exercise 13: *It's White's turn. Should he capture the knight on d7?*

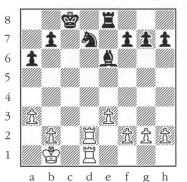

Exercise 14: *It's White's turn. Should he capture the knight on d7?*

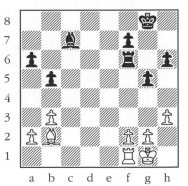

Exercise 15: *It's Black's turn, and the rook on f6 is attacked by the bishop on b2. Does Black have any other way to defend against this threat than by moving the rook?*

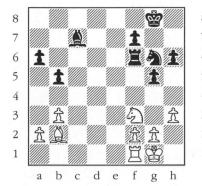

Exercise 16: *It's Black's turn, and once again the rook on f6 is attacked by the pesky bishop on b2. Does Black have any way to defend against this threat than by moving the rook?*

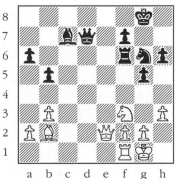

Exercise 17: *Once again it's Black's turn, and once again the rook on f6 is attacked. Now does he have any other way to meet the threat of its capture than to move it?*

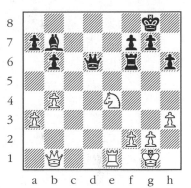

Exercise 18: *It's Black's turn. What is his best move?*

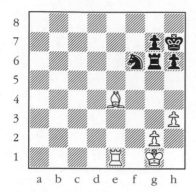

Exercise 19: *It's Black's turn. What is his best move?*

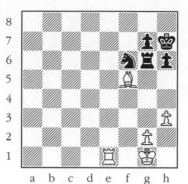

Exercise 20: *It's Black's turn. Can he prevent White from capturing his rook next turn?*

Exercise 21: *It's Black's turn. How can he prevent White from capturing his rook next turn?*

Exercise 22: *What happens if Black tries to save the rook the same way he did in Exercise 21?*

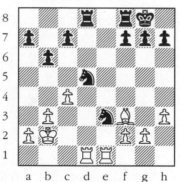

Exercise 23: *It's White's turn. Which knight should White capture, and why?*

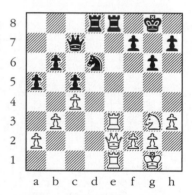

Exercise 24: *It's White's turn. Can White win material by capturing the rook on e8?*

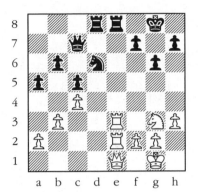

Exercise 25: *It's White's turn. Can White win material by capturing the rook on e8?*

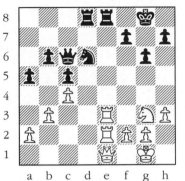

Exercise 26: *It's White's turn. Can White win material by capturing the rook on e8?*

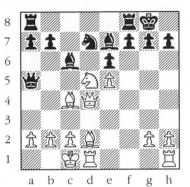

Exercise 27: *Black to move. White has just played his knight from c3 to d5. Black's queen is now attacked, as well as his bishop on e7. How can Black defend both pieces at once? What is his best move?*

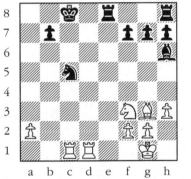

Exercise 28: *Black to move. What should Black play? Who will be ahead in material?*

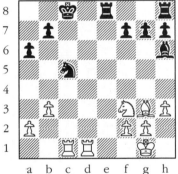

Exercise 29: *Black to move. What should Black play? Who will be ahead in material?*

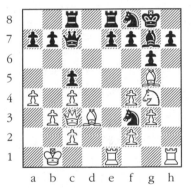

Exercise 30: *This is a very hard one! Black has just played his knight to f3 from d4. How can White save his queen (attacked by the bishop on g7) and rook (attacked by the rook on f3) at the same time? What is White's best move?*

The Least You Need to Know

♦ Having a material advantage is all about having a more powerful army to fight with.

♦ Chess is such a finely balanced game that when grandmasters play, having a material advantage of one pawn is often enough to win.

♦ Knowing how to judge who has a material advantage is a crucial skill, so always remember the scale of the relative value of the pieces.

♦ Practice the skills you need to judge when a capture wins or loses material.

♦ Practice the skills you need to recognize when one of your pieces (or pawns) is attacked, and how to parry the attack.

Chapter 6

Tricks of the Tactical Trade

In This Chapter

- The "fork"
- The "pin"
- The "skewer"
- Two attacks at once

What is a tactic? A *tactic* is a sequence of moves, at most a few moves long, played with some goal in mind. The most dramatic tactics have the goal either of giving checkmate or of winning material. In this chapter and the next, I'll show you some of the most important tactics for winning material. Of course, no two positions are exactly alike, but you'll see that there are some typical tactics that fall into patterns you can recognize in many different positions. Once you learn these patterns, you'll be able to anticipate them from your opponent, and you'll be able to use them to your advantage.

The Fork

When one piece attacks two pieces at the same time, it's called a *fork*. I'll show you examples of forks by each different piece. Let's start with the pawn.

Chess Talk

A **tactic** is a sequence of moves played to accomplish some goal, often winning material or giving checkmate.

Chess Talk

A **fork** is when one piece attacks two pieces at the same time.

Pawn Forks

Consider Diagram 1. It's White's turn to move. Black is threatening to capture the pawn on e4, so White could defend it with 1.Bd3 or exchange pawns with 1.exd5 exd5. But White has a much better move: 1.e5! White attacks both Black's bishop on d6 and knight on f6. There is no way Black can defend both of them. He must lose a bishop or a knight for a pawn, as is illustrated in Diagram 2.

The paradox of the pawn fork is that pawn forks are so dangerous precisely because pawns are worth so much less than the other pieces. It's useless to protect a piece against a pawn, because if you lose even a knight or a bishop for a pawn, you've lost a lot of material.

In fact, it's often worth a pawn to set up a pawn fork. Take a look at Diagram 3.

It's White's turn. Notice that Black's pawn on e5 is attacked twice by White's pawn on d4 and knight on d3, and defended twice by Black's knight on d7 and bishop on d6. But if White could get one of his own pawns to e5, and if that pawn were protected, Black's knight on f6 and bishop on d6 would be forked. Do you see a way to do that?

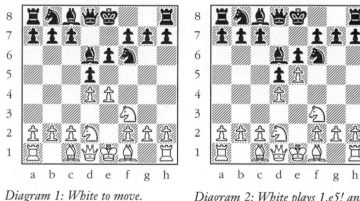

Diagram 1: White to move.

Diagram 2: White plays 1.e5! and forks Black's knight and bishop.

White cleverly plays 1.f4! (see Diagram 4), which attacks the pawn on e5. Because it's attacked by two pawns, it's useless to defend it with a piece, and there is no way to defend it with a pawn. Unless Black wants to lose a whole pawn for nothing, Black had better capture one of White's pawns. So in Diagram 5 Black plays 1...exd4.

But now White can carry out his plan to establish the pawn fork by playing 2.e5 (see Diagram 6). White has lost a pawn, but he's attacking two pieces and will win one of them for a pawn, so he'll come out ahead a piece for two pawns.

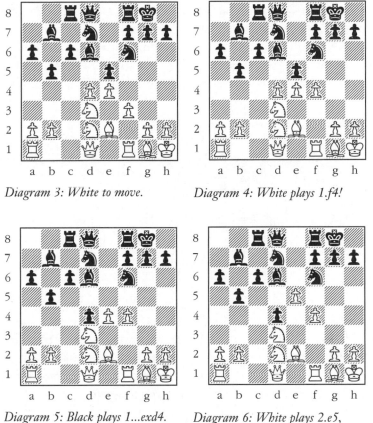

Diagram 3: White to move.

Diagram 4: White plays 1.f4!

Diagram 5: Black plays 1...exd4.

Diagram 6: White plays 2.e5, forking Black's knight and bishop.

Knight Forks

Knights strike terror into the hearts of the rooks and the queen, because they're so tricky. Two pieces that seem to be far apart and out of range of anything can suddenly find themselves forked by a knight. Watch out for these guys!

Consider Diagram 7, where it's White's turn. What danger could there possibly be to Black in this position? All the danger in the world after 1.Ne4, as you can see in Diagram 8. Both Black's queen and rook are attacked by the knight, and Black has no way to remove the threat to both pieces in his next turn, so he must lose material. By the way, Black should make the best of a bad deal by moving the queen to a square where it can recapture the knight once it captures the rook on c5. For example, 1...Qe7 is a good move.

Part of the danger of knights is that because they don't move like any other piece, when they fork two (or more) pieces, they often do not have to be defended. (Compare to the pawn fork in Diagram 2, for example.) Diagram 9 shows the most deadly knight fork of all: the "family fork," so called because the knight forks both the king and queen. Black is in check, so he must move the king, and White will win a whole queen!

Diagram 7: White to move.

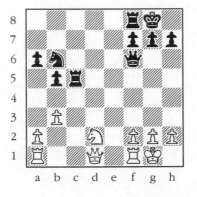

Chess Talk

When a knight forks the king and the queen, it's called a **family fork**.

In fact, this brings us to an important point. Why would you want to promote a pawn to anything other than a queen? The most common reason is to promote to a knight to set up a *family fork*. Promote to a queen, and you just gain a queen. Promote to a knight while setting up a family fork at the same time, and you gain a knight, plus you capture a queen. Diagrams 10 and 11 demonstrate this.

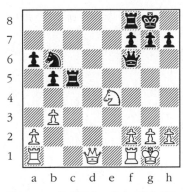

Diagram 8: White plays 1.Ne4!, forking the rook and queen.

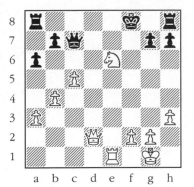

Diagram 9: White's knight forks Black's king and queen.

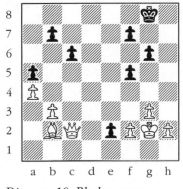

Diagram 10: Black to move.

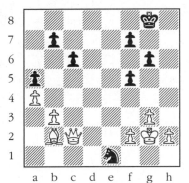

Diagram 11: Black plays 1...e1=N+, forking the king and queen.

Bishop Forks

The other pieces may not be quite as dangerous forkers as the pawn and the knight, but they are not to be trifled with! Consider Diagram 12. It's White's move, but Black has a material advantage of a knight, rook, and pawn. How much damage could White possibly do?

Lots! White starts with 1.Bxc6+ (see Diagram 13), which not only captures a knight, but also forks Black's rook on d5 and king on e8. Black responds with 1...Ke7. Maybe Black figures that even after losing the knight and the rook, he will still have a material advantage of a pawn.

But Black doesn't notice that after 2.Bxd5, White is again forking two pieces: the knight on g8 and the rook on b3 (see Diagram 14). Black must lose one or the other, which will leave White with the large advantage of a bishop for a pawn. Notice that Black's pawns on b6 and g7 are getting in his way. If Black didn't have the pawn on b6, he could play 2...Rb8 to move the rook out of the attack and also protect the knight. If Black didn't have the pawn on g7, then if he played 2...Rg3 he would move the rook out of the attack and also protect the knight at the same time. But the pawn on b6 prohibits 2...Rb8, and the pawn on g7 blocks the g-file, so that 2...Rg3 doesn't protect the knight. What a bishop!

Diagram 12: White to move.

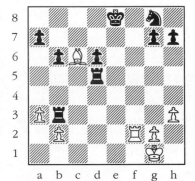

Diagram 13: White plays 1.Bxc6+.

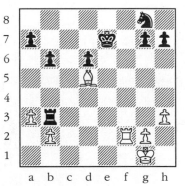

Diagram 14: Black plays 1...Ke7 and White plays 2.Bxd5.

Rook Forks

Whenever you see two pieces along the same file or the same rank, and a rook nearby, watch out! There may be a fork just waiting to happen.

Consider Diagram 15. Material is just about equal. In a game between two grandmasters, a draw would be the most likely result. However, in this case Black isn't satisfied with a draw, so to be aggressive, Black plays 1...Ne2?? (see Diagram 16) to attack the rook.

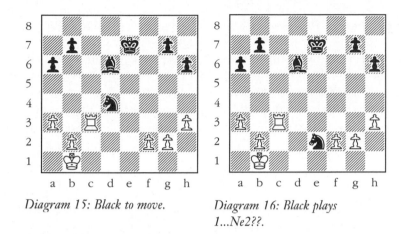

Diagram 15: Black to move.

Diagram 16: Black plays
1...Ne2??.

But this is a horrible blunder! Notice how Black has carelessly put the knight into the same file as the king without considering the consequences. White snatches the opportunity to fork the two pieces by playing 2.Re3+. Black must get out of check, and then White captures the knight (see Diagram 17) in the next move, leaving Black with a lost position.

Diagrams 18 and 19 give another example of a rook fork. Here Black even has a material advantage, but it will not last. White plays 1.Rd7!, and attacks both the knight on e7 and the bishop on b7. One or the other must go: The fork will give White a winning material advantage.

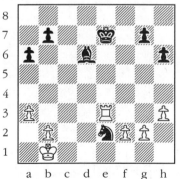

Diagram 17: White plays 2.Re3+,
forking king and knight.

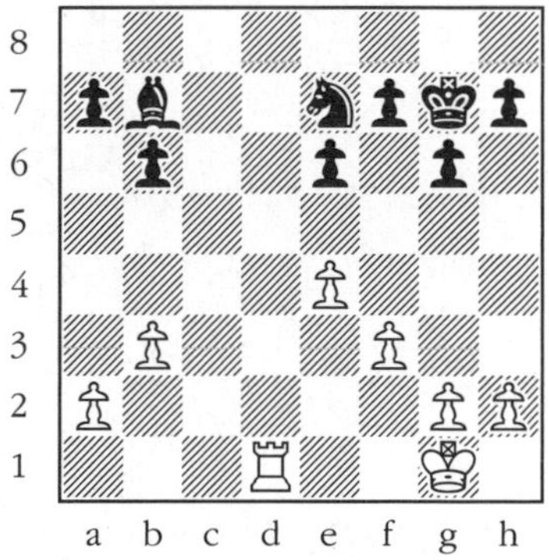

Diagram 18: White to move.

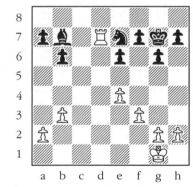

Diagram 19: White plays 1.Rd7!,
forking knight and bishop.

Queen Forks

You can never be too careful with the queen. When thinking about your opponent's queen, always check twice to make sure that there is not a fork hiding somewhere. And when thinking about your own queen, look to see whether an opportunity for a queen fork might be present. Because the queen combines the power of the rook and the bishop, it can attack two or more pieces from almost any square on the board.

Diagrams 20 through 22 show one example of how the queen's ability to combine the rook's move and the bishop's move makes it such a dangerous piece. Black decides to play 1...Ng5??, but this is a grave error. White spots the flaw and plays 2.Qd8+! forking the king and the knight. Black must defend against the check, for example, by 2...Kh7, and then White wins a knight for free by 3.Qxg5.

Here's another example. In Diagram 23, Black wants to move the bishop. A good move would be 1...Be6, which puts the bishop on the sensitive diagonal in front of the king on g8. But Black plays 1...Bb7?? (see Diagram 24), a terrible mistake. White pounces on the error by playing 2.Qb3+! (see Diagram 25), forking the bishop and the king. Black must defend against the check, which will leave the bishop defenseless to the queen. (Notice that blocking the check with the bishop by playing 2...Bd5 fails to save the bishop, because White can safely capture the bishop on that square with the pawn, knight, or queen.)

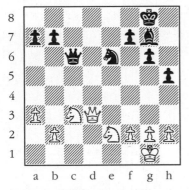

Diagram 20: Black to move.

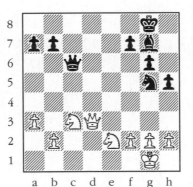

Diagram 21: Black plays 1...Ng5??.

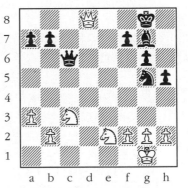

Diagram 22: White plays 2.Qd8+, forking the king and knight.

King Forks

Because the king is so vulnerable, it's unusual for the king to be used aggressively before many pieces have been exchanged, so it is not common for the king to fork pieces or pawns. But it can happen, just the same!

Consider Diagram 26. Black notices that his rook is attacked by the knight on g4, so he should move the rook away from the attack. Where should it go?

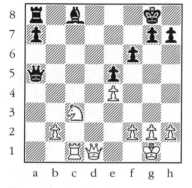
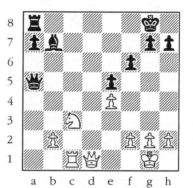
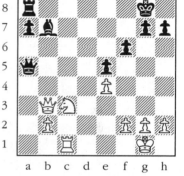

Diagram 23: Black to move. *Diagram 24: Black plays 1...Bb7??* *Diagram 25: White plays 2.Qb3+!, forking king and bishop.*

A good move would be 1...Re7, but Black tries to be too aggressive. He figures if he can give a check, why not do it? So Black plays 1...Rg3+? (see Diagram 27), and only after 2.Kf2! does he realize that his rook and knight are forked by the king (see Diagram 28). The best Black can do is to play 2...Rxg4, but after 3.Rxg4, Black has lost the exchange (rook for knight).

A more typical king fork occurs when there are very few pieces left. Then it's safer for the king to be used aggressively, and it will sometimes fork pawns. In Diagram 29, Black's king has managed to make it all the way behind White's pawns. Now Black reaps the benefits by playing 1...Kb2! (in Diagram 30), which attacks three pawns at the same time. Now that's a fork fit for a king! (See Chapter 14 for more about how the king can be used aggressively when there are only a few pieces left on the board.)

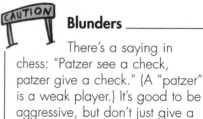

Blunders _____

There's a saying in chess: "Patzer see a check, patzer give a check." (A "patzer" is a weak player.) It's good to be aggressive, but don't just give a check because you can. Make sure you take your opponent's response into account.

Diagram 26: Black to move.

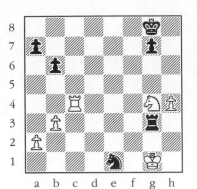

Diagram 27: Black plays
1...Rg3+?.

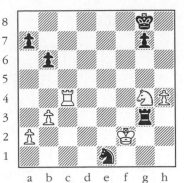

Diagram 28: White plays 2.Kf2!,
not only removing the king from
check, but also forking Black's
rook and knight.

Patrick's Pointers

The king does not like to be exposed along a rank, file, or diagonal! Among the many dangers of being so exposed is that there might be a fork lurking. And a fork that involves the king is doubly dangerous: Because the king must be protected at all costs, the other piece that is forked is often helpless. So if you notice that your opponent's king is exposed along an open rank, file, or diagonal, look for a way to take advantage of it. And if your own king is so exposed, try to get it out of harm's way.

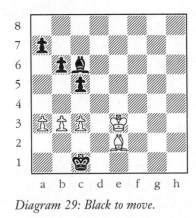

Diagram 29: Black to move.

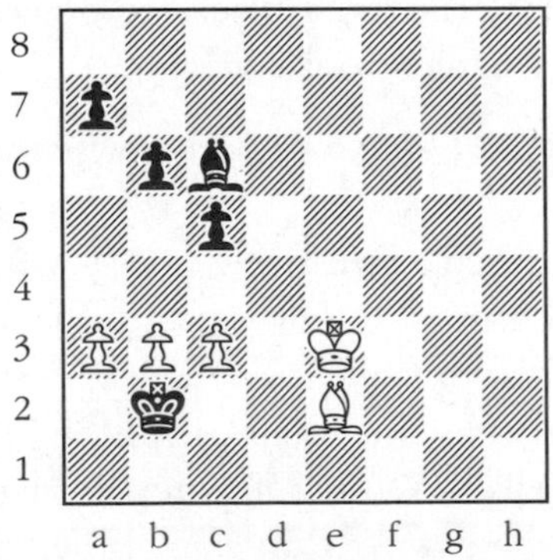

Diagram 30: Black plays 1...Kb2!,
forking all three of White's pawns.

The Pin

When you attack a piece, and that piece cannot move without exposing another piece behind it to capture, you are *pinning* the first piece to the piece behind it. Only the long-range pieces—the bishop, the rook, and the queen—can pin one piece to another. The ability to pin one piece to another is part of what makes those long-range pieces so dangerous!

I'll show you some common ways for bishops, rooks, and queens to pin pieces. But keep this in mind: There's a difference between pinning a piece to any ordinary piece, and pinning a piece to the king. When a piece is pinned to the king, the pinned piece can never move off the line of attack (because that would be exposing the king to check). Therefore, pinning a piece to the king is especially effective for the player doing the pinning—and dangerous for the player being pinned! In contrast, if a piece is pinned to an ordinary piece, you should always remember that it's legal, though often undesirable, to move the piece.

Chess Talk

When one piece is attacked, and it can't move without exposing a piece behind it to attack, the first piece is **pinned** to the piece behind it.

What should you do if your opponent is pinning one of your pieces and you want to remove the pin? There are four ways to "break" a pin:

- ◆ Capture the piece that is doing the pinning.

- ◆ Attack the piece that is doing the pinning, and force it to move away.

- ◆ Block the pin: either put something between the pinning piece and the piece that is pinned, or put something between the pinned piece and the piece it's pinned to.

- ◆ Get out of the way. If all else fails, you can move the piece "behind" the pinned piece out of the line of fire.

Patrick's Pointers
The fork is not always an automatic winner. When you use more valuable pieces to fork, you must watch out for the possibility that one piece may be able to move out of the attack and simultaneously protect the other piece. (Remember, the reason that pawn forks are so deadly is that it's impossible to protect a piece from a pawn, because the piece is worth so much more than the pawn.)

Bishop Pins

The position in Diagram 31 is the position from Exercise 20 in the last chapter. The bishop on f5 pins the rook on g6 to the king. Black cannot move the rook from attack, because that would expose the king to check. So White will win the rook for the bishop.

When a piece is pinned to your opponent's king, sometimes it's better not to capture it right away, but to bring another piece over to reinforce the attack. That way, you can win the pinned piece without allowing your opponent to recapture the piece that captured it. Or, alternatively, you can capture the pinned piece with a piece of lower value than the one you are pinning it with.

The next few diagrams illustrate what I mean. It's Black's move in Diagram 32. Black can only hope that White would be so foolish as to capture the rook right away with the bishop—then Black would recapture the bishop, and material would be equal. But Black realizes the real danger is that White might play 1.Ne5!, attacking the rook again, so that White can win it for nothing. It's Black's move, and he plays 1...Nd5 (Diagram 33). Black's idea is that if White plays 2.Ne5, Black can play 2...Ne7, defending the rook and even attacking the bishop, thereby gaining time to remove the king from the pin while still protecting the rook by playing 3...h5 and 4...Kh6.

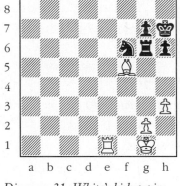

Diagram 31: White's bishop pins Black's rook to the king.

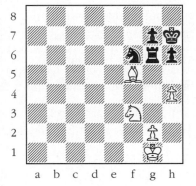

Diagram 32: Black to move.

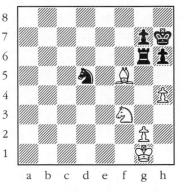

Diagram 33: Black plays 1...Nd5.

It's a good plan, but it fails, because White plays 2.h5! in Diagram 34, attacking the rook with a pawn. There is nothing for Black to do. If Black plays 2...Ne7 (see Diagram 35), White plays 3.hxg6+, and if Black is so foolish as to recapture the pawn with 3...Nxg6? (see Diagram 36), White will play 4.Ne5, winning the knight as well. What a pin!

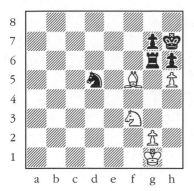

Diagram 34: White plays 2.h5!, attacking the pinned rook with the pawn.

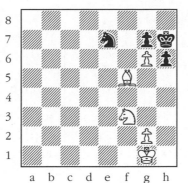

Diagram 35: Black plays 2...Ne7, and White plays 3.hxg6+.

Diagram 36: If Black plays 3...Nxg6?, White wins the knight by playing 4.Ne5.

Diagrams 37 and 38 show something else to watch out for. Suppose you pin your opponent's rook to his queen with your bishop. Make sure that the rook can't move away and give check at the same time, especially if your bishop isn't protected! This is really a version of "two attacks at once," which I will explain to you later in the chapter.

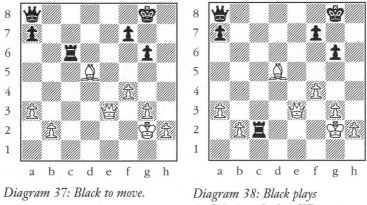

Diagram 37: Black to move.

Diagram 38: Black plays 1...Rc2+!, and when White moves the king, Black will play 2...Qxd5.

Finally, here are some typical pins: Bishop pinning knight to king (see Diagram 39) or queen (see Diagram 40). Notice that there is no reason for the side with the pinned knight to panic yet. Although there is a pin, there is no threat to win the pinned piece. Even so, the bishop is often quite usefully employed in such a pin, because not only is the bishop being used actively, it's also cutting down the effectiveness of the knight.

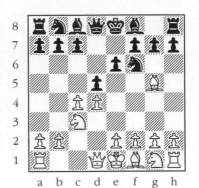

Diagram 39: Bishop pinning
knight to king.

Diagram 40: Bishop pinning
knight to queen.

Rook Pins

Diagrams 41 through 43 show some examples of rook pins. Notice in Diagram 43 that
if the rook is going to pin the queen, it had better be protected! (The same holds true
for a bishop pinning the queen, of course.)

One of the most common uses of the rook pin is to pin a piece to the uncastled king along
the open e-file, if one side has castled early and the other side has not. (By the way, this is
one very good reason to castle early!) Diagrams 44 and 45 show you what I mean. In
Diagram 44, White has castled, and Black has not. Black's knight and king are precariously
placed on the same file! In Diagram 45, Black pays the price. White attacks the knight,
which cannot move because it is pinned. Even if Black defends the knight, it can't be
saved, because next move White will attack the knight with a pawn, and the knight will
have to stand his post while he is slaughtered by the pawn. Don't let this happen to you!

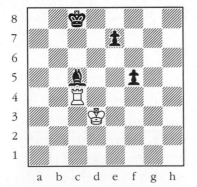

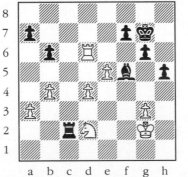

Diagram 41: White's rook pins
Black's bishop to the king.

Diagram 42: Black's rook pins
White's knight to the king.

Diagram 43: Black's rook pins
White's queen to the king.

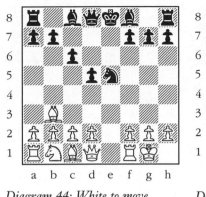

Diagram 44: White to move.

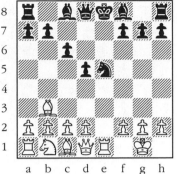

Diagram 45: White plays 1.Re1!, which wins material.

Queen Pins

The queen moves like the rook and the bishop, so it can pin like the rook and the bishop: along ranks, files, and diagonals. Diagrams 46 shows an example.

Keep in mind that because the queen is so powerful, if your opponent is able to protect the piece that is pinned, you won't want to capture it with the queen. But that doesn't stop you from attacking the piece with something else, perhaps even a lowly pawn. The queen holds the piece down, and the other piece or pawn goes in for the kill. Diagram 47 shows an example of this.

Patrick's Pointers
I can't stress this enough: Castle early! Nothing but trouble awaits the king sitting in the middle of the board in the early part of the game, before pieces have been traded. Plus, if you castle, it's much easier to use your rooks. You may even be able to pin one of your opponent's pieces to a still-uncastled king!

I have been concentrating on showing you how to use pins to win material. But keep this in mind. Pins are also effective ways to immobilize your opponent's pieces. Even if there's no immediate way to win the piece being pinned, just by pinning it you have severely limited its ability to move.

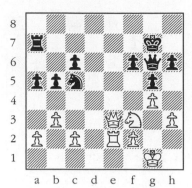

Diagram 46: White pins the knight to the rook, and Black must lose a piece.

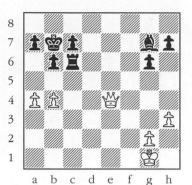

Diagram 47: White pins the rook to the king, and threatens to play 1.b5.

The Skewer

The *skewer* is a variation on the pin. In a skewer, you attack a piece, force it to move, and then win the piece behind it. Usually the piece you force to move away is more valuable than the piece behind it.

Chess Talk

A **skewer** is the name for the tactic of attacking a piece, forcing it to move away, in order to capture the piece behind it.

Diagrams 48 through 51 show some examples of skewers. Keep in mind that king skewers (skewers where you give check because when the king moves you want to capture the piece behind the king) are the most dangerous skewers of all.

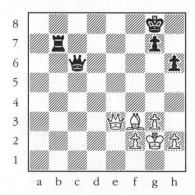

Diagram 48: White skewers the queen and rook with the bishop.

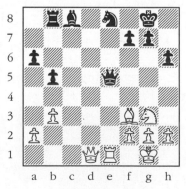

Diagram 49: White skewers the queen and knight with the rook.

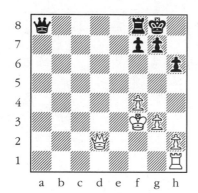

Diagram 50: Black skewers the king and rook with the queen.

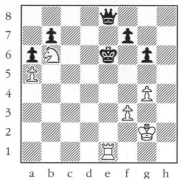

Diagram 51: White skewers the king and queen with the rook.

Two Attacks at Once

When you give two attacks at once, one move creates two attacks by two different pieces at the same time. Notice how this is different than the fork, where one piece attacks two pieces at the same time.

Does that sound impossible? The idea is simple, really. One piece moves and attacks something, and after it is out of the way, another piece behind it is "discovered" to be attacking something else. Let's take a look at two examples of this.

In Diagram 52, Black notices that the bishop would attack the queen if the knight were not in the way on c6. This gives Black an idea. Is there some useful square to move the knight to, so as to use the fact that the bishop will be attacking the queen?

> **Patrick's Pointers**
>
> When I was a kid, someone gave me a great piece of advice: "When you see a good move, don't make it right away; sit on your hands and make sure there isn't a better move." Diagrams 54 through 56 show White benefiting from this advice.

In Diagram 53, we see the answer. Black plays 1...Nb4!, an extremely strong move. Because the bishop on b7 now attacks the queen, White must meet this threat. But the knight on b4 also attacks the rook. White cannot meet both threats at the same time and so must lose material.

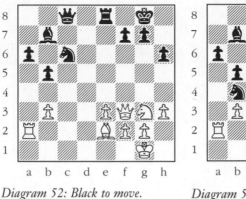

Diagram 52: Black to move.

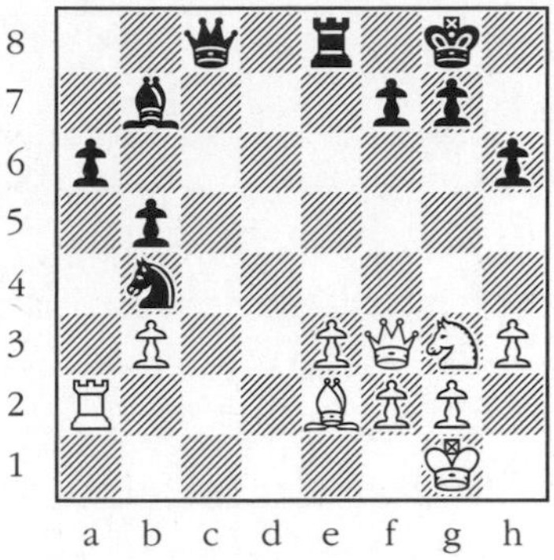

Diagram 53: Black plays 1...Nb4!, attacking the rook with the knight and the queen with the bishop.

Our second example shows that the discovered attack is such a strong tactic that there may be more than one good move. In that case, always look for the strongest possible discovered attack.

One possible discovered attack is to capture the pawn on a6 (see Diagram 54). The bishop can't be captured (see Diagram 55), because of the threat to the queen. But this only wins a pawn; isn't there a stronger move? Yes there is! White can play 1.Bg4! (see Diagram 56) which attacks the rook on c8. Black must move the queen, and White will win the rook for the bishop.

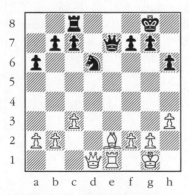

Diagram 54: White to move.

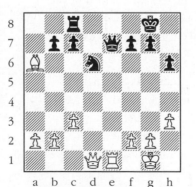

Diagram 55: White plays 1.Bxa6. This wins a pawn, but White had a stronger move.

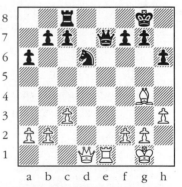

Diagram 56: White plays 1.Bg4! This wins the rook for the bishop.

Discovered Check

The most potent way to give two attacks at once is the discovered check. When you give discovered check, you move one piece, and thereby uncover a check by another piece to the king. (The king suddenly "discovers" that it is in check!) I cannot emphasize strongly enough how powerful this tactic is. Every grandmaster has deep respect for the discovered check—so much respect that if he can give discovered check he assumes that there must be something very powerful he can do, and if he sees that his opponent can give discovered check, he assumes there's going to be trouble!

Diagrams 57 through 60 show how powerful discovered check can be. Diagrams 58 and 60 show a discovered check that wins the queen, because there is no way to remove the king from check and also prevent the queen from being captured. (In particular, notice in Diag-ram 60 that 1...Qc7 can be answered by 2.Nxc7.)

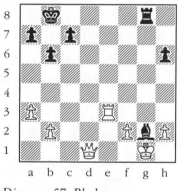

Diagram 57: Black to move.

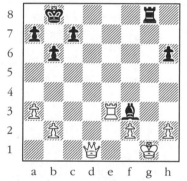

Diagram 58: Black plays 1...Bf3+!, which wins the queen.

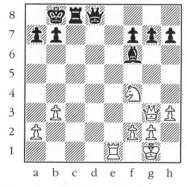

Diagram 59: White to move.

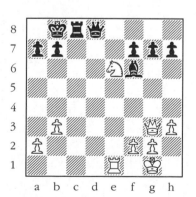

Diagram 60: White plays 1.Ne6+!.

Double Check

A *double check* is an interesting twist on discovered check. The double check is a discovered check, where the piece moving away decides to attack—the king! The king finds itself being checked by two pieces at once, and so there is no other way to meet the check than to move.

Chess Talk

A **double check** is when two pieces check the king at the same time. Double check is only possible as a form of discovered check.

Basically, the double check is not a tactic to win material, but a tactic to attack the king. Still, because it's a variant of the discovered check, I might as well introduce you to it in this chapter—and that gives me a chance to show you a beautiful execution of an attack against the king!

Diagrams 61 through 66 show an example of double check leading to checkmate. At the moment, in Diagram 61, Black has an extra knight. Probably he expected White to just win back the piece by using the pin on the e-file and playing 1.Re1. Instead, White plays a move that begins a forced sequence leading to checkmate!

In Diagram 62, White plays 1.Qd8+!!, catching Black off guard. What is White up to? Well, it doesn't matter—there is only one legal move anyway—so Black captures the queen with 1...Kxd8 (see Diagram 63).

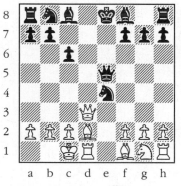

Diagram 61: White to move.

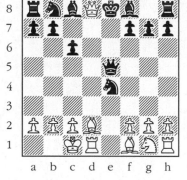

Diagram 62: White plays 1.Qd8+!!.

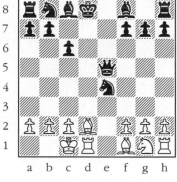

Diagram 63: Black plays 1...Kxd8.

But now White's clever plan is revealed: He plays 2.Bg5+!! (see Diagram 64), putting Black in double check. Because Black is in check from two pieces at once, he must move the king. The king has only two moves, to c7 or to e8. But no matter which way the king goes, White will give checkmate.

I urge you to figure out for yourself how White would give checkmate if Black moved the king to c7. (Here's a hint: White gives checkmate with his bishop.) Black decides to play 2...Ke8 (see Diagram 65). Now White has only one check, but it's the check that ends the game: 3.Rd8# (see Diagram 66). What a finish!

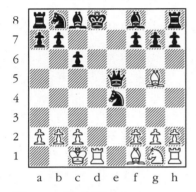

Diagram 64: White plays 2.Bg5+!!.

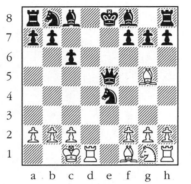

Diagram 65: Black plays 2...Ke8.

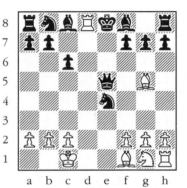

Diagram 66: White plays 3.Rd8#.

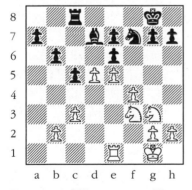

Exercise 1: *White to move. How can White win a pawn by threatening a pawn fork between Black's knight and bishop?*

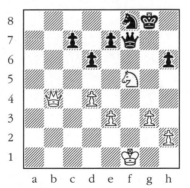

Exercise 2: *White to move. Should Black be worried about 1.Nxh6+, or should White be worried because the knight is being attacked?*

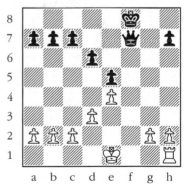

Exercise 3: *White to move. What is White's best move?*

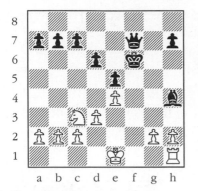

Exercise 4: *White to move. Can White win Black's queen? What is White's best move?*

Exercise 5: *Black to move. Who should win this position?*

Exercise 6: *White to move. What is White's best move?*

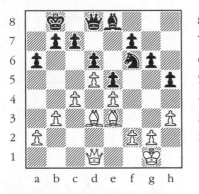

Exercise 7: *White to move. White plays 1.Bg5 in this position. What is his threat? Can Black defend?*

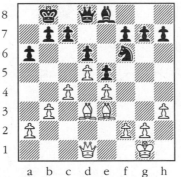

Exercise 8: *White to move. White plays 1.Bg5 in this position. Does Black have the same problem as he had in Exercise 7?*

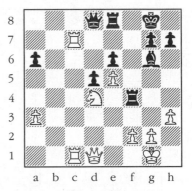

Exercise 9: *White to move (Wolff–Sagalchik, North Bay, 1996). I played 28.Nxe6, forking the queen and the rook on f4. What was my idea if Black played 28...Rxe6?*

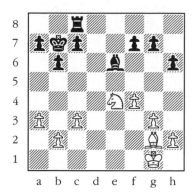

Exercise 10: *White to move. What is White's best move?*

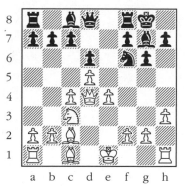

Exercise 11: *Black to move. What is Black's best move? (Hint: The solution involves combining two different tactics.)*

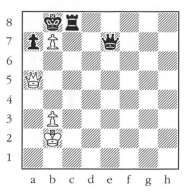

Exercise 12: *White to move. This is a tough one! White thinks about playing 1.bxc8=Q+ Kxc8, giving both sides equal material and the position should be a draw. But White also sees the possibility to do better. How?*

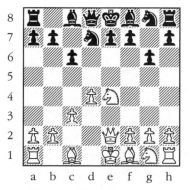

Exercise 13: *White's last move was 1.Qe2. What is his threat? Should Black play 1...Ngf6 or not?*

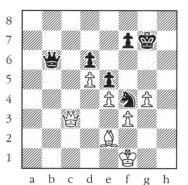

Exercise 14: *Black played an amazing move in this position, 1...Qg1+. What on Earth was his idea after White captures the queen with his king?*

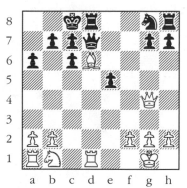

Exercise 15: *White to move (Volchok–Kreslavsky, USSR, 1970). It looks like Black will win back the bishop because of the pin against the rook. But White found a terrific way to turn the tables and win.*

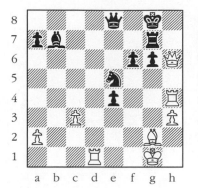

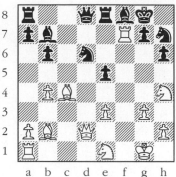

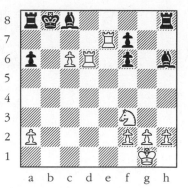

Exercise 16: *White to move (Szabo–Bronstein, Zurich, 1953). Material is roughly even in this complicated position, but White found a way to cut through the complications and get a winning material advantage. How? (Hint: 1.Qh8+ is not the right first move, but it is the right idea.)*

Exercise 17: *White to move. White wins if he finds the right way to give discovered check with the rook.*

Exercise 18: *White to move (Sznapik–Bernard, Poznan, 1971). White could capture Black's f-pawns, but then Black defends with 1...Ra7. Instead, White found a beautiful way to win. How?*

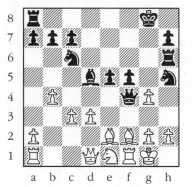

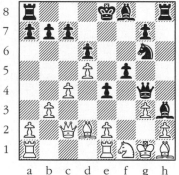

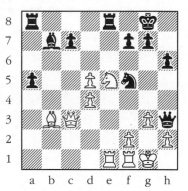

Exercise 19: *Black to move (Kosalopov–Nezhmetdinov, Kazan, 1936). Black found an incredible way to win with 1...Qxh2+!! 2.Kxh2. What should Black play now?*

Exercise 20: *White to move (Yermolinsky–Abroskin, Leningrad, 1972). How did White win Black's queen?*

Exercise 21: *Black to move (Morozevich–Adams, Holland, 2001). How did Black force White to resign in one move?*

The Least You Need to Know

- The fork, the pin, the skewer, and two attacks at once are very effective tactics for winning material.

- A discovered check is especially potent. Every grandmaster uses it when he can, and avoids falling victim to it whenever possible!

- The double check is a version of discovered check. It is a very useful tactic for giving checkmate.

- Practice recognizing these tactics with the exercises, and then use them to win material in your games.

Chapter 7

Dirtier Tricks

In This Chapter

♦ Distracting your opponent's pieces

♦ Sometimes your own pieces get in the way

♦ How some chess pieces can have x-ray vision

♦ The importance of the "in between" move

In Chapter 6, you learned the most basic tactics you can use to win material. Now I will show you some tactics that are more sophisticated. You will probably see the tactics in Chapter 6 more often than the ones in this chapter, but the ones here are pretty common, too. You'll have plenty of chances to use them against your opponents!

Getting an Enemy Piece Out of the Way

Many times, if you could only force your opponent to move one of his pieces to another square, you could take advantage of some weakness in his position. Forcing your opponent to move a piece to a different square is called "deflecting" that piece. *Deflection* comes in many different forms, but it falls roughly into two different categories.

Attacking the Defender

In Diagram 1, does White have any way to win material? Well, the only piece that is attacking any of Black's pieces is the knight on e5, which attacks Black's bishop on d7

Chess Talk

When you force your opponent to move a piece away in order to take advantage of some weakness in his position, it's called **deflection**.

and his pawn on f7. But if White captures either one, Black can recapture the knight. Taking the pawn on f7 by playing 1.Nxf7?? would be a bad idea, because after 1...Kxf7, Black wins material, capturing a knight and only losing a pawn. Taking the bishop on d7 by playing 1.Nxd7+ is not so bad, but after 1...Nxd7 White has only exchanged a knight for a bishop, which is basically an even trade.

Okay, so there is nothing for White to capture right away that will give him a material advantage. But is there any way for White to deflect one of the black pieces that is crucial for the defense? Suppose Black's knight could be driven away from the f6 square, so that it wouldn't defend the bishop any more. Then White could capture the bishop for free! Do you see how to do it?

White plays 1.g5, in Diagram 2, attacking Black's knight with a pawn. Black is really in trouble now. Because Black's knight is attacked by a measly pawn, there is no way to defend it. In vain, Black looks for some way to attack White, but there is nothing to do. Black is caught between a rock and a hard place: Either White captures a whole knight for only a pawn, or—even worse—Black moves the knight so the bishop is no longer defended, allowing White to win a whole bishop for free!

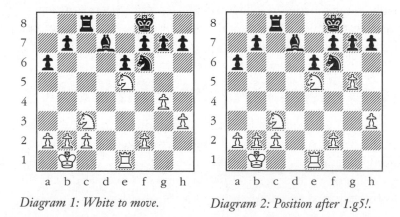

Diagram 1: White to move.   *Diagram 2: Position after 1.g5!.*

There's another example in Diagram 3. It's Black's turn to move. Is there any way for Black to use deflection to his advantage? Well, what does Black attack? Black attacks the pawn on h3 with the bishop, but that doesn't look very promising, because that pawn is defended by the pawn on g2, and how would you deflect that pawn? But Black attacks something else that looks much more promising: the bishop on e2. Black's queen attacks it, and it is only defended by White's queen. If there were only some way to drive the queen away, Black could take the bishop.

Sure enough, Black can play 1...Rd8! (see Diagram 4) to attack White's queen. What can White do? He can't take the rook, because it's defended by Black's queen. Is there any square to which White can move the queen where it still defends the bishop? No: The queen can only move to c1 or b1, and neither of those lets it defend the bishop. The only chance is to block the attack, so White plays 2.Bd3 in Diagram 5. (White could also block the attack by playing 2.Nd3, but this move would lose material in the same way that 2.Bd3 does.)

White figures he has killed two birds with one stone: He has defended the queen from attack, and he has moved the bishop off the sensitive e2 square. "I'm completely safe now," he thinks. But Black has seen farther! Even though he can't use deflection any more, he can use one of the ideas from last chapter to win material. Do you see how?

Black plays 2...c4! in Diagram 6, to attack the bishop. Black realizes that White's bishop is pinned to the queen, so White must either lose the bishop or let his queen be captured. (Notice that if White had played 2.Nd3, then 2...c4 would have won the knight because of the pin in a similar way.)

> **Patrick's Pointers**
>
> Always look for a way to combine the tactics you have learned! You will see several examples of combining tactics in this chapter, and I guarantee that you will have many opportunities to combine tactics in your games.

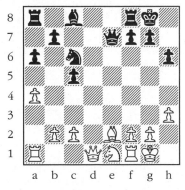

Diagram 3: Black to move.

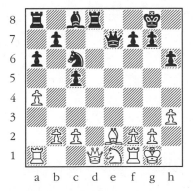

Diagram 4: Position after 1...Rd8!.

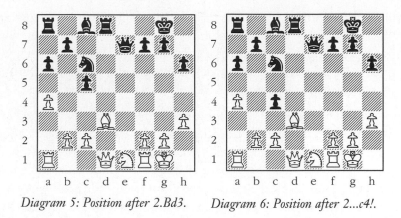

Diagram 5: Position after 2.Bd3.   *Diagram 6: Position after 2...c4!.*

Overloading the Defender

Everyone knows how hard it can be to do two things at once. Well, the same is true for chess pieces. If one piece has to defend two things at the same time, sometimes the piece is unable to do both.

In Diagram 7, Black has two possible captures: 1...Rxc2 or 1...Qxe3+. White defends both pieces with the queen, which means the queen is doing double duty. Black takes advantage of this by playing 1...Rxc2! in Diagram 8.

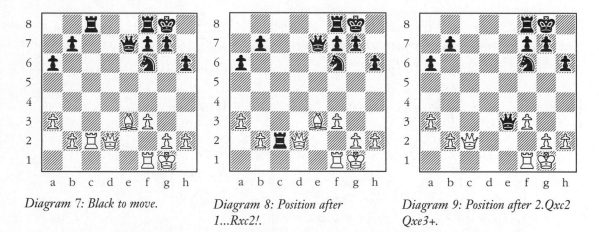

Diagram 7: Black to move.   *Diagram 8: Position after 1...Rxc2!.*   *Diagram 9: Position after 2.Qxc2 Qxe3+.*

When White recaptures with 2.Qxc2, the queen leaves the defense of the bishop, and Black wins a whole piece for nothing with 2...Qxe3+ (see Diagram 9).

Sometimes when a defender is overloaded, it's worth taking a piece of lesser value instead of one of greater value, even though the piece will be recaptured. This can work to your advantage because the defender is deflected from the defense of another piece that you can capture, and the two pieces together are worth more than the one piece you lost. Here is an example.

In Diagram 10, White has counted the material, and assumes things stand about equal: A knight and a bishop add up to six points (maybe even a little more), and are at least as good as a rook and a pawn. White sees that Black's rooks are attacking the knight and bishop, but it seems that everything is defended well enough by the rook—the knight is even defending the bishop to boot! What could go wrong?

Black plays 1...Rxe3! in Diagram 11, and suddenly the roof caves in. White has no choice but to recapture the rook with 2.Rxe3, whereupon Black plays 2...Rxc4 (see Diagram 12). Black has won two pieces for a rook, and now has an extra pawn and all the chances to win.

Keep in mind that a defensive piece can be overloaded in ways other than just having to defend another piece from capture. For example, sometimes it might have to defend against check or checkmate.

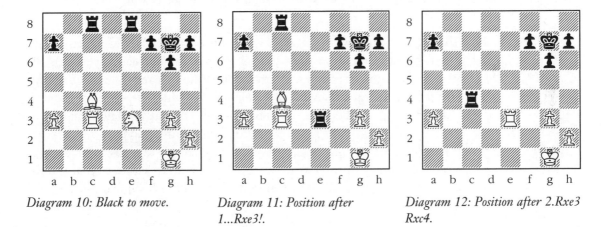

Diagram 10: Black to move.

Diagram 11: Position after 1...Rxe3!.

Diagram 12: Position after 2.Rxe3 Rxc4.

In Diagram 13, White attacks only one piece, the knight on e7, and it is defended by the bishop on f8. But White is alerted to the possibility of decoying the bishop away from defending the knight because he notices that Black's king is exposed to check along the diagonal, and the only defense to the check is to block it with that same bishop on f8. White plays 1.Bf6+! (see Diagram 14), and after 1...Bg7 he plays 2.Bxe7 (see Diagram 15), winning the knight for nothing.

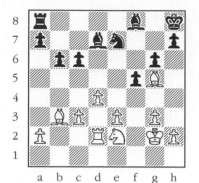

Diagram 13: White to move.

Diagram 14: Position after
1.Bf6+!.

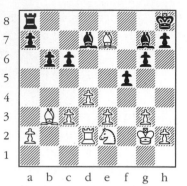

Diagram 15: Position after
1...Bg7 2.Bxe7.

When You Are Your Own Worst Enemy

Sometimes one of your pieces is on a square which another one of your pieces would just love to reach. When that happens, you should look for the most advantageous way possible to get the piece out of the way. Sometimes the best way to get the piece out of the way is to *sacrifice* it. When you sacrifice a piece to get it out of the way, it's called a *clearance sacrifice*.

Let's see how this works by taking two examples from two former World Chess Champions. The first example is a position from the game Tal–Parma, played in Bled, 1961 (see Diagram 16). Bruno Parma was a very strong grandmaster in his day, but he was no match for the Latvian genius Mikhail Tal, known as "the Wizard from Riga"

Chess Talk

A **sacrifice** is when you voluntarily let your opponent get a material advantage. A **clearance sacrifice** is when you sacrifice a piece in order to get it out of the way.

because of his brilliant and inventive play. (You can read more about Mikhail Tal in Chapter 16.) Tal sees that he has a rook for a bishop and a pawn, giving him a material advantage. But he also sees that if only his knight were on e6 instead of his queen, he would be forking Parma's Black king and queen. What's the best way to get the queen out of the way? For a genius like Tal, it couldn't have taken more than a millisecond to find 29.Qxf5! (see Diagram 17).

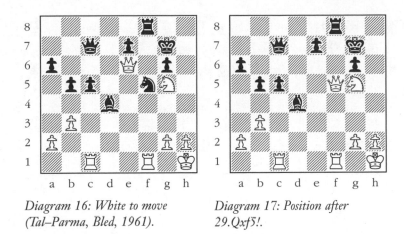

Diagram 16: White to move
(Tal–Parma, Bled, 1961).

Diagram 17: Position after
29.Qxf5!.

Tal captures the knight with his queen, because even though Black can recapture the queen, White will follow up with 30.Ne6+ and win back the queen, pocketing the knight as profit. Parma resigned, yet another victim to Tal's magic.

When Tal played that game, he had just the year before taken the World Championship title from Mikhail Botvinnik, a man almost 30 years his senior. Yet Botvinnik would retake the title from Tal later in 1961. (You can read more about Mikhail Botvinnik in Chapter 16.) Let's take a look at a game Botvinnik played before he reached his full strength. Even though he was not yet World Champion, he was good enough to teach us a thing or two!

Botvinnik played White against G. Stepanov in this game in 1931. (see Diagram 18). Perhaps Stepanov hadn't suspected anything yet, but we can assume that Botvinnik already noticed that his opponent's queen was in a precarious position. How did Botvinnik take advantage of this circumstance? Are any of his own pieces in the way?

In Diagram 19, Botvinnik played 19.Bxf7+!!, which at first blush seems crazy. What could the idea of this move possibly be? After all, Black had the square f7 securely defended, so that it looks like White is simply trading bishop and knight for a rook and pawn. However, the real point was revealed after Black recaptured the bishop, 19...Rxf7. (Because Stepanov was in check, he had nothing better than to take the bishop.)

It turns out that f7 was not White's real target at all, as now Botvinnik played 20.Nc4!, as shown in Diagram 20, attacking the black queen. What Botvinnik had noticed and his opponent had missed is that the queen has no safe square to run to. If you can't believe it, try to find a safe square for the queen. But don't forget that because the knight has moved from e5, the bishop on g3 controls the c7 square! The young Botvinnik exploited his material advantage and eventually won the game.

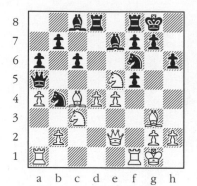

Diagram 18: White to move (Botvinnik–Stepanov, USSR, 1931).

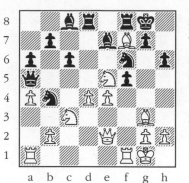

Diagram 19: Position after 19.Bxf7+!!.

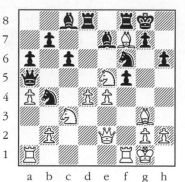

Diagram 20: Position after 19...Rxf7 20.Nc4!.

Wishing Can Help You Make It So

It often takes a flash of inspiration to find a clearance sacrifice, because it's hard to see the possibility of putting one of your pieces on a square that another one of your pieces already occupies. You can help that flash of inspiration to come by asking yourself this question:

"What move do I wish I could play?"

Sometimes you may find that the only thing preventing you from making your wish come true is one of your own pieces. And if that's the case, maybe you can do something about it.

In Diagram 21, suppose you were Black in this position. Things look pretty dismal. White has an extra pawn, and Black doesn't have any obvious threats. Maybe you even start daydreaming here: "Man, I was so stupid to lose that pawn. Not only am I behind in material, my pieces don't look that great. My knight is the only piece beyond the first rank, and the only one doing any good for me! Well, maybe my queen is doing a little good, because it's attacking the rook on c6. Come to think of it, White's rook and queen are lined up in a typical knight fork position, if only I could play 1...Nb4. I wish I could play 1...Nb4, but my pawn on b4 blocks that hope."

Even though White has an extra pawn, Black has a killer move here, and daydreaming has taken Black halfway to finding it. If your pawn offends you, push it: 1...b3! is deadly (see Diagram 22). Actually, this move begins a sequence that combines three tactics: a fork, a clearance sacrifice, and a deflection. Because White's bishop and queen are forked, the pawn can't be ignored. Because Black's queen attacks White's rook on c6, 2.Qxb3 simply loses the rook to 2...Qxc6 (see Diagram 23). So White plays 2.Bxb3, but then Black forks the queen and rook with 2...Nb4 (see Diagram 24).

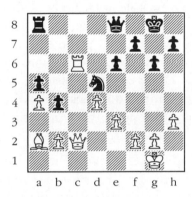

Diagram 21: Black to move.

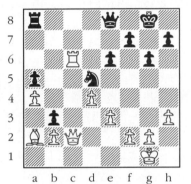

Diagram 22: Position after 1...b3!.

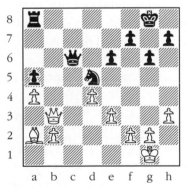

Diagram 23: Position after 2.Qxb3 Qxc6.

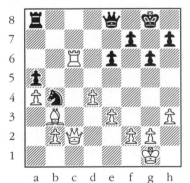

Diagram 24: Position after 2.Bxb3 Nb4!.

Superman's Not the Only One with X-Ray Vision!

I used to love reading comic books (okay, I still love reading them), and Superman was one of my favorite heroes. In fact, I first started reading comic books around the same time I first started learning how to play chess! Maybe that's why I have a special fondness for this next tactic, the *x-ray*. The name comes from the idea that sometimes a piece can "see through" an enemy piece.

Let me illustrate what I mean with a simple example in Diagram 25. It might look as though Black's bishop on d5 adequately protects the rook on a8, so if White plays 1.Rxa8+, Black can just recapture the rook with 1...Bxa8, and the result will be an even trade. But look at the position after 1.Rxa8+ Bxa8 (see Diagram 26), and it becomes easier to see that White will play 2.Bxa8 and win a bishop for free! The white bishop on f3 can "see" the a8 square through the black bishop on d5, because if the black bishop ever captures anything on that square, the white bishop on f3 suddenly has a clear path to a8. That is the nature of the x-ray tactic.

Chess Talk

Sometimes if an enemy piece captures one of your pieces, another one of your pieces suddenly has its scope increased so that whereas before it didn't defend the piece that was captured, now it can capture the enemy piece on the same square. This tactic is called an **x-ray**.

The idea behind the x-ray is pretty simple, but being able to spot these tactics can be hard and takes practice. What makes it hard is that somehow it just doesn't seem natural that a piece that is "blocked off" from a square (like the white bishop was blocked off from the a8 square in Diagram 25) can have any control over it. The key to the x-ray is if the piece that is blocking some piece from controlling a square is itself used to capture something on that square, it suddenly no longer blocks access to that square.

Diagram 25: White to move.

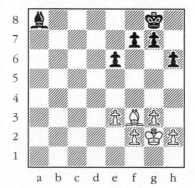

Diagram 26: Position after 1.Rxa8+ Bxa8.

Whew, that last sentence was a mouthful, wasn't it? Maybe I'd better just show you what I mean. The next position is taken from a game played by the most famous chess player of all time: Bobby Fischer. Fischer played this game in the 1963–64 U.S. Championship, which was just one of the eight U.S. Championships Fischer won! (Even more incredible is that he only played eight times!) Fischer's brilliant career culminated in his becoming World Champion in 1972 by crushing the champion from the Soviet Union, Boris Spassky. (You can read more about both Fischer and Spassky in Chapter 16.)

In this game, Fischer is playing another American grandmaster, Arthur Bisguier (see Diagram 27). Bisguier has calculated that the pawn on d3 is adequately protected. He figures that if White captures the pawn, he will maintain material equality as follows: 34.Rxd3 Qxd3 35.Rxd3 Rxd3. White will have traded two rooks for a queen and one pawn, which amounts to about an even trade.

Sure enough, Fischer took the pawn, and Bisguier recaptured the rook (see Diagram 28). Now Bisguier expects Fischer to capture the queen on the next move, after which Bisguier will recapture the rook. This is only an even trade for Fischer, but what else could Fischer have been thinking?

Fischer's idea was to use the x-ray tactic to his advantage! Instead of taking the queen on d3, he captures the rook on d7 (see Diagram 29). The method to his madness is that the queen is now protected by the rook on d1. If Black plays 35...Qxd7, White just plays 36.Rxd7. After the dust settles from all the captures, White emerges with an extra pawn.

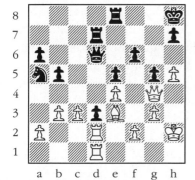

Diagram 27: White to move (Fischer–Bisguier, U.S. Championship 1963-64).

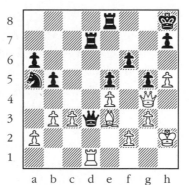

Diagram 28: Position after 34.Rxd3 Qxd3.

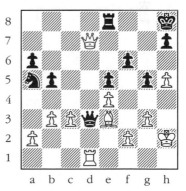

Diagram 29: Position after 35.Qxd7!.

The "In Between" Move

Huh? What's this? In between what?

No, this doesn't mean in between the squares, or in between the lines, or in between the king and the queen. The *in between* refers to a move that comes in between two moves that you expect your opponent to have to play consecutively. Suppose you capture one of your opponent's pieces, which is protected. You naturally expect him to recapture. But you must always be careful not to overlook the possibility that he may have some move he can play "in between," perhaps a threat to another one of your pieces, or a check. And that little "in between" move may make a world of difference ....

Chess Talk

An **in between move** is a move that comes in between two moves you expect your opponent to have to play consecutively. Sometimes such a move is called a **zwischenzug,** which is German for "in between move."

Patrick's Pointers

Powerful "in between" moves are often checks, so you should always be extra careful when you see that your opponent can give a check. And always take a careful look at a check that you can give: It might be a good move!

Take the position in Diagram 30, for example. Black has every reason to be happy. He has a material advantage of a rook for a bishop, and so he is looking to win. Black decides to exchange off a pair of rooks, figuring that after 1...Rxh4, White has nothing better than to recapture with 2.Qxh4. Black notices that White could also give check with 2.Qd8+ (see Diagram 31), but there doesn't seem to be any point to it, because Black can just move the king with 2...Kh7.

But Black has failed to take into account the power of this "in between" move! Black just assumed that White would have nothing better than to recapture the rook. But had Black thought more carefully about the consequences of allowing the check, Black might have realized that the queen on d8 is forking the king and rook, so White is not giving up on recapturing the rook. Even worse, once Black moves the king to h7, White will capture the rook on h4 with check (see Diagram 32).

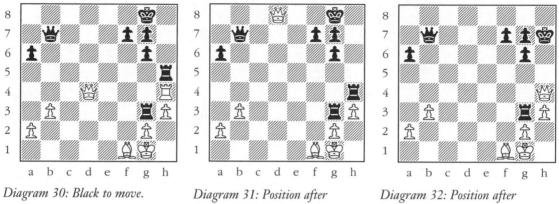

Diagram 30: Black to move.

Diagram 31: Position after
1...Rxh4?? 2.Qd8+!.

Diagram 32: Position after
2...Kh7 3.Qxh4+.

And it's not just check: it's another fork of the king and the rook! Black is obliged to move the king back to g8, and then White will capture the rook on g3, winning a rook for nothing, and gaining a decisive material advantage. Carelessly thinking that White had nothing better than to recapture, Black went from a winning position to a losing position!

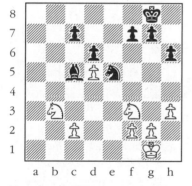

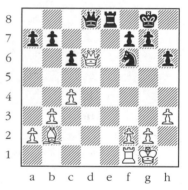

Exercise 1: *White to move. White wants to take advantage of the fact that the pawn on d6 defends two pieces at the same time. How can White win material?*

Exercise 2: *Black to move (Spassky–Fischer, World Championship Match, 1972). Bobby Fischer knew how to take advantage of deflection in this game. Can you find the winning move?*

Exercise 3: *White to move. Would it be a good idea for White to play 1.Rd1 to protect the queen? If not, then why?*

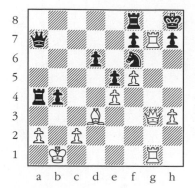

Exercise 4: *White to move. Would White prefer to have another piece on g7 besides the rook? How should White arrange for it to happen?*

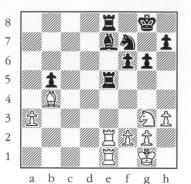

Exercise 5: *White to move. Can White win material by using the x-ray attack with 1.Bxe7? Does it matter which rook Black recaptures the bishop with?*

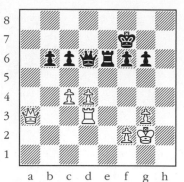

Exercise 6: *White to move. White can win a pawn with 1.Qa7+, but he has an even better move. The two keys here are deflection and the "in between" move!*

Exercise 7: *White to move. How can White win material?*

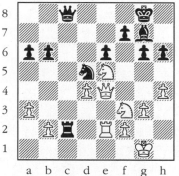

Exercise 8: *Black to move (Illescas–Wolff, Biel, 1993). Miguel Illescas is a tough grandmaster, but I was able to win a pawn by using a variation of deflection and a clearance sacrifice to set up a fork. Can you see what I played? (This is a tricky one!)*

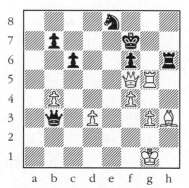

Exercise 9: *Black to move (Shirazi–Wolff, U.S. Championship, 1992). I wanted to capture White's rook, but my pawn was pinned to my king. How did I manage to deflect the queen away, so that I could pocket some extra material?*

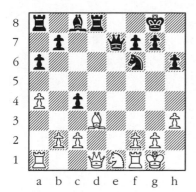

Exercise 10: *White to move. This position is identical to Diagram 3 of this chapter, except that the knight is on f6 instead of c6. That small difference allows White to save the bishop. How?*

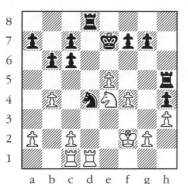

Exercise 11: *White to move (Kasparov–Kramnik, Holland, 2001). Kasparov rejected 1.g4, because he did not want to allow 1...hxg3+ 2.Nxg3 Rxh3. However, he missed that at this point he would have a crushing move. What is it? (Hint: White has the same move no matter which square Black moves the rook to along the h-file after 2.Nxg3.)*

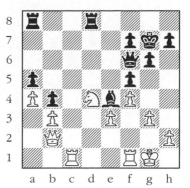

Exercise 12: *White to move and win.*

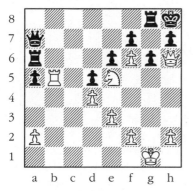

Exercise 13: *White to move (Gauzel–Ginting, Novi-Sad, 1990). It looks like Black has everything defended, but White was able to overload and deflect the defending pieces to win. How?*

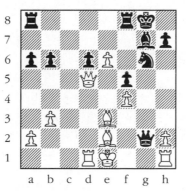

Exercise 14: *Black to move (Ehlvest–Yermolinsky, Las Vegas, 1994). White, a top grandmaster, has just played 1.Qd5. Yermolinsky, another top grandmaster, captured the queen and lost the game. What strong "in between" move did both grandmasters miss?*

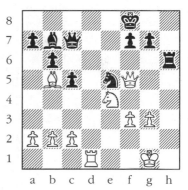

Exercise 15: *White to move (King–Benjamin, USA, 1962). How did White win a piece by exploiting the overloaded black queen?*

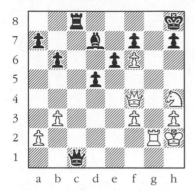

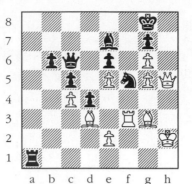

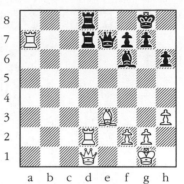

Exercise 16: *White to move. If 1.Qg3 or 1.Qg4, then 1...Qh6 defends. Nor does 1.Qxc1 Rxc1 2.Rg7 Be8 make headway. How can White force either checkmate or decisive win of material?*

Exercise 17: *Black to move. It looks like White has a crushing attack. But Black can not only defend, he can win! How? (Hint: Black needs to nudge the white king to the right square.)*

Exercise 18: *Black to move. Can Black win material by capturing either rook? Why or why not?*

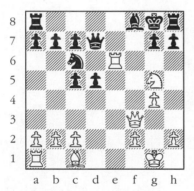

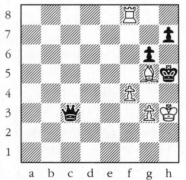

Exercise 19: *White to move (Maroczy–Vidmar, Ljubljana, 1922). White is attacking, but Black has an extra pawn and if he beats back the attack will win. White found an incredible winning move. What is it? (Hint: White combines deflection with getting Black to block the defense of a key square.)*

Exercise 20: *White to move. If White could play g3-g4, it would be checkmate. But Black's queen pins the g-pawn. How can White deflect the queen and win?*

The Least You Need to Know

◆ If you attack a piece, but that piece is defended by some other piece, look for a way to attack the defending piece.

◆ If one piece defends two or more other pieces, it might be overloaded.

◆ Pay attention to whether one of your pieces wants to get to a square that another one of your pieces is on. If so, you might be able to get it there with a clearance sacrifice.

◆ X-ray tactics are easy to miss, so watch out for them!

◆ Be careful for those little "in between" moves—especially checks—when you are calculating a sequence of moves.

◆ Always keep in mind that tactics can be combined!

Chapter 8

Hunting Down the King

In This Chapter

- ◆ "Relative" versus "absolute" material advantage
- ◆ How to use a relative material advantage to attack the king
- ◆ An example of an attack against the king from a grandmaster game
- ◆ Tactics for attacking the king

In the previous three chapters, I stressed the importance of having a material advantage, and I showed you some useful tactics for gaining a material advantage. In this chapter, I expand on these two concepts a little more.

First, I explain another way to think about having a material advantage, and how to use it to attack the king. Then I show you some special tactics that are useful in attacking the king, as well as some ways to use the tactics you've already learned!

When a Material Advantage Is All Relative

Let's start by thinking a little more about having a material advantage. What good is having more material? Remember in Chapter 5, I said the point of having more material is that when you have more material, your attack overwhelms your opponent's defense, and your defense turns his attack.

Now this is certainly true, in the long run, for attacks in general. But in the short run, the success of a particular attack doesn't depend on overall material, but on how much material the players have in the *relevant* part of the board.

Think of it this way. If you have more material overall, then as long as "nothing is happening" right away, you have an overall advantage in force. But if "something is happening" somewhere, the person with more material where that "something" is taking place will have the advantage in force as far as that "something" is concerned.

Does it matter to have an advantage in force in one particular part of the chessboard? Well, it matters if there is something important in that part of the chessboard. And nothing is more important than the king, so it can *really* matter when attacking the king! Take a look at Diagram 1 to see what I mean.

Diagram 1: White has a winning attack against Black's king.

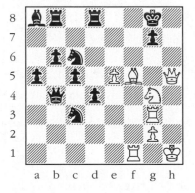

Black has a huge material advantage. If his position were generally secure, he could expect to win with his extra material, because in the long run, he would be able to mount successful attacks against White. But there isn't going to be a long run, because White is about to slaughter Black's king!

Even though White has much less material than Black, all of it (except for the one pawn on g2 and the king) is right near the Black king, ready to go for the kill. And notice that Black has only one measly pawn in front of the king to beat back the attack. One pawn is no match for a queen, two rooks, a knight, and a bishop! Because Black's pieces are too far away to help, and aren't coordinated to attack the White king, there is nothing Black can do to distract White.

I suggest that you play around with this position on your own, to convince yourself that White's attack is overwhelming. Here's a hint to get you going: If it's White's turn, 1.Be6# is checkmate, so you had better assume it's Black's turn to move!

This was a pretty exaggerated example just to make my point. Now we'll look at some more realistic situations where one side can launch a successful attack against the king because he has more material near the opponent's king.

The Emperor Has No Clothes!

One way that having more material near the opponent's king can make a difference is if the opponent's king has very few pieces or pawns around it for defense. When this happens, we say that the king is "exposed." When your opponent's king has few clothes on, it's your job to point this out with an attack! Keep in mind that it may not always be immediately obvious that the king is exposed.

You can see what I mean in Diagram 2. At first glance, it might look like Black's king is not in danger. But take another look: White's knight on e5, rook on g3, and bishop on c2 all control squares that are very close to the king. And Black has only two pawns in front of the king to shield it. Furthermore, Black's queen on b8 and his two knights are very far away from the king, so they may not be useful for defense. Is there some way White can bring more material near the black king to attack it?

Blunders

Don't let your king become too exposed! As a general rule of thumb, when your king is castled, it's a good idea to have at least two connected pawns in front of the king and at least one minor piece (knight or bishop) near the king for defense.

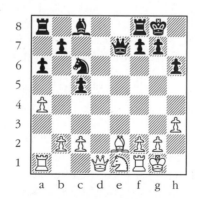

Diagram 2: White to move.

Yes, there is! In Diagram 3, White plays 1.Qh5! to attack the pawn on h7. Suddenly, White's material advantage near the king is huge. In fact, Black has no adequate defense and is lost. I'll show you two plausible tries for Black to defend himself, and how White defeats both of them. You may want to try to find other defenses for Black, and how White defeats those as well.

The first try is for Black to play 1...h6 (see Diagram 4). Black removes the pawn from attack on h7 and puts it on a square where it is protected by the pawn on g7. Except it isn't really protected, because the g7 pawn is pinned by the rook on g3 to the black king! White can simply play 2.Qxh6 in Diagram 5, capturing the pawn, renewing the threat of mate on h7, and creating a new threat on g7. Black can't meet all these threats. (If this is not clear to you, you should set the position up on a board and try to find a defense for Black.)

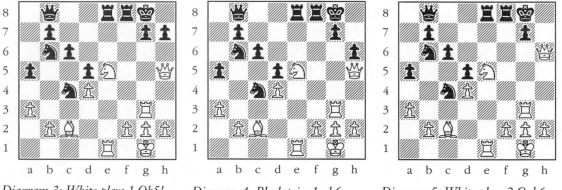

Diagram 3: White plays 1.Qh5!, which threatens 2.Qxh7#.

Diagram 4: Black tries 1...h6.

Diagram 5: White plays 2.Qxh6.

The second try is for Black to play 1...g6 (see Diagram 6). This blocks the attack to the h7 pawn. Black figures if White captures the pawn on g6, when Black recaptures the piece with the h7 pawn, Black will gain a material advantage. But who cares about material if you can give checkmate? White plays 2.Bxg6! in Diagram 7, renewing the threat to the h7 pawn, and creating new threats of discovered check. Black has nothing better than 2...hxg6, when 3.Rxg6# is checkmate (see Diagram 8).

Black's troubles were caused by having too few pieces close enough to the king to help in its defense. (And in this case, the pieces near the king—the rooks on f8 and e8—weren't much help.) If we make two minor changes, things become much better for Black. Let's suppose that the knight on b6 is now on f6, and the queen on b8 is now on c7, as shown in Diagram 9. Suddenly, Black has two more pieces near the king for defense. The queen on c7 protects the sensitive pawn on g7 and can travel along the second rank to protect the king. The knight on f6 protects the sensitive pawn on h7 and also prevents the white queen from coming to h5. Now Black's king is much safer and White has no prospects for a sudden attack.

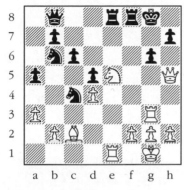

Diagram 6: Black plays 1...g6.

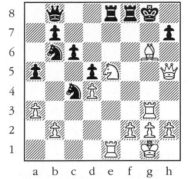

Diagram 7: White plays 2.Bxg6!.

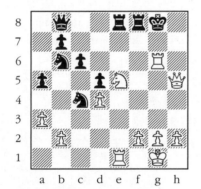

Diagram 8: Black plays 2...hxg6, and White plays 3.Rxg6#.

Diagram 9: Black's king is safe.

Exposing Your Opponent's King

Because your opponent may not be so obliging as to leave the king so open to attack, you'll often have to work at making your opponent's king more exposed. Now I'll show you an example from a game between grandmasters where one player saw an opportunity to expose his opponent's king and used that chance to go for the kill.

Let me warn you: for this example, I'll examine many more moves than I've been doing thus far. I'll make it as easy to follow as possible, but if you haven't been using a chess set, you may want to get one to follow this example. If you don't have one, don't worry; just follow along as best you can. The most important thing is that you understand the main ideas.

Anand–Kasparov, 1995

This example is forever etched in my memory because it comes from the 1995 World Championship match, where I was one of Viswanathan Anand's coaches in his bid to challenge the World Champion, Garry Kasparov. Anand unfortunately lost that match, and this game is one reason why.

Kasparov, playing Black in Diagram 10, is temporarily behind one pawn. He can recapture the pawn by playing 20...Qxe6 or 20...fxe6, which would restore the material balance. But Kasparov plays a much stronger move: 20...c4! in Diagram 11.

The idea behind his move is to prevent White from castling either on the kingside or the queenside. White can't castle kingside, because now the black queen controls the g1 square. White could castle queenside, but it would be a bad idea, because after 21.O-O-O, Black would play 21...cxb3 22.axb3 Qxb3 with a winning position.

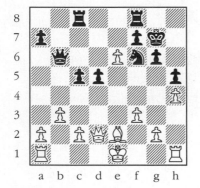
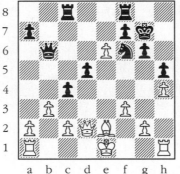
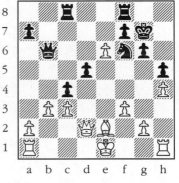

Diagram 10: Black to play (Anand–Kasparov, New York, 1995).

Diagram 11: Black plays 20...c4!.

Diagram 12: White plays 21.c3.

Anand was afraid of allowing Black's pawn to c3, but he didn't want to play 21.bxc4 dxc4 because he felt this would expose his queenside to Black's queen, so he played 21.c3 in Diagram 12. Now Kasparov could have captured either of White's pawns on b3 or e6, but doing so would have slowed down his attack against the king. Instead, Kasparov brought more material to bear against White's increasingly precariously positioned king by playing 21...Rce8! (see Diagram 13). One danger of leaving your king in the center of the board too long is that your opponent can put pressure on the king by putting a rook or two, or even the queen, on the same file as the king.

Now Anand did not want to play 22.exf7, because after 22...Rxf7, the rook on f8 would join the attack. Not only would the f-file suddenly be open, but also the rook would be ready to play 23...Rfe7, threatening to capture the bishop on e2, which is pinned to White's king. But Anand felt that he needed to have some material to compensate for Black's growing attack, so he played 22.bxc4 in Diagram 14. Kasparov responded by bringing his rook into the action by playing 22...Rxe6 (see Diagram 15).

Patrick's Pointers

Castle early! If your opponent has castled and you haven't, you're risking having your king attacked. If you have castled and your opponent has not, look for a way to attack his king. In particular, it is often worth a pawn to keep your opponent's king stuck in the center of the board for a while.

Diagram 13: Black plays
21...Rce8!.

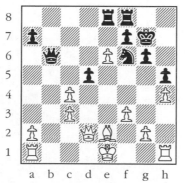

Diagram 14: White plays 22.bxc4.

Diagram 15: Black plays
22...Rxe6.

After 22...Rxe6, Black was threatening to play 23...Rfe8, which would win material by attacking the pinned bishop. Anand moved his king out of the pin by playing 23.Kf1 (see Diagram 16). This move did meet the threat, but it had the drawback of giving up the right to ever castle, which practically ensured that White's king would not soon find safety. Black played 23...Rfe8! anyway (see Diagram 17). Even though this move doesn't win the bishop anymore, it is still a very good move. It brings another piece closer to White's king, forcing White to defend against a specific threat (to capture the bishop on e2), and stopping White from improving his position in any other way. White defended against the threat by playing 24.Bd3 in Diagram 18.

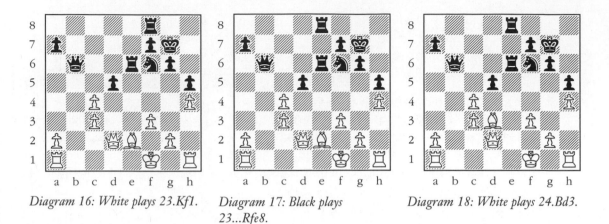

Diagram 16: White plays 23.Kf1.

Diagram 17: Black plays
23...Rfe8.

Diagram 18: White plays 24.Bd3.

Kasparov now spots a magnificent way to expose White's king even more, and goes in for the kill. He begins with what is basically a deflection tactic: 24...dxc4 (see Diagram 19). White recaptures the pawn in Diagram 20 with 25.Bxc4. Then Kasparov shows why he wanted to deflect the bishop from the defense of the e4 square (see Diagram 21) with his next move: 25...Ne4!!.

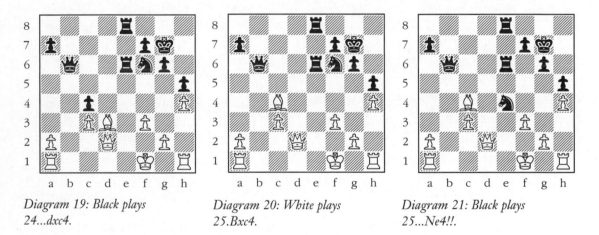

Diagram 19: Black plays
24...dxc4.

Diagram 20: White plays
25.Bxc4.

Diagram 21: Black plays
25...Ne4!!.

Black's rook is attacked, but he ignores that threat and moves his knight to a square where it can be captured! Yet the move is so strong that Anand resigned. I hated to watch Anand lose, but I have to take my hat off to Kasparov for playing a beautiful game. He gave us all a valuable lesson in how to conduct an attack against the king.

Blunders

Some amateurs emulate grandmasters too closely by resigning at the first sign of trouble. This is a big mistake. It made sense for Anand to resign in Diagram 21, because for him and Kasparov these variations were easy to see. But for you and your opponent such variations would not be so easy to see, so you could still hope your opponent would make a mistake. Don't give up the ship unless it's really, truly, hopeless!

Perhaps it isn't obvious to you why White should resign this position. (Don't worry: It wasn't obvious to many of the spectators at the match, either!) I urge you to take a chess set and play over the variations that follow which explain why White resigned in Diagram 21. As you do so, keep in mind how Black is using all of his pieces in the attack, while White's two rooks stand on the sidelines doing nothing.

Black threatens to capture the queen on d2 with check. How does Black break down each of White's defenses?

Variation 1: 26.fxe4 Rf6+ 27.Ke1 (If 27.Ke2 Rf2+ 28.Kd1 Rxd2+ 29.Kxd2 Rxe4 not only gives Black a material advantage, but with White's king so exposed to attack, Black would win quickly); 27...Rxe4+ 28.Kd1 (28.Be2 Qf2+ 29.Kd1 Rxe2! 30.Qxe2 Rd6+ gives Black a huge material advantage); 28...Rxc4 is hopeless for White; Black threatens both 29...Rd6 and 29...Rf2, and White cannot last in the face of Black's attack. Notice how exposed White's king is, and notice how active Black's rooks are, while White's rooks are so passive!

Variation 2: 26.Qd4+ Qxd4 27.cxd4 Nd2+ forks the king and bishop, giving Black a winning material advantage. This demonstrates two very important ideas about attacking the king. First, White tries to defend by exchanging queens, thereby removing Black's most powerful attacking piece. Second, Black's attack is made all the more dangerous because he combines the attack against the king with threats against other pieces. (Note the use of the fork!) Black is willing to break off the attack against the king if he spots a way to gain a large material advantage (without, of course, allowing his opponent to start attacking his own king!).

Variation 3: 26.Qf4 Qf2#.

Variation 4: 26.Qc2 Ng3#.

Variation 5: 26.Qe1 (This move defends both f2 and g3, so it is a better try than variations #3 and #4.) 26...Rd6! and White is helpless. Black threatens

27...Nd2+. If White plays 27.Rd1 to protect the d2 square, then 27...Rxd1 28.Qxd1 Ng3# is the end. If White plays 27.fxe4, then 27...Rf6+ 28.Ke2 Rxe4+ wins material and keeps the attack going.

Useful Tactics for Attacking the King

Good for you if you had the patience to read through all of the last example (including the variations at the end)! I know it's hard work, but it will really pay off. Now, I'm going to show you a couple of useful tactics to keep in mind for attacking the king.

I may have given the impression so far that a successful attack always involves having more material near the king, but that's not so. Having more material near the king is useful, but that's all. It doesn't guarantee a successful attack, and it's not always necessary for an attack to succeed. Sometimes an attack succeeds not because you have more pieces near the king but simply because the pieces you do have near the king work really well. There are many ways this can happen, and I can hardly show you all of them in a few pages. But I want to show you two of the most common ways it can happen.

Nowhere to Run!

When the king is castled, often it has three pawns right in front of it blocking all the squares it could move to. That's often a good thing: the pawns provide very good shelter for the king. However, having the pawns all in a row can also be a problem. Because the king is already on the edge of the board, it has only one rank it can move along. If a rook or queen should come along and give check, and there is no way to capture it or block the check, the king will be checkmated! That is called the *weak back rank*, and it is an incredibly common theme. You've already seen this theme in this book; for example, the very first checkmate I showed you (Chapter 3, Diagram 21), was a checkmate on the weak back rank. But the idea is so important, I'll show you another example.

Chess Talk

The **back rank** refers to the rank at the bottom of your position (first rank for White, eighth rank for Black). The back rank is **weak** when a rook check or queen check along that rank would be checkmate.

In Diagram 22, White has moved his h-pawn from h2 to h3, thereby giving the king a square to move to. But this square is attacked by the black bishop on c7, so White's king still suffers from a weak back rank, which Black exploits with 1...Ra1+. White can block the check with his rook or his knight, but these pieces will be captured, and the check will soon be checkmate.

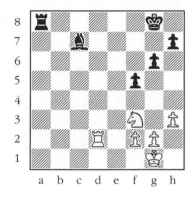

Diagram 22: Black to move.

Death by Suffocation

You would think that the king would be safe if it surrounded itself with lots of pieces, right? Well, that certainly blocks any check from most pieces, but not the knight! You can't block a knight's check. And if you've taken away all the squares the king can move to, that one check might be mate. When that happens, it's called the *smothered mate.*

Chess Talk

A **smothered mate** is when the knight checks the king, and because the king is completely surrounded by its own pieces, it's checkmate.

A quick look at Diagram 23 gives the impression that Black is in no danger of smothered mate here. But in fact, White can force checkmate in just a few moves, by combining no fewer than four tactical ideas: deflection, the weak back rank, double check, and smothered mate. If you think that White might have a way to force checkmate, and you're looking for the way to do it, it's good to look at a check. So that suggests that the right first move is 1.Nf7+, as shown in Diagram 24. Now Black can't capture the knight, because that would leave the queen on c8 unprotected, and White would play 2.Qxc8+, with mate to follow on the back rank. (Here is where deflection and the weak back rank play their role.)

Because Black can't capture the knight, he must play 1...Kg8 (see Diagram 25). Now what? Again we should look for a check, but no ordinary discovered check will work, because the queen on c4 is attacked by the queen on c8. So we have to use double check and play 2.Nh6+ in Diagram 26, after which Black has only one possible response: 2...Kh8 (Diagram 27).

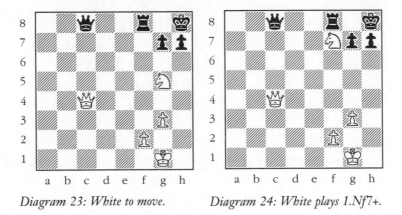

Diagram 23: White to move.   Diagram 24: White plays 1.Nf7+.

You might think that White should force perpetual check now, by playing 3.Nf7+ Kg8 4.Nh6+ Kh8 5.Nf7+, and so on. After all, White is behind in material, and how could Black be vulnerable to attack? But think about this: When White plays Nf7+, Black has only one square to move the king—g8. Is there a way White can force Black to occupy this square with the rook? If so, when White plays Nf7+, Black's king will be smothered by its own pieces, and it will be checkmate.

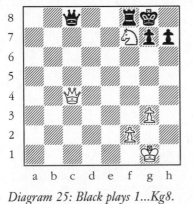

Diagram 25: Black plays 1...Kg8.   Diagram 26: White plays 2.Nh6+.   Diagram 27: Black plays 2...Kh8.

And yes, there is a way to do it: the queen sacrifice 3.Qg8+!! (see Diagram 28). Black's only move is to capture the queen with 3...Rxg8, as shown in Diagram 29, and then in Diagram 30, 4.Nf7# is checkmate. Notice that not only did White force Black to occupy the g8 square with his rook, but also when he did so, it took the rook away from the defense of the f7 square.

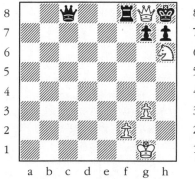
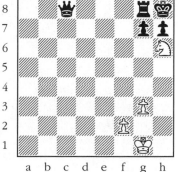
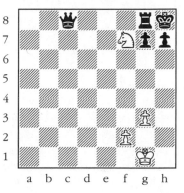

Diagram 28: White plays 3.Qg8+!!.   *Diagram 29: Black plays 3...Rxg8.*   *Diagram 30: White plays 4.Nf7#.*

The Infinite Variety of Checkmates

The weak back rank and smothered mate are two of the most important tactics to keep in mind when looking for checkmate. But there are literally thousands of other checkmate tactics. In the following exercises, I'll challenge you to find ways to give checkmate that may not fit into some of the tactics you've already seen. It's up to you to learn these tactics and keep them in mind for future use. (I'll give you a hint if the exercise uses a new tactic.) One very important way for you to improve your chess skills is always to be on the lookout for new tactics to use, both to win material and to checkmate the king.

And remember this, too, *always* look for ways to combine tactics!

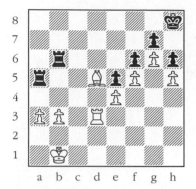

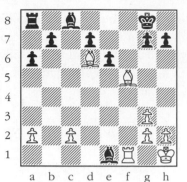

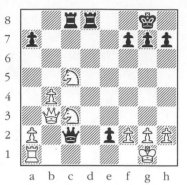

Exercise 1: *White to move (Wolff–Rao, Philadelphia, 1992). Black has a weak back rank. What is the best way for White to take advantage of it? (Hint: White uses a tactic called "interference," using one piece to physically block another piece from being able to move to a certain square.)*

Exercise 2: *White to move (Wolff–Dimitrijevic, Boston, 1994). Again Black has a weak back rank! How can White force checkmate in two moves using that back rank?*

Exercise 3: *Black to move (Krum Georgiev–Gulko, Canada, 1988). Boris Gulko, playing Black, has been one of the strongest American grandmasters for over 15 years. In this game he found a beautiful idea: 25...Rd1+! Show how Black wins after either 26.Nxd1 or 26.Rxd1. (Hint: After 26.Rxd1, find a deflection.)*

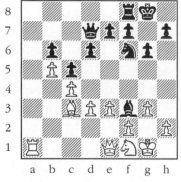

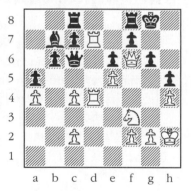

Exercise 4: *White to move. Why can't White capture the queen? If White plays 1.Qe1, then 1...Qxh2# is checkmate. Suppose White plays 1.Qg3 instead, to protect h2. How does Black force checkmate using a deflection?*

Exercise 5: *Black to move wins, but White to move can defend. If it's Black's turn to move, how can he force checkmate in two moves? (Hint: Bring the most powerful piece into the attack.) If it's White's move, how should he defend against the threat?*

Exercise 6: *White to move (Short–Timman, Holland, 1991). Here's an amazing position from a game between two recent world championship contenders, which uses the same idea as the last exercise, with a twist. White played 32.Kg3, and after 32...Rce8 he played 33.Kf4. What was White's idea? Can Black defend?*

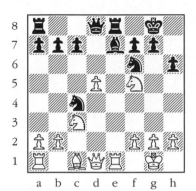

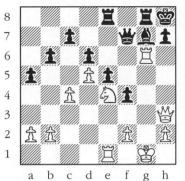

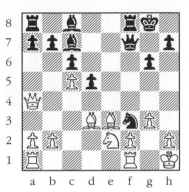

Exercise 7: White to move (Wolff–Formanek, Chicago, 1994). This is a tough one! I would like to bring my queen over to g3, to work together with the knight on f5 to attack Black's king. But if White plays 14.Qd3, to attack the knight on c4 and also to play 15.Qg3, Black plays 14...Nd6, which drives the white knight from its strong post on f5. I need a way to expose the black king so that the same idea will be stronger. Can you see how? (Here are two hints: First, don't overlook the white bishop on c1. Second, consider that if, after 14.Qd3 Nd6, 15.Qg3 were check, Black's king would be in great danger.)

Exercise 8: White to move. It looks like White will have to retreat the rook, giving Black time to defend. But White has a deadly blow. What is it? (Hint: White uses deflection to deliver smothered checkmate.)

Exercise 9: Black to move. How can Black combine an attack against a White piece to reposition himself for a deadly blow against White's king?

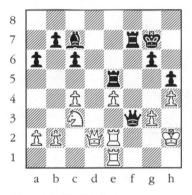

Exercise 10: Black to move (Rohde–Yermolinsky, Philadelphia, 1992). Two of America's strongest grandmasters are battling in this position. Black missed a brilliant sacrifice to rip open White's king and then give checkmate. Can you find it? (Hint: Think about how to draw the White king out and maximize the power of the bishop on c7.)

Exercise 11: White to move. Does White have a stronger move than retreating the knight to e4 or f3?

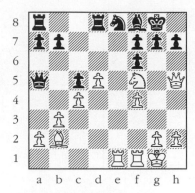

Exercise 12: *White to move (Khalifman–Seirawan, Holland, 1991). White, a top grandmaster, started a brilliant winning combination with 1.Nh6+!! gxh6. How should White continue the attack against the king?*

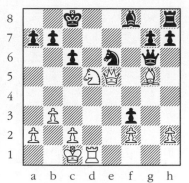

Exercise 13: *White to move. How can White deliver checkmate on d8? (Hint: White needs to get his knight out of the way, and he needs to make sure the king will not have access to the c7 square when the knight has moved out of the way.)*

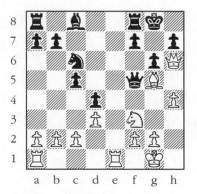

Exercise 14: *White to move. How can White exploit the back rank to force checkmate?*

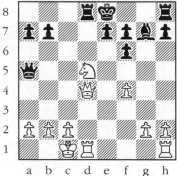

Exercise 15: *White to move (Girsch–Man, Canada, 1963). Once again, White can exploit the weak back rank, this time with a deflection sacrifice.*

The Least You Need to Know

♦ Even if you don't have an absolute material advantage, a particular attack can succeed if you have more material in the part of the chessboard where you are attacking.

♦ An exposed king is always potentially in danger.

♦ The weak back rank and smothered mate are two very common tactics to use in the attack against the king.

♦ There are literally thousands of tactics to use in the attack against the king. Part of learning to play better chess is recognizing these tactics and applying them in your own games.

♦ Always look for a way to combine threats to win material with the attack against the king.

Part 3

Strategy

If there's no move to capture one of your opponent's pieces, and you can't see how to attack the king, how can you know what move to play? Which positions are good for you, and which are bad? How can you tell? The answers to these questions come from knowing chess strategy, and that's the subject of this part.

The traditional way to teach chess strategy (and who am I to break with tradition?) is to divide the course of a chess game into three phases: the beginning phase (called the opening), the middle phase (called the middlegame), and the final phase (called the endgame). Similar strategies apply to each phase, but there are some differences in how the strategies should be applied in each phase. By the time you finish this part, you'll know what to do and when to do it!

GET OUT THERE AND *PROTECT* ME!

In the Beginning

In This Chapter

- The three phases of a chess game
- The difference between "the opening" and "an opening"
- Your goal in the first 8–12 moves
- Important principles for the first 8–12 moves

So far, we've looked at lots of different kinds of chess positions that might arise in a game. But we haven't looked at the one chess position that always arises in every game: the starting position. "All these tactics are fine and dandy," you might think to yourself, "but what the heck should I actually do when I start the game?" That's the subject of this chapter. I explain to you what your goal should be in the first 8–12 moves, and some of the crucial principles you should keep in mind as you achieve that goal.

The Beginning, Middle, and End of a Chess Game

Chess can be divided into three distinct phases. The first phase is called the opening, and is the first 8–12 moves of the game. The third phase is called the endgame, which is that phase of the game where there are relatively few pieces left for each side. And the second phase, the one that comes between the opening and the endgame, and which is most of chess, is called the middlegame.

So why do special considerations apply to the opening? At the beginning of a chess game, all the pieces and pawns are crammed into two ranks for each side, and there are four ranks of unoccupied squares. It would be foolish to rush out and attack your opponent before you brought out your pieces and pawns to good squares. After all, would a general mount an attack on the enemy before his army was ready to fight? If you're going to be a good general to your chess army, you have to know how to bring out your pieces and where they belong. That's what the opening is all about. Once you have your army fairly well mobilized, the middlegame begins. And although the number of moves it takes to reach that stage varies from game to game, 8–12 moves is a good rough estimate.

"The Opening" or "an Opening?"

"The opening" refers to the general phase of the game where you're bringing out your pieces and pawns, getting ready to make plans and mount attacks. But we can also talk about "an opening," which is a specific sequence of moves that one plans in advance to start the game with. There are literally hundreds, even thousands of such sequences of moves. The more advanced one becomes at chess, the more time is spent studying these sequences of moves. In a game between grandmasters, sometimes the whole game can be won or lost because of a new idea—even just one new move—that one grandmaster plays against another in an opening sequence.

If you want to progress beyond this book, you need to learn more about these specific openings. In Chapter 15, I tell you how to do that. But you must learn to walk before you can run. Before you learn any specific openings, you must learn the basic principles for playing the opening. Those principles are the subject of this chapter.

When Does the Beginning End?

When do you know the opening has ended? The simple answer is that you know it's over when you've achieved the goal of the opening. Your goal in the opening has two parts: To get most of your pieces and some of your pawns off their starting squares and onto better squares, and to get your king into safety. There are five basic principles (discussed in the following sections) to keep in mind for the opening while you achieve that goal.

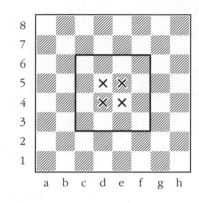

Diagram 1: The square in bold outlines the center of the board; the X's show the four most important center squares.

The Center Is Where All the Action Is

Okay, so you want to bring your pawns and pieces into play. That makes sense, but where should you put them? The answer is simple: you want to put them on squares where they control the center of the board. Diagram 1 shows the center.

Why control the center? Basically, there are two reasons. First, when you control the center, you can switch your pieces from one part of the board to any other in the most efficient way possible, because the easiest way to move from side to side is to go through the middle. Second, controlling the center gives you more control over the sides of the board. So it comes down to flexibility and raw power, both of which are increased by controlling the center.

Keep in mind that occupying the center is not always the same thing as controlling it, because a piece or pawn does not control the square it's sitting on. That doesn't mean that you shouldn't put pieces or pawns in the center! It just means that when you do, you have to make sure that those pieces or pawns are adequately supported by other pieces or pawns.

Center Pawns First

If you should control the center, which pieces and pawns should you bring out first to do it? Different considerations apply to pieces and pawns, so I'll talk about them separately.

Blunders

Center pawns are worth a little more than noncenter pawns because they can influence the center. Don't exchange a center pawn for a noncenter pawn without good reason!

For the pawns, the rule of thumb is to use the e-pawn and the d-pawn first, and maybe the c-pawn. The reasons to push the e-pawn and the d-pawn are that they are the center pawns and have a bigger influence on the battle for the center, and pushing them lets the bishops and queen get into the game. The reasons to push the c-pawn are that it can have some effect on the center (although less than the center pawns), and pushing it also opens a diagonal for the queen to use. (Even if the queen does not use it right away, it may be useful later in the game.) Pushing the f-pawn is tricky; there are times when it can be good to push the f-pawn, but there are also times when it's bad to do so, because pushing this pawn exposes the king. An experienced player will often know when it's good to push this pawn and when it's bad, but even an experienced player can come to regret pushing his f-pawn too early in the opening.

> **Patrick's Pointers**
>
> Take another look at the Anand–Kasparov game in Chapter 8. Because Anand's pawn was on f3, Kasparov's queen on b6 was able to prevent him from castling, which made Black's attack against the white king possible. This is a perfect example of the problems that result from pushing the f-pawn too soon!

What about the other four pawns? There are times when you want to push them; in particular, later in the chapter I mention what is called the "fianchetto," which can be quite good, and requires you to push either your g-pawn or your b-pawn. But in general, the pawns on either side of the board shouldn't be pushed until you have finished the opening, and certainly not without a very good reason.

Minor Pieces Before Major Pieces

The rule of thumb for *developing* pieces is to develop the less powerful pieces first, and the more powerful pieces later. Develop the knights and the bishops first (some people even stress that you should develop the knights before the bishops), then the rooks, and then the queen.

> **Chess Talk**
>
> When you move a piece for the first time, we say that you **develop** it. For some reason, though, you don't "develop" the pawns, only the pieces. And no one talks about "developing" the king, because in the opening, the king shouldn't be developed, it should be put away in a safe place!

Some beginning players think they should bring the queen out right away. I understand the thought: because the queen is so powerful, why not use it right away to attack? But often, this is wrong. You're not going to be able to attack anything before you get the rest of your army into action, so you'll just waste time. And even worse, the queen will be exposed to attack by your opponent's pieces. Your opponent will be able to gain time to develop more of his pieces, because he'll be able to develop a piece and attack the queen at the same time, forcing you to move the queen out of the way.

Of course, any rule has its exceptions, and there are openings grandmasters play where the queen plays a role early in the opening. But these cases are rare, and they have been carefully thought through in advance. You will learn the exceptions to the rules as you learn more about chess. For now, keep the queen home in the opening!

Time Is of the Essence

I said that one reason you should not bring the queen out too early in the opening is that your opponent will "gain time" to develop his pieces by attacking your queen. Actually, time is always important in chess, especially in the opening.

Think of it this way. Suppose you and I are playing a game. Suppose that in my first few moves, I move each center pawn once, each knight once, and each bishop once, and then I castle; in your first few moves, you move one center pawn and take two moves to develop each piece. Obviously, I'm going to be able to have more pieces and pawns playing a role in the game earlier on, and that's going to give me an advantage in any early skirmishes we might have. Not to put too fine a point on it, you've wasted time in the opening.

Of course, there will be times when you just have to move the same piece twice or even more in the opening (for example, if you have to recapture a piece). But as much as possible, you should develop each piece to a good square, and then turn your attention to developing the other pieces.

Castle Early!

Castling is a wonderful move. It does two things: it hustles the king out of the center of the board and to one of the wings, where it will be out of the way of the other pieces; and it makes it easier to develop the rooks.

Maybe it's not obvious why castling helps develop the rooks. If you are following my advice, you'll be pushing the e-pawn, the d-pawn, and maybe the c-pawn in the opening. Now if the rooks are going to get into the game, they're going to need *open files*, and the open files will be those whose pawns have been pushed forward, or maybe exchanged (the e-pawn, the d-pawn, or the c-pawn). So you need to get the rooks to those files, and castling helps do that.

Chess Talk

An **open file** is a file that has no pieces or pawns obstructing the rook's mobility along it; it can also be a file whose pawns or pieces are far advanced, so that even though the file is not completely open, the rook still controls a lot of squares along it.

You might wonder which side you should castle on. The answer is always going to depend on the particulars of the position, but an extremely important consideration is which side the king will be safer on. Remember from last chapter that the castled king should have at least two and preferably three pawns in front of it to keep it safe. You should make sure that you haven't moved so many of the pawns on the side where you want to castle that the king will be exposed once it gets there.

Two Openings to Illustrate the Principles

This section shows examples from actual openings that grandmasters might play, to illustrate good play in the opening according to the principles you've just learned.

Queen's Gambit Declined

The first opening we look at is called the Queen's Gambit Declined. White begins Diagram 2 by playing 1.d4, to which Black responds 1...d5 (see Diagram 3). With his first move, White stakes out territory in the center and opens up the diagonal for the queen's bishop. Black does the same.

White's next move is 2.c4 (see Diagram 4). The purpose of this move is to fight for the central square d5. White uses the c-pawn to intensify the struggle for the central squares; but the move also places the pawn on a square where Black can capture it. This is why the opening is a gambit: White offers Black a pawn as part of his opening strategy.

Diagram 2: White plays 1.d4.

Diagram 3: Black plays 1...d5.

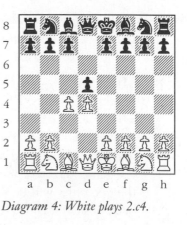
Diagram 4: White plays 2.c4.

Chess Lore _____

It's interesting that the chess word "gambit" has passed into everyday usage, yet most people use the word in a way that is inconsistent with its chess usage. In chess, a "gambit" is a sacrifice, usually of one or two pawns, in the opening. If the sacrifice doesn't happen in the opening, it's not a gambit. Furthermore, for the sacrifice to be a gambit, it has to be known to the player beforehand. If a player is struck with inspiration and decides to sacrifice material in the opening without having thought about it before the game, it is not a gambit; but if the sacrifice is good, it may become a gambit when other people decide to copy the idea.

Black decides not to capture the pawn and plays 2...e6 (see Diagram 5). (It is also possible for Black to capture the pawn: then the opening is called the Queen's Gambit Accepted.) Notice that Black's second move not only helps develop the king's bishop, it also enables Black to recapture on d5 with a pawn if White should play cxd5. This is important, as it means that Black can maintain the very strong pawn on d5.

The next several moves by each player are excellent, straightforward developing moves aimed at controlling the center. In Diagram 6, White plays 3.Nc3, and Black plays 3...Nf6; in Diagram 7, White plays 4.Bg5, and Black plays 4...Be7. (If Black were to play 3...dxc4 or 4...dxc4, White would respond strongly with 4.e4 or 5.e4; Black would not be able to keep the pawn, and would lose control of the center to boot.)

Notice, in particular, that White's fourth move pins Black's knight to the queen, while Black's fourth move breaks the pin by putting the bishop between the knight and queen.

In Diagram 8, White plays 5.c3, and Black plays 5...O-O. Now that White has developed the queenside minor pieces, he begins to focus on developing the kingside minor pieces. Black, on the other hand, hurries to castle kingside.

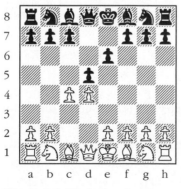

Diagram 5: Black plays 2...e6.

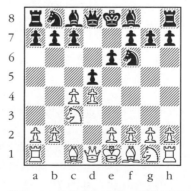

Diagram 6: Position after 3.Nc3 Nf6.

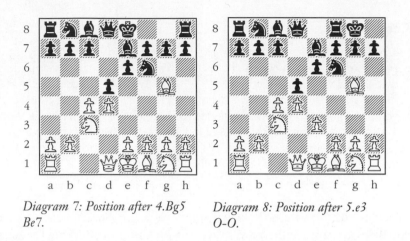

Diagram 7: Position after 4.Bg5 Be7.

Diagram 8: Position after 5.e3 O-O.

White's next move is 6.Nf3, developing the knight to an excellent square. Black responds with 6...Nbd7 (see Diagram 9). This move puts the knight into the fight for the center, but the black knight is not as strong here as White's queen's knight on c3. Black decides to develop the knight to this less active square rather than to c6 because he wants to be able to use the c-pawn in the fight for the center, either by pushing it to c5 to attack White's pawn on d4 or by pushing it to c6 to support the pawn on d5.

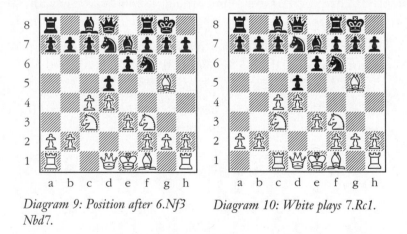

Diagram 9: Position after 6.Nf3 Nbd7.

Diagram 10: White plays 7.Rc1.

In Diagram 10, White plays 7.Rc1. Perhaps this move seems surprising; it might seem that White would do better to play 7.Be2 or 7.Bd3, to develop the bishop and to castle before developing the rook. The explanation is that White wants to make the best possible use of time by anticipating Black's idea. White realizes that one plan for Black is to capture the pawn on c4 and then to play ...c5 himself.

For example, if 7.Bd3, then Black would play 7...dxc4 8.Bxc4 c5; although Black has exchanged a center pawn for a noncenter pawn, it is all right because Black will soon exchange a noncenter pawn for a center pawn again. White anticipates this idea by developing his rook first; now if Black captures the pawn on c4, when White recaptures he will have gained the Rc1 move over the previous sequence. Black decides that it is not in his interest to allow White to gain time in that way, so he chooses instead to support his center by playing 7...c6 (see Diagram 11).

Now White plays 8.Bd3 (see Diagram 12), developing the last minor piece. How should we evaluate this position? White's control of the central squares is somewhat stronger than Black's, but Black has still secured a good stake in the center. White has not yet castled, but soon will. Because White's pieces control the center a little better than Black's, and because White's pawns are slightly farther advanced than Black's, it's fair to say that White has a small advantage. But this advantage is not much; and if Black plays well, a good position can be secured. (And in fact, in Chapter 12, I show you Black's best way to continue.)

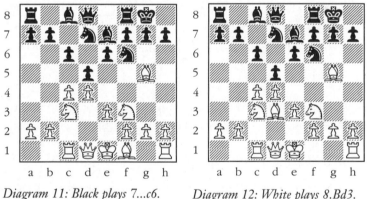

Diagram 11: Black plays 7...c6.   *Diagram 12: White plays 8.Bd3.*

Sicilian Defense

The second example comes from the Sicilian Defense Opening. White plays 1.e4, a move that fights for the center in a similar way to 1.d4; but in contrast to the last example, Black does not mimic White's first move and plays 1...c5 instead (see Diagram 13). Black decides to grab territory on the side of the board that White's first move slightly neglected. On the plus side, Black may stand better on the queenside than White because of this bold strike; but on the minus side, Black's first move does not help develop pieces, and the pawn on c5 controls less of the center than the pawn on e4. This provocative opening often leads to very exciting games!

In Diagram 14, White's next move is 2.Nf3, while Black plays 2...d6. White's move develops the knight toward the center, while Black's move prepares to develop the queen's bishop.

White's third move is quite bold: 3.d4 (see Diagram 15). On the plus side, this move fights for control of the d4 square, and it enables White to develop the queen's bishop. On the minus side, it allows Black to exchange a noncenter pawn for a center pawn. Such dynamic imbalances are typical for this opening.

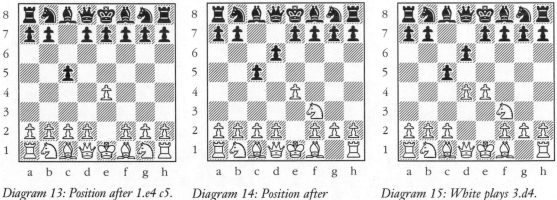

Diagram 13: Position after 1.e4 c5.

Diagram 14: Position after 2.Nf3 d6.

Diagram 15: White plays 3.d4.

Black takes White up on the offer to exchange pawns (see Diagram 16), and White recaptures with his knight. (He doesn't take the pawn with his queen with 4.Qxd4, because then the queen would be exposed to attack by 4...Nc6, which would enable Black to develop his knight with gain of time.)

In Diagram 17, Black develops his knight to an excellent square with gain of time by playing 4...Nf6, and White defends the pawn by developing his knight with 5.Nc3. Now Black wants to develop his king's bishop and then castle. What's the best way to do this?

Black plays 5...g6 (see Diagram 18), with the intention of putting the bishop on g7 next move. This is not the only solution to his problem, but it is a good one. This move defines this particular variation of this opening, called the Dragon Variation.

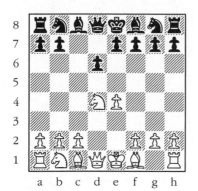

Diagram 16: Position after
3...cxd4 4.Nxd4.

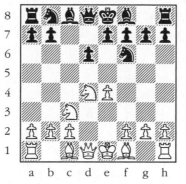

Diagram 17: Position after
4...Nf6 5.Nc3.

Diagram 18: Black plays 5...g6.

Chess Lore

Openings often have many variations with separate names; in no opening is this so true as in the Sicilian Defense, which has more than a dozen different variations. The Sicilian Dragon is one of the most exciting of all of these Sicilian variations. There is some disagreement about where the name comes from. Some people say that the name comes from the resemblance of Black's pawn structure of d6, e7, f7, g6, h7 to the constellation Draco. But other people say that it gets its name from the fearsome power of the bishop on g7, which breathes fire along its diagonal which cuts across the middle of the board! Whichever is the case, this variation has been played by many grandmasters, including Garry Kasparov in his 1995 World Championship match against Viswanathan Anand in New York.

A Brief Digression: Fianchettoing the Bishop

Moving either the g-pawn or the b-pawn up one square and then putting the bishop onto the square the pawn used to be on is called "fianchettoing the bishop." (*Fianchetto* is Italian for "little flank.") You should be careful about adopting this strategy for two reasons:

◆ The pawn move does little to fight for control of the center squares, so it loses time in the opening.

◆ Once you advance the pawn, it no longer guards the squares it used to. This is especially important if the king castles to that side of the board, because the king might be more exposed because the pawn has advanced.

Diagram 19: Position after
6.Be2 Bg7.

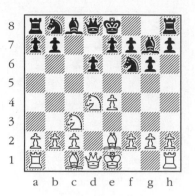

Nevertheless, the fianchetto is often a good way to develop the bishop. In the position in Diagram 19, it is especially effective because White's d-pawn has been exchanged and no longer stands on d4, so the black bishop's diagonal will be relatively unobstructed by White's pawns. That means the bishop will have a powerful post on g7.

Back to the Sicilian Defense

Both sides continue their development. White plays 6.Be2, and Black plays 6...Bg7; White castles (see Diagram 20), and then Black castles. For his eighth move, White decides to develop his queen's bishop to e3, where it fights for control of the d4 square, and Black develops his queen's knight to c6, where it also fights for control of d4 (see Diagram 21).

White's ninth move, in Diagram 22, will not make sense unless you understand Black's intention. Black would like to advance his d-pawn to d5. This would exchange White's last center pawn, weakening White's control of the center, and leaving Black with only one center pawn. Therefore, White decides to retreat his knight to b3 with 9.Nb3. Although this takes a piece away from the center, it also increases the scope of White's queen, in particular increasing the control of the d5 square. Besides, White was nervous about the possibility of the knight on d4 coming under heavy pressure because of the knight on c6 and the bishop on g7. Although at the moment this bishop is cloaked by the knight on f6, it always has the potential to strike!

Black develops his last minor piece by playing 9...Be6 (see Diagram 23). This move reinforces Black's control of the d5 square and prepares the possibility of playing 10...d5.

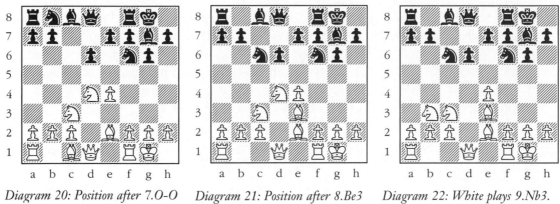

Diagram 20: Position after 7.O-O O-O.

Diagram 21: Position after 8.Be3 Nc6.

Diagram 22: White plays 9.Nb3.

White responds by playing 10.f4 in Diagram 24. Although this move goes against the caution of not pushing the f-pawn in the opening, in this position it is justified. Remember that the reason not to play the move is that it exposes the king. But in this position, White's king is already castled, and the diagonal which this pawn move exposes is shielded by the bishop on e3. Besides, this move has a specific point: now if Black plays 10...d5, White does not have to allow Black to exchange this pawn, but instead can respond by playing 11.e5, because now the e5 square is protected by the f-pawn. Finally, White is also poised to cause trouble for Black's bishop on e6 by pushing the pawn to f5 at some point.

Once again it's time to take stock of the result of the opening for both sides. White's pawns are more aggressively posted, but Black's position has no weaknesses, and his pieces are well placed. Chances are about equal, and a tough fight lies ahead in the middlegame.

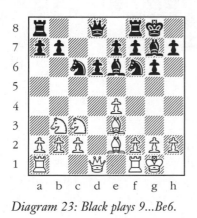

Diagram 23: Black plays 9...Be6.

Diagram 24: White plays 10.f4.

Use the following exercises to develop your understanding of the principles discussed in this chapter. Above all, remember that your goal in the opening is simply to develop your pieces to good squares as quickly as possible, control the center, and get your king to safety. You don't have to worry about learning specific opening sequences at this point. If you decide at some point that you do want to learn more about such specific opening sequences, I explain how to do so in Chapter 15.

Exercise 1: White to move. White has played 1.g4, to which Black responded 1...e5. Who has played better in the opening so far, and why? White is thinking about playing 2.f3. Why would this move be a terrible mistake?

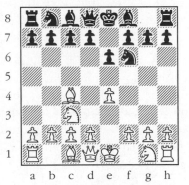

Exercise 2: Black to move. Black is thinking about playing 1...d5. Would this be a good move or a bad move? Why?

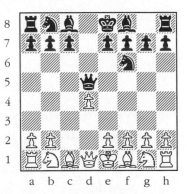

Exercise 3: White to move. This position was reached after 1.d4 Nf6 2.c4 d5 3.cxd5 Qxd5. Black's first move is excellent, but his second and third moves are not; give at least two reasons why, and suggest a good move for White to play next.

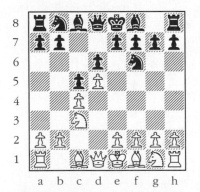

Exercise 4: Black to move. Do you think this is a good position for Black to fianchetto his king's bishop? Why or why not?

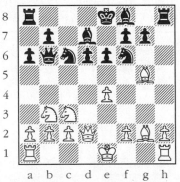

Exercise 5: White to move. It's been a pretty wild opening so far; now White wants to castle. Should he castle kingside or queenside? Why?

Exercise 6: White to move. This position was reached by 1.e4 c5 2.Bc4 Nc6. Is 3.Qh5 a good move or a bad move? Why?

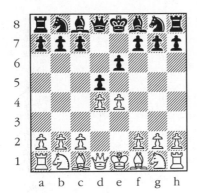

Exercise 7: *White to move. This position was reached by 1.e4 e6 2.d4 d5. List all the moves that you would consider for White here. Why do you list those moves? What are the best moves to consider? Is 3.f3 a good move or a bad move? Why?*

Exercise 8: *Black to move. This position was reached after 1.d4 Nf6 2.c4 e6 3.Nc3. Black is considering three moves: 3...Bb4, 3...Be7, and 3...d5. One of these moves is a bad move, the other two are good moves. Which is the bad move and why?*

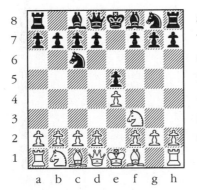

Exercise 9: *White to move. This position was reached by 1.e4 e5 2.Nf3 Nc6. Here White usually plays 3.Bb5 or 3.Bc4. Why do people not play 3.Bd3 or 3.Be2? Explain why these two moves are not as good as the normal moves.*

Exercise 10: *Black to move (Kasparov–Kramnik, London, 2000). This position was reached several times in the World Championship match after 1.e4 e5 2.Nf3 Nc6 3.Bb5 Nf6 4.O-O Nxe4 5.d4. Every time, Kramnik played 5...Nd6, which after 6.Bxc6 dxc6 7.dxe5 Nf5 8.Qxd8+ Kxd8 leads to a complicated endgame. Why do you think Kramnik did not play 5...exd4? Analyze this position and find a good way for White to continue.*

The Least You Need to Know

♦ A chess game can be divided into three phases: the opening, the middlegame, and the endgame.

♦ As a beginner, focus on understanding the general principles for playing the opening, and don't worry about learning specific opening sequences.

♦ Your goal in the opening is to bring your pieces and center pawns out to fight for the center quickly and efficiently, and to get your king out of the center by castling as soon as possible.

♦ Just because the opening is a special phase doesn't mean that the other things you've learned about playing good chess don't apply here! In particular, always remember the importance of material and king safety.

Making the Most of Your Pieces

In This Chapter

◆ The importance of mobility and attacking your opponent's weaknesses

◆ Tips on how to use each piece more effectively

◆ How to tell whether the knight or the bishop is the better piece in any particular position

The middlegame is where most of the action is, so we spend the next four chapters on it. In this chapter, you learn how to use your pieces more effectively. Later in the chapter, we consider each piece separately: knight, bishop, rook, and queen. (We talk about the pawns in Chapter 11; and as for the king, you should be keeping him in a safe place until the endgame!) But first, let's talk about two very important concepts that apply to all the pieces.

Mobility: Give Me Room!

A piece tends to be more powerful if it controls more squares. And when it controls more squares, we say it's more mobile. Of course controlling more

Patrick's Pointers

Controlling the center isn't just important in the opening (as discussed in Chapter 9); it's also very important in the middlegame. So make sure your pieces control the center!

squares isn't the only thing that's important, obviously it matters *which* squares your pieces control. We'll come to that in a moment. But right now, I want you to appreciate the importance of making sure your pieces control more squares, rather than fewer squares. It's a simple idea, but it's very important.

Do Be Cruel: Attack Your Opponent's Weaknesses

You want your pieces to be as effective as possible. Part of being more effective is making sure that you attack weak spots in your opponent's position. A weak spot can be the king, a pawn or group of pawns, a piece, or even a particular square. The point is: don't attack your opponent where he is strongest; attack him where he is weakest!

A lot of the challenge in chess is identifying the weak spots in your opponent's position. Later in this chapter, I give you specific examples of well-placed and poorly placed pieces, so you can see examples of what are weak spots and strong spots in a position.

Now let's look at each piece and see how to increase its mobility and use it to attack your opponent's weak spots.

The Knight

The disadvantage of the knight is that it is not a long-range piece like the bishop, rook, or queen. It has to be relatively close to the action in order to have any effect, and it takes a knight a lot longer to get somewhere than it takes a bishop, rook, or queen. But the knight also has one big advantage. It can hop over other pieces. Once you get the knight close to the action, it doesn't matter whether the squares next to it are occupied or not—it still has the same power.

What does this mean? Well, the knight wants to find a strong square somewhere in the middle of the board or close to some weak spot in the opponent's position, and then the knight wants to sit there. The knight doesn't care about getting a "clear view" of anything, because it always has the same view no matter what. But the knight also doesn't want to have to move around too much, because it is so much slower than the other pieces.

In Diagrams 1 and 2, both players follow this advice. Each side has played well so far. (Notice how well each side controls the center!) Now White sees a way to increase the power of his knight on f3 and plays 1.Ne5! This is an excellent move; the knight now occupies a powerful post in the center and it won't be easily dislodged. Notice in particular that Black cannot easily attack the knight with a pawn.

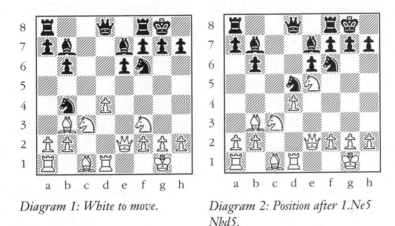

Diagram 1: White to move.   *Diagram 2: Position after 1.Ne5 Nbd5.*

But Black also has the opportunity to increase the power of one of his knights, and so he plays 1...Nbd5!, also an excellent move. Each side has found a good square for the knight, where it is relatively secure, and where it controls many important squares. (Note that Black could move either of his knights to d5, and he correctly chooses the one that's farther from the center.)

Your pawns and knights can often work very well together. A knight may be able to occupy a square deep in the heart of your opponent's territory if it is supported by a pawn. Diagram 3 shows an example of this. In the diagrammed position, I had just managed to maneuver the knight to d6, where it stands very well thanks to the pawn on e5. Notice how the knight attacks Black's pawns on f7 and b7. Even though these pawns are protected, the fact that they are attacked still causes Black serious problems, because Black is forced to divert his pieces to defend these pawns. In particular, notice the bishop on e8, forced to languish on the edge of the board because it has to protect the pawn on f7. And of course, Black's king is

Blunders

There is an old saying in chess, "A knight on the rim is dim," which means that a knight on the edge of the board is usually not well placed, because it controls fewer squares on the edge than in the center. Don't put your knights on the edge of the board without a very good reason!

none too happy about having an enemy knight so close to it! In fact, it took me fewer than 10 more moves to win this game, thanks largely to my powerful knight on d6.

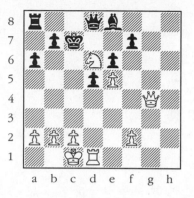

Diagram 3: Wolff–Olszewski, Canada, 1996.

A knight often stands very well when it attacks two connected pawns at once, as long as one of the pawns is not defended by a pawn. This is illustrated in Diagram 4. If Black's h-pawn were on h7 instead of h6, Black could play 1...g6 to dislodge the knight on f5, and the game would be about equal.

Patrick's Pointers

A piece that defends a pawn or another piece, particularly when it controls few squares, is called a passive piece. A piece that attacks another pawn or piece, particularly when it controls many squares, is called an active piece. For example, in Diagram 3, the knight on d6 is active, whereas the bishop on e8 is passive. In general, you want your pieces to be active and your opponent's pieces to be passive!

But because his pawn is on h6, he cannot get rid of the knight so easily, because if he plays 1...g6?, White wins a pawn with 2.Nxh6+. White therefore has an advantage, because the knight on f5 is very powerful, not only controlling important central squares, but also putting pressure on Black's king position (see Diagram 4). In fact, if it's White's move, he can immediately exploit the strong position of his knight by playing 1.Qg3!, which threatens checkmate on g7, and to which Black has no adequate response. (For example, if 1...Nh5, then 2.Qg4! attacks the knight, and 2...g6 loses the pawn to 3.Nxh6+, whereas 2...Qg6?? is even worse because of 3.Ne7+.) If Black's h-pawn were on h7, Black could respond to this move with 1...g6, but here this move loses the h-pawn.

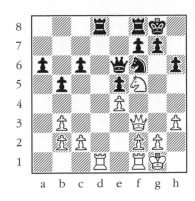

Diagram 4: White's knight on f5 is very powerful.

It is important to be able to tell when a knight that *looks* well placed is not. Look at Diagram 5. Is Black's knight well placed on c6? At first it would appear so, because it controls the center and is hardly in any danger of being dislodged from its post. But in fact, it is badly placed because White's pawns on c3 and d4 "control" the knight. That is, they control many of the squares the knight attacks, and this lessens the knight's effectiveness considerably. White's knight, although at the moment it sits on the first rank, has a much brighter future because it can maneuver to a very strong square.

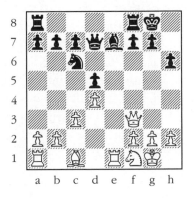

Diagram 5: White to move.

White plays 1.Ne3! Rfd8 (Black must move one or the other rook to d8, or else he will lose the d-pawn) 2.Nf5, and suddenly the white knight occupies a terrific square (see Diagram 6). In fact, working with the bishop on c1, the queen on f3, and the rook on e1, this knight leads a powerful attack against Black's king.

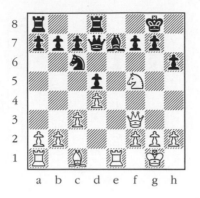

Diagram 6: Position after 1.Ne3 Rfd8 2.Nf5.

The Bishop

In many ways the bishop is the knight's opposite. Whereas the knight moves slowly, the bishop zooms across the board. So the bishop doesn't care so much about getting right up next to the action because it can influence things from far away. But unlike the knight, who hops over pieces, the bishop can be blocked. So the bishop cares very much about its diagonals being clear of pieces or pawns.

In Diagram 7, even though White's bishop is away from the action on g2, it is extremely powerful because it controls a long, unobstructed diagonal, along which it attacks Black's pawn on c6. (Notice how badly Black's knight on g6 is placed, because it is forced to defend the pawn on e5, and because it is controlled by the white pawn on g3. Also notice that White's queen is more active than Black's queen.) Black's bishop, on the other hand, is very passive, as it is forced to defend the pawn on c6. Each bishop has moved only one square from its starting position, but White's fianchettoed bishop is much more powerful, because it attacks a weakness whereas Black's bishop must defend the same weakness.

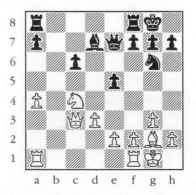

Diagram 7: White's bishop is stronger than Black's bishop.

Bishops can be "good" or "bad." As the name suggests, you should avoid the *bad bishop* and aim for the *good bishop*. Diagram 8 shows the contrast; Black's bishop is blocked by its own pawns and is therefore terribly passive. White's bishop, on the other hand, is very active as it is perfectly centralized and controls many squares on both the kingside and the queen-side. You should not put too many pawns on the same color square as your bishop, as this will tend to make your bishop bad.

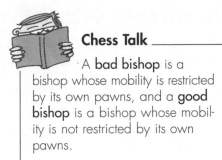

Chess Talk

A **bad bishop** is a bishop whose mobility is restricted by its own pawns, and a **good bishop** is a bishop whose mobility is not restricted by its own pawns.

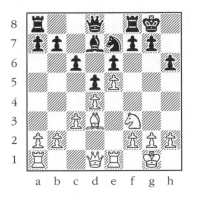

Diagram 8: White's bishop is good, whereas Black's bishop is bad.

But just because your pawns are on the same color as your bishop doesn't necessarily mean that your bishop is bad. In Diagram 9, Black's bishop is no longer constrained by the pawns; even though Black's pawns are on the same color squares as the bishop moves on, the bishop is active. You should always be careful about putting pawns on the same color squares as your bishop moves on, but if you do, it is usually better to get the bishop "outside" the pawns so that it can be active.

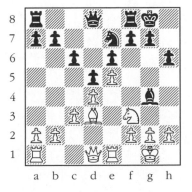

Diagram 9: Black's bishop is not bad because it's actively placed outside the pawns.

Which Is Better: Bishop or Knight?

Many positions are equally suited for the bishop or the knight, but some positions definitely favor one or the other.

Diagram 10 shows an example of a position that clearly favors the knight. The player of the white pieces was Emanuel Lasker, who was World Champion for almost 30 years! (You can read more about Lasker in Chapter 16.) Lasker knew that Black's bishop, so badly hemmed in by its own pawns, was a weak piece in this position. But Lasker also understood that his own knight was not the strongest piece at the moment either, because it was being controlled by Black's pawns. (That is, Black's pawns controlled many of the squares the knight controlled.) And Lasker also knew that the knight is happiest when it finds a secure square from which it can control lots of central squares. Lasker saw a way to improve the position of his knight.

Lasker played 1.Na4! (see Diagram 11). This violates the rule about not putting the knight on the edge of the board, but it's okay here, because the knight isn't going to stay there long; it's going to c5.

Black's queen is attacked, so he retreated it to e7, to which Lasker responded 2.Qd4! (Diagram 12). This move controls the c5 square, so White can play Nc5 next move. The knight will stand very well on this square, and it is totally secure; not only does the queen protect the knight, but also the knight can be supported by the b-pawn by moving it to b4 if necessary.

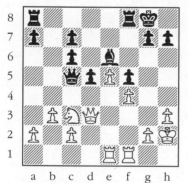

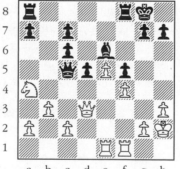

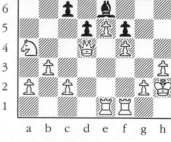

Diagram 10: White to move (Lasker–Cohn, St. Petersburg, 1909.)

Diagram 11: White plays 1.Na4!.

Diagram 12: Position after 1...Qe7 2.Qd4!.

Notice how Black's bishop, restricted to the white squares, is incapable of fighting for control of the black squares. In positions where the knight is stronger than the bishop, it is common for the knight to find a strong square of the opposite color of the enemy bishop. Notice also that the center is *closed*, meaning that there are lots of pawns in the middle of the board blocking the files, ranks, and (most importantly as far as the bishop is concerned) the diagonals. This is another common feature of positions where the knight is stronger than the bishop.

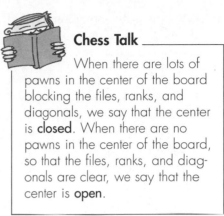

Chess Talk

When there are lots of pawns in the center of the board blocking the files, ranks, and diagonals, we say that the center is **closed**. When there are no pawns in the center of the board, so that the files, ranks, and diagonals are clear, we say that the center is **open**.

When the center is clear of pawns and the knight lacks any strong squares to settle on, the bishop tends to be the stronger piece. Diagram 13 shows an example of this. Black's bishop has a magnificent diagonal, at the end of which lies a white pawn and the white king; perfect targets. Clearly, the relevant area is the kingside, but White's knight is practically a spectator to any kingside activity. Notice, in particular, how the black pawns on b6 and c5 control the white knight. Even though material is equal, Black has a very large advantage in this position.

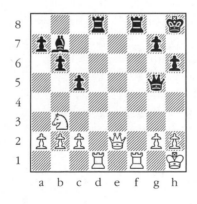

Diagram 13: Black's bishop is much stronger than White's knight.

The Two Bishops

Often, the bishop's power is felt most strongly in the middlegame when it joins forces with its companion bishop. It is not always an advantage to be the only player with both bishops, but it often is. Some people go so far as to say that having both bishops is worth an extra half-point of material! (Recall the chart in Chapter 5.) You should remember that everything depends on the position; when the position is not one that favors bishops in general, having an extra bishop is often not an advantage. Still, even blocked positions may open up, so one must never underestimate the potential—or danger—of the two bishops.

Diagram 14 shows a typical situation where the two bishops constitute an advantage. White may be able to attack Black on either the kingside or the queenside. Black's minor pieces are passive; the knight is on a stable square, but it does not attack any important points in White's position, and it is hard to see how it could do so soon. Black's bishop is good for the defense of the king, but it also attacks nothing in White's position.

Diagram 14: White has the better position thanks to the two bishops.

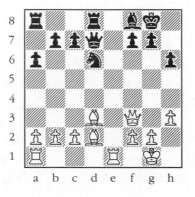

But a small change in the position can improve Black's game. For example, suppose that Black's bishop was on e6, rather than f8, as in Diagram 15. In this case, the bishop and the knight coordinate much better together, so Black's position has improved. For example, if it is Black's move, he might play either 1...Bc4 or 1...Bf5. Not only would this exchange White's strong bishop on d3, it would also enable the knight to reach a more active square, because it was the bishop on d3 that restricted Black's knight.

Diagram 15: Here the two bishops are not so large an advantage, because Black's knight and bishop work well together.

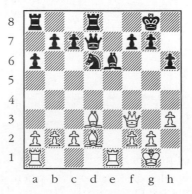

If an opposing knight is off to the side of the board, the two bishops may be worth a pawn or more. Diagram 16 shows a position where Black has a large advantage, even though White has a pawn more. Black's bishop on e4 totally dominates the board, in particular preventing the white knight from maneuvering to a position that is closer to the center. (In fact, this position is taken from a game I played as White several years ago, except in that game Black did not have a pawn on g7, so he was behind by two pawns. But even with two extra pawns, I only drew!)

The two bishops do not always confer an advantage, however. In particular, when one or both of the bishops is blocked by pawns, the position may favor knights. In Diagram 17, White's bishops are clearly not playing a very active role at the moment. If it were Black's turn to move, he could play 12...c5!, which would ensure that the White's black-squared bishop would be locked away for the foreseeable future. As it was White's turn, he stopped this move by playing 12.c5 himself, but even so, Black gained the advantage after 12...dxc5, and won by attacking White's king.

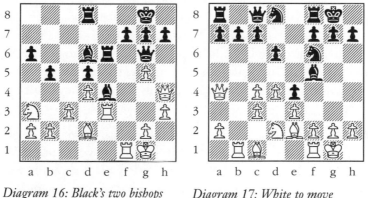

Diagram 16: Black's two bishops are worth at least a pawn.

Diagram 17: White to move (Ivanov–Wolff, Bermuda, 1991).

Notice that White has two pawns on the same file in Diagram 17; it's quite common for one side to exchange a bishop for a knight to create this pawn formation, called "doubled pawns." (You'll learn more about doubled pawns and other pawn formations in Chapter 11.)

Here are some general rules to follow for playing positions where one side has the two bishops.

If you have the two bishops …

◆ Create open diagonals; sometimes it's worth a pawn to do it.

◆ Don't let the center become blocked with pawns.

◆ Keep the enemy knights away from wherever you are attacking, and keep them from settling on secure squares in the center.

If you are playing against the two bishops …

◆ Block the center with pawns.

◆ Put most of your pawns on the opposite color of your bishop. (This will not only strengthen your bishop, it will also blunt the power of the enemy bishop for which you have no counterpart.)

◆ Find a strong square for the knight, or at least keep it close to wherever the bishops might attack.

Opposite-Colored Bishops

You'll see in Chapter 14 that even if one side has the advantage of one or two pawns, and the players have *opposite-colored bishops*, the game may be drawn. In the endgame, opposite-colored bishops often favor the defender. But exactly the reverse is true in the middlegame. In the middlegame, opposite-colored bishops favor the attacker. The reason is that when you use your bishop to attack, your opponent can't use his bishop to defend any of the threats your bishop creates, because they all occur on the wrong-colored squares.

There are many ways the opposite-colored bishops can favor the attacker, but the general idea is always the same; Diagram 18 shows you what I mean. White threatens 1.Bxf7+, because if Black captures the bishop, he loses the rook on d8. Black can defend only by moving the rook away from d8, but then White still maintains the attack against f7, and has also gained the d-file for his rook to boot. White is probably winning. Notice how Black's knight and bishop simply fail to attack anything in White's position, whereas White has fastened on the pawn on f7 with deadly effect.

Chess Talk

When each side has only one bishop, and each bishop travels on different-colored squares, we say that the players have **opposite-colored bishops**.

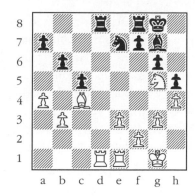

Diagram 18: Black to move.

The Rook

There are three very simple things to keep in mind about the rook: 1. Rooks crave open files. 2. If you can penetrate with your rook into one of the first three ranks of your opponent's position, it will often be very strong for you. 3. Rooks work very well in pairs; if there is something to attack along a file or a rank, think about putting both rooks there. (Putting two rooks on the same file or rank is called "doubling the rooks.")

We can continue the analysis from Diagram 18 to show the first two principles. Diagram 19 shows the position after Black plays 1...Rxd1 and White recaptures with 2.Rxd1. (Black could also defend by moving the rook to another square, such as e8, but that does not really change the nature of White's advantage.) Now White's rook is clearly much more active than its counterpart on f8, which is forced to defend the pawn on f7. In addition, White threatens to play 3.Rd7, which will attack the knight on e7 and the pawn on a7 as well as put pressure on the pawn on f7. How can Black defend?

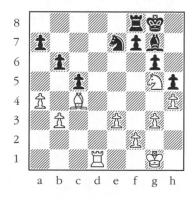

Diagram 19: Position after 1...Rxd1 2.Rxd1.

Actually, there is no good defense. The following three diagrams show one possible sequence of moves: i've chosen this particular variation to highlight how strong it can be for the rook to penetrate to ranks deep within the enemy position. Black tries to defend the knight with the bishop by playing 2...Bf6, but White attacks the bishop with 3.Ne4 (see Diagram 20). Black defends the bishop with the king with 3...Kg7, but White attacks the a-pawn with 4.Rd7 (see Diagram 21). If Black defends the pawn by playing 4...a5 (there is no better move), White forks the bishop on f6 and the pawn on b6 along the sixth rank by playing 5.Rd6 (see Diagram 22).

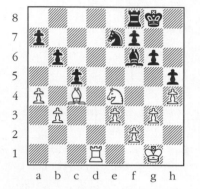

Diagram 20: Position after 2...Bf6 3.Ne4.

Diagram 21: Position after 3...Kg7 4.Rd7.

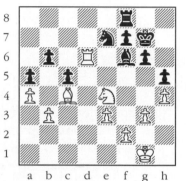

Diagram 22: Position after 4...a5 5.Rd6.

Keep in mind that moving a rook to an already open file is not the only way to put the rook on an open file; you can also open the file by pushing the pawn in front of the rook, or by capturing with the pawn in front of the rook. You'll read more about this in Chapter 11, but here's one example to show you what I mean. This is another position from the Dragon Variation of the Sicilian Defense (which you learned about in Chapter 9). It is White's turn to move in Diagram 23. What is the best way for White to get the rook on h1 into the action?

Diagram 23: White to move.

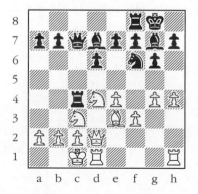

White plays 1.h5 in Diagram 24, with the intention of playing hxg6 soon. This will open the h-file and facilitate an attack against the black king. (In fact, this tactic of pushing the h-pawn in order to open the h-file is one of the most dangerous ways of attacking a king that has castled into a fianchettoed bishop's position.) The open h-file will help White's attack enormously, and so it is a very dangerous plan. (Notice that if Black plays 1...gxh5, White still opens the h-file with 2.g5! Ne8 3.Qh2! followed by 4.Qxh5.) But Black may have one small compensation: if he recaptures the pawn on g6 by playing ...fxg6, he will open the f-file for his own rook!

> ### Patrick's Pointers
>
> One especially effective way to use the rooks is to double them on the next-to-last rank. (That is, if you are White, to double them on the seventh rank, and if you are Black, to double them on the second rank.) Sometimes doubled rooks so placed are called "greedy pigs," because they "eat" (capture) everything in their path!

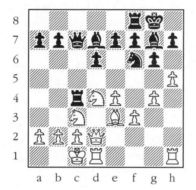

Diagram 24: White plays 1.h5.

The Queen

Because the queen is so valuable, you have to be a little careful about how you use it. Just as in the opening, if you put the queen in the center of the board, it may find itself harassed by enemy pawns, minor pieces, or rooks.

The queen's power makes it difficult to define general principles for its use. Because it is so powerful, it can serve almost any purpose. The best way to use the queen is to put it on a flexible square, where it is out of harm's way, but also capable of quickly moving to wherever it may be useful. It is often a great advantage if the queen can safely occupy a central square. If you can establish it in the center without it coming under fire, you must have strong control of the center to begin with. And if the queen can occupy such a post, it will greatly increase your control of the rest of the board, because it can attack squares in all directions.

One important thing to keep in mind is that because the queen is so powerful, it's often worth a lot to try to trap it. If you send the queen into the middle of your opponent's position, be careful that you don't allow your opponent to surround it—and if your opponent sends his queen into your position, look for a way to cut off its escape (and then its head)!

> ### Patrick's Pointers
>
> The queen is a tremendous attacking piece because it's so powerful, but it's not a great defender because it's always vulnerable to being captured. Try to use the queen for attack, and leave the defense to the minor pieces and the pawns.

Diagrams 25 through 30 show one example of how dangerous it can be to do a solitary raid with the queen. (The position comes from the opening, but the same principles apply here as in the middlegame.) Diagram 25 shows a position from another variation of the Sicilian Defense, called the Najdorf Variation, where it is Black's turn to play his seventh move. (The position arises after 1.e4 c5 2.Nf3 d6 3.d4 cxd4 4.Nxd4 Nf6 5.Nc3 a6 6.Bg5 e6 7.f4.) Black has several moves here; one of the most aggressive is to play 7...Qb6, as shown in Diagram 26.

Black clearly intends to capture the b-pawn. This is called the Poisoned Pawn Variation because of the danger to the queen of capturing this pawn. I should point out that this opening is in fact quite good for Black. Two former World Champions have made it a crucial part of their opening repertoires: Bobby Fischer (now retired), and Garry Kasparov (still very active). But please bear in mind that they would only play such a move because they convinced themselves after many, many hours of analysis that it is good for Black. Without preparation, you should not play such a dangerous move in the opening!

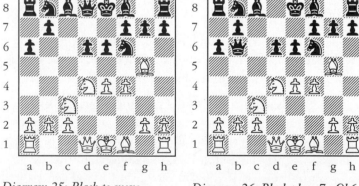

Diagram 25: Black to move.

Diagram 26: Black plays 7...Qb6.

The most common response for White is to gambit the pawn with 8.Qd2 Qxb2, as shown in Diagram 27. Then one plan for White is to protect the rook on a1 and simultaneously shut the queen in by playing 9.Nb3, as shown in Diagram 28.

Black has several moves here, the best perhaps being 9...Qa3. But above all, Black must see White's threat and suspect that there is a threat. When your queen only has one square to run to in case it is attacked, an alarm should go off in your mind that says: WARNING! QUEEN IN DANGER OF BEING TRAPPED!

Let's suppose Black does not see White's idea (do you see it?), and plays the simple developing move 9...Be7 (see Diagram 29). On general principles, this move is impeccable; Black wants to complete his development and castle. But general principles must give way to the problem of rescuing the queen.

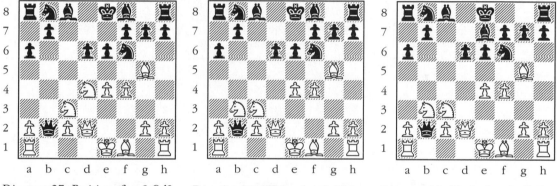

Diagram 27: Position after 8.Qd2 Qxb2.

Diagram 28: White plays 9.Nb3.

Diagram 29: Black plays 9...Be7.

Black pays the price in Diagram 30, where White plays 10.a3. Too late, Black now realizes that White threatens to win the queen with either 11.Ra2 or 11.Nd1. Now there is no antidote to the poison, and the queen must die.

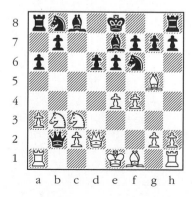

Diagram 30: White plays 10.a3.

You may find the upcoming exercises more difficult than the ones in previous chapters. Try your best to solve them, and then study the answers. My goal in giving you harder exercises is to teach you more than I could explain in the chapter.

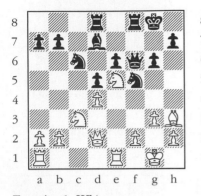

Exercise 1: *White to move (Wolff–Wen, Canada, 1991). Which minor pieces should White exchange in his next two moves? How would you then evaluate the position?*

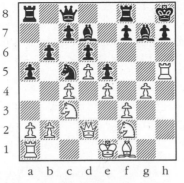

Exercise 2: *White to move (Nimzovich–Tartakower, Germany, 1929). The two players in this game were both among the finest of their day. White now played 17.Nh1. Why did White play this move? (There are at least two reasons.)*

Exercise 3: *Black to move (Morphy–Amateur, New Orleans, 1858). Morphy played this game blindfolded, while playing five other blindfold games. His opponent had to decide between 15...f6 or 15...f5. One is correct; the other (which he played) is a terrible mistake. Which is the better move, and why?*

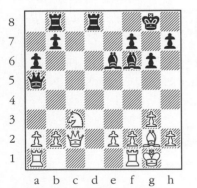

Exercise 4: *Black to move (Dzindzichashvili–Ehlvest, New York, 1990). Do the two bishops give Black enough compensation for his pawn deficit? What move would you play for Black, and what is the idea behind it?*

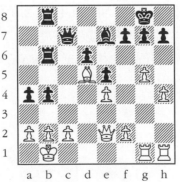

Exercise 5: *White to move. Can White use the opposite-colored bishops to his advantage? Suggest a way for White to play. (Hint: Try to identify Black's weakest point, and then figure out a good way to attack it.)*

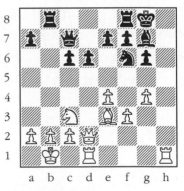

Exercise 6: *White to move. How can White use the open h-file to attack Black's king? (Hint: Find a way to exchange the piece that is best defending Black's king from attack along the file, and then combine the power of the queen and the rook.)*

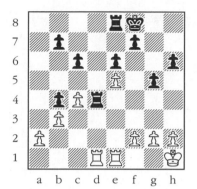

Exercise 7: *Black to move. How should Black use the open d-file to his advantage? Find Black's best move, and suggest how the game might continue.*

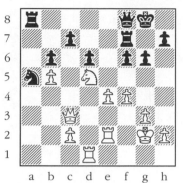

Exercise 8: *White to move. Explain why White stands better in this position. Suggest a way that White could press his advantage by exposing the black king to attack. (The details are difficult here, so don't worry too much about them. I want you to find the best idea, and try to analyze the resulting position the best you can.)*

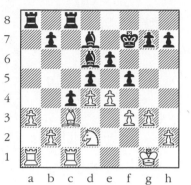

Exercise 9: *White to move (Janowski–Capablanca, New York, 1916). This is a famous game. Janowski played 1.e5 and lost a long endgame. GM Alex Yermolinsky suggests 1.exf5 exf5 2.f4 as an improvement. What is the idea behind Yermolinsky's suggestion? (Hint: White wants to activate a piece.)*

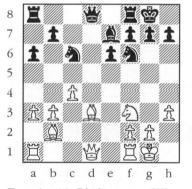

Exercise 10: *Black to move. Who has the advantage in this position, and why? Suggest a plan for Black.*

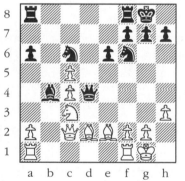

Exercise 11: *Black to move (Oll–Anand, Biel, 1992). Who has the advantage in this position, and why? Suggest a plan for Black.*

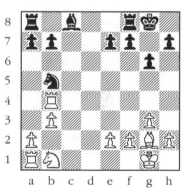

Exercise 12: *Black to move (Villamayor–Gallagher, Calcutta, 2001). Black's knight is attacked, but Black found a much stronger move than defending or moving the knight. What did he play?*

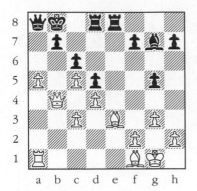

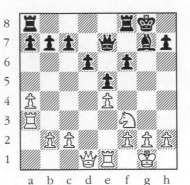

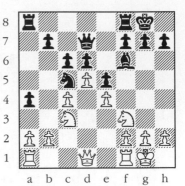

Exercise 13: Black to move (Anand–Hubner, Germany, 1992). Black has the advantage of the exchange, but his queen is passive and his king is exposed. Does White have enough compensation for the material? Why or why not?

Exercise 14: White to move. How can White exploit Black's bad bishop? Suggest a plan for White, involving repositioning the knight to a stronger square.

Exercise 15: Black to move. Black's bishop is passive, and is a "bad" bishop because it is trapped behind the e5 and d6 pawns. Can you suggest a way for Black to make this bishop more active?

The Least You Need to Know

◆ Try to maximize the mobility of your pieces. Very generally, the more squares a piece controls, the more powerful it is.

◆ Identify the weakest spots in your opponent's position, and try to maneuver your pieces to attack them.

◆ The knight likes to find a secure square in a closed position, and the bishop likes to find a powerful diagonal in an open position.

◆ Rooks are well placed on open files, or on ranks deep within your opponent's position.

◆ The queen is better for offense than defense. Be careful not to get your queen trapped!

Pawn Shop

In This Chapter

◆ Why pawns have been called "the soul of chess"

◆ Pluses and minuses of different pawn structures

◆ How to use pawns to your advantage

In Chapter 10, we looked at the pieces. Now it's time to look specifically at the pawns. Even though the pawn is the least powerful part of your chess army, in some ways it is the most significant. Many times, the way the pawns are arranged determines what is your best plan, and many times your best plan is to change the way the pawns are arranged! We'll soon get into the specifics of what you should do with different *pawn structures*, but first let's understand what makes the pawns so important.

"The Pawns Are the Soul of Chess"

There are three reasons why the pawns are especially important:

1. Because there are so many pawns, and because they are worth so much less than the pieces, the position of the pawns limits and determines how the pieces can move. Because a piece normally cannot allow itself to be captured by a pawn, the squares that the pawns control are off limits to the pieces, so to speak. And that means it's important to use your pawns to control as many squares as possible, and to control the right squares.

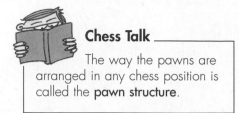

Chess Talk

The way the pawns are arranged in any chess position is called the **pawn structure**.

2. Because they move forward but capture diagonally, pawns often block each other. When this happens, they become a kind of fixed feature of the position, and the pieces have to move around them. So not only do the pawns limit and determine how the pieces can move by what squares they control, they also do so by what squares they're on.

3. Because pawns only move forward and never move backward, each pawn move is a commitment. Put a piece on a bad square and you can still reposition it later. Put a pawn on a bad square and you may be stuck with it for the whole game! So you have to be extra careful to handle your pawns well.

Keep these three things in mind as you read the rest of this chapter!

Chess Lore

Without a doubt the greatest chess player of the eighteenth century was the Frenchman André Philidor (1726–1795). At the young age of 22, when he was already considered one of the strongest chess players in Europe (and so, at that time, in the world), he wrote *L'analyze des Echecs* (The Analysis of Chess). This book is considered one of the classics of chess literature. In this book, Philidor introduced many of the strategic elements that grandmasters take for granted today. In particular, he thought that his contemporaries were weakest in how they played with the pawns, and so he urged their importance by writing, "The pawns are the soul of chess."

Philidor's genius was not limited to chess. He was also a composer of music, and was especially renowned for his comic operas. In his day he was famous throughout Europe for both his chess and his musical abilities, but today he is mainly remembered as the first truly great genius of the modern version of chess.

Chain Gangs

André Philidor was a Frenchman and the strongest chess player of the eighteenth century. One of Philidor's compatriots, the great philosopher Jean-Jacques Rousseau, wrote that people "are born free, yet are found everywhere in chains." The opposite is true of pawns. Pawns are born in a chain stretching from one side of the board to the other, but as they advance, they become separated. Often they form little groups, sometimes even becoming isolated from their fellows. Let's take a look at some of the common ways pawns form groups.

Side by Side Is Strongest

Generally speaking, pawns are best placed when they are two or sometimes three abreast. When they are in this formation, all the squares they control are lined up on the same rank, which maximizes their effectiveness. An example is shown in Diagram 1. This is a standard position from an opening called the Pirc Defense. Black does not stand too badly; he has developed about as well as White and he has good enough squares on which to develop his last two minor pieces. But most grandmasters agree that White has a small advantage in this position, thanks mainly to his powerful *pawn duo* on e4 and d4, which control the center squares very well. In fact, this pawn duo is so powerful that it is essential for Black to challenge it by advancing one of his pawns to the fifth rank after proper preparations: the d-pawn to d5 (rare), the c-pawn to c5 (uncommon), or the e-pawn to e5 (most common by far).

Chess Talk

When two pawns stand side by side as the pawns on d4 and e4 in Diagram 1 or the pawns on e4 and f4 in Diagram 2, they are called a **pawn duo**.

Another reason the pawns stand well side by side is that because each pawn controls the square in front of its neighbor, each pawn supports the other's possible advance. This gives the pawns maximum dynamic potential. Diagram 2 shows a position we've already seen in Chapter 9, Diagram 24. White has just played 10.f4, which supports both f5 and e5. For example, even though it would clearly be a mistake for White to advance his e-pawn to e5 if it were his turn to move (because it would lose a pawn), if Black plays 10...d5, the support of the f-pawn makes 11.e5 strong. And it would in fact be strong for White to advance his f-pawn to f5 if it were his turn, as this would chase Black's white-squared bishop away from the center, so Black must do something about this possibility. The move 10.f4 has enhanced White's chances, thanks to the creation of the pawn duo on e4 and f4.

When a pawn duo has few or no pawns opposing it, the duo can be terribly strong. Look for an example of this feature in the exercises at the end of this chapter.

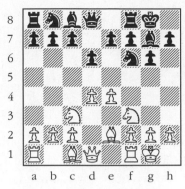

Diagram 1: White's pawn duo on e4 and d4 is strong.

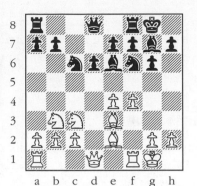

Diagram 2: White's pawn duo on e4 and f4 gives him dynamic play in the center.

Forward Pawns and Backward Pawns

Very often, one or the other pawn in a pawn duo will march forward, and the pawns no longer harmoniously control all the squares of both colors in front of them. Instead, the forward pawn controls two squares of one color, and the backward pawn controls two squares of the same color—including the square on which the forward pawn sits. This pawn formation has the potential to be either strong or weak, depending upon the situation.

A typical example is shown in Diagram 3, from my game against the Armenian grandmaster Smbat Lputian. White's forward pawn controls two squares deep in Black's position: d6 and f6. The f6 square is close to Black's king, and that, plus the fact that White controls many more squares on the kingside, indicates that White's correct strategy is to attack on the kingside. Black's forward pawn on d5 controls the squares e4 and c4. None of Black's pieces are able to take advantage of this pawn's control of e4, but on the other hand, they are well placed to control squares on the queenside. So one strategy that suggests itself to Black is to attack on the queenside. Another is for Black to attack White's strong pawn on e5 (and at the same time fight for control of the f6 square) by advancing his f-pawn to f6. In fact, my opponent combined both of these ideas, gained the upper hand, and won the game.

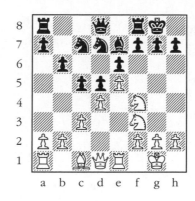

Diagram 3: (Wolff–Lputian, Holland, 1993).

To further understand this pawn structure, let's compare the backward pawns for each side—that is, the d4 pawn and the e6 pawn. The e6 pawn is defended by the f7 pawn, which is defended by the king. So Black's pawns are all well defended. White's pawn on d4 is defended by the pawn on c3, which is defended by the pawn on b2, so at first it may seem like White's pawns are at least as well defended. But Black could play ...cxd4, and if White recaptures with the pawn, this will leave the d4 pawn undefended by another pawn. In the middlegame, with all the pieces left on the board, this pawn is usually not in any danger. But now let's imagine a scenario like that in Diagram 4.

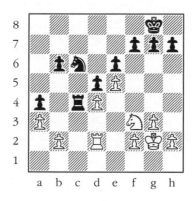

Diagram 4: White's pawn on d4 is weak.

Now the d4 pawn is under heavy fire from Black's pieces; White's rook and knight are passive because they are forced to defend the pawn, whereas Black's pieces are active, so only Black has any chance to win this position. One of the dangers of the backward pawn is that it can become weak if it loses support from its fellow pawns.

When judging the worth of different *pawn chains*, a crucial consideration is how easily one can advance the backward pawn to create a pawn duo again (see Diagram 5). Even though it's Black's move, he stands very poorly in this position, because White is poised to advance his e-pawn, whereas Black's c-pawn and d-pawn are blocked by White's pieces. When White advances his e-pawn, Black's pieces will be pushed back to his first few ranks. Not only will White's pawns on e5 and d5 be extremely strong, but their power will strengthen White's pieces behind them. (Notice that if it were White's move, he would win material immediately with 1.e5 because Black's knight would have nowhere to go.)

Chess Talk

Although we can think of a chain of pawns as being a string of pawns that touch one another, chess players actually use the term in a more restricted sense. A **pawn chain** is a string of pawns that protect one another from beginning to end. For example, in Diagram 3, White has a pawn chain that goes from b2 to e5, and Black has two pawn chains, one going from a7 to c5, and one going from f7 to d5.

Diagram 5: Black to move.

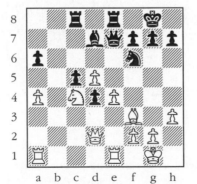

I've introduced the terms *forward pawn* and *backward pawn* to make things clearer; chess players don't usually have special names for these pawns. But chess players do sometimes use the phrase "backward pawn" for the specific case of when (what I've been calling) a backward pawn can't be defended by another pawn, the square in front of it is not occupied by an opposing pawn, and it can't advance forward safely. An example of this is shown in Diagram 6. Notice how much of a liability the backward d6 pawn is. It can't be defended by another pawn, so it must be defended by pieces, which makes those pieces passive. Furthermore, Black has almost no hope of safely advancing the pawn to d5 so as to exchange it for White's e4 pawn, so it will remain a weakness for a long time. Finally, because Black's e-pawn has advanced to e5, the square in front of the backward pawn (d5) lacks pawn protection and is therefore "weak." Think about how powerful White's knight would be on this square, and how difficult it would be for Black to chase it away!

The conclusion you might draw from this example is that it is always bad to have a backward pawn. But things are not so simple. Compare Diagram 6 to Diagram 7. (Diagram 7 is a position from the Najdorf Variation of the Sicilian Defense.) Black's position here is much better than in Diagram 6, for several reasons:

- ◆ Black's d-pawn is well defended by the bishop on e7, and although defending the d-pawn makes the bishop passive, in this case it's not too serious because the bishop is usefully placed to defend the kingside.

- ◆ Black has some influence over the d5 square, enough to prevent White from permanently occupying it with a piece. (See Chapter 13 for more explanation about this factor.)

Chess Talk

When one pawn in a pawn duo advances one square forward, the pawn that advanced is the **forward pawn**, and the pawn that remained behind is the **backward pawn**. However, the term *backward pawn* usually has a more restricted meaning, where it can't be defended by another pawn, and although the square in front of it is not occupied by an opposing pawn, it can't advance forward safely.

♦ Black's pawn on e5 helps to control White's knight on b3, which is a passive piece.

♦ Black's queen and rook are actively placed along the c-file.

For these reasons, the position in Diagram 7 is thought to offer approximately equal chances for both sides, in spite of Black's (true) backward d6 pawn.

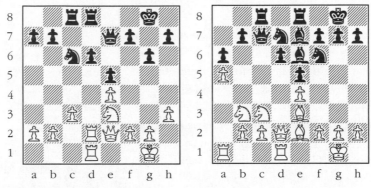

Diagram 6: Black's d6 pawn is a true backward pawn, and it is a liability.

Diagram 7: Again the d6 pawn is a true backward pawn, but here it's not so bad.

The bottom line: when one pawn advances forward and leaves the other behind, there are pluses and minuses. Unlike the pawn duo, it is not always a strong formation. Whom it favors, and why, always depends on the particulars of the position.

When One Pawn Holds Two

Notice in Diagrams 6 and 7 that White's e-pawn blocks Black's e-pawn from advancing, and also stops Black's d-pawn from advancing because it controls the square in front of it. In general, it is good for you to have one pawn serve double duty like this, because it allows you to use your other pawns to greater effect.

In Diagrams 6 and 7, the advantage of the e-pawn "holding" two pawns is not so great, because White can't really use his other pawns to strong effect. (This is especially true in Diagram 7; because White's c-pawn is blocked by the knight on c3, it plays little part in the center. But notice that in Diagram 7, White's a-pawn also holds two pawns! This serves White well, as it gives White better control of the queenside.) Diagrams 8 and 9 show a situation where "one pawn holding two" gives one side a large advantage.

Consider Diagram 8. White's best plan is to push his e-pawn. Not only will this give him strong control of the center, it will also establish one pawn duo (e4 and f4), and give him the potential to establish another, even stronger duo (d5 and e5). Another advantage of pushing the e-pawn is that it would enable White to push his f-pawn, which would threaten to expose Black's king, and would also allow White to bring his bishop to f4, which together with the strong knight on c4 would attack Black's weak d-pawn.

White has the advantage, and 1.e4 would not be a bad move. But pushing the e-pawn right away ignores Black's idea, which is to push his b-pawn to b5 so as to establish his own pawn duo (c5 and b5) and kick White's knight away from its strong post.

The best move is 1.a5!, shown in Diagram 9. This move stops Black from establishing his pawn duo (because 1...b5? now loses a pawn to 2.axb6 *en passant*), and so secures the knight's square at c4. Because White's a-pawn holds Black's a-pawn and b-pawn, White practically has an extra pawn, which he will use to great effect next move when he advances the e-pawn to e4.

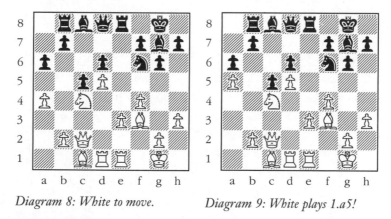

Diagram 8: *White to move.*   Diagram 9: *White plays 1.a5!*

Some Pawns Are Islands

Each group of pawns separated by a file with no pawns of the same color is called a pawn island. As a general rule, you want all your pawns working side-by-side, so ideally you want to have only one group of pawns. Don't take this to extremes, but a useful principle is to have as few pawn islands as possible.

Diagram 10 gives an example of the danger of having too many pawn islands. Black's pawn structure is free of any weaknesses, but White's pawns on a3 and c3 are weak. (If White's pawn on a3 were on b2 instead, there would be nothing wrong with his position.) However, White controls more squares on the kingside, so Black must be careful not to allow White to attack him there. Black's best move is 1...Bc4!, which does three things: 1. It forces the exchange of a piece that could potentially be very dangerous in an attack against the king; 2. It makes sure that the c-pawn cannot advance to c4 to establish a pawn duo; and 3. It clears the d5 square for the knight, so as to attack the c3 pawn again.

Diagram 10: Black to move.

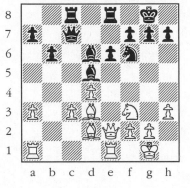

The Isolated Pawn

When there are no pawns of the same color on either of the files next to it, we say that the pawn is isolated.

The isolated pawn has the potential to be a bad weakness for two reasons. First, it must be defended by pieces, and that can be hard to do. Second, the side with the isolated pawn can't control the squares in front of it with pawns, so the opponent can use those squares more easily. Diagrams 11 and 12 show examples where the isolated pawn is a weakness for each of these reasons.

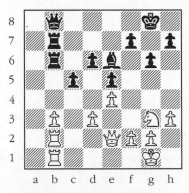

Diagram 11: White's isolated b-pawn can't be defended.

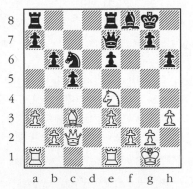

Diagram 12: The White knight on e4 is powerful.

However, the isolated pawn isn't always a bad thing. Diagrams 1 and 2 of Chapter 10 show a position where one side has the isolated pawn and the position offers roughly equal chances to both players, whereas Exercise 7 of Chapter 8 shows a position where the isolated pawn confers an advantage because it yields such good control of the center. Here are a few important rules of thumb to keep in mind for playing with and against the isolated pawn, especially when it is a center pawn:

> **Patrick's Pointers**
>
> Suppose two pawns can capture the same piece. Which one should you use? A good rule of thumb is that you should capture "toward the center"—that is, capture whichever way will bring a pawn closer to the center. Don't break this rule without a good reason!

♦ The isolated pawn usually wants to advance, both in order to gain space, and in order to exchange the pawn for another pawn. Therefore it's crucial for both players to control the square in front of the isolated pawn. (It's especially important for the player who does not have the isolated pawn!)

♦ The side with the isolated pawn wants to keep as many pieces as possible on the board, because with more pieces, he can use the extra space and central control to generate an attack somewhere.

♦ The side playing against the isolated pawn wants to exchange pieces, because this will lessen any possible attack, and so the weakness of the isolated pawn will become more important.

Double the Pleasure

Sometimes when a pawn makes a capture, you can get two pawns on the same file. Such pawns are called *doubled pawns*. Sometimes doubled pawns are a weakness, but sometimes they're not so bad, and in some cases they can even be advantageous.

The absolutely worst doubled pawns are isolated pawns on an open file, like Black's c-pawns in Diagram 13. These miserable creatures are easy targets for White. They are easy to attack along the open file, and they are hard to defend because there's no way to protect one of them with a pawn. Avoid these doubled pawns unless you have a very good reason.

It's also bad to have doubled pawns that are fixed as backward pawns, such as White's b-pawns held by Black's a-pawn in Diagram 14. The problem with doubled, backward pawns is that the second backward pawn (in Diagram 14 the b2-pawn) usually contributes very little. It doesn't protect any adjacent pawn as the b3-pawn does, and it can't advance because it's got a pawn in front of it. The only time when the extra doubled pawn does anything useful is when the squares it controls happen to be important for some reason, but that's usually a lucky accident.

When doubled pawns create more pawn islands, they're often a liability, as in Diagram 15. In this case, the extra pawn island caused by the doubled f-pawns is most significant because it weakens the squares around Black's king. Kevin Spraggett, a Canadian grandmaster who was Black in this game, has compensated by placing his bishops in front of his king, but this has the drawbacks of making his black-squared bishop passive and allowing White to gain the two bishops (by capturing the white-squared bishop) whenever he wants. In this case, the knight on h4 is well placed even though it is on the edge of the board, because it menaces the bishop and the king, and because it is secure on this square. I was at the tournament where this game was played, and I watched Michael Adams, a then-young British grandmaster playing White, win very nicely.

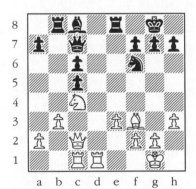

Diagram 13: Black's doubled, isolated c-pawns are very weak.

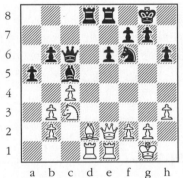

Diagram 14: White's doubled, backward b-pawns are not good.

Blunders

It's possible to get three (or more) pawns on the same file, which are called—what else?—tripled pawns. Unlike doubled pawns, which are sometimes okay, tripled pawns are almost always terrible. Avoid tripled pawns!

So when are doubled pawns not bad? Well, when they're not isolated, when they're not backward, and when they don't make extra pawn islands, they may be okay. Diagrams 16 and 17 show an example of this. In Diagram 16, White sees an opportunity to double Black's pawns, which he takes advantage of in Diagram 17. (Notice that Black captures toward the center with 1...hxg6.) But the pawn capture doesn't create any more pawn islands, or any more backward pawns, so it doesn't do much damage to Black's pawn structure after all.

There is a slight cost to the doubled pawns: The g5 square is weakened because Black has lost the possibility of controlling it by pushing his h-pawn to h6. But on the other hand, Black has gained control of the f5 square, which compensates for that slight weakening. Here the doubled pawns are acceptable.

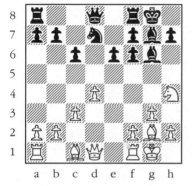

Diagram 15: (Adams–Spraggett, Hastings, 1989).

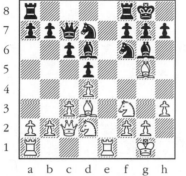

Diagram 16: White to move.

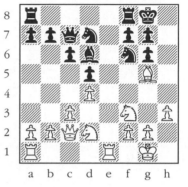

Diagram 17: Position after 1.Bxg6 hxg6.

Patrick's Pointers

You saw an example of doubled, backward pawns in Diagrams 10 through 12 of Chapter 10. Now I can tell you another reason that Lasker's knight maneuver in that game was so strong: It prevented Black from ever establishing a pawn duo on c5 and d5, thus ensuring that Black would be stuck with doubled, backward pawns.

There are two typical cases where doubled pawns are good: when doubling your pawns increases your control of the center, and when doubling the pawns opens a file or diagonal (usually a file) that you can use to your advantage. Diagrams 18 and 19 show an example of each of these. In Diagram 18, White's doubled pawns are otherwise healthy (not isolated, not backward, and not creating extra pawn islands), and the pawn on b4 (which has come from a3) helps White control the important square c5. (Notice that this formation of doubled pawns is extremely sturdy; the b4 pawn is protected by the c3 pawn which is protected by the b2 pawn, which is very hard for Black to attack.) These doubled pawns are good for White.

In Diagram 19, Black's position is littered with doubled pawns, but here they serve Black well because Black has used both the open files the doubled pawns have yielded (the d-file and the g-file) to attack White's position. In particular, White's king is coming under heavy fire, and even if it's White's turn to move, I doubt he can survive. (Black threatens 1...Nf4, after which a catastrophe will occur on d3, g2, and h3.) Notice here that the doubled pawns are all controlling important squares: d4, e5, and e6. In this case, the doubled pawns are good for Black because the piece activity they generate far outweighs the structural weakness they constitute.

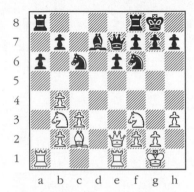

Diagram 18: The doubled pawns are good for White.

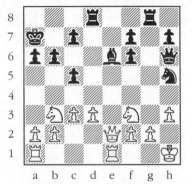

Diagram 19: The doubled pawns open important files for Black.

Pawns: What Are They Good For?

Unlike in the song, the answer is not "absolutely nothing." There are lots of ways to use pawns, so I can't possibly show you all of them. But I can show you some of their most important uses. It's up to you to pay attention in your games and any other games you see to look for other ways to use pawns.

Open Sesame!

Pawns are very useful for prying open a file or a diagonal. I've shown you one very common way this is done in Diagrams 23 and 24 in Chapter 10, but there are many other ways to open either a file or a diagonal.

Diagrams 20 through 22 show White opening both a file and a diagonal with the same pawn move. If White's h-pawn were moved back one square, and Black's h-pawn were moved up one square (so that White's h-pawn were on h4 and Black's h-pawn were on h5), then Black's king would be completely safe, because White would have no good way to open any files or diagonals to the king. But with the pawns where they are, 1.g4! is very strong. Because Black's f-pawn is attacked several times, Black must play 1...fxg4 2.Qxg4, when White has a powerful attack by all his pieces against the king.

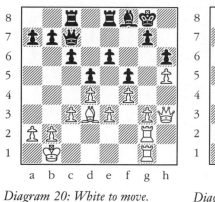

Diagram 20: White to move.

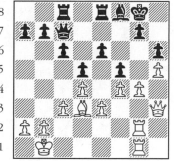

Diagram 21: White plays 1.g4!.

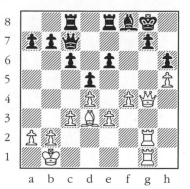

Diagram 22: Position after 1...fxg4 2.Qxg4.

"Reconstructive Surgery"

Another important way to use your pawns is to advance one of your pawns so that it can be exchanged for one of your opponent's pawns. That way you can change the pawn structure so as to get rid of some weakness in your position. This is different from the last case because there the reason for exchanging pawns was to open a file or a diagonal, whereas here the reason is just to get rid of one of your pawns.

In Diagram 23, White has backward doubled pawns. In fact, White is in great danger here, because if Black can play 1...b5!, White's bishop on b3 will be cut off completely from the center and kingside, and it will be reduced to complete passivity. If Black could play 1...b5, White would practically have to play without the use of his white-squared bishop.

Clearly, White must not allow this to happen, and the way to stop it is to play 1.c4! (see Diagram 24), and exchange one of the backward doubled pawns for Black's d-pawn. With his weak pawn ready to be exchanged and his bishop back in action, White's chances will be no worse than Black's.

In Diagram 25, Black has the advantage because of White's awful pawns on c3 and c4, and because the bishop on e2 is bad. Black has several good moves; maybe 1...Qc7 is the best. (Then 2.Bxa7?? would lose the bishop after 2...b6! 3.Qa4 Ra8.)

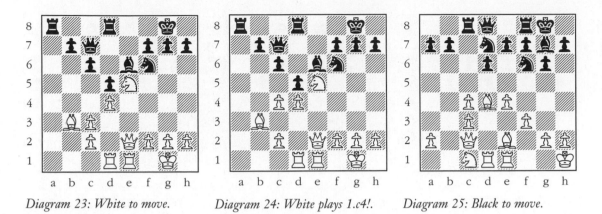

Diagram 23: White to move.   *Diagram 24: White plays 1.c4!.*   *Diagram 25: Black to move.*

But Black is too eager to attack the weak c4 pawn and pays a price: After 1...Nb6?, White plays 2.c5! (see Diagram 26). Black cannot capture the pawn because White wins material with a discovered attack (2...dxc5?? 3.Bxf6!), so he must retreat the knight back to d7. (It doesn't help to put the knight on the awful a8 square with 2...Na8, because after 3.cxd6, if Black tries to prevent his pawn structure from being weakened with 3...Qxd6?? he loses a piece to a pawn fork after 4.e5.)

Patrick's Pointers
When you attack a weak pawn, make sure that it can't move forward with strong effect. Usually the best way to do this is either to occupy the square in front of it (this is called "blockading the pawn"), or to control the square in front of it more effectively than your opponent does.

After 2...Nbd7, White plays 3.cxd6 exd6, reaching the position in Diagram 27. Now each side has the same number of pawn islands, and White's two bishops and better control of the center give him the advantage.

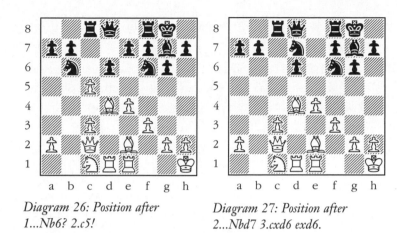

Diagram 26: Position after 1...Nb6? 2.c5!

Diagram 27: Position after 2...Nbd7 3.cxd6 exd6.

Damaging Your Opponent's Pawn Structure

Notice that in Diagrams 25 through 27, White didn't just repair his own pawn structure, he also damaged Black's pawn structure. Sometimes the opportunity will arise to do damage to your opponent's pawns by making one of them isolated, or by splitting them into more pawn islands. When you can do this without cost to your own pawn structure, it is usually a good thing to do.

Diagrams 28 and 29 show an example of this. In Diagram 28, neither side has any pawn weaknesses. However, White has the opportunity to create pawn weaknesses in Black's position, which he does in Diagram 29 with 1.b5!.

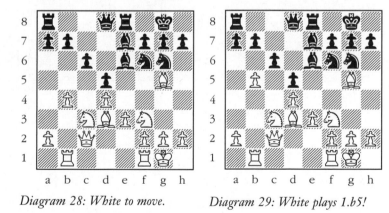

Diagram 28: White to move.

Diagram 29: White plays 1.b5!

No matter how Black responds to this pawn move, his pawns will be weakened, whereas White's will not:

- ◆ If Black plays 1...cxb5, then after 2.Bxb5, Black will have three pawn islands, and an isolated pawn on d5. White will have only two pawn islands, and although the pawn on a2 is isolated, it is so difficult for Black to attack that it hardly counts as a weakness.

- ◆ If Black plays 1...c5, then after 2.dxc5 Bxc5, Black's d-pawn will be isolated, and on an open file as well, which makes it even weaker.

- ◆ If Black ignores White's b-pawn, then after 2.bxc6 bxc6, Black will again have three pawn islands to White's two, and the c-pawn will be a backward pawn on an open file.

Diagrams 30 and 31 show another typical way a pawn structure can be damaged: While the previous example showed White attacking the "middle link" of the pawn chain, here White attacks its "base" with 1.a6!. By attacking the b7 pawn, White undermines the c-pawn's protection. In fact, Black cannot avoid some loss of material after this move. You might want to analyze this position for yourself to see why.

Diagram 30: White to move.   *Diagram 31: White plays 1.a6!*

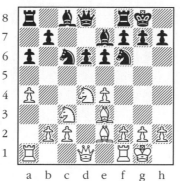

Exercise 1: *White or Black to move. If it's Black's turn, what should he play to get rid of an isolated pawn and damage White's pawn structure? If it's White's turn, what should he play to prevent Black's idea?*

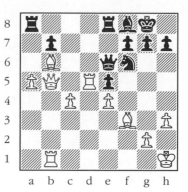

Exercise 2: *White to move (Anand–Kasparov, World Championship, 1995). What pawn move should White play and why?*

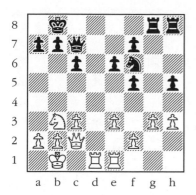

Exercise 3: *Explain what compensation White has for the material after 27...Nxd5 28.exd5, and suggest what White's plan for the next several moves will be. (Note: This is an extremely difficult position. Kasparov himself misjudged it! Try your best to understand this position, and then study the explanation in the answers to the exercises.)*

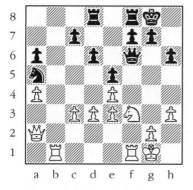

Exercise 4: *Black to move (Kasparov–Anand, World Championship, 1995). Has White worsened his position by accepting doubled pawns? Explain why or why not.*

Exercise 5: *White to move (Anand–Kasparov, World Championship, 1995). Has Black worsened his position by accepting doubled pawns? Explain why or why not.*

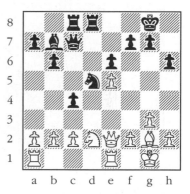

Exercise 6: *Black to move. How can Black do great damage to White's pawn structure?*

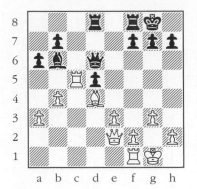

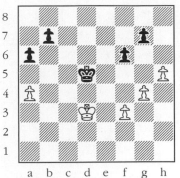

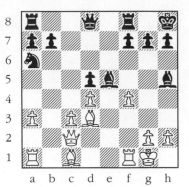

Exercise 7: *White to move (Gligoric–Euwe, Zurich, 1953). Black is hoping to give White an isolated pawn after the rook on c5 retreats, for example, 21.Rc3 Bxd4 22.exd4. But does White have to move the rook on c5? Suggest a move for White that protects d4 so he can avoid the isolated pawn. Evaluate the position after that move.*

Exercise 8: *White to move. Even though you may not yet have read Chapter 14, I bet you can solve this position using your knowledge of pawn structures! Each side wants to promote a pawn; if White can stop Black from promoting a pawn on the queenside, then he can win by promoting one of his own on the king-side. What is White's best move?*

Exercise 9: *White to move (Kasparov–Shirov, Holland, 2001). Black has just captured a knight on e5. Which way should White recapture? Why?*

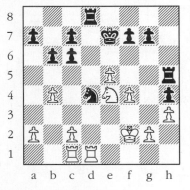

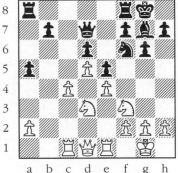

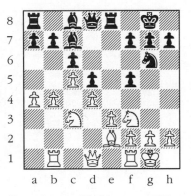

Exercise 10: *White to move (Kasparov–Kramnik, Holland, 2001). If you have done Exercise 11 in Chapter 7, you know that Kasparov rejected 1.g4 because he did not see the key tactic preventing Black from playing 1...hxg3+. Suppose you saw that you could play 1.g4 without allowing 1...hxg3+. Why is it to White's advantage to play this move?*

Exercise 11: *White or Black to move. If it is White's move, what move should he play, and why? If it is Black's move, what move should he play, and why?*

Exercise 12: *Black to move. What pawn move should Black play? Why?*

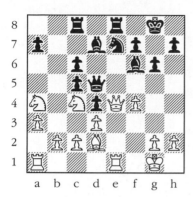

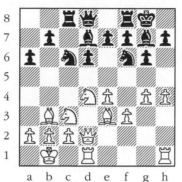

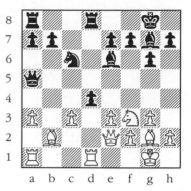

Exercise 13: *White to move (Kveinys–Yermolinsky, Vilnius, 1979). In this position, White played 1.b4. Is this a good move or a bad move? Justify your answer.*

Exercise 14: *White to move. White wants to attack on the kingside. What is the best move to start his attack? Why?*

Exercise 15: *White to move (Arnett–Yermolinsky, New York, 1998). Black has just captured a pawn on d4. How should White recapture? Why?*

The Least You Need to Know

- The pawn duo is almost always a strong formation.

- Controlling the square in front of a backward pawn is important for both sides.

- Be on the alert for ways to use your pawns to open useful files or diagonals for your pieces.

- You should always look for ways to use pawn moves to correct your pawn structure or damage your opponent's pawn structure.

- Doubled pawns are often a weakness, but if they do not create any new pawn islands, and if they are not doubled backward pawns, they may not be weak. If they help control the center, or open lines you can use, they may even be good.

Chapter 12

The Final Frontier

In This Chapter

- The importance of having more space
- Grabbing space
- Exploiting your extra space
- What to do when you have less space

In Chapter 10 we talked about the pieces, and in Chapter 11 we talked about the pawns. In the next two chapters, we talk about the squares. (You've got to agree this will take care of the whole chess set!) More specifically, we talk about two very important ideas: how many squares you control and which squares you control. As you read through this chapter and the next, think about the ideas you've learned in the previous three chapters. You'll find that what you've learned about the opening and about the pieces and the pawns has a lot to do with how many squares you control and which squares you control.

The Advantage of Space

The amount of space you control is the total number of squares you control with your pieces and pawns. Generally speaking, the more you control, the better it is for you. When you control more space, your pieces are more powerful because they have more squares to go to. Although who has more space is determined by the squares controlled by both pieces and pawns, as you go through the examples in this chapter you should notice that the pawn structure often determines who has more space. The player whose pawns are farther advanced usually has more space because pawns limit where the pieces can go. (Recall Chapter 11.) Because the pawns largely determine the mobility of the pieces, the side whose pawns are farther advanced will have more room to maneuver, and so more space.

Grabbing Space

One way to take more space is to occupy the center with your pawns. In some cases, it can be worth taking time away from developing your pieces to stake some ground in the center with pawns. Let's see how Bobby Fischer did this in a game he played on the way to winning the 1972 World Championship title.

Diagram 1 shows the position of Petrosian–Fischer, sixth game of the final qualifying match for the World Championship. It would seem at first that White has a good position. He has developed two pieces, and they both control squares in the center. Black has yet to develop a piece, although we must admit that both his pawn moves fight for the center. Because Black hasn't developed a single piece, we might expect him to do so now, say with 3...Nc6 or 3...Nf6, and that's probably what Petrosian expected, too. Instead, Fischer played an extraordinary move: 3...f6! (see Diagram 2). Fischer is breaking all our opening rules! How can we explain this?

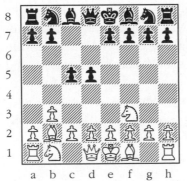

Diagram 1: Position after 1.Nf3 c5 2.b3 d5 3.Bb2 (Petrosian–Fischer, Buenos Aires, 1971).

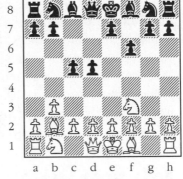

Diagram 2: Black plays 3...f6!.

Fischer realizes that although pushing the f-pawn often puts the king in jeopardy, here his king is safe. Furthermore, the pawn move has an important idea behind it: Black wants to put a pawn on e5. Then Black will control more space with his pawns. White has no good pawn moves to fight against Black's pawns, and he can't do anything with his pieces, so Black will be able to develop his pieces behind his pawns. Black's strategy will enable him to control the lion's share of the board. (Notice in particular how establishing a pawn on e5 protected by a pawn on f6 will drastically reduce the power of White's knight on e5 and bishop on b2.)

Chess Lore

Fischer became World Champion in 1972 by beating then-champ Boris Spassky in a 24-game match. (Fischer won so decisively that only 21 games were necessary: He had such a large lead that even if Spassky had won the last three games, Fischer would still have won more games!) To qualify for that match, Fischer had to win three preliminary matches against some of the best players of the day. The first two matches were played to the best of 10 games, the third to the best of 12. (A win counts as a full point, a draw counts as a half point, and a loss counts as zero.)

In one of the most dominating results in chess history, Fischer won his first two matches with a score of 6-0! Nobody could believe it at the time—remember that his opponents were some of the very best players of the day. Fischer's third opponent, Tigran Petrosian, was the man from whom Spassky had taken the World Championship title in 1969, so people expected that Petrosian would give Fischer more trouble. And he did: Fischer won the first game, Petrosian won a game, and the next three games were drawn. But then Fischer went into overdrive, winning the next four games to win the match. Not since the days of Paul Morphy had the chess world seen such domination—and once again from an American genius!

Let's see how Fischer's strategy worked. White decided to fight for the center with his pawns after all, but he didn't want to play 4.d4, because after 4...cxd4 followed by 5...e5, Black would keep his grip in the center, and White would have exchanged a more valuable center pawn for a less valuable noncenter pawn. So he played 4.c4, and after 4...d4 5.d3 e5, reached the position in Diagram 3. White controls some of the center squares with his pawns, but Black controls many more with his pawns.

Both sides then continued developing their pieces with 6.e3 Ne7 7.Be2 Nec6, reaching the position in Diagram 4. Although it looks strange for Fischer to develop his king's knight in two moves to a square he could have developed his queen's knight to in one move, the maneuver makes sense because Fischer has decided that most of his play will be on the queenside (remember Silman's Rule from Chapter 11: Black's pawn chain points to the queenside), so he wants to have both knights on that side of the board. In particular, if White exchanges pawns on d4, Black will recapture with his c-pawn toward the center, and then he will maneuver his queen's knight to the c5 square, where it will attack the two squares in front of the d4 and e5 pawns.

More development and then castling ensued, reaching the position in Diagram 5 after 8.Nbd2 Be7 9.O-O O-O. Notice that even though White has developed more pieces, Black's pieces have much more mobility: White controls only four squares in Black's territory, whereas Black controls seven in White's territory. (Plus, Black controls the d4 square four times.) That is what a space advantage can do for your pieces!

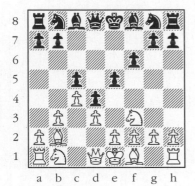

Diagram 3: Position after 4.c4 d4 5.d3 e5.

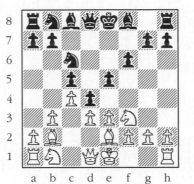

Diagram 4: Position after 6.e3 Ne7 7.Be2 Nec6.

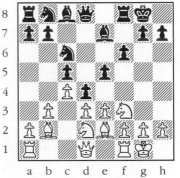

Diagram 5: Position after 8.Nbd2 Be7 9.O-O O-O.

What to Do with More Space

Wherever you have more space, your pieces have more mobility than your opponent's, so an attack in that part of the board has a good chance of overcoming your opponent's defense.

Let's zoom forward in this instructive game to see how Fischer used his space advantage. Diagram 6 shows the position after Black's twenty-third move. With our knowledge of pawn structure, we can see that Fischer's plan is to push his c-pawn forward. After exchanging Black's b-pawn and c-pawn for White's b-pawn and d-pawn, White will have an isolated a-pawn.

Petrosian decided to force Fischer's hand immediately, rather than wait for Fischer to break through at his pleasure. He played 24.a4, and after 24...bxa4 25.bxa4 c4 reached the position in Diagram 7. Petrosian put up a tough defense, but eventually Fischer won the weak a-pawn and then the game.

Another good thing to do when you have space is: Take some more space! A good example comes from this game of *The New York Times* chess columnist, grandmaster Robert Byrne. In Diagram 8, White clearly has more space than Black, but what is he to do with it? It's hard to see any way to attack on the queenside, so maybe he should attack on the kingside. But how to do that? Well, if he's going to attack the king, he's going to need open lines, so he played 16.f4 (see Diagram 9), trying to entice Black to capture.

> ### Patrick's Pointers
>
> When the center is closed, the power of the pieces is reduced, so you can afford to take more time (without wasting time!) to maneuver each piece to its best square. But always watch out that the center doesn't suddenly open up: if that happens, and you're behind in development, your opponent will be able to attack you!

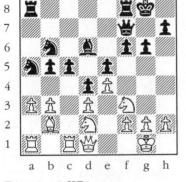

Diagram 6: White to move.

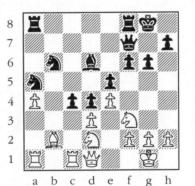

Diagram 7: Position after 24.a4 bxa4 25.bxa4 c4.

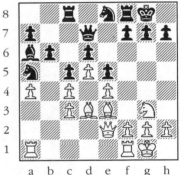

Diagram 8: White to move (Byrne–Kotov, USA–USSR Team Match, 1954).

Black was too clever for that. He realized if he captured the pawn with 16...exf4, after 17.Rxf4 he would just be asking for White to move all his pieces to the kingside and give checkmate. So he kept the position tightly closed by playing 16...f6. But that gave White the opportunity to take even more space by playing 17.f5. Compare Diagram 10 to Diagram 8, and you can see how much more space White has taken: Now he can more easily attack on the kingside. Although the game was eventually drawn, White had the better position.

Patrick's Pointers
The danger of pushing your pawns forward too quickly is that your opponent will be able to smash the center open with a well-timed pawn move, and then his superior development will bring you nightmares. Make sure the center will stay closed if you push your pawns at the expense of developing your pieces!

But Don't Forget the Center!

Games like Petrosian–Fischer can give a misleading impression: Just fling your pawns forward and you'll squeeze your opponent to death. Actually, it's much trickier than that. What grandmasters found so impressive about Fischer's play in the game against Petrosian was his realization that he had an exceptional position where he could effectively push his pawns and ignore his development for a few moves because White had no way to fight back in the center.

You may remember Diagram 11; it's the same position as Diagram 11 from Chapter 9. When discussing this position in Chapter 9, I said that a good move for White is 8.Bd3, developing a piece. But after reading the first part of this chapter, you might prefer to neglect your development and gain space on the queenside by playing 8.c5 (see Diagram 12). Is this a good idea?

Diagram 9: Position after 16.f4.

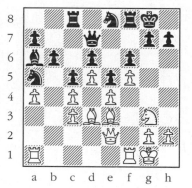

Diagram 10: Position after 16...f6 17.f5.

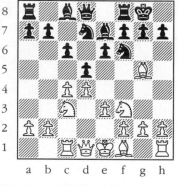

Diagram 11: White to move.

The answer is a resounding no. In addition to neglecting development, this move has two other problems. It relieves the pressure on Black's vital d5 pawn, and White's c-pawn becomes weak.

Maybe that sounds strange, because the pawn on c5 is protected by the pawn on d4, so how can it be weak? The answer becomes clear after 8...e5! (see Diagram 13). Black would love to push this pawn to e4, because then suddenly he would be the one with more space. White thought he had stopped this move, but now he realizes that he had been counting on the d4 pawn to control e5, but once the d4 pawn captures on e5, then the c5 pawn becomes weak.

Diagram 14 shows the result; after 9.dxe5 Ne4! 10.Bxe7 Qxe7 Black will win back his pawn, and White has lost any advantage he might have had. In fact, Black is better, because White must find a way to protect two weak pawns and complete his development and get his king to safety, whereas Black has no problems.

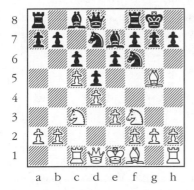

Diagram 12: White plays 8.c5.

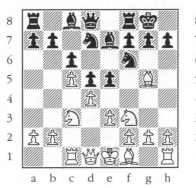

Diagram 13: Black plays 8...e5.

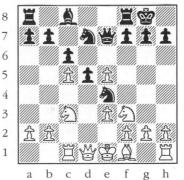

Diagram 14: Position after 9.dxe5 Ne4 10.Bxe7 Qxe7.

Relieving a Cramp

We'd all like to have more space, but there are only so many squares on the chessboard, and someone's going to control more of them. Sometimes that's okay: having less space doesn't necessarily mean that you can't attack your opponent, and having more space doesn't necessarily mean that you can. But sometimes having less space is a real problem and you need to solve it.

Here are three good strategies to adopt if you have less space:

♦ Exchange pieces

♦ Take some space of your own

♦ Challenge your opponent's space advantage

Exchange Pieces

If you've got less space to maneuver your pieces in, it stands to reason that you'd like to trade a few pairs of pieces, so the pieces you're left with can move around more easily (and your opponent has fewer pieces to take advantage of the extra space). Trading pieces is the first strategy you can adopt when your position is cramped.

Diagram 15 shows the opening position we saw in Chapter 9, Diagram 9. Black unquestionably has less space, which in particular means he has trouble developing his queen's bishop. But Black can solve that problem by exchanging some pieces.

Patrick's Pointers

If you've got more space, your opponent might be trying these strategies himself, so you should aim for the opposite: Avoid any unnecessary exchanges!

Black starts by playing 8...dxc4 9.Bxc4 Nd5 in Diagram 16. By trading pawns, Black gives his knight a post on d5. If Black didn't have a specific strategy in mind, this would be risky, because it also gives White an extra center pawn. But Black knows what he's doing.

White exchanges bishops with 10.Bxe7 Qxe7, and then decides to play than 11.O-O, whisking his king out of the center (see Diagram 17).

Black continues his strategy of exchanging pieces in Diagram 18, with 11...Nxc3 12.Rxc3. At first it seems that Black hasn't accomplished anything. White still has more space, and Black seems to have surrendered control of the center to boot. But Black has benefited by trading pieces, because his queen now joins the knight in supporting the important pawn push 12...e5! (see Diagram 19). With this move, Black fights back in the center and gains more space. Plus, Black's white-squared bishop finally has its diagonal cleared of the e6 pawn so it can be developed as soon as the knight moves. Black's position improves because of the pawn push 12...e5, but Black couldn't have accomplished it without first trading pieces.

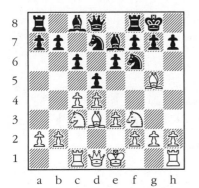

Diagram 15: Position after 8.Bd3.

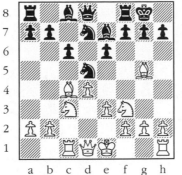

Diagram 16: Position after 8...dxc4 9.Bxc4 Nd5.

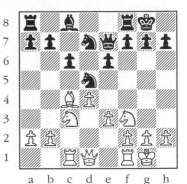

Diagram 17: Position after 10.Bxe7 Qxe7 11.O-O.

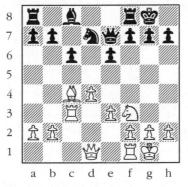

Diagram 18: Position after 11...Nxc3 Rxc3.

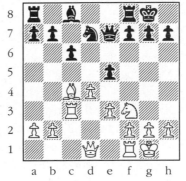

Diagram 19: Black plays 12...e5.

Take Some Space of Your Own

Another strategy to adopt is pretty straightforward. If you have less space, go out and claim some territory! We can see this strategy in action in an opening called the "King's Indian Defense."

Diagram 20 shows a standard position from this opening. (It arises after 1.d4 Nf6 2.c4 g6 3.Nc3 Bg7 4.e4 d6 5.Nf3 O-O 6.Be2.) There is no doubt that White has more space. How should Black play?

Black begins by striking in the center with 6...e5 (see Diagram 21). Black isn't going to let White's pawn duo in the center (a pawn trio, even!) remain unchallenged. In Diagram 22, White castles (7.O-O), because he can't win a pawn by taking twice on e5. (If 7.dxe5 dxe5 8.Nxe5 then 8...Nxe4! wins the pawn back. Can you see why?)

Black develops his knight to c6 to put more pressure on White's d4 pawn (7...Nc6). This finally forces White to advance the pawn (8.d5), which attacks the knight, so Black retreats it to e7 (8...Ne7).

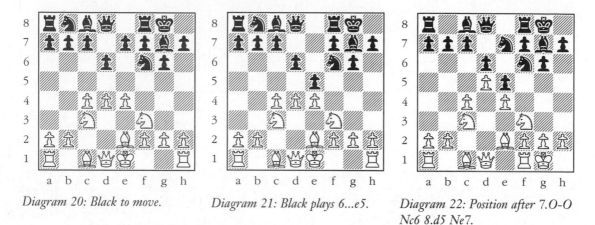

Diagram 20: Black to move.   Diagram 21: Black plays 6...e5.   Diagram 22: Position after 7.O-O Nc6 8.d5 Ne7.

White's next move looks strange at first: 9.Ne1 in Diagram 23. This is by no means the only reasonable move in this position, but it's a good one. White's idea is that because his space advantage is on the queenside, that's where he should attack. The best way to do that is to push his c-pawn to c5, so that a future cxd6 will weaken Black's pawns and open the c-file. To support this advance, he decides to maneuver his knight to d3 and his bishop to e3. So 9.Ne1 is the first move in that plan. (Note that the reason both sides can afford to engage in some maneuvering at the expense of development in this position is that the pawn structure in the center is completely closed.)

Black's next move, 9...Nd7 (Diagram 24), has both a defensive and an offensive idea behind it. The defensive idea is to lend support to the c5 square. If White wants to press his queenside advantage by pushing his c-pawn to c5, Black wants to stop it! The offensive idea is to strike in the center and to gain space on the kingside by pushing his f-pawn to f5. Notice that one of the benefits Black gets by pushing the e-pawn to e5 is that it stakes out territory on the kingside, a benefit Black is quick to use to his advantage.

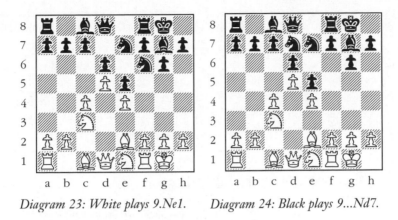

Diagram 23: White plays 9.Ne1.   *Diagram 24: Black plays 9...Nd7.*

Both sides proceed with their plans. White plays 10.Be3 to lend more support to the eventual c4-c5 push, and Black strikes in the center and the kingside with 10...f5 (see Diagram 25). White's next move, 11.f3, has two purposes. The first is to support the e-pawn with another pawn: Now if Black captures on e4, White can recapture with a pawn, so Black won't have eliminated one of White's center pawns (and Black's knight on e7 won't be able to use the nice f5 square). The second idea is to give the bishop the f2 square to retreat to if Black advances his pawn to f4. From f2 the bishop will still control the vital c5 square.

Sure enough, Black plays 11...f4 (see Diagram 26), taking more territory on the kingside. White retreats the bishop with 12.Bf2, and then Black takes even more space on the kingside with 12...g5. Compare Diagram 27 to Diagram 20 or 22, and see the difference in space. White still has more space, but now Black has definitely marked out a side of the board to attack on. And because the kings live on that side of the board, you can bet the game will be exciting!

Diagram 25: Position after 10.Be3 f5.

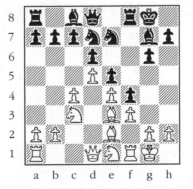

Diagram 26: Position after 11.f3 f4.

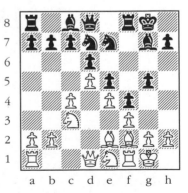

Diagram 27: Position after 12.Bf2 g5.

> ### Patrick's Pointers
>
> Notice in Diagrams 20 through 27 that even after gaining space on the kingside, Black still has less space than White. That's because White's farthest advanced pawn (on d5) is a center pawn, whereas Black's farthest advanced pawn (on f4) is not. So when White's pieces control more center squares they naturally control more squares overall. One more reason that the center pawns are so valuable is that you gain maximum space by advancing a center pawn!

Challenge Your Opponent's Space Advantage

The third strategy for addressing a disadvantage in space is to try to take back the territory your opponent has claimed. Usually, this is done by exchanging one of your opponent's far-advanced pawns for one of yours that is close to home, thereby doing two things: removing the enemy pawn's influence over squares in your own territory and opening lines for your own pieces.

Diagrams 28 through 32 illustrate how this strategy can (and can't) work. Diagram 28 shows a position from an opening called the "French Defense." (The position arises after 1.e4 e6 2.d4 d5 3.Nd2 Nf6 4.e5 Nfd7 5.c3 c5.) It's White's turn and he has two strategies he can adopt. The first is to play 6.f4, as shown in Diagram 29. By supporting the e5 pawn with a second pawn, White ensures that Black can't force White to exchange it for his f-pawn: Because the e5 pawn is twice protected by pawns, White can simply allow Black to capture it with the f-pawn, and then White will recapture with his own f-pawn. (The situation is similar to Diagrams 20 through 27, and there it's precisely because Black can't hope to force White to exchange his d-pawn that Black doesn't bother to attack it by advancing his c-pawn.)

Diagram 28: White to move.

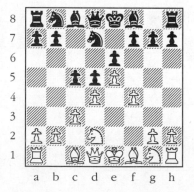

Diagram 29: Position if White plays 6.f4.

But 6.f4 has drawbacks as well. The move does nothing to contribute to White's development, and the pawn push makes the queen's bishop bad. So, although 6.f4 is a perfectly respectable move, many grandmasters prefer to play 6.Bd3, as shown in Diagram 30. Then after 6...Nc6 7.Ne2 cxd4 8.cxd4, Black almost always plays 8...f6: This position is shown in Diagram 31. (White plays 7.Ne2 because if 7.Ngf3 then 7...Qb6! is a strong move; if White defends the d-pawn with 8.Nb3?? he loses a piece to 8...c4. Notice that after 7.Ne2, 7...Qb6 can be effectively met by 8.Nf3.)

The move 8...f6 is a perfect illustration of the strategy of challenging the opponent's space advantage. White's best move is to capture the pawn with 9.exf6, and then after 9...Nxf6, Black controls as much space as White, as you can see in Diagram 32. It should be said that Black has paid a price for equalizing space. In particular, Black has two new problems in Diagram 32 that he didn't have before: His pawn structure has been weakened because he now has a backward pawn on e6, and his kingside has been weakened because of the lack of the pawn on f7. On the other hand, Black has also made some gains in addition to equalizing space. Once Black castles kingside, his king's rook will be very active down the open f-file, and the bad bishop on c8 has a chance to escape into the outside world by playing ...Bd7-e8 and then ...Bg6 or ...Bh5. All in all, a tough fight is in store for both players, which is why there are grandmasters willing to play each side of this position.

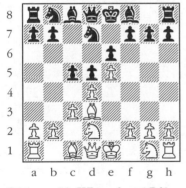

Diagram 30: White plays 6.Bd3.

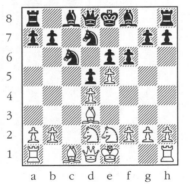

Diagram 31: Position after 6...Nc6 7.Ne2 cxd4 8.cxd4 f6.

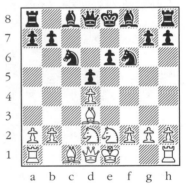

Diagram 32: Position after 9.exf6 Nxf6.

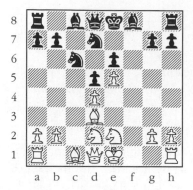

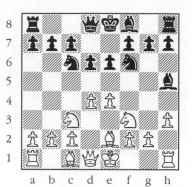

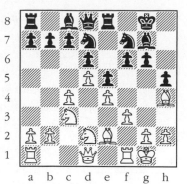

Exercise 1: *Black to move. This exercise is a review of your tactical skills. (Tactics are still important, you know!) The position comes from Diagram 31 if White plays 9.f4? fxe5 10.fxe5??. Can you see how Black wins a pawn? (Hint: Black uses a fork.)*

Exercise 2: *White to move (Wolff–Minasian, Los Angeles, 1994). White has two pawn moves to take more territory in the center. What are they? Which move is better, and why?*

Exercise 3: *White to move (Reshevsky–Kavalek, Netanya, 1971). Who has more space? Assess the position, and suggest what White's next move might be and why.*

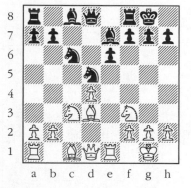

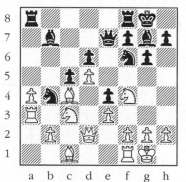

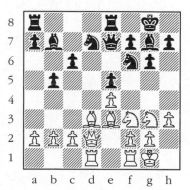

Exercise 4: *An example of the iso-lated pawn. Who has more space? Review the rules of thumb for playing with or against the isolated pawn in Chapter 11. How do they relate to the rules of thumb for playing with more or less space?*

Exercise 5: *Black to move (Davies–Wolff, Preston, 1989). White has more space on the queenside, and Black has more space on the kingside. At the moment both players control about the same amount of space. Where should Black attack and why? Suggest how Black should play.*

Exercise 6: *White to move (Wolff–M. Gurevich, Holland, 1993). Who has more space? I played 14.c4. Is this a good move or a bad move? Explain why or why not.*

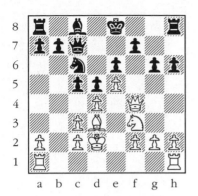

Exercise 7: *White to move (Fischer–Rossolimo, U.S. Championship, 1965–66). Fischer, in his classic book* My 60 Memorable Games, *wrote that he should have played 13.Qf6 Rg8 14.h4 to attack on the kingside (where he has more space). Instead Fischer played 13.h4 right away. Do you see what Black played to gain more space on the kingside? (Hint: He used a pin to his advantage.)*

Exercise 8: *Black to move (Letelier–Fischer, Germany, 1960). Another of Fischer's memorable games shows the danger of rushing your pawns forward too quickly at the cost of development. White's center looks imposing, but Fischer smashed through it by playing 7...c5! 8.dxc5 Nc6!. Analyze this position and convince yourself that Black has a good position. Compare your analysis with the answer to this exercise when you're ready. (This is a tough one! Do the best you can.)*

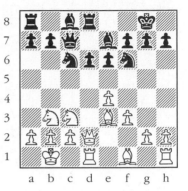

Exercise 9: *Black to move. What move can Black play to gain more space for himself and to challenge White's spatial control? (Notice the connection between controlling the center and controlling more space.)*

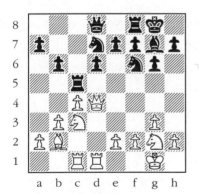

Exercise 10: *Black to move (Andersson–Portisch, Iceland, 1991). Who has more space? Do you think 14...Nd5 is a good move for Black? Why or why not?*

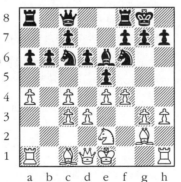

Exercise 11: *White to move (van Wely–Fritz Computer, Dutch Championship, 2000). Who has more space? How can White increase his space advantage, and what should his plan be once he does so?*

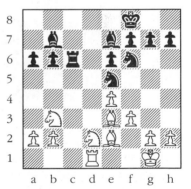

Exercise 12: *White to move (Kramnik–Kasparov, London World Championship match, 2000). How can White increase his space advantage? How might play continue?*

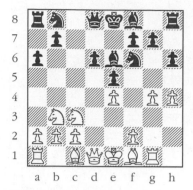

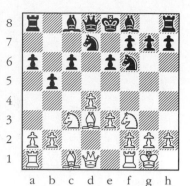

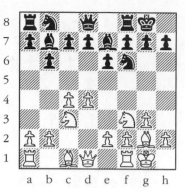

Exercise 13: Black to move. White's plan is to play g4-g5 to push the knight away from the center and gain space. How should Black meet this plan?

Exercise 14: Black to move. White's d pawn gives him more space in the center. Plus, if he is allowed to, White will play e4-e5, gaining even more space in the center. How can Black fight for more space and stop White from taking more?

Exercise 15: Black to move. Black is considering two moves to neutralize White's space advantage: 1...Ne4 and 1...c5. Which is better, and why?

The Least You Need to Know

♦ The pawn structure largely determines who has more space.

♦ Whoever controls more squares, particularly within the opponent's half of the board, has more space.

♦ Where you have more space, your pieces are more mobile, so you should generally attack on the part of the board where you have more space.

♦ When you have less space, you should either take more space on some other part of the board or you should challenge your opponent's space advantage.

♦ The player with less space wants to exchange pieces; the player with more space wants to avoid exchanging pieces.

Chapter 13

Weak Squares

In This Chapter

- ◆ How a square can be weak
- ◆ Recognizing which squares are weak
- ◆ Exploiting weak squares in your opponent's position
- ◆ Repairing weak squares in your own position

In Chapter 12, we talked about the importance of controlling more squares than your opponent. But not all squares are equally important. Some squares are difficult (or impossible) for one player to control with his pawns. Such squares have the potential to be *weak squares*, especially if the other player can control them with his pawns.

Recognizing Weak Squares

To recognize which squares are weak, just see which squares you or your opponent can't easily (or ever) control with pawns.

For example, let's look at Diagram 1. Does White have any weak squares? Obviously, we can ignore the first two ranks, because White's pawns can never control those squares anyway. The only square that could potentially be weak is d3, because White can no longer control that square with a pawn. But that's probably not something to worry about in this position, because Black is hardly able to control that square himself.

Now what about Black? Even if we ignore the eighth and seventh ranks, we see that Black has no fewer than four weak squares; d6, d5, f6, and h6. (Did you remember to count d6? Remember that no piece or pawn controls its own square!) Should Black worry about these squares? Well, White certainly controls d5 and d6, so White might be able to take advantage of those squares. White doesn't control f6 at the moment, but if the knight goes to d5, it will control f6; plus, it's not hard to imagine White's queen controlling f6 by going to f3. So White might be able to take advantage of the weak f6 square. The hardest square for White to control is h6, so that's probably the least weak of the bunch. On the other hand, h6 (like f6) is very near the black king, so Black should be especially careful about these two squares. If any white pieces land on those squares, they could be a serious menace to Black's king!

Chess Talk

A **weak square** is a square that one player can control but the other player can't. Often a square is weak because one player has permanently lost the ability to control it with his pawns, but sometimes a square is weak because one player can't move a pawn to where it would control the square without making some serious concession in his position.

In Diagram 1, White controls the weak square d5 more than Black does. In addition, White attacks the d6 pawn several times, which forces Black to defend it several times. For these reasons, Black's weak squares are a serious liability. (Another thing that makes the weak squares a serious liability for Black is that two of them are so near the king. We'll come back to this theme later in the chapter.) But now compare Diagram 1 to Diagram 2.

Once again Black has some weak squares: b6, d5, and d6. But these weak squares are much less of a problem than in Diagram 1, because Black controls these squares much better. The b6 square is controlled by the knight on d7 and the queen on c7. The d6 square (and the pawn sitting on it) is defended by the bishop on e7 and the queen on c7. And the d5 square is controlled by the knight on f6 and the bishop on e6. In addition, because it's impossible to see right now how White could attack the d6 pawn with a minor piece, the pawn is very well defended just by the bishop on e7. All in all, even though Black has weak squares, they are not too much of a liability because they are well controlled by his pieces.

One of the important contrasts between Diagrams 1 and 2 is that in Diagram 1, White can play his knight to d5 without allowing it to be captured; whereas in Diagram 2 if White plays his knight to d5, if it were captured, White would have to recapture with a pawn, which would eliminate the weak square on d5. (Notice that such an exchange would also change the status of the d6 pawn; it would no longer be a "backward pawn" in the specific sense of the phrase, because the square in front of it would be occupied by a white pawn.) Actually, White can't even play the knight to d5 anyway because Black would win the pawn on c2. But in Diagrams 3 and 4, I've changed the position slightly to show what happens if White plays his knight to d5 and has to recapture with a pawn.

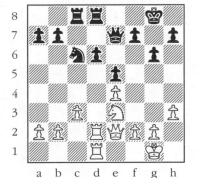

Diagram 1: White has no weak squares, but Black has four: d6, d5, f6, and h6.

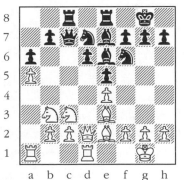

Diagram 2: Black has three weak squares: b6, d5, and d6.

When White plays 1.Nd5, Black plays 1...Nxd5, and after 2.exd5 the d5 square is no longer weak, because it's been occupied by a white pawn. I'm not saying that there's never any reason for White to carry out this exchange. For example, after the pawn goes from e4 to d5, White gains more space on the queenside. All I'm saying is that the d5 square is no longer weak for Black because White occupies it with a pawn.

Weak Squares and Pawn Structure

Perhaps you've noticed that weak squares and backward pawns seem to go together. That's not an accident. Because pawns capture diagonally and not forward, the square in front of a pawn is always a potentially weak square. I strongly suggest that you review Chapter 11 and look for all the weak squares that go with each pawn structure. Keep in mind that when pawns are lined up side by side, there are no weak squares in front of them! That's one big reason the pawn duo is such a strong pawn formation.

In addition to backward pawns, one of the pawn structures that most naturally gives rise to weak squares is the isolated pawn. Because there are no pawns on the files adjacent to the isolated pawn, the square in front of the isolated pawn is weak. So for example in Diagram 5, the d4 square is weak, and White can use it for his pieces.

Diagram 3: White to move.

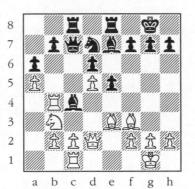

Diagram 4: Position after 1.Nd5 Nxd5 2.exd5.

Diagram 5: The d4 square is weak, and White can use it for his minor pieces.

The Hole

Sometimes a weak square is called a "hole." Think of it this way: when pawns are side by side, they control all the squares in front of them; but when one advances ahead of another, there is a hole in the pawn structure because that square can no longer be controlled by a pawn. Diagram 6 gives an example of such a hole. White's knights occupy two of Black's weak squares: c5 and e5. The c5 square is not a hole because Black could eventually play his pawn to b6 and control c5. But the e5 square can never again be controlled by a Black pawn, so it is a hole in Black's pawn structure. The white knight has a splendid post on this weak square, where it controls squares deep in Black's position.

Actually, it's worth pointing something out about the weak square on c5. Although Black could, in theory, control this square by advancing his pawn to b6, the pawn on c6 makes it especially hard to do this, because if the b-pawn advances to b6 it will leave the c6 pawn undefended. Therefore, the c6 pawn actually makes the c5 square weaker by making it harder to control that square without losing the pawn. This idea—a square being made weaker because control-ling the square would leave another pawn (or square) undefended—is very important and comes up many times. (Chapter 10 has at least two examples of this: Diagram 4 and Diagram 6.)

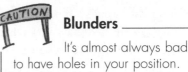

Blunders _____

It's almost always bad to have holes in your position. Avoid holes! If you must allow one, make sure your opponent can't put a piece on it, as White has done in Diagram 6.

The Weak Color Complex

White has two other advantages in Diagram 6. One is his space advantage; the other is his opponent's "weak color complex." This is a fancy way of saying that Black has a lot of weak squares of the same color—in the case of Diagram 6, a lot of weak black squares, such as e5, c5, d6, and maybe also f4 and g5. When one player has put a lot of pawns on squares of one color, it's usually important for him to keep the bishop that moves on squares of the other color. That's not to say that you can't have a weak color complex even if you have the bishop, or that not having the bishop means you will; it's just better to keep the bishop that travels on the color of weak squares. (Notice that in Diagram 6 Black no longer has his black-squared bishop. That fact makes his dark-square complex easier for White to take advantage of.)

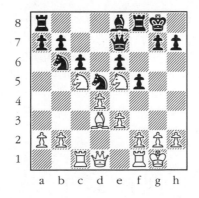

Diagram 6: (Janowski–Kupchik, Havana, 1913).

If it's important for the player with lots of pawns on the same color to keep his bishop, it makes sense for his opponent to exchange those bishops. That was the strategy I used in a game at the North Bay Open in Canada. In Diagram 7, Black has just played his queen to c7 in order to prevent White from moving the bishop to f4 and exchanging it for Black's bishop. I decided to play 12.g3 (see Diagram 8) to increase my control of the f4 square so I could carry out the idea of exchanging bishops. Moving this pawn carries some risk with it, because it weakens f3 and h3, two squares close to my king. But I had analyzed this position at home before playing it in this game, and I had decided that it was more important for White to try to exploit Black's weak black squares than to be worried about the white squares near his king.

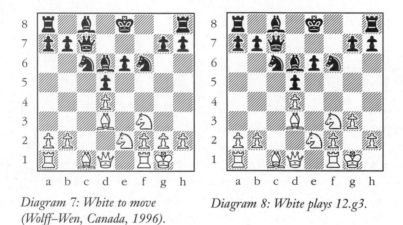

Diagram 7: White to move
(Wolff–Wen, Canada, 1996).

Diagram 8: White plays 12.g3.

Diagrams 9, 10, and 11 show how I carried this idea out. Notice that in Diagram 11, White has several advantages, such as more space and more pieces developed. But one of the most important advantages is that my pawns are almost all on black squares and I have a white-squared bishop, while Black's pawns are almost all on white squares and he has a white-squared bishop. My pawns and bishop work harmoniously together, whereas Black's don't. As a result, his black squares are much weaker than my white squares, and my bishop is good, while his is bad. (If you did Exercise 1 in Chapter 10, you saw a later position in this same game. Can you see how the color-complex advantage I gained here helped set up the strategy I was able to carry out later in that exercise?)

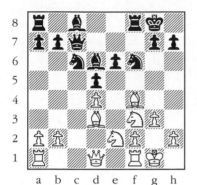

Diagram 9: Position after
12...O-O Bf4.

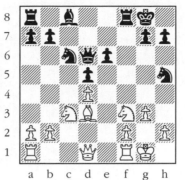

Diagram 10: Position after
13...Nh5 14.Bxd6 Qxd6 15.Nc3.

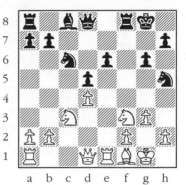

Diagram 11: Position after 15...g6
16.Re1 Qd8 17.Bf1.

Weak Squares and the King

Leaving weak squares near your king practically invites your opponent to attack. Your opponent's pieces can use those weak squares, and without pawns to repel them, it becomes much harder to survive an attack. Let's look at an example.

There are a lot of good things about White's position in Diagram 12. He has an extra pawn, the two bishops, and a very strong pawn center. (Even the doubled pawn is a strength, because it helps control the center and it gives White the open a-file for his rook.) But White has a hole on g3, and this invites Black to line up his queen and bishop to set up a checkmate threat on h2. If White's h-pawn were on h2, he would have a large advantage. In Diagram 12, with the pawn on h3, he is lost after 1...Qg3! (see Diagram 13).

Black threatens checkmate by 2...Qh2#. White's only defense is to run away with 2.Kg1, but then Black forces checkmate by playing 2...Qh2+ 3.Kf2 Bg3# (see Diagram 14). Every move of Black's attack was on one of those two squares, g3 or h2!

> ### Patrick's Pointers
>
> When you're attacking the king, find ways to create weak squares near the king, and then move your pieces so that they can control or occupy those squares. Sometimes it's even worth sacrificing material to create weak squares near the king.

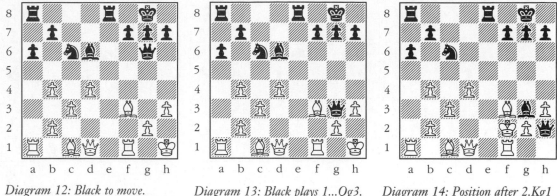

Diagram 12: Black to move. *Diagram 13: Black plays 1...Qg3.* *Diagram 14: Position after 2.Kg1*
Qh2+ 3.Kf2 Bg3#.

Even if there is no immediate checkmate, it's often wise to maneuver some of your pieces to any weak squares around the king. The pieces will then be well placed once the attack gets going in full. An example of this is my game against former World Championship Challenger David Bronstein (see Diagram 15).

Black is ahead one pawn. I could regain my pawn by playing 24.Nxe5, but this would open up the diagonal of his bad bishop on g7. Besides, his king is exposed, and with my queen on h5 and my rooks doubled, most of my pieces are in good position to attack. What I need is to maneuver my knight to Black's weakest square near his king: f5. To this end, I play 24.Nd6! as shown in Diagram 16.

Chess Lore

David Bronstein is one of the strongest players who never became world champion. He was born in Kiev, Ukraine (then part of the Soviet Union), in 1924. In 1951 he qualified to play a 24-game match for the World Championship with the current title holder, Mikhail Botvinnik. The match was hard fought and close all the way to the end. When Bronstein won game 22, he was ahead by one point; but Botvinnik won the next game, and the score was again even. Because the champion would keep the title in case of a tied match, Bronstein had to go all out for a win in game 24. He tried his best to win that game, but the pressure to win led him to attack prematurely, and Botvinnik soon had a winning advantage. Botvinnik offered a draw, and Bronstein, seeing that he had no chance to win, accepted. The match was tied, and Botvinnik kept the title.

Bronstein never again qualified to play for the World Championship, although he tied for second in the 1953 tournament that determined who would challenge in 1954. Bronstein then wrote a book where he analyzed most of the games of that tournament, a book recognized today as a classic.

Black plays 24...h6?, in an effort to offer the exchange of queens with 25...Qg5, but after 25.h4 (see Diagram 17) squelches that idea, the result is that Black weakens his king's position even more. He tries to activate his king's rook by playing 25...Rfb8, but after 26.Nf5 Qf8 in Diagram 18, my knight is on an ideal square and my attack is ready to go. In fact, White already has a move that wins a pawn by force. One of the exercises at the end of the chapter asks you to find that move.

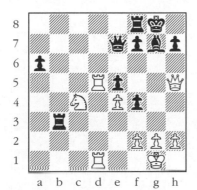

Diagram 15: White to move (Wolff–Bronstein, Holland, 1992).

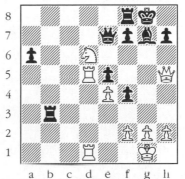

Diagram 16: White plays 24.Nd6!.

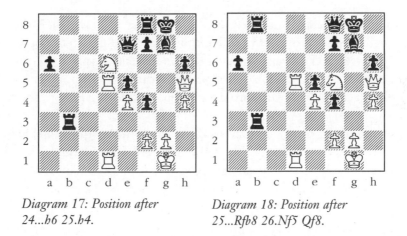

Diagram 17: Position after 24...h6 25.h4.

Diagram 18: Position after 25...Rfb8 26.Nf5 Qf8.

Because it's so dangerous to have weak squares near the king, it's obviously very much in your interest to create weak squares near your opponent's king if you're attacking it. One way to do this is to push one of your pawns up to the king's pawn cover. Even if the pawn is not protected, pushing it can put the defending side in a no-win situation. If he lets you capture his pawn, his king's position is compromised, but if he captures or advances his pawn, the effect is the same.

Diagrams 19 and 20 show an example of this. White has slightly more space and Black has a bad bishop, so we'd expect White to have a small advantage. But White's advantage is larger than one might expect because he can make a powerful strike at Black's castled position with 1.h6!.

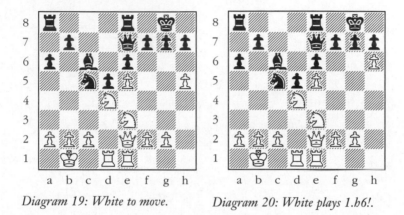

Diagram 19: White to move.   Diagram 20: White plays 1.h6!.

White threatens to capture the pawn on g7. If Black plays 1...gxh6?, then 2.Ng4! is very strong, because White will win back the h-pawn and gain the open h-file for his attack. (Notice that White also threatens to win material by playing Nf6+.) An attempt to counterattack the pawn on e5 doesn't work either, for example 1...Qg5 is well met by 2.Ng4!. Black's best move is probably 1...g6, to keep the king as sheltered as possible, but then after 2.Ng4 Nd7 (2...Ne4? 3.f3 Ng3 4.Qf2 Nh5 5.Rh1 forces the knight off to the side of the board, and makes Black's king more vulnerable, because White will be able to expose the king with the sacrifice Rxh5 at the right time) 3.Qe3 allows White to increase his space advantage. Notice that Black's knight has been forced to a more passive square because of the need to defend the weak square f6.

Repairing a Weak Square

Once you've pushed a pawn, you can't pull it back. But there are other ways to cope with having a weak square, and when you have weak squares, you should look for an opportunity to do so.

Diagram 21 shows a position that arises from a gambit called the "Marshall Attack," named after the great American player Frank Marshall. White has an extra pawn, but Black has more pieces developed, and White's kingside is weakened. How can White cope with the weak white squares around his king?

In Diagram 22, Tal finds a brilliant answer with 16.Bd5!, which serves both a defensive and offensive purpose at the same time. Its offensive purpose is to attack the rook on a8. Its defensive purpose is to stop Black from taking the long white-square diagonal for himself by putting the bishop on b7.

Black plays 16...Bf5, and after 17.Qe3! he has to move the rook on a8; he can't move it to e8 because White would win material (two rooks for a queen) by capturing it. So Black plays 17...Rad8, and after 18.Bg2 (see Diagram 23), White succeeds in largely repairing the weak white squares around his king. Tal is then able to develop the rest of his pieces, and he quickly gains a large advantage because of his extra pawn.

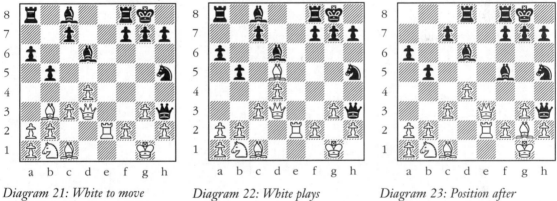

Diagram 21: White to move (Tal–Witkowski, Riga, 1959).

Diagram 22: White plays 16.Bd5!.

Diagram 23: Position after 16...Bf5 17.Qe3 Rad8 18.Bg2.

Another way to cope is to exchange whichever of your opponent's pieces is best able to take advantage of the weak square.

Suppose you are playing the black side of Diagram 24. Without question, Black is worse: Black's bishop is inferior to White's knight, and Black has a glaring weak square on d5, and another weak square on f5. (White's knight would be very strong if it got to f5.)

But Black can solve most of his problems by playing 1...Ba5!. Because of the pin to the rook on e1, White can't avoid the exchange of bishop for knight. Black still has a worse pawn structure, but after exchanges Black will be only a little worse, and should probably draw (for example, 2.Re3 Bxc3! 3.Rxc3 Rxc3 4.Qxc3 Qe7). Certainly the weak squares at d5 and f5 will be much less of a problem once White's knight is off the board.

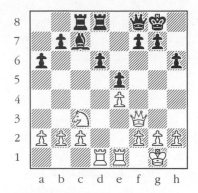

Diagram 24: Black to move.

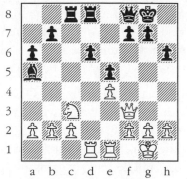

Diagram 25: Black plays 1...Ba5!.

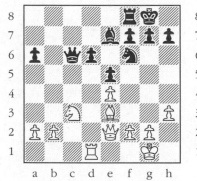

Exercise 1: *White to move. How can White weaken Black's control of the d5 square? (Hint: Find a way to use White's black-squared bishop.)*

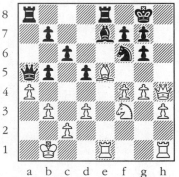

Exercise 2: *White to move. Each side is attacking the other's king. How can White use a weak square near Black's king to make sure his attack gets through first? If Black's g6 pawn were on h7, what difference would this make?*

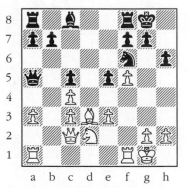

Exercise 3: *White to move (Botvinnik–Kan, USSR Championship, 1939). Botvinnik plays 16.Ne4!, and after 16...Qd8 the game continues 17.Nxf6+ Qxf6. What is Botvinnik's idea? Do you see what weak square Botvinnik wants to exploit and which piece he wants to put there?*

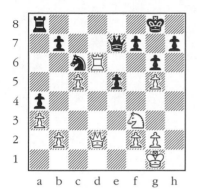

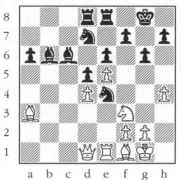

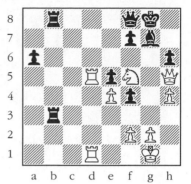

Exercise 4: White to move (A. Ivanov–Gulko, U.S. Championship, 1995). Black has just played 24...e5. Which squares near Black's king are weak? How can White maneuver a piece to control those squares?

Exercise 5: White to move (Adams–Wolff, New York, 1996). My last move is 25...Bc6?. This move is a mistake because it allows White to maneuver one of his pieces to a very weak square near my king while attacking the bishop at the same time. How?

Exercise 6: White to move (Wolff–Bronstein, Holland, 1992). Here is Diagram 18 again, after 26...Qf8, where we see White reap the benefit of maneuvering his knight to the weak f5 square. How can I win a pawn and also expose Black's king even more? (Hint: White makes a move that creates two threats at once.)

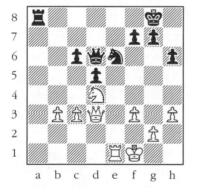

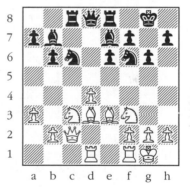

Exercise 7: Black to move (Bernstein–Lasker, St. Petersburg, 1914). White has many weak squares near his king, which Black should try to exploit. The best move is either 35...Qg3 or 35...Qh2. Which is the right move, and why? (This is a hard exercise: Lasker himself played the wrong move! Here's a hint: the key is to determine which move works out better for Black if White plays 36.Nxe6.)

Exercise 8: Black to move (Illescas–Wolff, Switzerland, 1993). It's my turn to play my seventeenth move. How can Black repair the weaknesses caused near the king by playing the g-pawn to g6?

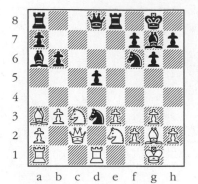

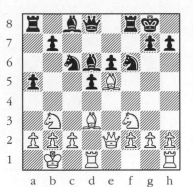

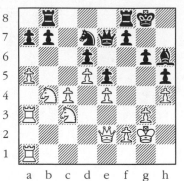

Exercise 9: *Black to move (R. Byrne–Fischer, U.S. Championship, 1963–1964). This is a very, very hard exercise. I've included it because it's very instructive, and I also think it's one of the most beautiful games I know. Fischer finds an incredible way to exploit the potentially weak white squares around White's king. He plays 15...Nxf2!! 16.Kxf2 Ng4+ 17.Kg1 Nxe3 18.Qd2 Nxg2!!. (Fischer writes, "Removing this bishop leaves White defenseless on his white squares.") 19.Kxg2 d4! 20.Nxd4 Bb7+. Here Fischer writes, "The king is at Black's mercy." Analyze this position and convince yourself that Black has a winning attack against all of White's replies. Then compare your analysis with the analysis given in the answer.*

Exercise 10: *Black to move (Shirov–Kramnik, Holland, 2001). How can Black induce a weakness in White's castled position?*

Exercise 11: *White or Black to move. If it is White's turn, what move should he play to create a very weak square that he can exploit? If it is Black's move, how should he defend against White's threat?*

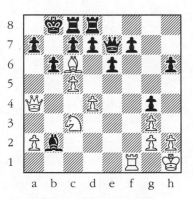

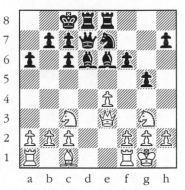

Exercise 12: *White to move. White has an attack, but he is behind in material and several pieces are attacked. How does White press home the attack by exploiting the weak squares around Black's king?*

Exercise 13: *White to move. What squares are weak around the king? How can White exploit them?*

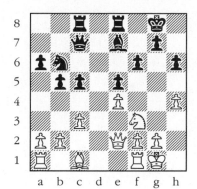

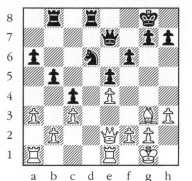

Exercise 14: *White to move. How can White exploit Black's weak squares?*

Exercise 15: *Black to move. How can Black exploit White's weak squares?*

The Least You Need to Know

- ◆ When a square can't easily be controlled by a pawn or can't ever be controlled by a pawn, it's a weak square.

- ◆ You should exploit weak squares in your opponent's position by controlling those squares with pawns or pieces or by occupying the square with a piece.

- ◆ If you have a weak color complex, you should keep the bishop that controls those squares; if you want to exploit a weak color complex in your opponent's position, you should capture the bishop that controls those squares.

- ◆ Weak squares around the king are an invitation to attack.

- ◆ You can compensate for weak squares in your position by controlling them with your pieces.

All Good Things Must Come to an End

In This Chapter

◆ Knowing when the middlegame becomes the endgame

◆ General principles for the endgame

◆ Some specific endgames

As the middlegame progresses, opposing forces come into contact with one another. If neither side manages to mount a decisive attack, more and more pieces will tend to be exchanged. When material for each side is reduced enough, the middlegame has ended, and the third phase of a chess game—the endgame—has begun.

"How reduced does material have to be? How much is enough?," you might ask. Unfortunately, there's no easy answer to those questions. I can't give you a simple way to tell when enough material has been exchanged so that the middlegame has become the endgame. But I can tell you the two general principles that apply to the endgame. What you should do when some material has been exchanged is ask whether those principles seem to apply to the position you're playing. If they do, the endgame has begun.

But Don't Forget What You've Learned Up to Now!

Before I explain these two general principles, I must make one thing very clear:

> All the principles and strategies you've learned for playing the middlegame still apply to the endgame!

Controlling the center, king safety, the advantage of active over passive pieces, pawn structure, space, weak squares, and more: all still apply. Middlegame principles are principles for playing good chess, and the fact that there's less material on the chessboard in the endgame doesn't mean that those principles no longer hold true. However, the reduced material does have some effect on how the principles are applied. The most important changes are listed here:

◆ Controlling the center. It's still important to control the center. In fact in many endgames it's absolutely essential to occupy the center before your opponent. But when material is drastically reduced, the center may become less important. For example, if all the pawns are on one side of the board, all of the action will probably be on that side of the board, so the center will lose most of its importance. Diagram 1 shows an example of such a position.

Diagram 1: Example of a position where control of the center is not important.

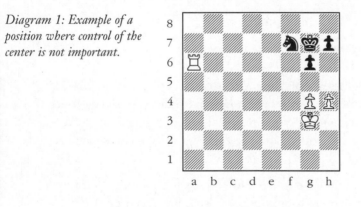

◆ Active vs. passive pieces. In the endgame, it's more important than ever to keep your pieces active. The reason is simple. In the middlegame, when each side has lots of pieces, the rest of the army can compensate for one passive piece; in the endgame, that one piece may be practically your whole army! For example, in Diagram 2, White's rook and king are active, whereas Black's rook and king are passive. That means White's whole army is active, whereas Black's is passive. Because his pieces are more active, White will be able to win Black's a-pawn, which will give him a winning advantage.

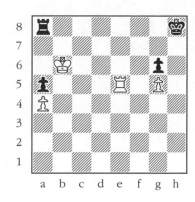

Diagram 2: Example of a position where having the more active pieces is even more important than in the middlegame.

♦ "Good" bishop vs. knight. For similar reasons as above, whether the bishop or the knight is the better piece becomes more important as fewer pieces remain. The bishop is the better piece when it can roam freely, and there are pawns on both sides of the board. In such cases, its greater mobility is an advantage over the knight. Diagram 3 shows such a position, taken from a world championship game between Kasparov and Karpov. Karpov drew, but Kasparov had good winning chances throughout. (Notice that Kasparov also has more space and better control of the center!)

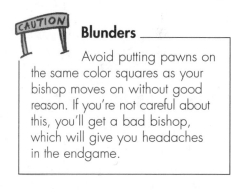

Blunders

Avoid putting pawns on the same color squares as your bishop moves on without good reason. If you're not careful about this, you'll get a bad bishop, which will give you headaches in the endgame.

♦ "Bad" bishop vs. knight. Sometimes the knight is the better piece. This happens most often when the bishop is "bad." (Recall Chapter 10.) Some endgames are lost just because of the bad bishop. Diagram 4 shows an example of this, taken from another World Championship match game between Karpov and Kasparov. Black's bishop can only attack one white pawn, whereas all of Black's pawns are targets for White's knight. Furthermore, the mobility of the bishop is reduced by having so many pawns on white squares. Karpov was able to exploit Black's ineffectual bishop and win this endgame. (But notice that part of White's advantage is also his very active king, which is invading behind enemy lines and will attack Black's pawns.)

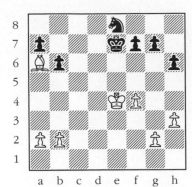

Diagram 3: Example of a position where the bishop is better than the knight (Kasparov–Karpov, World Championship match, 1986).

Diagram 4: Example of a position where the knight is better than the bishop (Karpov–Kasparov, World Championship match, 1984).

These are the most important ways that middlegame principles have to be adjusted to fit the endgame. Experience will teach you others.

The King Is a Strong Piece: Use It!

The first principle is a quote from Reuben Fine. It was one of the pieces of advice he offered in his classic book, *Basic Chess Endings*, "In the middlegame, with so much material on the board, the king should be kept out of harm's way. But when material is reduced, the danger to the king decreases accordingly, and then the king should be used like any other piece."

Two examples will help me make this point. First, look at Diagram 5. White has an extra pawn, but his rook is passive and Black's is active. White wants his most powerful piece to be active. The solution? Bring the king over to help! White should play 1.Kf1, 2.Ke1, 3.Kd1, and 4.Kc2 to protect the pawn and drive away Black's rook. By using the king, White can get more out of his rook.

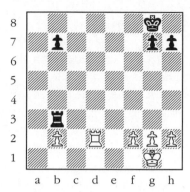

Diagram 5: White needs to activate the king to exploit his extra pawn.

Diagram 6: White to move (Khmelnitsky–Wolff, U.S. Championship, 1995).

Diagrams 6 through 9 show the second example. Diagram 6 shows the position of one of my games just at the moment that queens have been exchanged. (My last move was 25...bxc5, capturing White's queen.) While the queens were still on the board, it was much too dangerous for either side to bring the king to the center. But Diagram 7 shows that as soon as queens were exchanged, each of us rushed the king to the middle of the board as fast as possible!

Diagram 8 shows the game at a much later stage. Although I have since won a pawn, it's difficult to see how to win. The solution was to activate my king by playing 62...c4+! 63.Bxc4 Kc5 as shown in Diagram 9. Because his bishop was attacked, White had to allow the black king to reach d4, and then the activity of my king and knight were enough to force a win by attacking and winning White's pawns.

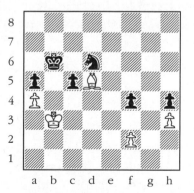

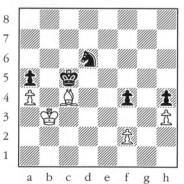

Diagram 7: Position after 26.Ke2 g5 27.Bc2 Kg7 28.Kd2 Kf6 29.Kc3 Ke5.

Diagram 8: Black to move (Khmelnitsky–Wolff, U.S. Championship, 1995).

Diagram 9: Position after 62...c4+ 63.Bxc4 Kc5.

The Passed Pawn Rules the Endgame!

When there are no longer any opposing pawns that can block a pawn, or that control any of the squares between the pawn and the edge of the board, we say that the pawn is *passed*. (The name comes from the idea that the pawn has "passed" all of the opposing pawns.) In the middlegame, with lots of material on the board, it's hard to promote a passed pawn. (That doesn't mean that passed pawns are unimportant in the middlegame, just that they rarely dominate the position.) But in the endgame, with much less material on the board, the passed pawn becomes much more important. Ultimately, endgame strategy is usually all about creating and promoting a passed pawn. This is precisely why the advantage of even one pawn is often enough to win a game. One extra pawn usually makes very little difference in a direct attack against the king. But one extra pawn makes all the difference when that one extra pawn promotes to a queen! Let's look at some of the most important aspects of passed pawns.

Chess Talk

If no opposing pawn occupies or controls any of the squares between a pawn and the edge of the board, the pawn is a **passed pawn**.

Patrick's Pointers

The king is a strong piece and you must use it in the endgame. But when material is reduced, the king can still find itself in jeopardy! Even when the absolutely right thing to do is to use the king, you must always be on the lookout for possible checkmates.

The Pawn Majority

When a larger number of pawns faces off against a smaller number of pawns, it's called having a pawn majority. Where you have a pawn majority, you have the potential to make a passed pawn.

In Diagram 10, each side has a pawn majority on one side of the board. White has a pawn majority on the queenside, whereas Black has a pawn majority on the kingside. But White's pawns are much farther advanced than Black's, so White is much better positioned to make a passed pawn with 1.b6!

After 1...cxb6 2.cxb6 (see Diagram 11), White already threatens to play 3.b7 and 4.b8=Q. (Notice how well White's rook supports the passed pawn from behind it.) The only way Black can try to stop the pawn from promoting without giving up the rook is to play 2...Rb7, but then in Diagram 12, White uses his more active king to drive the black rook away by playing 3.Ke6! White will play 4.Kd6 and 5.Kc6; then using the king to drive the rook away and the rook to support the pawn, he will push the pawn. Black cannot defend and must lose.

There are many, many ways to use a pawn majority. You should always look out for new ways to use the pawn majority in your own games, and in any other games you see.

Patrick's Pointers

The rook is almost always very well placed in the endgame behind a passed pawn, because if it's your passed pawn, the rook supports its advance, whereas if it's your opponent's passed pawn, the rook inhibits its advance.

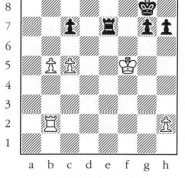

Diagram 10: White to move.

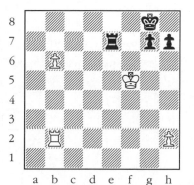

Diagram 11: White plays 1.b6! cxb6 2.cxb6.

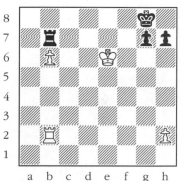

Diagram 12: Position after 2...Rb7 3.Ke6.

Patrick's Pointers

In almost any endgame, the winning strategy is to create a passed pawn and then push that pawn to the far side of the board to promote it to a queen. Once you have a queen, checkmating your opponent should be easy. If you're trying to win, this is what you must do. If you're trying to draw, this is what you must prevent your opponent from doing.

The Outside Passed Pawn

In earlier chapters, I've stressed that center pawns are more powerful than noncenter pawns. That's definitely true in the opening and the middlegame, and it's still sometimes true in the endgame when control of the center is important. But in the endgame, the *outside passed pawn* can be a definite advantage. There are two reasons for this:

◆ Because the outside passed pawn is so far away from other pieces, it's harder for the defending side to get over to it and stop it from advancing. (Diagrams 10 through 12 give an example of this.)

♦ Even if the defending side can get over to stop the pawn, his pieces may have been led away from many other important squares. In other words, the outside passed pawn can act as a decoy.

Diagrams 13 through 15 show how, by acting as a decoy, the outside passed pawn can be deadly. White plays 1.a6. Black must stop this pawn, so he must play 1...Kc6 (or 1...Kc7). But then White's king can infiltrate Black's pawns on the kingside by playing 2.Ke5. Because Black had to move the king over to catch the outside passed pawn, the kingside pawns are left defenseless to the white king.

Diagram 13: White to move.

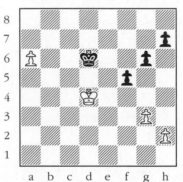

Diagram 14: White plays 1.a6.

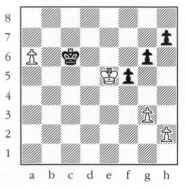

Diagram 15: Position after 1...Kc6 2.Ke5.

The Protected Passed Pawn

A protected passed pawn is simply a passed pawn that is protected by another pawn. In the endgame, the protected passed pawn can be very powerful indeed. The point is that because the passed pawn is so powerful, you want it to be securely defended. And what better way for it to be defended than by another pawn?

Diagrams 16 through 19 show an example of the power of the protected passed pawn. Each side has a pawn majority, but only Black has a protected passed pawn. Because the pawn is protected, White has no way to attack it with the king. (If White's king ever goes beyond the fourth rank, Black will play 1...b3 and make a queen, so the white king can never attack Black's queenside pawns.) Because the pawn is passed,

White must keep his king close enough to catch it if Black should start advancing it. So the protected passed pawn severely limits the mobility of the white king. This turns out to be a large enough advantage for Black to win this position.

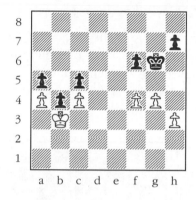

Diagram 16: Black to move.

Black starts by playing 1...f5! in order to break up White's pawns. His plan is to loosen the pawns so that he can attack them with his king. If White plays 2.g5, then after 2...Kh5 (as shown in Diagram 18) Black will play 3...Kh4 and capture White's h-pawn, after which the other pawns will fall. (I haven't shown 2.gxf5+ Kxf5 in a diagram, but can you see that Black could then immediately capture White's pawn on f4?) So White plays 2.Kc2, and after 2...fxg4 3.hxg4 h5! Black succeeds in exposing the pawns to attack by the king. Exercise 12 at the end of this chapter will challenge you to figure out how Black wins the position in Diagram 19.

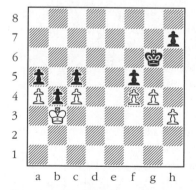

Diagram 17: Black plays 1...f5!.

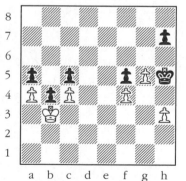

Diagram 18: Position if play continues 2.g5 Kh5.

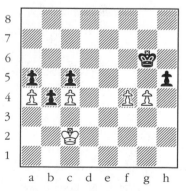

Diagram 19: Position after 2.Kc2 fxg4 3.hxg4 h5!.

Blockading the Passed Pawn

When your opponent has a passed pawn, you should make sure that it doesn't have the chance to advance. The best way to do that is to stick a piece in front of it. When you do this, it's called blockading the passed pawn.

Diagram 20 shows an example of the blockade. White's e-pawn is passed, but because Black's knight is in front of it, it's not going anywhere. White can attack the knight with his king, but then Black will defend it with his king. Because White's bishop moves on black squares, it can't attack the square in front of the pawn, so Black can maintain the blockade indefinitely.

Diagram 20: White to move.

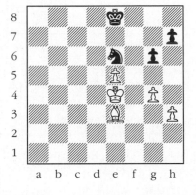

The only other way for White to win is to use his king to attack Black's pawns, but so long as Black keeps his knight on e6 and his pawn on g6, all the fifth-ranked squares on the kingside are guarded and White's king can't get at the black pawns. If White plays 1.Kd5 as in Diagram 21, Black plays 1...Kf7, defending the knight with his king. Then he moves the knight back and forth from e6 to another square, then back to e6. By following this plan, Black can only lose if he runs out of a safe square to move the knight to; but this will never happen, so the position is a draw. (Try playing this position out with a friend or a computer to see for yourself!)

When employing the blockade, make sure you leave yourself enough space so you don't run out of moves. This danger is shown in Diagrams 22 and 23. Black has blockaded the passed pawn just one square before promoting. Because White has a black-squared bishop, you might think that Black is safe. But Black's knight is on the edge of the board, which means it has very few squares to move to. Now White plays 1.Be5! and Black discovers, to his horror, that he has no good move! If Black could "pass" and not move, he would be fine because White still has no threat. But there's no such thing as "passing" in chess, so Black is in for it. If he moves the king, he loses the knight; but if he moves the knight, White will capture it with the bishop, and then promote the pawn next move.

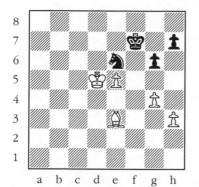

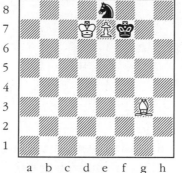

Diagram 21: Position after 1.Kd5 Kf7.

Diagram 22: White to move.

Diagram 23: White plays 1.Be5!.

Connected Passed Pawns

Recall from Chapter 11 that the pawn duo is very strong. Well, imagine how strong a pawn duo of passed pawns must be! When two pawns on adjacent files are passed, they are called "connected passed pawns." Connected passed pawns are very, very powerful. Sometimes they are worth a lot of material.

Diagram 24 shows a special case that illustrates the power of connected passed pawns. White to move wins by playing 1.c6!, because Black can't stop White from making a queen. For example, play could continue 1...Rc8 2.b7 Rxc6 3.b8=Q+, and so on. Black to move wins by playing 1...Rb8!, which stops White from advancing his pawns. Then Black moves the king over to the queenside and captures the queenside pawns. Notice that 1...Rc8?? loses to 2.b7! Rb8 (2...Rxc5 3.b8=Q+) 3.c6 and 4.c7.

Connected passed pawns are so strong because they're so hard to blockade. Diagram 24 shows that sometimes they can overcome a lot of material all by themselves. With some support with other pieces, they are fearsome.

Diagram 24: Whoever
moves wins.

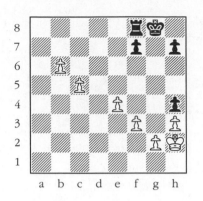

In Diagram 25, Black has two passed pawns of his own. If one of them were far advanced, he might have a chance of promoting it in time to stop White. But instead, they sit on their original squares, and White's connected passed pawns are far advanced. With White's king and knight nearby, Black has no chance of stopping them even though his king and knight are right in front of them. White wins by playing 1.e6+ followed by 2.d6, followed by advancing the pawns with the support of the knight and king. One sample line goes: 1.e6+ Kd8 2.d6 Ne8 3.Kc6 (White threatens 4.e7+ and 5.d7+.) 3...Nf6 4.Kb7 a5 5.Nc6+ Ke8 6.Kc8! (Not 6.d7+?? Nxd7 7.exd7+ Kxd7 and White has no pawns left!) followed by 7.d7+ and wins.

Diagram 25: White to
move.

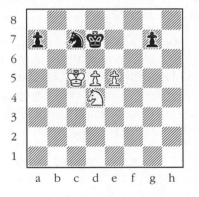

If you don't support your connected passed pawns well enough with your pieces, your opponent may be able to blockade them by getting one of them to advance and then blockading the backward pawn. Watch the exercises at the end of this chapter for an example of this.

Three Specific Endgames

Remember in Chapter 9 we had to distinguish between the opening and an opening. The opening is the opening phase of the game, whereas an opening is a specific sequence of moves one plans ahead of time to start the game with. In a similar way, we have to distinguish between the endgame and an endgame. The endgame is the endgame phase of the game, for which you've been learning general principles. An endgame refers to a specific kind of endgame that one learns how to play ahead of time. Of course, unlike the opening, you can't really plan to play a particular endgame ahead of time: It all depends on how the game goes! Nevertheless, it turns out that it is very valuable to learn how to play certain specific, typical endgame positions. Because endgames have such a small number of pawns and pieces, the positions can be classified into certain types. Often the plans and even specific tactics associated with those types of positions come up again and again.

There are many endgames to learn. A grandmaster knows thousands of them. I'm going to show you three. Each one helps to illustrate certain principles, and is also useful in its own right.

King and Pawn vs. King, and the Opposition

Our first specific endgame is shown in Diagram 26. Notice the position of the two kings. When there is one square between the kings (horizontally or vertically), they're said to be *opposed*. Whichever side does not have to move has the *opposition*. So in Diagram 26, if it's White's turn, Black has the opposition; if it's Black's turn, White has the opposition. The opposition is often a big advantage because when you have the opposition you can force the other king to give ground. In Diagram 26, if Black has the opposition, he draws; but if White has the opposition, he wins.

Chess Talk

Occasionally, whichever side has the move is at a disadvantage. Such a position is called **zugzwang**. (Chess has some pretty weird words, doesn't it?) The position in Diagram 26 is zugzwang. If it's White's move, the game is a draw; if it's Black's move, he loses. The **opposition** is not the only case of zugzwang, but it's one of the most common.

Diagram 26: White to move draws; Black to move loses.

Diagrams 27 and 28 show how. If it's White's turn to move, he has no better move than 1.d7+. Black plays 1...Kd8, and now unless White wants to lose his only pawn he must play 2.Kd6. But then it's a draw, because Black is stalemated.

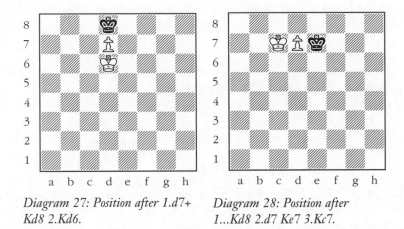

Diagram 27: Position after 1.d7+ Kd8 2.Kd6.

Diagram 28: Position after 1...Kd8 2.d7 Ke7 3.Kc7.

If it's Black's turn to move, he has to move his king to either d8 or b8. If he plays 1...Kb8, after 2.d7 he can't control d8 in his next move, so White will promote the pawn and win. So Black plays 1...Kd8, and White plays 2.d7. Now the only legal move is 2...Ke7, after which White plays 3.Kc7, as shown in Diagram 28. White controls the d8 square, so White will again promote the pawn.

Suppose in Diagram 26, instead of pushing his pawn, White played his king back with 1.Kc5. Black might play 1...Kd7, and then after 2.Kd5 we get Diagram 29. Now where should Black move his king? Wherever Black moves it, he should be able to take the opposition when White brings his king to either e6 or c6.

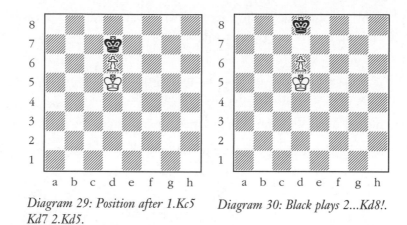

Diagram 29: Position after 1.Kc5 Kd7 2.Kd5.

Diagram 30: Black plays 2...Kd8!.

Black should play 2...Kd8! as shown in Diagram 30. This is the only move to draw, because otherwise White can take the opposition himself. But now if White moves the king to either c6 or e6, Black can take the opposition and draw. And if White moves the king to some other square, say e5, then Black just moves the king back to d7, and White is making no progress.

These king and pawn versus king endgames can get pretty tricky, and in the exercises I will give you a couple more to cut your teeth on. But you can figure them out if you remember the importance of having the opposition.

King, Rook's Pawn, and Wrong-Colored Bishop vs. King

This next endgame is either tragic or comic, depending on your point of view. In Diagram 31, White has an extra pawn and an extra bishop. Surely Black should resign. But no: White can't win even with all his extra material! The problem is that White can't force the king out of the corner with just the king and pawn because even if he takes the opposition, Black will be stalemated. And the bishop is of no help, because White has the wrong-colored bishop—that is, the bishop that doesn't control the corner where White wants to promote the pawn.

Diagram 32 shows a typical position that might arise if White tries to win. White can advance the pawn to h7, but he can't force the king out of the corner. The best he can do is give stalemate. Notice that the bishop is useless because all it can do is control g8, which just helps stalemate Black.

But don't think that having a bishop and a pawn always leads to a draw! Bishop and pawn against king is only a draw when all of these (very) special circumstances hold true:

◆ The pawn is a rook's pawn—that is, the pawn is on a file where a rook starts the game, for example, either the h-file or the a-file.

◆ The bishop does not control the corner square where the pawn promotes.

◆ The lone king can occupy the corner square where the pawn promotes.

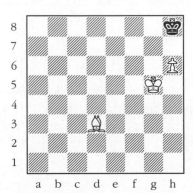

Diagram 31: Even with an extra bishop and pawn, White can't win.

Diagram 32: The best White can do is stalemate Black; there's no way to force the king out of the corner.

Opposite-Colored Bishops

In Chapter 10, I said that having opposite-colored bishops favors the attacker, because what one side's bishop attacks, the other side's bishop can't defend (so it's like having an extra piece in the attack). But in the endgame, having opposite-colored bishops favors the defender, because the attacker's bishop often can't attack the defender's pawns, whereas the defender's bishop often can blockade the attacker's passed pawns.

Diagram 33 shows how this can work. White has two extra connected passed pawns, but how can he make progress? White can't advance either of the passed pawns, because they're blockaded by the black king and bishop; and White can't break the blockade because his black-squared bishop is useless for controlling c6 or d5. If White could make another passed pawn, he might be able to advance that pawn, which Black couldn't blockade because his king and bishop would be too far away. But as the pawns stand, there's no way to make another passed pawn. And there's no way to attack Black's pawns, because Black's g6 pawn is protected by the f7 pawn, and the f7 pawn is protected by the bishop, and White's bishop is useless for attacking Black's pawns. White's black-squared bishop is practically a spectator! Black draws because even with two extra pawns, White can neither destroy Black's blockade nor capture Black's pawns.

Opposite-colored bishop endgames can get pretty complicated. The important thing to realize is that Black draws in Diagram 33 only because White can't destroy the coordination of Black's pieces. A slight change can give White a winning position. For example, in Diagram 34, White wins by playing 1.d7! Kxd7 2.Kxd5, and in Diagram 35, White wins by playing 1.h5! gxh5 2.gxh5 Bb3 3.h6 Bc2 4.d5+ Kd7 5.Kf6, and Black's defense collapses. (White's h-pawn distracts Black's bishop, forcing it to patrol the diagonal from which it can control the h7 square. With the bishop taken away from the queenside, White will have no trouble advancing his pawns to create a queen.)

So opposite-colored bishop endgames aren't always drawn. However, they do give much better drawing chances than almost any other kind of endgame, because the defending side can more easily defend his pawns and blockade the opponent's pawns.

> ### Patrick's Pointers
>
> If you're trying to win an end-game, don't exchange down to opposite colored bishops unless you have a very good reason. And if you're trying to draw, grab any chance to exchange down to opposite-colored bish-ops. It might even be worth one or two pawns to do it!

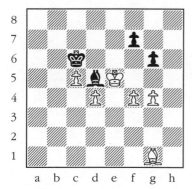

Diagram 33: Even with two extra pawns, White can't win.

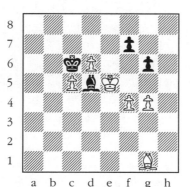

Diagram 34: White wins with 1.d7.

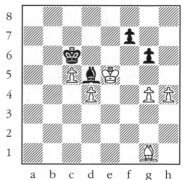

Diagram 35: White wins with 1.h5.

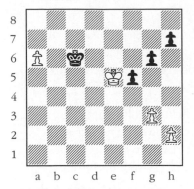

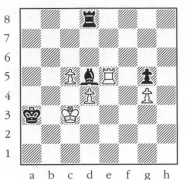

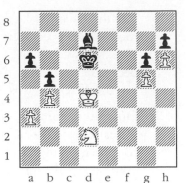

Exercise 1: *Black to move. This is Diagram 15 again, and your task is to show how White wins even against Black's best defense. (Hint: Black is going to play 2...Kb6 to capture the a-pawn. While he does that, capture Black's kingside pawns, but be careful not to let him use his pawn majority while you do so!)*

Exercise 2: *White to move. It looks like Black has White's pawns blockaded. Can White break Black's blockade and push his connected passed pawns? How?*

Exercise 3: *White to move. Who is better and why? How should White play?*

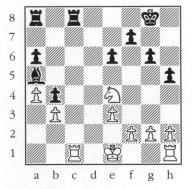

Exercise 4: *White to move (Capablanca–Germann, Miller, and Skillcorn, London Exhibition, 1920). In the old days, grandmasters used to play matches against teams of wealthy amateurs. This is one such game that Capablanca played against a team of three players. It's Capablanca's turn to make his twenty-third move. Which move is better: 23.Ke2 or 23.O-O? Why?*

Exercise 5: *White wants to win, Black wants to draw. If it's White's turn, does he win? If it's Black's turn, does he draw? Justify your answer by showing how the game should continue if it's White's turn and if it's Black's turn.*

Exercise 6: *White wants to win, Black wants to draw. If it's White's turn, how does he win? If it's Black's turn, how does he draw? (Hint: Remember the importance of having the opposition!)*

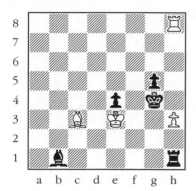

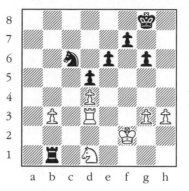

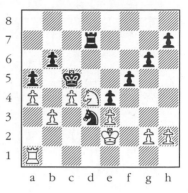

Exercise 7: *Black to move (Wolff–Browne, U.S. Championship, 1995). This is one of the strangest games I ever won. Clearly Black can't lose after 55...Rxh3 56.Rxh3 Kxh3 57.Kf2, but he can't win either. (Why?) So Browne decided to play 55...Kf5?? to prevent the exchange of rooks. But this move is a terrible blunder. How did I take advantage of Browne's mistake?*

Exercise 8: *White to move (Lasker–Capablanca, World Championship, 1921). Evaluate this position. Who do you think is more likely to win, and why?*

Exercise 9: *Black to move (Merenyi–Capablanca, Budapest, 1928). Capablanca played 30...Rxd4! 31.exd4+ Kxd4. Explain why this is a good sacrifice for Black to play.*

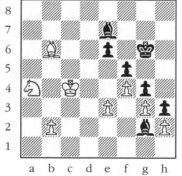

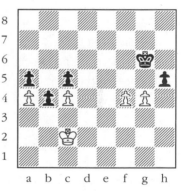

Exercise 10: *(Gutman–Wolff, Paris, 1987). It's White's turn, but rather than make a move, he resigned. Does the fact that I had a rook's pawn and the wrong-colored bishop mean that White should have been able to draw? If White had played 57.Kd2, how should Black play?*

Exercise 11: *Black to move (Chow–Wolff, Sioux Falls, 1996). This is a tricky exercise! How does Black win this position despite being down a pawn? (Hint: Find a way—any way at all—for Black to make his h-pawn a passed pawn.)*

Exercise 12: *White to move. This is Diagram 19 again (which came from Diagram 16 after 1...f5 2.Kc2 fxg4 3.hxg4 h5), and your job is to show how Black wins no matter how White plays. This is a long and difficult exercise: Analyze the position the best you can, and then compare your analysis with the answer in the appendix.*

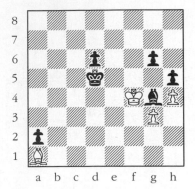

Exercise 13: *Black to move. This endgame is a draw. Analyze this position. After 1...Kc4, what is White's drawing strategy?*

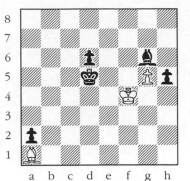

Exercise 14: *Black to move. Can White draw this position also?*

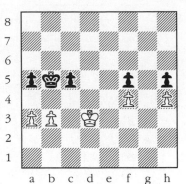

Exercise 15: *Black to move (Kasparov–Bareev, Holland, 2001). Black resigned in this position, but Kasparov later demonstrated that the position is completely drawn! Can you demonstrate how? (Warning: This is hard!)*

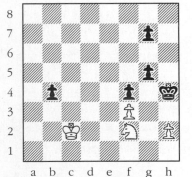

Exercise 16: *Black to move (Turner–Pert, British Championship, 2000). It looks like White has stopped Black's king and pawns and is poised to use his king to take Black's pawns. But Black found an extraordinary idea: 1...g4! What was Black's idea? Can Black draw?*

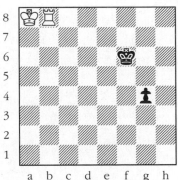

Exercise 17: *White to move. Black will try to draw by advancing his pawn and forcing White to give up his rook for it. Can White win? (Hint: This is hard until you find the right idea, but if you find the right idea the endgame is easy. Look for a way to cut off the black king.)*

Exercise 18: *White to move. Can White win? (The variations can get long, but once you understand the basic idea the analysis is straightforward.)*

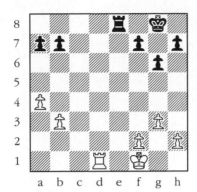

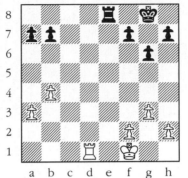

Exercise 19: White to move. What is White's strongest move, and why?

Exercise 20: White to move. Even after White plays the strongest move, Black has a resource in this position that he does not have in Exercise 19. What is it?

The Least You Need to Know

♦ Middlegame principles and strategies still apply to the endgame, although the reduced material modifies slightly how they should be applied.

♦ In the endgame, the king is a strong piece, so you should use it offensively. (But you should still always be careful about checkmate possibilities!)

♦ When an endgame is won, it's almost always by making a passed pawn and promoting it to a queen.

♦ When an endgame is drawn, it's almost always by preventing the opponent from making a passed pawn, blockading his passed pawns, or forcing stalemate.

♦ In endgames with just kings and pawns, having the opposition is extremely important, and often enough for the stronger side to win or the weaker side to draw.

♦ Two endgames that offer very good chances for the weaker side to draw are opposite-colored bishop endgames and the rook's pawn and wrong-colored bishop versus the king.

Part 4

Beyond the Basics

If you've studied the first three parts, you've learned how to play chess well. But you've only scratched the surface of the possibilities chess has to offer. This part is your platform for diving into the world of chess.

Now that you've learned the basics, you're ready for more. I give you tips for how to keep improving your skill at chess. You can learn about the superstars of chess: the world champions. I also tell you how to meet more people to play chess with. You even learn how the computer plays chess—and how to take advantage of its weaknesses. Are we having fun yet?

Training Camp

In This Chapter

- ◆ Studying the opening and the endgame
- ◆ Learning more about tactics and strategy
- ◆ How to use www.wolffchess.com
- ◆ Lessons from the superstars
- ◆ Reviewing your own games

At this point, you've learned all the basic tactics and strategies for chess. You can probably beat most or all of your friends, and you can certainly play better than most people who haven't studied the strategies and tactics you have learned so far. If your newspaper has a chess column, you can read it and appreciate it. You might be every bit as good at chess as you've ever wanted to be.

But then again, maybe not. Maybe even after studying this book there's somebody you know who still beats you, and you'd like to be able to turn the tables. Or maybe you've really gotten hooked on chess, and you'd like to get to the level where you feel comfortable competing at a club or in tournaments. Or maybe there isn't any reason you'd like to get even better except that chess is a great game, and it's satisfying to be able to play such a great game really well.

Whatever the reason, it doesn't matter: If you've studied all the chapters up to here, and you want to become even better at chess, this is the chapter where I tell you how to do it. Note that this chapter describes and recommends certain products, but it doesn't give you any specific addresses of people who sell or provide them. I tell you more about who supplies chess products in Chapters 17 and 18 (see especially "Finding and Entering a Chess Tournament" in Chapter 17), and you can find the contact addresses in Appendix A.

Studying the Opening and the Endgame

From previous chapters, you'll remember that it's important to distinguish between the opening or the endgame and an opening or an endgame, and that there are lots of specific openings and endgames to learn. If you want to get better at chess, you have to start studying openings and endgames. If you get your hands on a chess catalog, or if your local bookstore or library has a good chess section, you'll quickly discover that there's a huge amount of literature—mostly books—about openings and endgames.

Patrick's Pointers

Some chess books, particularly those written some years ago, use another kind of chess notation called descriptive notation. You can learn how to read descriptive notation in Appendix B. Appendix B also describes some of the minor variations in the kind of chess notation this book uses (the universal chess notation for books written today) that you may encounter from book to book.

Chess Talk

An **opening repertoire** is a set of opening variations one prepares in advance to be able to reach a playable middlegame no matter how the opponent plays in the opening. Every grandmaster spends much of his studying time refining his opening repertoire in order to get the jump on the opposition at the start of the game.

Studying the Opening

If you want to play chess competitively, you must develop an *opening repertoire*. That is, you must learn a set of specific opening sequences that allow you to reach a playable middlegame no matter how your opponent plays in the opening. Developing an opening repertoire is a lot of work. I don't recommend it unless you're sure you want to put some real effort into improving your chess game. If you don't want to play competitively, you could probably spend your time more efficiently studying other aspects of chess. But if you want to compete for prizes in club competitions or amateur tournaments, it's essential that you have an opening repertoire.

> **Patrick's Pointers**
>
> An excellent way to improve your game is through private instruction with a strong player, perhaps even a grandmaster. Such instruction is not cheap, and it involves a serious time commitment, but it's a tremendous way to get better. You may find such instruction at your local chess club, or you can receive instruction over the phone, through the mail, or by Internet. Look in chess magazines or on the Internet for advertisements or other information about private instruction.

Developing an opening repertoire is a personal thing. There's no right or wrong repertoire except whatever gives you middlegame positions you like and play well. For that reason, I can't tell you what openings to play; and when I teach amateurs I never try to tell them what to play. But I can tell you how to decide what to play, and then how to learn it.

First, get an opening encyclopedia. I recommend that you get one of the following two books:

1. *Nunn's Chess Openings*, written by Joe Gallagher and John Emms, edited by John Nunn.

2. *Modern Chess Openings, 14th edition*, written by Nick deFirmian, edited by Walter Korn.

Modern Chess Openings is much better at general explanation and still quite comprehensive, whereas *Nunn's Chess Openings* is even more comprehensive with slightly better analysis. If this will be one of your first openings books, I strongly recommend *Modern Chess Openings*. However, if you already have some experience with opening books, you may prefer *Nunn's Chess Openings*. In either case, use the book you get to browse through the openings and figure out which ones you like and how you'd want to fit them together.

> **Patrick's Pointers**
>
> A good way to help you decide which openings you like is to look through grandmaster games and see whether you like the kinds of middlegames and endgames the various openings give rise to.

I should mention that grandmasters use an advanced encyclopedia called the *Encyclopedia of Chess Openings* (ECO). This five-volume set gives a detailed analysis of all chess openings. For especially popular or topical openings, there are dedicated monograms published in the same format. Each book is over 500 pages long and is in either its third or fourth edition, which says a lot about how valuable grandmasters consider them! The set is supplemented by a journal called *Chess Informant*, which comes out three times a year and features grandmaster analysis of many of the most important grandmaster games played around the world. I do *not* recommend these for you yet, because the analysis is extremely dense. Right now, you need something that is easier to understand. But if you ever get *really* serious about studying chess openings, you should know that the ECO and the *Chess Informant* are the most advanced materials around.

After you decide which openings to learn, you might want to get some books written on specific openings. Be careful in your purchases. There's an enormous number of opening books, and not all of them are good. I can tell you that any opening book by John Nunn is of superb quality, but his books are often written at a very high level, and you might not be ready for him yet. Beyond that, I can only urge you to get recommendations from someone you trust before buying too many opening books. You can waste a lot of money here if you're not careful!

> **Patrick's Pointers**
>
> See Chapters 17 and 18 for ideas on how to find sources of chess books and other kinds of chess supplies.

Studying the Endgame

Fortunately, you only need to study a few books to learn just about everything you need to know to play the endgame well.

Two books that are superb are:

1. *Chess Endings: Essential Knowledge*, written by Yuri Averbakh.

2. *Essential Chess Endings Explained Move by Move, Volume 1*, written by Jeremy Silman.

There is another book that I highly recommend, although it's more difficult than either of the two listed above—*Practical Chess Endings*, written by Paul Keres. If you learn everything in this book, you'll be playing endgames as well as a grandmaster!

Finally, I highly recommend anything written by Edmar Mednis. Edmar was my teacher for several years, and I learned a lot about endgames from him. Sadly, Edmar passed away in 2002, but during his lifetime he wrote many books on the endgame, and in my opinion they're all very good.

Magazines and Periodicals

In addition to the many books on chess, there are also many magazines and periodicals you can subscribe to. If you really want to explore the world of chess, there's no better way to find out what's out there and what's going on than to read some magazines. In addition, most magazines have games analyzed by grandmasters, as well as articles intended specifically for instruction. Some magazines also have articles on related topics, intended more for fun than for instruction. There are lots of magazines you can get, but the following are some of the best:

♦ *Chess Life*, the official magazine of the U.S. Chess Federation. (See Chapter 17 for more about that organization.)

♦ *New In Chess*, a Dutch publication, is probably the best chess magazine in the world. This magazine has lots of games analyzed by grandmasters, plus interviews with the movers and shakers of the chess world.

♦ *Chess*, a British magazine featuring annotated games, book reviews, news, opening theory, quizzes, and more.

Using www.wolffchess.com and Other Websites

As I've mentioned previously, the Internet is an incredible boon for chess. Its potential has only just been scratched so far, and I predict that the future holds even more tremendous benefits for chess! The web is great for transmitting, displaying, and manipulating information. Chess is a game of pure information. It's a match made in heaven.

I no longer play chess professionally. In 1997, I started a new career in business. From 1999 to 2001 I worked at two web companies, where I learned to appreciate what the Internet can offer. With that in mind, I built an instructional chess website. If you're reading this now and you're looking for a way to keep getting better at chess, you may want to check out my website.

WolffChess is an online chess-training resource. Its URL is www.wolffchess.com. There you have access to over 500 exercises you can do online. The exercises are organized according to themes you have seen in this book. My goal is to provide a more interactive chess instructional experience than a chess book can provide. At WolffChess you can play through the exercises without using a chessboard, and you can get comments and feedback while doing them.

You can read much more about using the Internet in many, many other ways in Chapter 18, but I'll give you a sneak preview here of some other websites you can visit for chess information:

- The Week in Chess is a terrific resource. Its URL is www.chesscenter.com/twic/twic.html or go to www.chesscenter.com and click the "TWIC" tab. TWIC started as an e-mail newsletter and grew into a chess news website. You can go there to find daily reports and games from every important ongoing tournament or match, anywhere in the world.

- The Chess Café is chock full of interesting, in-depth articles. Less news-driven than TWIC, Chess Café is more oriented toward historical retrospective, reviews, opinion, and commentary. Chess Café is also the web outlet for House of Staunton, the premiere maker of fine chess sets. The Chess Café URL is www.chesscafe.com.

- Grandmaster Chess is an attractive site with a lot of information. Its URL is www.gmchess.com.

- Chessville.com is a site geared toward chess instruction. In addition to original material produced especially for Chessville.com, it monitors other chess sites and maintains up-to-date links to instructional articles from all over the web. The URL is www.chessville.com.

This really is just a taste of what's available online, though. Chess is blossoming on the web!

Studying Tactics

An excellent way to improve your game is to learn more tactics and exercise your ability to find the tactics that are hidden in any chess position. There are many good books on the subject. Here are two classics to get you started: *1001 Chess Sacrifices and Combinations*, and *1001 Brilliant Ways to Checkmate*, both written by Fred Reinfeld. As the names imply, there are 1001 chess positions in each book, so they should keep you occupied.

Patrick's Pointers
Many newspapers have a chess column with a diagram that challenges you to find the winning tactic. But I think the web is a perfect medium for training yourself. Online, there is no limit to the number of exercises you can use, and you can see the moves without needing a chessboard. That's exactly why I designed www.wolffchess.com the way I did.

Studying Strategy

One of the best ways to develop your strategic sense in chess is to study annotated grandmaster games, especially games with comments by one of the players himself. One terrific book for learning strategy that is not just a collection of annotated chess games is *My System*, written by Aron Nimzovich in 1925. The most recent publication of this book is edited by Lou Hays, and I highly recommend it.

Another classic is *The Art of Attack in Chess*, written by Vladimir Vukovic. This is one of the first books I ever read, and it made me a much better player.

Although this next book is a collection of games, the title makes it clear that it's intended for instruction in strategy. *The Most Instructive Games of Chess Ever Played: 62 Masterpieces of Chess Strategy*, written by Irving Chernev, is a wonderful book. This is another book I read when I was young.

Among contemporary chess authors, Andrew Soltis is particularly good. You have to be a bit careful with his work: He has written several dozen books, and some of them show that they were done quickly. But the ones that he took his time with are splendid. I especially recommend three Soltis books, *The Art of Defense in Chess*, *Pawn Structure Chess*, and *The Inner Game of Chess*. The topics of the first two books are self-explanatory; the third book is all about how to calculate the consequences of your moves. Each is excellent, and I myself learned a lot from them.

One recent book that I recommend highly is *The Road to Chess Improvement* by Alex Yermolinsky. Alex emigrated from Russia to the United States many years ago. He is a great chess player, and is very personable. That personality really comes through in the book. He explains things very clearly, in a genuine and engaging tone. *The Road to Chess Improvement* is an interesting mix between strategy and autobiography, with a lot of well-annotated games. It's a unique book, both enjoyable and instructive.

All of these authors are grandmasters. Almost all of the good books on chess strategy are written by grandmasters. But there is one exception I know of, *Best Lessons of a Chess Coach*, written by Sunil Weermantry and Ed Eusebi. Weermantry has many years of experience as a coach for children of all ages. Although he is not a grandmaster, he is a strong master. I have worked with him several times instructing children, and I think he's an excellent teacher. This book features some of his best lectures in a clear and enjoyable format.

Reading for Pleasure

So far you must be getting the impression that the only reason to read chess books is to improve your play. That's one good reason to read about chess, but it's not the only one. Chess books aren't always for instruction: Some are just for fun! I recommend the following books for many hours of amusement:

◆ *Karl Marx Plays Chess*, another book written by Soltis. Soltis is a genius at digging up fun facts. Suffice it to say that history recorded only one game by Karl Marx, and Soltis found it. The book also has puzzles, trivia, and lots of funny stories.

◆ *The Even More Complete Chess Addict*, written by Mike Fox and Richard James. Loads of trivia!

◆ *The Oxford Companion to Chess*, written by David Hooper and Kenneth Whyld. Everything you need to know about chess, and lots that's just fun.

◆ *Soviet Chess 1917–1991*, again, written by, Soltis. As the title suggests, this is a historical review of chess in the Soviet Union. The book is expensive and dense, so it's not a casual purchase. But if you are fascinated by the relationship of chess to either history or the Soviet Union (or both), you'll love this book.

> **Patrick's Pointers**
>
> People often ask me how to help kids get better. I think the best way generally is to give them exactly the same books that adults should study. However, there are books written specifically for kids, and especially if you have someone under 10 in mind, you might want to check some of them out.

And don't think that the list ends here! There are lots of other books out there that are fun to read. I couldn't hope to list them all, but here's a tip: Any book written by Irving Chernev or Andrew Soltis that includes stories, trivia, and so forth is likely to be lots of fun.

Collections of Games

There are at least two very good reasons to read books of the games played by great players. One is simple pleasure. Just as every sport has its great moments, chess has its great games. If you love basketball, then you love watching a beautiful no-look pass or an overwhelming slam dunk. If you love chess, you'll love playing through the best chess games ever played. The second reason is that studying the games of the great players is a great way to improve your own play. Every move offers instruction. Many of the world champions (see Chapter 16 for a complete list of who they are) have written books in which they analyze their own games. Any of those books is worth buying and studying! I'll highlight a few that are especially good:

♦ *My 60 Memorable Games*, written by Bobby Fischer. This may be the single best book ever written on chess. Every chess player should read it. Period.

♦ *Tal–Botvinnik 1960: Match for the World Chess Championship*, written by Mikhail Tal. Many grandmasters think this is the best book ever written on a World Championship match. Tal not only analyzes the games brilliantly, he also honestly relates what it was like to play for the title of world champion. An extraordinary book.

♦ *New World Chess Champion* and *London-Leningrad Championship Games*, each written by Garry Kasparov. Those grandmasters who don't think Tal's book is the best ever written on a world championship match think one of these is. In these two books, Kasparov analyzes the games of the match where he won the world championship title from Anatoly Karpov, and then defended that title from Karpov in a revenge match.

♦ *My Great Predecessors*, by Garry Kasparov and Dmitry Plisetsky. In a monumental project, Kasparov analyzes the most important games of all the world champions. Along the way, he also attempts to trace the evolution of chess technique throughout the history of modern chess. Even if his historical arguments are not always convincing, an anthology of the greatest chess games, annotated by perhaps the strongest player ever, is an indispensable work! At the time of this writing, the first three volumes (of a projected four or five) have been published.

♦ *My Best Games*, by Victor Korchnoi. Korchnoi may be the greatest chess player who never became world champion. He is also the greatest chess player over the age of 70 of all time. In 2001, at the age of 70, he wrote a two-volume series of his best games: one book with his best games with White, the other book with his best games with Black. Not only are the games terrific, but the personality of this great player really comes through in the annotations.

♦ Finally, I will mention a book I wrote about a World Championship match. It is *Kasparov versus Anand: The Inside Story of the 1995 World Chess Championship Match*. I spent several months helping the challenger, Viswanathan Anand, first as a trainer before the match, and then as a coach during the match. This book provides a brief history of the World Championship matches, some background on each of the players, and a running commentary on the match, as well as analysis of every game.

I wish I had space to list dozens more books, because they all deserve to be read! In my opinion, a collection of well-annotated games by one of the great grandmasters is almost always the best value for your dollar. Here is a (partial) list of some of the great players who have written such a collection. If you get your hands on a book by any one of them about their own games, it will be a terrific book:

Emanuel Lasker	José Capablanca
Alexander Alekhine	Mikhail Botvinnik
Vasily Smyslov	Bent Larsen
Viktor Korchnoi	Garry Kasparov
Vladimir Kramnik	Viswanathan Anand
Alexei Shirov	Anatoly Karpov

Studying Your Own Games

In a chess tournament, each player in each game is usually required to write down all the moves as they are played. This is called keeping score. Each player is supplied with a special sheet of paper for recording the moves, called a score sheet. The following figure shows a copy of one of my score sheets from a tournament.

So far I've been suggesting which books (or magazines or websites) to study about different aspects of chess or about other peoples' games. But you should also study your own games—the losses as well as the wins. In fact, you should study your losses more carefully than your wins, because if you were beaten it means your opponent was doing something right that you were doing wrong!

I strongly urge you to record some of your games and study them. Every grandmaster does this with all his games. In fact, most of the time when two grandmasters finish a game, they will immediately go back over it together. Do as the grandmasters do.

Patrick's Pointers

When you play, get in the habit of writing down the moves of the game as they're played. (Write down both your moves and your opponent's moves.) Then later on, you can play through your games—especially your losses!—and learn from them. It can sometimes be hard to learn on your own from your games. This is one area where private instruction can be a big help. However, another (cheaper) way to learn is to go through your games with a friend who plays chess. Two can often learn better than one!

An example of a chess tournament score sheet.

CHESS FEDERATION OF CANADA

Event _North Bay Open_ Date _Aug. 11_
Round _9_ Time Controls _40/2; 50/1_

□ White _Wolff_   ■ Black _Sagalchik_
Rating _____   Rating _____

	□	■		□	■
1	e4	e5	26	Rec3	Re8
2	Nf3	Nc6	27	Rc7	Qd8
3	Bb5	a6	28	Nxe6	
4	Ba4	Nf6	29		
5	O-O	Nxe4	30		
6	d4	b5	31		
7	Bb3	d5	32		
8	de	Be6	33		
9	Nbd2	Nc5	34		
10	c3	Bg4	35		
11	Bc2	Qd7	36		
12	Re1	Rd8	37		
13	Nb3	Ne6	38		
14	h3	Bh5	39		
15	Bf5	Be7	40		
16	a4	ba	41		
17	Nbd4	Nxd4	42		
18	cd	a3	43		
19	ba	c5	44		
20	dc	Bxc5	45		
21	Be3	Bxe3	46		
22	Rxe3	O-O	47		
23	Rc1	Bg6	48		
24	Bxe6	fe	49		
25	Nd4	Rf4	50		

The Least You Need to Know

♦ You can improve your game by getting instruction; studying books, magazines, or websites; and analyzing your own games either alone or with a friend.

♦ You don't need to worry too much about developing an opening repertoire if you want to play casually, but if you want to compete, it's essential.

♦ Studying games played and analyzed by the great players is one of the best ways to improve your game—and it's great fun, too.

♦ You should get in the habit of recording your games so that you can study them afterward. Study your losses especially well.

Chapter 16

Hall of Fame

In This Chapter

- World champions during the classical era
- World champions during the period of Soviet dominance
- World champions in the age of the "Fischer Revolution"
- The split of the World Championship title: Will the real World Champion please stand up?

Just like every other sport, chess has its champions. A small number of extraordinary people have played so well that they're immortalized by many generations of chess fans.

In this chapter, I briefly introduce you to each of the official World Champions in the history of chess, and along the way I tell you a little about the history they helped make. Then I tell you about the curious state of the World Chess Championship in the year 2004.

The Classical Era

The first half of the nineteenth century is called the "romantic era" of chess. There were no international chess tournaments and no official world champions. This lack of structure was reflected also in the style of play of the time. Each player would attack the king as quickly as possible. Many beautiful games were produced, but the overall quality of chess strategy was low. Defense was not as well understood as offense, so many games were lost that should not have been.

Chess Lore

Just like baseball, basketball, football, and other sports, chess has its own national hall of fame and museum. The U.S. Chess Hall of Fame opened in 1986, relocated in 1993 to the U.S. Chess Center in Washington, D.C., and relocated again in 2001 to its present home at the Sidney Samole Museum in Miami, Florida. The hall includes exhibits on great American players such as Bobby Fischer and Paul Morphy, as well as individuals who contributed greatly to American chess in other ways, such as Arpad Elo, inventor of the current chess rating system, and John Collins, mentor to Fischer and teacher of hundreds of other young players. New members are inducted each year.

In the middle of the century, things began to change. A new generation of players formulated more sophisticated chess principles. Attack, yes—but only when you possess certain strategic advantages, and only when you direct your attack against your opponent's weaknesses. Maybe this conceptual revolution was part of a more general change in how people thought about chess. The game was no longer only for coffeehouses; now there were national and international tournaments for the best players to compete in. National champions began to be recognized. There was not yet an official world champion, but there soon would be. The classical era of chess had begun.

Wilhelm Steinitz (1836–1900)

Steinitz was the strongest of the new generation of chess players that marked the beginning of the classical era. (With one exception: Paul Morphy was undoubtedly stronger during his brief career; but Morphy played for so short a time that he's usually not associated with the start of the classical era.) Steinitz grew up in Prague, Czechoslovakia, but moved to Vienna, Austria, as a young man. His initial ambition was to be a journalist, but when he won the Vienna championship of 1861–1862, he devoted more of his energy to chess. He played in the London international tournament of 1862, finishing in sixth place. This convinced him to play chess professionally, and he settled in London. Over the next 10 years his results improved, and by 1872 he was recognized as the world's strongest player. However, there still wasn't any official world championship title. What was needed for that was an official challenge to the man generally acknowledged as the best in the world.

That challenge came in 1883, from the Polish-born Johann Zukertort (1842–1888), who had just won the London international tournament of that year. A match was arranged between the two players, where the first person to win 10 games would be declared the winner. Each player agreed that the winner could call himself the world champion, and the chess public recognized the claim.

Steinitz had moved to the United States in 1883 (and eventually became an American citizen), so the match was played in New York, St. Louis, and New Orleans. The match occurred in 1886, and Steinitz won it by the score of +10 =5 −5 (that is, 10 wins, 5 draws, 5 losses) and became the first official world champion.

Emanuel Lasker (1868–1941)

Steinitz had been the world's best player since 1872, but he would only possess the official title for eight years until the German Emanuel Lasker would challenge him and take the laurels away. Lasker studied mathematics as a young man, and in fact made some significant contributions there; however, chess was the primary medium of his genius.

Lasker recognized, as no one else had, the significance of Steinitz's contributions to chess thinking. Late in his life, Lasker wrote a chess primer where he praised Steinitz as a great chess thinker and acknowledged the debt he owed to the great man for his own development as a player. In 1894, at the young age of 25, he challenged Steinitz and defeated him +10 =4 −5.

At first the chess public was reluctant to believe that Lasker really deserved to be called world champion. But Lasker solidified his claim with a string of tournament victories. And he did so while earning a Ph.D. in mathematics!

Chess Lore

Although Lasker is now remembered primarily for his chess achievements, during his life he wrote philosophy and studied mathematics. He was good friends with Albert Einstein, who wrote the foreword to Lasker's biography. Lasker and Einstein discussed mathematics and relativity with one another; unfortunately, we have no records of any chess games they might have played!

Lasker kept the world championship title for 27 years, much longer than anyone has since. Most people think that he was no longer the world's best after about 1915, but World War I prevented Lasker from meeting his preeminent challenger, José Capablanca, until 1921. Even so, he dominated the chess world for a very long time during a period when there were a lot of strong players. Even after finally losing the title, Lasker remained among the world's strongest for many years. In 1924 he took first prize ahead of nearly all the world's elite players, including his World Championship successor Capablanca, in a legendary tournament in New York. One of his most remarkable feats in the later part of Lasker's life was to take third place in the international tournament in Moscow, 1935, ahead of many of the world's best players, at the age of 66! No wonder Lasker is considered one of chess's all-time great fighters.

Emanuel Lasker.

José Raul Capablanca (1888–1942)

Capablanca was born and raised in Havana, Cuba, and to this day he is the only Latin American ever to become World Champion. Capablanca is considered by many people to be, alongside Paul Morphy, the greatest natural chess talent ever. There is a story that he learned chess by watching his father play against friends. And he learned well enough to beat his father in his first-ever game! Whether or not this tale is true, there's no doubt that Capablanca had a fantastic "feel" for the game. Often he could find the right move without being able to explain why it was correct.

Capablanca was in many ways the opposite of the man he defeated to become world champion. Whereas Lasker was by nature an intellectual, Capablanca was bored with his studies. For Lasker, chess was first and foremost a struggle. For Capablanca, it was an art. But they shared this in common: Capablanca, like Lasker, challenged the World Champion at a very young age. Capablanca issued his challenge in 1911, at the age of 22.

Negotiations for the match broke down, and many people felt that Lasker was demanding unfair terms. But in 1911 Capablanca probably wasn't yet ready for the title anyway. The two men played for the first time at St. Petersburg in 1914, in one of the strongest tournaments ever held. Capablanca surged to an early lead, but Lasker came roaring back, defeating Capablanca 2–1 in their three games, to win the tournament just one half point ahead of his rival. Lasker's triumph impressed Capablanca, but Capablanca's performance impressed the rest of the world, and the chess public demanded a rematch.

Unfortunately, World War I intervened, and the match wasn't held until 1921. By this time, Lasker's skills had faded, and Capablanca won decisively (+4 =10 –0). Capablanca followed this victory with a series of tournament successes over the next several years, and most people thought his reign would be as long as Lasker's. But Capablanca would lose the title after only six years to Alexander Alekhine.

Alexander Alekhine (1892–1946)

Alexander Alekhine was born in Moscow, the son of aristocratic parents. He emerged as a chess talent at the same time as Capablanca, but in the early part of their careers the Cuban eclipsed Alekhine. For example, Alekhine also played in the great St. Petersburg tournament, but he came in a distant third behind Capablanca and Lasker.

The popular view is that Alekhine did with hard work what Capablanca did with raw talent. I'm not sure that's really fair to Alekhine, but there's no doubt that he had an enormous capacity for work and a near obsession for chess. There is a famous story (perhaps exaggerated) that when an English chess fan took Alekhine and Capablanca to a London theater in 1922, Capablanca never took his eyes off the chorus line, and Alekhine never took his eyes off his pocket chess set!

Alekhine was severely affected by the Russian Revolution of 1917, when he lost his family fortune. Details of his life during this period are sketchy, but we know that he went abroad in 1921 and eventually settled in Paris. (He later became a French citizen.) Once there, he again worked very hard on chess.

In 1927, he challenged Capablanca for the world championship. Everyone expected Capablanca to win, but Alekhine had analyzed Capablanca's chess very well, and he purposefully adopted a style that Capablanca had trouble with. Alekhine won the match by the score of +6 =25 –3. In his later years, Alekhine had difficulties with alcohol. Some people think this explains his loss to Max Euwe in 1935 in their World Champi-onship match. Although this may not be fair to Euwe, it's true that after that loss Alekhine abstained from drink, challenged Euwe to a rematch in 1937, and won back the title. Then came World War II and chess activity stopped until 1945. Alekhine was negotiating the conditions of a World Championship match in 1946 with Mikhail Botvinnik when he died. Alekhine is the only man ever to die while still World Champion.

Machgielis (Max) Euwe (1901–1981)

Max Euwe (pronounced "OY-vuh") lived his whole life in Holland, and he is the only Dutch World Champion. He is often dismissed as the weakest of the world champi-ons, and that's a pity, because it's unfair to remember this remarkable man as second-rate in any way.

Euwe became a professor of mathematics in 1924 and continued in that career until 1957. Throughout all the time that he played chess, he did so as an amateur. Even though he wrote many fine chess books, and was noted as an openings analyst—all of this aside from winning the World Championship!—chess remained for Euwe a hobby, along with swimming, boxing, and languages.

When Euwe challenged Alekhine for the World Championship, no one expected him to win. Perhaps due to Alekhine's alcohol problems, however, Euwe did win by the score of +9 =13 –8. Before 1948, when it was still a champion's privilege to choose his own challengers, it was rare for a new champion to allow his vanquished predecessor a rematch. But Euwe was a gentleman, and there was no question of denying the great Alekhine a second chance. Alekhine won the rematch +10 =11 –4.

Euwe continued playing chess for many years after that match, garnering many suc-cesses, although never again being a serious contender for the World Championship. In 1970, Euwe was elected president of FIDE, where he served for eight years. He was a good president, who served the interests of chess above all else.

Chess Lore

"FIDE" is an acronym for *"Féderation Internationale des échecs,"* which is French for "International Chess Federation." This organization was founded in 1924, when delegates from 15 countries met at Paris and established it for the purpose of promoting the game of chess around the world. It established an Olympiad, to be held every two years, where each member country would send a team of its best players to compete for medals. FIDE also established a separate world championship for women. Both events have continued in one form or another up to the present day.

In 1948, two years after Alexander Alekhine died, FIDE organized a tournament to determine the World Championship. It also drew up rules for a qualification series to identify legitimate challengers for future World Championship matches and standardized the conditions under which World Championship matches would be played.

FIDE can claim credit for several important achievements in the development of chess over eight decades. In addition to the Olympiad and World Championship events described above, FIDE organized other events such as youth championships and women's championships. In addition, FIDE established criteria for bestowing such honors as the title of grandmaster, so that these became official titles and FIDE implemented an international rating system to rank players by a mathematical formula, so that there could be some objective way to measure players' results.

Soviet Dominance

From 1930 to 1970, prizes in chess tournaments were too low for professionals to make a good living. Some full-time chess players supplemented their income by teaching lessons, writing, and giving exhibitions. But it's difficult to rise to the very top if you have to take time away from tournament preparations for such activities, and those who had to do so didn't make it to the top.

But beginning in the 1930s, one group of chess players didn't have to take time away from their preparations. They were the Soviets. Lenin had decided that one way he would prove the superiority of the communist system was to give state support to Soviet chess players. A new generation of chess players emerged from the Soviet Union, and they dominated the World Championship for 25 years.

Mikhail Moiseyevich Botvinnik (1911–1995)

Botvinnik was the first of this generation. He was already one of the strongest players in the world in the mid-1930s, but World War II made a challenge for the World Championship impossible until 1946, and then Alekhine died before the match could be arranged.

Alekhine's death left the world without a champion, so FIDE organized a tournament to determine who would hold the title next. The six best players in the world were invited, but one (Reuben Fine—see Chapter 14) declined, so only five players participated. Botvinnik won, and was declared world champion.

Botvinnik kept the title for most of the next 15 years, even though he lost more games in his World Championship matches than he won! The secret to his success was the rematch. FIDE decided to follow Euwe's example and establish a rematch clause, so that a defeated world champion would be entitled to a rematch one year after losing the title. Botvinnik spent much of his time working at his engineering, and by the 1950s he was past his prime anyway, so he lost some of the matches he played to defend his title. But he was deadly in the rematch! All world championship matches played from 1951–1972 were 24 games long, with the champion keeping his title in event of a tie. Botvinnik tied his first match, tied the second, and lost the third but then won the rematch, and lost the fourth but then won the rematch. By the time he played the fifth match, FIDE had decided the rematch was too great an advantage and eliminated it. Botvinnik lost this fifth match, and never again played for the World Championship.

Vasily Vasiliyevich Smyslov (1921–)

The first person to "borrow" Botvinnik's title was Vasily Smyslov. Smyslov was probably the strongest player of the 1950s, but he was world champion for only one year. He first challenged Botvinnik in 1954, but their match ended tied +7 =10 –7, and Botvinnik retained the title. Smyslov won the title from Botvinnik by the score of +6 =13 –3 in 1957, but Botvinnik won the rematch in 1958 by the score of +7 =11 –5.

Smyslov is a friendly man with a terrific sense of humor, which made him a striking contrast to the dour Botvinnik. I got a chance to experience the contrast firsthand in 1992. Botvinnik and Smyslov were analyzing a chess game together. I joined in the analysis, and at one point I made a move on the chessboard to suggest that it might be strong. Botvinnik wordlessly put the piece back on the square I had moved it from. Smyslov laughed and said, "Mikhail Moiseyevich does not allow such moves at his board!"

Smyslov's affability seems to be part of his spiritual nature, and his general love of life. Perhaps this explains how he has been able to play such strong chess even in his 60s and 70s! Most grandmasters lose the ability to play genuinely strong chess once they enter their 50s, but Smyslov is an exception. In 1984, he came within one step of playing again for the World Championship, and even today he continues to produce top-flight chess.

Mikhail Tal (1936–1992)

Tal was known as "the wizard from Riga" because of his ability to create an attack seemingly out of nothing. As the nickname suggests, he was Latvian and not Russian like Botvinnik and Smyslov, but in the days of the Soviet Union they were all compatriots. Tal's genius was extraordinary, but sadly it came in a body afflicted with disease. Tal's love of smoking, drinking, and partying didn't help his health either. Tal defeated Botvinnik in 1960 by the score of +6 =13 −2, and then wrote a wonderful book where he described his feelings during the match and analyzed each of the games. But when the inevitable rematch came, Tal was drained from a bout with kidney disease earlier that year. Botvinnik won +10 =6 −5, and although Tal would have a brilliant tournament career afterward, he was never again within reach of the World Championship title.

Those who knew him said that Tal had more energy than he knew what to do with, but he never fully succeeded in channeling that energy. After their rematch, Botvinnik said, "If Tal would learn to program himself properly then it would become impossible to play him." But Tal lived life the way he played chess: always trying to do the impossible, and often succeeding.

Mikhail Tal.

Tigran Vartanovich Petrosian (1929–1984)

The poet Robert Frost mused whether the world would end in fire or ice: Botvinnik overcame the fire of Mikhail Tal's sudden attacks against his king, but he withered in the icy chill of Petrosian's defensive style. Tigran Petrosian took the title from Botvinnik in 1963 with the score of +5 =15 –2. FIDE had eliminated the champion's right of rematch, and Botvinnik decided he was too old to try to qualify for the World Championship the normal way, so this time Botvinnik finally lost the title for good.

Petrosian was raised in Armenia, making him the second non-Russian Soviet World Champion after Tal. (The third and last non-Russian Soviet World Champion is Garry Kasparov, who is Armenian, but was born and raised in Azerbaijan.) Unlike Tal, Petrosian's games lack the excitement of a mad rush at the king. Petrosian's style was subtle. He wanted to make sure all his opponent's active possibilities were extinguished before doing anything active himself. Many people find his games boring, but a close study of them can be very instructive.

Chess Lore

"Where are the women?" you might be asking yourself. That's a good question. Throughout history, no women have attained the same level of skill as the world champions. And few women have even tried.

FIDE has run a separate women's world championship since 1927 and it established a separate women's grandmaster title in 1977, both done for the purpose of encouraging more women to play chess. But many people feel it may have had the opposite effect by appearing condescending to women. Unlike football or basketball, there is no physical barrier stopping women from competing directly against men in chess, so why should they be treated differently?

The fact remains that very few women have competed in international chess, and fewer still have achieved the level of (men's) grandmaster. Some people suggest this may be explained by differences of brain structure: Men are supposed to be more proficient at mathematical activities, and chess is thought to require math-like skills. Others suggest that social factors are the explanation. Men are encouraged to be aggressive, and chess, as the cerebral form of warfare par excellence, demands an aggressive personality. A final possibility is that the lack of women at the top of chess is explained simply by the smaller number of women who play chess overall. Because fewer women choose to play, there's a smaller chance that any one woman will be extraordinary, which discourages more women from trying to reach the top. No one really knows the answer, but I like this final possibility the best, because it suggests an obvious remedy: Encourage more women to play chess!

Petrosian's style was not well suited for tournaments, because he drew too many of his games, so his tournament career was never as distinguished as that of his peers. But in a one-on-one match format, he was very tough to beat. Boris Spassky found that out when he challenged Petrosian for the World Championship in 1966, and Petrosian won +4 =17 –3. Petrosian never seemed clearly the world's best player, as Botvinnik was in the 1940s and Smyslov was in the 1950s, and he didn't possess the raw genius of a Mikhail Tal, but his style was ahead of its time. Ten years later, Anatoly Karpov would adopt Petrosian's style of dampening the opponent's active play, and it would enable him to dominate the chess world for a decade.

Boris Vasiliyevich Spassky (1937–)

Boris Spassky is widely remembered only as the guy who lost to Bobby Fischer, and that's a shame. Nobody was going to be able to beat Fischer in 1972, but Spassky gave it a much better try than anyone else could have done. Spassky's loss to Fischer obscures the fact that Spassky was probably the strongest player of the later 1960s, including both Petrosian and Fischer. For example, Spassky had won three games from Fischer, drawn two, and lost none during the 1960s. In 1966, Spassky won the very strong Piatagorsky Cup Tournament in Santa Monica, ahead of both Petrosian and Fischer.

Spassky was born in St. Petersburg (then called Leningrad), and raised in Russia. (The fact that he was a true Russian, unlike both Tal and Petrosian, further encouraged the "Cold War" storyline that the media attached to the 1972 match between Fischer and Spassky.) He won the World Junior Championship in 1955, and soon thereafter became one of the strongest players in the world. In contrast to Tal and Petrosian, Spassky's style was universal; he could attack or defend equally well. This style finally enabled him to triumph +6 =13 –4 over Petrosian the second time he challenged for the title, in 1969.

After losing the World Championship to Fischer, Spassky had to absorb the brunt of the disappointment of the Soviet officials who felt he had let down communism itself. Spassky could no longer live happily in the Soviet Union, but he was permitted to emigrate in 1975 to live in Paris.

Spassky never again played in a World Championship match after losing to Fischer, but he remained near the top of world chess for over a decade more. He still plays occasionally, but he is no longer one of the best in the world. Spassky made over a million dollars from a second match against Fischer (see the following) in 1992, and now he enjoys a less stressful life of tennis and relaxation, rather than enduring the nervous tension necessary to play chess at the very top.

The Fischer Revolution

There was very little money in chess during the 1950s and 1960s. For example, the total purse for the World Championship match between Petrosian and Spassky in 1969 was about $2,500.

Why was this? Well, virtually all the top players were Soviet, and there was no need to pay them much. Not only were they supported by the state, they weren't allowed to keep whatever they might be paid outside the Soviet Union anyway. Besides, there wasn't much interest for the general public (that is, the general public in the West) in seeing Soviet players compete against other Soviet players. It was doubtful that the situation would change until a charismatic superstar emerged from a non-Soviet country. But how could that happen when there was no money in chess anyway? Such a superstar would have to be completely devoted to chess, to be willing to do it to the exclusion of all else, and to be good enough to beat the Soviets. "All I want to do, ever, is play chess," is what the young man who would be that superstar said. He is Robert James (Bobby) Fischer, and he changed chess forever.

Robert James ("Bobby")
Fischer.

Fischer wasn't just great: He was phenomenal. He was brilliant at a young age, he was outspoken, he was headstrong. In short, he was exciting. People were willing to pay to see him play. And he was willing to make people pay to see him. Several times in his career he walked out of tournaments because his conditions weren't met. Because of him, throughout the 1960s, money came into chess. And when he finally challenged Spassky for the World Championship in 1972, the money flooded in. The purse for that match was originally $125,000, but Fischer refused to play until it was doubled to $250,000. Because of Fischer, chess had become a professional sport. In 1995, the purse for the World Championship match between Kasparov and Anand was $1.35 million. They, like all grandmasters, have Fischer to thank for their livelihood.

Robert James (Bobby) Fischer (1943–)

Bobby Fischer was born in Chicago, but raised in New York City. His development as a chess player is one of the most remarkable ever. At the age of 12, he was good—but nothing more. Many teenagers and preteens are as strong as Fischer was at that age. But then he made a colossal leap. At 14, in 1957, he won the U.S. championship, the youngest person ever to have done so. But even more incredible, at the age of 15, in 1958, he qualified for the tournament to determine the challenger to the World Champion! (Tal was the challenger who emerged from that event.) Nobody had ever before made such a tremendous result at such a young age.

Fischer quickly catapulted into the ranks of the top few players in the world. Everyone could see that he had incredible talent—maybe even more than Capablanca. Yet his development was not smooth. Partly this was due to his own temperament. For example, because of a dispute with the tournament organizers he walked out in the middle of the 1967 tournament to determine who would qualify to challenge for the 1969 World Championship, even though he was leading his competitors by one and a half points! After that incident, he didn't play a single serious game for 18 months.

But in 1970, he got it all together. He didn't walk out of any more tournaments. Instead, he simply beat everybody. His margins of victory were so wide that people couldn't believe it. He won the first two of the three matches he had to win to qualify to challenge Spassky without allowing his opponent a single win or draw! The third match, played against the super-solid former world champion Petrosian, he "only" won with the score of +5 =3 −1. The match against Spassky was tougher, but not by much. The final score: +7 =11 −3. (By the way, a fun book that tells the story of this match is *Bobby Fischer Goes to War*, by David Edmonds and John Eidinow.)

Three things stand out to explain Fischer's success:

- He had an indomitable will to win.

- He worked harder than almost anyone before ever had—harder maybe even than Alekhine had.

- He had a crystal-clear classical understanding of chess.

Fischer would not be tempted by brilliant but wacky attacks, like Tal; nor would he put off his own plans just because he spotted a hint of possible activity by his opponents, like Petrosian. Fischer had a clear conception of what the position demanded, and he would calculate the consequences of each move with absolute precision.

When Fischer won the World Championship, people thought he wouldn't be beaten for some time. In a sense, they were right: Fischer walked away from chess, never again to play a serious competition. He played no tournaments after he won the title, and when the next challenger, Anatoly Karpov had been selected, Fischer demanded extensive changes to the rules and format of the World Championship. FIDE could not agree to all of them, at which point Fischer resigned the title and Karpov became the champion.

For many years thereafter, people tried to coax Fischer into playing somewhere, anywhere. Finally in 1992, Fischer played a rematch against Boris Spassky. On principle he insisted that the match be for the "World Championship," although nobody took that claim seriously. Nobody knew how good Fischer was after twenty years away from organized chess, and everybody knew that Spassky was no longer among the top grandmasters. Even so, the match attracted a purse of $5 million, much more than the "real" world championship that was contested between Kasparov and Anand in the same year. Fischer won his match by the score of +10 =15 −5, which shows at least that he could still play pretty well. Sadly, he shows no signs of wanting to play with other grandmasters, so chess players have had to accept that Fischer is really and truly gone from the game. Many people consider Fischer the greatest chess player of all time, and in my view, it's either him or Kasparov. But between the two came Anatoly Karpov, himself a formidable World Champion.

Anatoly Yegenyivich Karpov (1951–)

Karpov is the only World Champion to gain his title by default. Born and raised in Russia, he was the Soviet system's response to Fischer's victory against Spassky three years earlier. But when he challenged in 1975, almost everyone agrees he would likely have lost had Fischer played. This may have left Karpov feeling he needed to prove that he was truly a worthy champion.

He did so by doing what no World Champion had done for 40 years: He won practically every tournament he played in. After fighting off a ferocious challenge from Victor Korchnoi in 1978 (+6 =21 −5), he easily defeated the same Korchnoi in 1981 (+6 =10 −2). By the middle of the 1980s he was considered unbeatable. If Garry

Kasparov had never been born, Karpov would probably have kept the World Championship title for 10 years longer than he did. Unlike many of his predecessors, after losing the title, Karpov didn't fade from the top. Instead, he remained indisputably number two in the world until 1995.

Anatoly Karpov.

Karpov's style is remarkable, and it's no exaggeration to say that he has singlehandedly contributed significantly to our current understanding of chess. The genius of his style is *active prophylaxis*, which is a fancy way of saying that he simultaneously restricts his opponent's active play while promoting his own. He incorporated the essence of Petrosian's style, but somehow avoided its inherent defensiveness. This hybrid style of Karpov has frustrated grandmasters for two decades, and the first time Kasparov faced it, he was nearly destroyed.

Garry Kimovich Kasparov (1963–)

Kasparov won the World Championship title from Karpov in 1985 and held it for an extraordinary fifteen years. Alongside Fischer, he is arguably the strongest World Champion ever. He certainly has the most impressive career of all time. Although Lasker and Alekhine reigned longer, each was champion at a time when one could duck the strongest challenger for years. (Each also had a World War interrupt chess activity during their reign.) Kasparov, by contrast, had to defend his title three times against Anatoly Karpov after beating him in 1985. Furthermore, also unlike his predecessors, Kasparov completely overpowered his competition in tournaments for many years after becoming world champion. He literally won or shared first in every tournament he played in for eight years after winning the title in 1985. Although he did not maintain that level of supremacy throughout the 1990s, he was indisputably the strongest player in the world until 2000. Even after losing the World Championship match to Vladimir Kramnik in November 2000, he remains the number one player in the world by tournament results. It's no exaggeration to say that Kasparov dominated chess the way Michael Jordan dominated basketball.

Yet it could have been very different. Kasparov first challenged Karpov for the World Championship in 1984. The format of the time called for the winner to be the first to win six games outright, with draws not counting in the scoring. After the first nine games, Karpov had won four (with five drawn), giving him a seemingly insurmountable lead. Then both players dug in their heels: Karpov apparently wanted to win the match without a loss, and Kasparov seems to have been determined not to lose too quickly. After 17 consecutive draws, Karpov won another game. Then Karpov missed a clear opportunity to win again and put away the match. Finally, Kasparov broke through and won the thirty-second game. There followed 14 more draws, after which something strange happened. Karpov appeared to crack. He lost two games in a row with very bad play. Suddenly the result of the match was very much in doubt.

Garry Kasparov.

At that point, the then-president of FIDE, Florencio Campomanes, did something so controversial it was condemned in newspapers around the world (including *The New York Times*). He stopped the match and declared that they would play another match, limited to 24 games, to start seven months later. Karpov would get a rematch if he lost, but the result of the 1984 match would be obliterated.

Kasparov howled with indignation, feeling that this was only being done for Karpov's benefit. Many people believe he was right, but ironically it may have benefited Kasparov more than Karpov. After all, he was still trailing 5–3, just one slip away from defeat. Plus, he had gotten to play a 48-game "training match" against Karpov—an invaluable learning experience! And indeed, Kasparov won the second match +5 =16 –3.

Whoever actually benefited more, the experience convinced Kasparov that another organization was needed, outside of FIDE, to run professional chess. His first attempt toward this end was to found the Grandmasters Association (GMA), a sort of professional player trade union. However, fractious internal politics led it to collapse. (Many people would insist that Kasparov himself was largely to blame.)

In 1993, Kasparov was to face a challenger who was not Karpov for the first time. The British sensation, Nigel Short had successfully fought his way through the qualification series, including a +4 =4 –2 defeat of the former champion. Short had his own dissatisfactions with how FIDE was handling his shot at the World Championship. During a fateful overseas telephone conversation, he and Kasparov essentially decided to secede from FIDE and to take the World Championship with them. They created a new organization, the Professional Chess Association (PCA), to run their match and the qualification series for future world championships.

Chess Lore

The Professional Chess Association (PCA) was established by Garry Kasparov and Nigel Short in 1993 because they were unhappy with how FIDE was organizing their World Championship match. For Kasparov, the PCA was a vehicle for fulfilling one of his dreams which was to promote chess to the level of a respected international sport like golf or tennis. From 1993 to 1995 the PCA had lined up a prestigious corporate sponsor in the Intel Corporation. During that time, the PCA held two World Championship matches (1993 and 1995), ran a Grand Prix cycle of rapid chess (in rapid chess, each player gets 25 minutes to play all his moves), and created its own rating system.

FIDE did not recognize the PCA's authority to administer the World Championship. During the life of the PCA, FIDE continued its own world championship cycle and organized its own matches. This obviously made life more difficult for the PCA, but most chess players regarded the PCA World Championship as the "true" cycle, because Garry Kasparov was indisputably the best player in the world.

After the 1995 PCA World Championship match between Kasparov and Anand, however, Intel withdrew its sponsorship, and the PCA subsequently collapsed. In my opinion, this was a sad development for professional chess. The PCA may have had some organizational challenges, but it was absolutely the right idea.

Ultimately, Kasparov would play two World Championship matches under PCA auspices: First against Short, which he won +6 =13 −1, and then against Viswanathan Anand, from India, which he won +4 =13 −1. (The match against Short was the best of 24 games, whereas the match against Anand was the best of 20 games.) Although the PCA subsequently collapsed, Kasparov and "his" title remained outside the FIDE World Chess Championship cycle for over a decade.

> **Chess Lore**
>
> One day perhaps, a woman will become the World Chess Champion. Who will that be? The most promising candidate today is the remarkable Judit Polgar. She is 28 years old and is ranked ninth in the world as of October 2004—easily the highest ranking any woman has ever attained. If she continues her progress, she may someday vie for the World Championship.
>
> Judit is the youngest of three sisters, all of whom were encouraged from an early age to play chess. Both she and her oldest sister, Zsuzsa, hold the men's grandmaster title. Judit does not play in women's competitions, but in 1996 Zsuzsa won the women's World Championship title.
>
> Having studied chess seriously since she was very young does not set Judith apart from other top chess players: almost every strong grandmaster showed a similar dedication at an early age. The example of Judit and Zsuzsa clearly shows that, whatever the reason so few women excel at chess, there is no inherent reason women can't play as well as men.

Will the Real World Champion Please Stand Up?

The demise of the PCA only served to further muddle a very confusing situation at the top of professional chess. FIDE had never accepted the legitimacy of Kasparov's breakaway championship events. On the contrary, already in 1993 they responded to the Kasparov–Short revolt by simply moving down the list, staging their own world championship match as scheduled, except the participants were Karpov and Dutch grandmaster Jan Timman. Karpov won, thereby earning the odd distinction of twice becoming FIDE World Champion without defeating his predecessor at the board!

The FIDE candidate's cycle also continued, anointing American Gata Kamsky as challenger in 1996. The Karpov–Kamsky match was duly held and Karpov defended successfully.

However, there was an unmistakably second-rate quality to these matches. Everyone knew that Kasparov was in fact the strongest player, and his PCA challengers Short and Anand seemed superior to the FIDE challengers. Moreover, the FIDE events were beset with rumors of uncertain sponsorship, checks bouncing, and contracts not being met. In 1998, FIDE decided on radical change. Ditching a century of chess tradition, FIDE that its version of the World Championship would no longer be decided in a match between the defending champion and a worthy challenger. Rather, an annual tournament with about 100 of the world's top players would decide the title.

In a strange sort of deference to tradition, however, FIDE decided to seed the defending champion to the finals of their inaugural championship tournament in 1998. That is, at the end of the tournament, the winner would play Karpov in an abbreviated (eight games) World Championship final. Supposedly the champion would receive no such advantage in subsequent years.

Whether or not it changed anyone's opinion about the true, legitimate "World Chess Championship," the new FIDE event did gain the participation of most top grandmasters. (Kasparov was a notable absentee, however.) No less a player than Kasparov's former challenger Anand fought his way through to win that 1998 tournament. But just a couple days later he had to begin the final versus a fully rested Karpov, who beat him.

The 1999 FIDE tournament was held in Las Vegas after numerous delays and schedule changes that resulted from attempting to satisfy Karpov's demands. In the end the defending champion skipped the tournament anyway, insisting that he still ought to be seeded to the final! Kasparov and Anand were among the other top players who declined to participate this time. Russian grandmaster Alexander Khalifman—a very good player but manifestly not of the Kasparov–Karpov–Anand class—emerged as champion.

Chess Lore

If two World Chess Champions aren't enough, there are still people who consider Bobby Fischer the undefeated world champion. There is evidence that Fischer himself holds to this view. He's getting older now and hasn't played since granting the 1992 rematch to Boris Spassky. Because Fischer won that match, it's true that he has never been actually defeated at the board since claiming the then-undisputed 1972 World Championship. For his most ardent and faithful fans, that's all that matters.

Meanwhile, Kasparov did not just fold up his tent after the PCA disbanded in 1996. Naturally he refused to play in the FIDE World Chess Championship events, but otherwise he remained active on the tournament circuit and was clearly still the man to beat to become the true world champion.

In 1998, Kasparov thought he'd lined up a sponsor for a match between the world's second and third-ranked players with Anand and yet another Russian, Vladimir Kramnik. The plan was that the winner of this match would then play Kasparov for the traditional World Championship. However, for various reasons Anand declined to participate. Another leading grandmaster, Alexei Shirov, was hastily plugged in as a substitute. Then Shirov proceeded to upset the whole plan by beating Kramnik in the qualifier, whereupon the sponsorship deal evaporated! Shirov is unquestionably a super-class grandmaster and a worthy world championship candidate in principle. However, his head-to-head record against Kasparov, over a great many tournaments, was so abysmal that no one gave him a chance in the proposed match. That's probably why efforts to fund it failed. The match that Shirov had fairly won the right to play was never held.

To add insult to injury, in 2000 Kasparov signed on to play Kramnik. By this time Kasparov was feeling the pressure to play *someone* to justify his title in the face of the ongoing FIDE events. Kramnik was the best, highest-rated challenger available. Moreover, he had a pretty good record in past encounters with Kasparov. Their match was staged in London, and to the surprise of most people, the challenger emerged victorious by the score of +2 =13 –0. Kasparov, and most chess fans, immediately acknowledged Kramnik as world champion, the latest entry to the line that extends forward all the way from Steinitz.

However, the larger question of how to determine future title matches became, if anything, more confused. The original contract for the Kasparov-Kramnik match envisioned a subsequent candidates event to select the next challenger for that version of the World Championship. Kramnik continued to hold to this idea even after it became clear that there was no sponsorship for it. The biggest problem in trying to fund a candidates event was that Kasparov was agitating for a direct rematch instead. Because the consensus remained that he and Kramnik were the best pair of players (only Anand stood on the same tier), it has been hard for the idea of a broader qualifying event to gain traction.

Meanwhile, just one month after Kramnik defeated Kasparov, another FIDE World Chess Championship tournament was completed with Anand as the winner. At the end of 2001 (actually running over into 2002) the FIDE tournament was contested yet again. With Anand choosing to sit this one out, another Russian, young Ruslan Ponomariov, emerged as the winner.

It's too bad that world-class chess is in such a confusing state. But we are very lucky to have so many outstanding chess players active today. Either Kramnik or Anand could have been World Champion during any of the previous eras. The relentlessly objective chess rating system gives its own interpretation. As of October 2004, Kasparov remains the top-rated player, Anand is number two, and Kramnik is third. Each one deserves the same "World Champion" attention as others have received in this chapter.

Viswanathan Anand (1969–)

Anand was born in Madras, India, and is the first world champion from Asia (assuming you count Russia as part of Europe). He learned chess from his mother at the age of six, but it was in 1978 that he became fascinated with the game. He had gone to Manila when his father had an assignment in the Philippines, and Anand became enthralled by the Karpov–Korchnoi World Championship match taking place there. When he returned to India, he became passionate about chess.

Viswanathan Anand.

Anand entered the international scene in 1983. He quickly developed a reputation for being immensely talented. For example, he often would take less than half as long to think about his moves as his opponents – and he would still beat them! In 1986, he became the Indian national champion, the youngest person ever to do so. In 1987, he became the World Junior (under 20) Champion, and in December of the same year, he became the world's youngest (at that time) grandmaster.

The amazing thing is that Anand was having all this success while being pretty undisciplined. Not only did he play all his games very quickly, but he didn't even study chess on a regular basis. But in 1990, he began to focus his energies. He started taking more time for his games and studying more diligently.

Results soon followed. By 1993, Anand was among the top half-dozen players in the world. In 1995, he challenged Kasparov for the World Championship. After losing that match, he scored a number of first places in top tournaments around the world (some including Kasparov in the field). From 1997 to early 2001, Anand has consistently been either number two or three on the rating list, trading places with Kramnik at various times.

Anand's style is active and pragmatic. He plays many different types of positions equally well. Anand is extremely good at judging the fine points of material imbalances, either on attack or defense. And he still calculates with terrifying speed and accuracy. Unlike Kasparov, Anand generally will not go to great lengths to strike first when playing Black. Rather, he is generally content to equalize the position against another strong grandmaster. And most grandmasters are happy to let him do so!

Vladimir Kramnik (1975–)

Vladimir Kramnik was born in Moscow and is Russian through and through. He is relatively quiet and reserved. (Almost anyone seems quiet in contrast to the flamboyant Kasparov! But even compared to the chatty and sociable Anand, Kramnik is reserved.) Like Anand, Kramnik demonstrated extraordinary talent at a young age, but he was more disciplined, with extraordinary results to match his talent. He was a grandmaster by the age of 16, and was winning major competitions.

Observing these results, Kasparov famously remarked, "Kramnik will be the next World Champion." Yet it was a hard road for Kramnik. Although his tournament results were outstanding, his results in matches were unconvincing. During the years 1993–1998, Kramnik lost a number of World Championship qualifying matches to other grandmasters. Although he was, of course, facing strong grandmasters, Kramnik was the favorite in each case, so his difficulties were puzzling to the chess world. Still, in tournaments he continued to rack up success after success.

Vladimir Kramnik.

Going into their match, Kramnik was the only player in the world to have an even score in games against Kasparov. (Anand had a heavy minus score.) The Kasparov "intimidation factor" seems not to have any effect on Kramnik. This may be because Kasparov has mentored Kramnik at various points in his career. In fact, Kasparov even hired Kramnik to help him in his 1995 match against Anand! So Kramnik enjoyed the benefit of an "inside view" of Kasparov's war room for a previous World Championship match.

Perhaps this experience was critical for his success. But also critical was a brilliant match strategy. Kramnik effectively steered the games into positions that favored his style and were ill suited for Kasparov's. That, plus excellent technique, enabled the amazing victory of two wins and no losses out of 15 games! Kasparov lost his title without a single victory.

Kramnik's style is similar to Karpov's. He defends extremely well but combines this with an active style. He focuses less on prophylaxis than Karpov, however, and is capable of much sharper attacking play. He also has an extremely narrow opening repertoire. (This is in direct contrast to Anand, who can play almost anything under the sun, it seems.) But you won't find anyone better prepared in the openings that he plays! Kramnik managed to outplay Kasparov in the openings in their match, which is saying something pretty impressive.

What Next?

With its various champions and sanctioning bodies, I'm afraid the World Chess Championship has come to resemble boxing in some respects. Some people are even saying that the very idea of a world champion is a twentieth century relic that does not fit chess for the twenty-first century.

What will the future bring? I don't know. In October, 2004 Kramnik defended his title against a top grandmaster, Peter Leko, by narrowly drawing a fourteen game match. (They had agreed beforehand that Kramnik would keep the title in event of a tie.) Leko is a top chess player (he is ranked number six as of November 2004) and still young at twenty-five, but there is no question that Kasparov and Anand are still the top two contenders for Kramnik's "title" of World Champion, so the fact that Kramnik played Leko is disappointing.

Meanwhile, FIDE continues to hold its World Championship tournaments, but the very top players continue not to compete so it is impossible to count the winner as a "world champion" in any serious way.

Perhaps in the end the fans will decide. If chess fans around the world care enough to see a World Championship event amongst the very top players, the money will be there to motivate all the players to compete. If not, then perhaps that is evidence that the twenty-first century no longer needs an official World Champion. Time will tell.

The Least You Need to Know

♦ The classical era is when the current style of chess really began.

♦ Each of the World Champions was a great player who contributed much to our understanding of chess.

♦ The Soviets dominated chess for many years, until Bobby Fischer revolutionized the game.

♦ The World Championship title is currently in dispute, and the chess world may be moving away from the idea of an official World Champion.

♦ Although he is no longer World Champion, Garry Kasparov is still the number-one ranked player after 16 years.

Getting Competitive

In This Chapter

◆ Finding stronger opposition

◆ Special rules for tournament play

◆ How chess tournaments work

◆ Long-distance competition

◆ Chess activities for children

In this chapter, I tell you how to find new opponents and test your skills against players in local, national, and even international competition. To visit or contact anyone listed in this chapter, consult Appendix A, where I've listed all the necessary information including Internet addresses.

Finding Stronger Opposition

If you've absorbed everything I've taught you so far, you can probably beat your family and friends by now, and they'll be as happy as you will be when you find some stronger competition! If you live in a large city, one way to do this is to look for outdoor chess scenes where people gather to play—sometimes for money but often just for fun—when the weather is good. Here are some of the best places to do this in the big cities of the United States:

- Boston: Harvard Square (Cambridge)
- New York: Bryant Park, Washington Square Park
- Washington, D.C.: Dupont Circle, Lafayette Park
- San Francisco: Market Street near Powell Street

There are many other public areas that reserve space for playing chess, including cafés, bookstores, and office buildings. But for more serious, organized, and year-round competition you should consider joining a chess club. There are thousands of clubs throughout the United States where you can meet other chess players and find all kinds of information about chess in the area. Most chess clubs meet on particular days and times in community centers, schools, office buildings, student unions, churches, and so on, but some of the bigger clubs have their own dedicated facilities. Some of the largest and oldest of these are:

- Boston: Boylston Chess Club.
- New York City: Marshall Chess Club, Village Chess Shop, Chess Forum.
- Rochester, New York: Rochester Chess Center.
- Philadelphia: Franklin Mercantile Chess Club.
- Washington, D.C.: U.S. Chess Center.
- Atlanta: Atlanta Chess Center.
- Phoenix: Chess Emporium.
- Los Angeles: Chess Palace (Los Alamitos).
- San Francisco: Mechanics Institute Chess Club.

But this only scratches the surface. Thanks to the Internet, you can access a comprehensive list of chess clubs throughout the United States and find a club near you no matter where you are. For a directory of chess clubs, go to www.uschess.org/clubs/.

This website is part of www.uschess.org, the online home of the U.S. Chess Federation (USCF), the principal national organization for chess. (Virtually every other country in the world has a national chess federation; you can find the address for the Chess Federation of Canada in Appendix A.) The USCF can also put you in touch with your state's chess association (every state has one), which will have more information about clubs and places to play near you. If you are serious about playing chess, I recommend that you join both the USCF and your state chess organization.

The USCF offers many services to its members, but the most important may be its sanctioning of chess tournaments. A USCF-sanctioned tournament is played according to the official rules of chess and the results are entered in the USCF rating system, which gives each member a way to measure his competitive strength and track his progress as he improves.

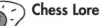

Chess Lore

One reason chess has become a popular game in recent decades is a clever rating system that measures the abilities of players who compete in tournaments. In some sports, the number-one ranking goes to the player who earns the most money or the team that a panel of journalists votes for. But in chess, just as the player who makes the best moves always wins the game, the player who achieves the best competitive results always earns the top ranking. The American physicist Arpad Elo (1903–1992) invented a system under which each player receives a numerical rating between 0 and 3000. A higher-rated player is more likely to defeat a lower-rated player, or at least outscore him in a series of games, depending on the difference between their ratings. A difference of 200 points corresponds to an expected score of 75 percent of the possible points for the higher-rated player, or a victory margin of 3 to 1 in a match. When you win a game (or draw against a higher-rated opponent), your rating increases in proportion to how much you exceeded your expected result; when you lose (or draw a lower-rated opponent), it decreases accordingly.

Elo originally developed his rating system for the USCF. It was so successful that other chess organizations (particularly FIDE) and even some activities apart from chess (for example, Scrabble) adopted some form of Elo ratings.

In the version of Elo's system currently used by FIDE, official ratings are published twice per year. In the USCF system, ratings are updated after every tournament and they are published as "official" every two months. The average tournament player in the United States has a rating of about 1400; achieving a rating of 2200 earns you the title of National Master, and a rating of 2400, Senior Master.

The International Grandmaster title is awarded only by FIDE and requires certain results in high-level tournaments in addition to a specific FIDE rating level. Roughly speaking, the International Grandmaster title corresponds to about a 2600 USCF rating or higher.

Special Chess Rules for Tournament Play

In most chess tournaments, a few additional rules are in force beyond the ones explained in Chapters 2 and 3. They don't change the game itself—how the pieces move, when checkmate occurs, or the like. These rules mainly exist to regulate the length of the game and to prevent disputes between the players. Each tournament is run by at least one and sometimes several tournament directors, who register the players, track the results, enforce the rules, and resolve the occasional dispute. The official rules for tournament play are explained in detail in *U.S. Chess Federation's Official Rules of Chess, 4th edition*, which I recommend you read if you want to play in tournaments. I'll explain the most important rule changes to look for.

Time Controls and Chess Clocks

In a tournament game, you can't think about your move forever; your time is limited. There are two basic types of time controls, or time limits, in use today. The simplest to understand is so-called sudden death, where each player is allotted a fixed amount of time to complete all moves. For example, each player might have 30 minutes to finish the entire game. If either player goes over his limit, he loses, just as though he resigned the game or was checkmated. So each game played under this time control is guaranteed to end within one hour.

The second type of time control allocates a certain amount of time to each player for a certain number of moves. For example, you might have two hours to complete the first 40 moves. If either player exceeds the limit before making the required number of moves, the other can stop the clock and claim a time-forfeit victory. If both players make it past move 40 without exceeding two hours, another time control begins. This might be similar to the first, such as one hour for the next 20 moves, or it might be a sudden-death control, such as 30 minutes to each player for the rest of the game.

Time controls are enforced using a special device known as a chess clock, which actually contains two clocks, one for each player. The clocks, which can be digital or analog, are connected by a mechanism that enables only one of them to run at any given time. Atop each player's clock is a button. When a player completes a move, he presses his button, which stops his clock and starts his opponent's. Thus, each player's clock measures exactly how much of his allotted time he has used (or has remaining). Don't forget, every time you make a move, press your clock! (And you should press it with the same hand you used to move the piece.)

Once you get used to using a clock, you'll probably never want to play without one again, even when you're just playing for fun. It adds an extra dimension to the game, keeps the action moving along, and makes chess more like other sports. (Can you imagine basketball without the shot clock?) The most popular time limit for casual chess is just five minutes per player for the entire game! This may seem like a very small amount of time, but once you get used to it, the fast time control makes the game very exciting. I love five-minute chess, also known as blitz or speed chess.

> **Patrick's Pointers**
>
> The first time you play chess with a time control, you might find it awkward. Beginners often become flustered by the pressure of needing to move within a specified time, or they find the clock itself distracting. However, this will quickly pass as you come to realize that even just a couple of minutes can seem like a long time. In tournaments with normal, longer time controls, lower-rated players typically wind up using just a fraction of their allotted time anyway, so don't get too hung up worrying that you will run out of time.

Other Ways to Draw the Game

In tournaments, there are two more ways that the game can end in a draw besides the ones mentioned in Chapter 3 (stalemate, perpetual check, insufficient material to checkmate, and friendly agreement).

The first is called threefold repetition. If the same position occurs three (or more) times during the same game, a draw may be claimed. The position must be the same in every way: The pieces must be in the same locations, the same moves must be legal (remember the castling and *en passant* rules), and the same side must be on move, for a true repetition to occur. To claim a draw by triple repetition, you should not actually make the move that brings about the position for the third time. Instead, you must stop the clock and tell your opponent, "By playing Bf5 I will repeat the position for the third time, so I am claiming a draw," or words to that effect. If you play the move and press your clock button, it's not your move anymore and so it's too late to claim the draw; you must hope the position repeats yet again and that you remember the procedure the next time!

The second additional way a tournament game can be drawn is called the 50-move rule. If 50 consecutive moves for each side have passed during which neither side has captured a piece or moved a pawn, either player may claim a draw. The point of this rule is to prevent someone from playing forever even when he has no realistic chance of winning. However, another practical effect is to highlight the importance of mastering basic endgame technique. For instance, in Chapter 4 I explained how to give checkmate with just a rook plus your king versus a lone king. You learned that this ending should always be won by the side with the rook; wouldn't it be a shame to miss out on a deserved victory because you couldn't finish your opponent off in under 50 moves?

The procedure for claiming the draw under this rule is the same as for the triple repetition: Stop the clock and point out that by making a certain move, 50 moves (or more) will have passed with all the criteria met, so you claim a draw.

Keeping Score

In tournaments, both players are generally required to keep an accurate score of the game. (Of course, you should want to do this anyway, so you can study and learn from your games later on!) You can also see how a complete score sheet may be required to verify a triple repetition, 50-move rule claim, or a time forfeit victory under the rules above.

Etiquette

The *touch-move* rule is always in force in tournament chess. This rule says that if it's your move and you touch a piece on the board with the intention to move it, you have to make a move with that piece. If you touch one of your opponent's pieces, you must capture it. (But if there is no legal move involving the touched piece, you're off the hook.) Also, once you release your hand from the piece you have moved, you cannot change the move. It is considered impolite to *hover* over a piece with your hand or to keep your hand on a piece for too long once you've moved it while you convince yourself it's not a mistake. If you want to adjust the positioning of a piece on its square, you must say "I adjust" or "*j'adoube*" (a term that comes from French) to let your opponent know you aren't planning to move it. I strongly urge you to get in the habit of reaching out to touch a piece only after you have made a final decision about what move you want to make. Then execute your move quickly, quietly, and confidently.

It is also forbidden to speak to your opponent or disturb him in any way except to resign or propose a draw. When resigning, it is customary to stop the clock and offer a handshake while saying "I resign." For an old-style touch you can also tip over your king. To offer a draw in a tournament game, you must first make a move, and then say "I offer a draw" or words to that effect, after you complete the move but *before* you press your clock button. Your opponent may accept the offer verbally, accept by offering to shake hands, decline the offer verbally, or make a move himself (which automatically declines the offer). He can think for as long as he wants (within the constraints of the time control) before accepting or declining your offer, and you cannot change your mind and retract the offer while waiting for him to decide. If your opponent declines your draw offer, it is considered poor etiquette to repeat the offer again the very next move.

You might find these rules of behavior a bit ponderous, but the more you play competitively the more you'll appreciate the way such conventions protect you from distraction and help you play at your best.

How Chess Tournaments Work

There is a USCF-sanctioned chess tournament going on somewhere in the country pretty much every hour of every day. On weeknights and weekends, there are probably dozens. The weeknight tournaments are usually held at chess clubs. Sometimes these begin and end on the same night, and sometimes they stretch over more than a month, with one round held per week. Weekend tournaments usually last either one or two days, and sometimes include a Friday-night round as well.

Patrick's Pointers

If you enjoy playing chess, I strongly suggest that you try playing in a chess tournament. Not only is it the most intense way to enjoy playing the game, you can also meet lots of other people who love chess. Plus, especially at the bigger tournaments, you can find all sorts of chess books and equipment for sale. And at the really big tournaments, you may even meet a grandmaster or two!

Many tournaments, especially the ones held over the weekend, are divided into several sections by ability level, so players only face opponents near themselves in strength. Each section functions essentially as a separate tournament, with its own score table and prizes. Ratings are usually used to determine section eligibility. The sections ensure that everyone encounters a fair set of opponents and doesn't just get slaughtered by masters (or bored by a bunch of novices).

Most chess tournaments run according to formats you might not be familiar with. In professional sports, the knockout (single-elimination) tournament, used in tennis and football, and the match, used in a baseball or basketball playoff series, are the most common. These are used in chess as well, but usually only in grandmaster events like the World Championship cycle. In amateur-level chess, most events use either the round-robin or the Swiss-system format. In either case, the player who has the most points (1 for each win, ½ for each draw, 0 for each loss) at the end of the tournament wins. Here's how these systems work.

Round Robin

In a round-robin tournament each player meets every other player the same number of times, usually once. Chess clubs that meet regularly often use this format for their championship tournaments, and many of the top international chess tournaments use it as well. It would seem to produce the fairest result. Every player faces the same opposition, all the scores should be directly comparable. An obvious drawback is that a round robin takes a long time to complete if there are a large number of players. However, small round robins are often finished in a single day. "Quads," for example, group players into four-person sections and run round robins within each section. If the grouping is done according to ratings, each player will wind up facing three other players near him in strength. In a double round robin, each player plays each other player twice—once with the white and once with the black pieces.

Swiss System

The vast majority of rated chess games in the United States are played in Swiss-system format tournaments. The Swiss system ingeniously incorporates the building drama of a knockout format (players who win play other players who win) without requiring all the losing players to watch from the sidelines the rest of the way. In the first round, players are ranked by rating, and the top half of the draw plays the bottom half. For all subsequent rounds, this procedure is repeated separately for each score group; thus, first-round winners play first-round winners, first-round losers play first-round losers, and so on. At each stage, you are playing someone who has the same score as you, no matter how good or bad that score is. If you lost your first two games and won your next two, in round five you will play someone else with two points, even if he won his first two and lost his next two. Crucially, players never play each other more than once, and nobody is eliminated—not even the occasional odd man out, who gets a free point and is back in the competition by the next round.

Finding and Entering a Chess Tournament

The best way to find USCF-sanctioned chess tournaments is to look in the "Tournament Life" section of *Chess Life* magazine, published by the USCF. (A subscription is included with membership.) Each month, the magazine lists hundreds of tournaments, with full information on how to enter, what the format and prizes are, where the games will be played, and even what hotels are nearby. This information is also available via the Internet at the U.S. Chess Online website at www.uschess.org/tla/. Your state organization or local chess club may also publish a magazine, newsletter, or web page listing tournaments not included in the national sources.

Once you have found a good tournament, remember to bring everything you will need: your chessboard and set (make sure they are standard and not exotic looking; the picture in Chapter 2 shows standard chess pieces), a chess clock (very important), and something to write down the moves of your games with. Most of these are not provided, although score sheets usually are. If you don't have chess equipment, you can order the basics and an infinite variety of other stuff, including the books I recommended in Chapter 15, from the catalogs of the following vendors:

◆ Chess Digest (Ardmore, Tenessee); www.chessdigest.com

◆ Chessco (Davenport, Iowa); www.chessco.com

◆ The Chess House (Lynden, Washington); www.thechesshouse.com

◆ Your Move Chess and Games (Huntington Station, New York); www.icdchess.com

◆ The USCF; www.uscfsales.com

For chess books, I'm a big fan of Amazon.com (www.amazon.com). You can get just about any chess book you want there, and Amazon has great service. But it's not great on chess pieces, board, clock, or other equipment. For that, try one of the vendors just listed. Additionally, many of the full-time chess clubs listed at the beginning of this chapter sell supplies. Many stores specializing in games and hobbies have excellent chess selections as well; check your telephone book.

Long-Distance Competition

If you can't get to a local club or tournament, there's always long-distance chess. You can play correspondence chess through the regular mail, where each move takes a few days and a game typically lasts 18 to 24 months. Contact the USCF for information about its large program of postal chess tournaments with its own rating system and rules. The organizations below also administer postal chess competitions:

◆ American Postal Chess Tournaments; correspondencechess.com/apct/ (no "www" at the beginning of the address)

◆ Correspondence Chess League of America; www.chessbymail.com

◆ International Correspondence Chess Federation; www.iccfus.com

◆ Canadian Correspondence Chess Association; correspondencechess.com/ccca/

Chess by mail has a long and noble tradition, but personally, I think it's more fun to play over the Internet. You can send moves instantaneously and have an electronic chessboard in front of you. Why use stamps? I'll tell you all about how you can use the Internet to play chess in Chapter 18.

Chess Competition for Children

There's no reason why children can't compete in any chess tournament; virtually all are open to any qualified player regardless of age. But there are also many competitions just for kids. The annual National Scholastic Championships sponsored by the USCF attract thousands of players, and similar regional events have become nearly as popular. Chapter 21 tells a little bit about the explosive growth of scholastic chess in the United States.

Events for children are usually sectioned by age or grade level rather than rating. You can find out more about them in *Chess Life*, as well as from state and local publications. To locate school-based chess clubs and programs, and to find out about lessons for children, contact the USCF or your state chess association. (This is another great reason to go to the USCF website at uschess.org/scholastic/.) You might also contact the following organizations:

- Chess-in-the-Schools (New York, New York); www.chessintheschools.org
- National Scholastic Chess Foundation (White Plains, New York); www.nscfchess.org
- The U.S. Chess Center (Washington, D.C.); www.chessctr.org
- The American Chess School (Bradford, Pennsylvania); www.amchess.org

I should mention that these organizations tend to have a local focus. There are lots of people bringing chess and kids together, and they tend to focus on their own community. You'll probably want to find out about what's going on in your area. If you live in the United States, the best way to do that is by contacting the USCF, your state chess federation, or a chess club near you. If you live in another country, check out Appendix A for contact information of other national federations. There are also several chess camps for kids around the country. They operate mainly during the summer months, but also occasionally during other school vacations. Consult advertisements in *Chess Life* and other publications, or your local chess club, for more information.

The Least You Need to Know

◆ You can find casual chess competition in local outdoor scenes, full-time clubs, and weekly clubs.

◆ When you're ready to play in tournaments, remember the special rules and etiquette that apply to serious competition. (And don't forget your equipment!)

◆ The Internet is a fantastic way to learn more about chess and play others. You can learn more about this in Chapter 18.

◆ Children can participate in the same clubs and tournaments as adults, and there are many age-grouped events just for kids.

Chess in Cyberspace

In This Chapter

- ◆ Great websites for chess
- ◆ Playing chess online
- ◆ Getting chess news and information online
- ◆ Playing chess electronically in the palm of your hand
- ◆ Playing and studying chess with your computer

Computers are wonderful for storing, presenting, and transmitting information. Chess is a game of pure information. So, not surprisingly, computers are wonderful for chess. The more you play and enjoy chess, the more you will come to love what computers can do for you! And in particular, the explosion of the Internet has been an explosion of opportunity for chess players around the world.

In this chapter, I take you on a tour of what computers can do for you. I focus on the Internet because that is where most of the action is, plus, it's so easy to access and use. But toward the end of this chapter, I also give you an overview of some of the programs you can purchase for your PC.

Chess Websites

There are literally thousands of websites where a chess player could spend hours every day. I've organized the best ones I know into five categories. Let's go through the best ones in each category, how you can get there and how you can use them.

WolffChess (www.wolffchess.com)

Please excuse me if I make this one a category unto itself! I think it offers something really unique—once you establish an account, you have unlimited access to over 500 chess exercises. There is a fee for your account that is roughly the same price as a chess book, but I've tried to make the quality and quantity of content worth at least any book. (Including this one!) I think you will find that the exercises complement what you have learned in Chapters 2–14, and because you do the exercises online, you can do them at work or home without a chess set.

I hope you check out WolffChess online, and I hope it helps you improve your chess game!

Chess Portals

A "portal" is a website that tries to be your point of entry onto the Internet. So a chess portal is a website that could be the point of entry onto the Internet for the total chess nut (like me). Any one of these websites is a place you could visit on a regular basis for anything having to do with chess.

Here are some websites I would put in this category:

- **The Week In Chess (www.chesscenter.com/twic/twic.html).** This website started as an e-mail newsletter by a devoted chess fan, Mark Crowther. He did such a great job that it grew into one of the most popular and respected chess websites in the world. You can get all the latest chess news from around the world in a no-nonsense format; in addition, you can get tons of chess games every week. If you want to get all the games played by the world's best grandmasters on a regular basis, this is your place! However, it's not a very "pretty" website, and if you are not very interested in recent grandmaster games, it may be less useful.

- **Chessville (www.chessville.com).** An ever-changing bouquet of chess news, instruction, trivia, and links. By monitoring the latest in chess from all over cyberspace and presenting links to the most interesting developments right on the front page, Chessville makes itself an ideal first stop for chess fans online.

The Chessville home page is not exactly what you'd call pretty to look at, but you will find it chock full of interesting stuff.

♦ **Grandmaster Chess (www.gmchess.com).** This is one of the most attractive chess websites I know of. It is clean and relatively well laid out. You can get all kinds of information here, from articles to chess problems to deeply annotated games. You can also purchase chess items, from chess sets to chess instruction.

♦ **The Chess Café (www.chesscafe.com).** This isn't a portal in the same vein as the other websites above, but it is so interesting and special that I think it deserves to be in the same list. Here you can find several-page articles of very high quality on all kinds of chess topics. It really is a "chess café" in the sense that you could go to this website with a cup of coffee and relax with a good read for an hour!

> **Patrick's Pointers**
>
> Some of the websites I recommend have URLs (web addresses) that are hard to remember. I recommend that you create a folder in your browser for all the chess sites you want to visit, then bookmark each site when you go there and save it into that folder.

♦ **Chessopolis (www.chessopolis.com).** Chessopolis offers a chat room, chess files for download, an online chess store, and, most important, a massive collection of links to other chess sites.

Chess Organizations

Every major chess organization has its own website. I can't hope to list all of them, but here are two you should know about:

♦ **U.S. Chess Federation (www.uschess.org).** This is the U.S. Chess Federation's official site, featuring among other things an online catalog, tournament listings, and news about the federation's governance and activities. If you play chess in the United States, I highly recommend exploring this website to see what you can find that will be useful to you.

♦ **FIDE (www.fide.com).** This is the official site of the international chess federation. It may be a bit intimidating if you're not already familiar with FIDE. But it has a lot of information and resources and is worth knowing about.

Personal and Special Interest Sites

With so many people playing chess in the world, many of them also computer enthusiasts, it's only natural that some people would decide to share their love for the game by creating their own chess websites. Indeed, a few of the important professional sites that I've mentioned here started out as a for-fun efforts by amateur hobbyists. If you create something good, it will grow!

Obviously, there's a huge variety of such sites, in terms of both type of content and quality. Not all of them are useful, but there are quite a few "niche" sites that offer something of real interest. Here are a few that I can recommend:

◆ **Chessmetrics (www.chessmetrics.com).** This site displays the fruit of statistician Jeff Sonas's remarkable investigation of historical ratings.

◆ **Chess Curiosities (www.xs4all.nl/~timkr/chess/chess.html).** The name says it all: trivia, weird coincidences, bizarre positions, and not a few entries of genuine scholarly value. Can't figure why anyone would ever want to underpromote a pawn to a bishop? Webmaster Tim Krabbé has dug up numerous games where it actually happened. Has a grandmaster ever resigned in a winning position? Oh, yeah; you'll find a bunch of examples here…

◆ **Jeremy Silman (jeremysilman.com/chess.html).** Silman gathers together news, instruction, interviews, and lots of really thoughtful book reviews. (Also astrological charts for famous chess players, if you're into that sort of thing.)

◆ **Chess History Center (www.chesshistory.com).** This site is a clearinghouse for research into various questions of chess history.

◆ **Chess Graphics (www.chessgraphics.net).** All sorts of chess-themed artworks are organized and available for viewing or download. This is an excellent resource if you need art for a chess brochure or newsletter.

It's natural with amateur websites that they will come and go more quickly than professional sites. Sometimes a site will stay online but turn stale if its creator loses interest, lacks the time to make regular updates, or simply runs out of new material to post. But other new and interesting chess sites come online just as quickly as older ones disappear. A little work with your search engine will probably turn up a site that specializes in whatever aspect of chess interests you.

Chess Shopping

The Internet has given us endless opportunities to purchase almost anything we want. What about chess?

All the chess vendors I listed in Chapter 17 have websites, and you can order some products from them. As I write this, some of their websites provide an easier shopping experience than others, but I am sure all of them will continue to work on it, so you should definitely check all of them out and bookmark them for your future purchases.

Apart from dedicated online retailers, many organizational websites and other chess-related sites will offer particular products for sale. For example, among the sites mentioned previously, Grandmaster Chess has some offerings, and Chess Café is an outlet for The House of Staunton, a seller of fine chess sets.

Patrick's Pointers

If you start exploring chess websites, you will quickly encounter something called "PGN." These initials stand for "Portable Game Notation." This is a standardized computer format for encoding chess games. There are two ways to read games stored in PGN format.

Structurally, a PGN file is a text file, so one way to view such a file is simply to open it using your word processor. You will see the moves of one or more games presented sequentially in normal text form. At the top of each game you will see several lines enclosed in brackets ([]) containing game data—the names of the White and Black players, the date of the game, what tournament it was from, etc.

The second option is to use a software program that recognizes PGN and will display it on your computer. In the section called "Chess on Your PC," I list some of the programs that recognize PGN. There are two advantages to using this kind of software program with PGN files. First, it gives you a graphic representation of the board, so you can play through the moves on your screen without needing an actual board and pieces. Second, such programs often included offer database features for manipulating multiple games in PGN format. Again, I will have much more to say about this in the "Chess on Your PC" section.

You can download simple freeware programs whose only function is reading PGN games. One place to find such a program is at Pitt Chess described in the "Libraries and Resources" section later in this chapter. Click the header on the left side marked "Utilities," and then explore any of the files that start with "pgn." (Note: You will need the program WinZip to read and extract these files—they are "zipped" to make them easier to store and download.)

Otherwise, try major mainstream retailers for various chess products. For books, the situation is excellent. Amazon.com is my favorite online bookstore (although both Borders and Barnes & Noble are also good), and they have every chess book I have ever looked for. Unfortunately, for other chess equipment, it has been my experience so far that the major retailers (including Amazon.com) don't have a good selection.

Playing Chess Online

The Internet isn't just for being a chess fan, student, or spectator. It's also about playing! There are lots of ways you can use the Internet to find a chess game at any hour of the day.

General Games Sites

People love to play games. Chess is perhaps the most popular game in the world. So it stands to reason that there will be lots of websites for playing games, and all of them will have chess. If you're just looking for a casual chess game from time to time, you can find it at any of these websites:

◆ **Yahoo! Games (games.yahoo.com).** One of the most popular games sites on the web. You can play chess along with hundreds of other games here.

◆ **MSN Gaming Zone (zone.msn.com).** Another one of the most popular games sites on the web. Personally, I think Yahoo! does a better job, but that's just a matter of taste.

Loads of other websites are devoted just to games, and virtually all of them will have chess. You can find them using any good Internet search engine. If you want to go to general games sites, though, I recommend going to the ones with the most people, and those will probably be the ones affiliated with the major portals.

Chess Lore _____

One of the most amazing cases of an online chess game took place in the summer of 1999. Garry Kasparov literally took on the entire world! In this Microsoft-sponsored event, Kasparov played White, and the world had Black. Anyone could go to the website and register a single vote for a chess move. Whichever move won the vote would be played against Kasparov. Each side had one day to play a move.

You might think that the game would be a cakewalk for Kasparov, but it was a lot closer than that. Several professional chess players offered their advice to the world, so the move that won turned out to be quite good. Add to this that Kasparov was surprised out of the opening, and you can see how it became a real fight. In fact, the world could have drawn in an endgame, but there was disagreement over which move to play, and the wrong move won.

Garry Kasparov even wound up writing a fascinating book (published in October 2000) about this one game! He analyzes it in great detail, plus he gives a lot of details about what it was like "behind the scenes" to play this game.

Chess-Specific Sites

There are also websites that focus completely on enabling people to play chess with one another. Here are a few that I recommend:

- **Internet Chess Club (www.chessclub.com).** This is the longest-running and most active chess-playing website in the world. You can almost always find grandmasters playing here! (You'll also find some pretty strong computers playing here.) Besides live play, the ICC also hosts other events, such as real-time coverage of grandmaster tournaments, grandmaster matches played on the ICC, online simultaneous exhibitions, lectures, and lessons. The bottom line: If you're serious about playing chess online, you've got to go to the ICC.

- **Chess.net (www.chess.net).** Another full-service online chess club, similar to the ICC. A few grandmasters play here as well, although more play at the ICC. In my opinion, the ICC is the better bet, but you may also want to check out Chess.net.

- **Free Internet Chess Server (www.freechess.org).** As the name suggests, you can play here for free! The FICS lacks some of the advanced features and fancy extras of the ICC, but for casual play the basic experience is similar. If you just want an occasional game, 24 hours a day, check it out.

◆ **ChessManiac.com (www.chessmaniac.com).** This versatile site describes itself as follows: "ChessManiac.com offers player ranking and ratings, tournaments, chess teams, forums, graphical user interface chessboard, user game history, pgn chess game export, Multilanguage support in English, German, French, Polish, Portuguese, Russian, Italian, and Spanish."

Patrick's Pointers
"What about America Online (AOL)?" you might ask. To be honest, I have never used AOL, so I don't know a lot about what it has to offer for chess. It certainly does have a gaming area for its members, and there are certainly a lot of people who play chess there. But I do want to offer one piece of advice. Don't stay inside the AOL area—use AOL to get onto the World Wide Web! As convenient as AOL's proprietary area is for a lot of things, it just can't match what you can find on the web for chess.

◆ **USCF online (www.chesslive.org).** The USCF's online chess-playing website. It offers a discount to members of ICC and other for-pay chess clubs who want to switch.

If you are only looking for an occasional casual game, and you are not looking for the highest possible challenge, go to one of the general games sites. But if you are looking for hard-core chess, definitely check out the sites above, starting with the Internet Chess Club.

Chess by E-Mail

Sometimes you might want to play chess over a longer period of time. Maybe you can take 10 minutes at work to think about a move, and you would enjoy playing a friend over several days or weeks. In the "old days" (before the 1990s), your best option was to send moves by mail. That's how I used to play my grandfather when I was a little kid.

Today, if I were playing my grandpa (or anyone else), I would use e-mail. It's faster, cheaper, and better. Honestly, I don't know why anyone would use stamps anymore!

Here are the only two websites you need to know about to get started playing chess by e-mail:

◆ **Shockwave.com (www.shockwave.com).** This site has lots of fun stuff for web-based games and entertainment. One of the things it has is a really cool e-mail chess program. (The easiest way to find it from the front page is to type "chess" in the Search field at the upper right.) You make your move on the electronic chessboard, and send it to your opponent straight from there via e-mail.

♦ **International Email Chess Group (www.iecg.org).** This is an organization dedicated to chess by e-mail. Go here if you want to find new opponents to play by e-mail, or if you want to play in e-mail chess tournaments. It even maintains its own e-mail chess ratings.

Have fun!

Chess News and Information

If you have spent time exploring the Internet, you know that it is a treasure trove of information for just about anything you could imagine. It's the same for chess. Let's take a look at some of the things you can find.

Libraries and Resources

Are you looking for all the known games from the eighteenth century? How about a font for writing chess pieces and diagrams in your word processor? Or a program that will allow you to play through chess games on your PC? If you can imagine it, then it's likely that somebody has programmed it. Fortunately, many people who play chess are also people who are very computer-savvy, so there is a lot of chess out there to find with your computer!

Here are some of the most promising libraries and general resources:

♦ **Pitt Chess (www.pitt.edu/~schach/index.html).** When you get to this website, click the button that says "Chess Archives." If you're looking specifically for game collections, next indicate what format your database or game reader software uses. (Go for PGN if you're not sure or you have no special chess database software.) Game collections within each format are organized by player, tournament, opening, and so on. Other types of downloads include chess art, articles, fonts, and software. You could spend days exploring this website and still not find everything it has to offer! Here's a tip: Click the Index link ("allindex.txt" or "allindex.zip" if you have WinZip). This will give you a complete index of everything at the site. Go nuts!

♦ **About.com (chess.about.com/index.html).** About.com is one of my favorite websites for getting information about almost anything. Its twist is that it has real people who are dedicated to particular subjects, and those people gather all the links and information you might want in one place. It has a section dedicated just to chess, and I recommend it.

◆ **Steve Pribut's Chess Page (www.drpribut.com/sports/chess.html).** Steve maintains this page simply for the love of chess. It is really worth checking it out just to see all the links and other information he has.

◆ **ChessLinks Worldwide (www.chesslinks.org/).** Some news but mainly what the name implies: An up-to-date directory of all sorts of chess-related links from all across the Internet. This site helped me prepare this chapter!

Online Magazines

Would you rather read *The New York Times* (or whatever your newspaper of choice is) or go to *The New York Times* website? If you prefer the latter, you may want to check out the websites of some of the best chess magazines and journals.

I can hardly hope to provide a comprehensive list, because there are literally hundreds of chess magazines out there. But here are some of the ones I recommend the most:

◆ **New In Chess (www.newinchess.com).** *New In Chess* is probably the best chess magazine in the world. Mostly, the website is a vehicle to sell the magazine and other chess products (which are generally very high quality, by the way), but it also has some links and content to check out.

◆ **British Chess Magazine (www.bcmchess.co.uk).** This is the website for the *British Chess Magazine*, one of the two top chess periodicals in Great Britain.

◆ **Chess Monthly (www.chess.co.uk).** This is the website for the other top chess periodical in Great Britain. It is closely associated with the website "The Week in Chess," one of the portal websites listed earlier in the chapter.

◆ **Europe échecs (www.europe-echecs.com).** The French magazine *Europe échecs* is one of the best chess magazines in Europe. If you are comfortable reading French, it's worth checking out.

Chess in the Palm of Your Hand

The late 1990s saw the rise of another electronic device: handheld computers like the popular Palm Pilot, Handspring Visor, or any of the various devices that run on Microsoft's operating system. These devices are sometimes called personal digital assistants, or PDAs for short. You might get one of these devices to serve as an electronic date and phone book, but you will soon discover that you can download and run an entire universe of programs for them.

Chess has benefited greatly from the creation of this new universe. No matter which PDA you have, there are chess programs you can download and use. (At the time of writing, the Palm operating system used by the Palm Pilot and Handspring Visor is the most widely supported, but look for the Windows Mobile Pocket PC and Blackberry devices to gain ever more traction in the future.)

Currently, by far the most popular chess applications for the PDA are simple chess playing programs. These allow you to play against your device (which, after all, is just another kind of computer), or against another person using the PDA as your chess set. You can also get PDA applications whose purpose is chess notation; basically you use your PDA as an electronic score sheet. (You won't be allowed to use this in a tournament, however!) Another application presents you with chess problems you can solve, and still another allows your PDA to function as a chess clock! I predict that in the future there will be even more content for your PDA, such as chess articles and books, chess problems, and grandmaster chess games. It's just a matter of the devices getting more powerful and more people writing the content.

Soon, PDAs will connect directly to the Internet all the time. (Some already do, although the connection is still kind of clunky.) As I write this, however, the main way to download programs into your PDA is to visit a website via your PC, download the program onto your PC, and then sync the PC with your PDA.

Here are a few websites I recommend for finding great chess programs for your PDA:

- **Handango (www.handango.com).** This is a business that is trying to become an online "superstore" for PDA devices and downloadable PDA programs. A few are free; most cost money. Many are available for a trial period.

- **Tucows PDA website (pda.tucows.com).** Tucows is a resource that has been used by software experts for years. Tucows has a separate part of the website devoted to PDA devices. You'll find a lot here of very good quality, and a lot of it (currently) either free or available for a free trial.

◆ **VersionTracker (www.versiontracker.com/palmos).** This is another general-purpose software download center, similar to Tucows.

This is an area that is developing very fast, so expect many more changes over the next few years!

Chess on Your PC

With all the exciting things happening with the Internet and various other electronic gadgets, we shouldn't forget the "old classic" software for your PC. There are some very good programs you can get that will enable you either to play with or study with your computer—or both.

Playing Chess on Your Computer

Here are a few of my favorite PC programs for playing chess:

◆ **Chessmaster 9000 (Ubi Soft).** The latest edition of the longest-running and most popular series on the market, this package has a tremendous variety of features at a relatively low price. It offers instruction, a database of historical games, a powerful chess engine, and great graphics. It's available for several different platforms, including Windows and Mac. You can find out more (and even purchase a copy) by going to the website for this product: www.chessmaster.com.

◆ **Virtual Chess 64 (Nintendo).** To be honest, I don't know a lot about this program, and I have never played Nintendo. But if you've got a Nintendo game and you want a chess program for it, check this out.

◆ **MacChess (Wim Van Beusekom).** Mac users with the latest version of Apple's operating system don't need to look far for a chess playing program: You've already got a strong one, which comes as part of the standard installation of Mac OS X. But if you use the older Mac OS 7, 8, or 9, download MacChess from VersionTracker or Tucows. It's strong, and best of all, it's free!

*A screenshot from
Chessmaster 9000.*

Studying Chess on Your Computer

Yes, the computer can be your friend as well as your competitor! A number of programs will help you study and learn chess. For straightforward chess instructions, I
recommend the following products:

◆ **Maurice Ashley Teaches Chess (Davidson/Simon & Schuster).** Maurice is a
terrific teacher (as well as being a strong grandmaster), and the software design-
ers did a great job of translating his style into this program.

◆ **The Chess Mentor System (Aficionado).** This is really a whole suite of products offering computer-assisted chess instruction with individual modules on a
wide range of topics. You can find out more by going to its website:
www.chess.com. (What a great URL!)

◆ **Learn to Play Chess with Fritz and Chesster.** This program is specially
designed for children, and the buzz is that it is very good. If you are looking for
a way to teach a preteen, this might be the product for you.

Learn to Play Chess with Fritz and Chesster.

But that only scratches the surface! The hard-core chess player can use special-purpose chess database software to collect and organize his own games, as well as to review and study master games. One grandmaster said that after getting used to studying with his database, which moves the pieces around a diagram on the screen, he had trouble going back to the "old" way of reading moves in a book and making them by hand with his board and set. A word to the wise—Simply playing through hundreds or thousands of grandmaster games will do little to make you a better player; serious study of games, especially with good annotations to help you understand the ideas behind the moves, is essential.

That said, databases are useful for reference and browsing, and you can use them to store an enormous amount of information. Publishers are developing special instructional databases that teach specific openings, endings, and middlegame themes. Several of the chess-playing programs listed above also have some database capabilities built in. The leading standalone database packages are:

♦ **ChessBase (ChessBase USA).** The first commercial chess database and the one used by more top grandmasters than any other. (I use it to organize all of my games and analyses.) It can be integrated with the Fritz chess program so that the computer will analyze the game and answer your questions about it. Or you can just play against the Fritz computer for fun. (Many grandmasters do just that!) Quite simply, this is the premium chess database product. It is expensive, and it is not for everybody; I don't recommend it unless you are really serious about studying chess. But if you are, this is the product to use. You can find out more at its website at www.chessbase.com. Or try the USA website at www.chessbaseusa.com.

♦ **Bookup (Bookup).** This is a "positional" database that organizes data by specific positions rather than game scores and is best suited for developing and recording an opening repertoire. A bundle that includes Bookup and a chess playing program called "Crafty" is sold under the name MasterChess 3000. I have less experience with this product than with ChessBase, but I have heard good things about it. And it is less expensive.

♦ **ExaChess (Exant).** If you're a Mac user, ExaChess is the way to go. It features a very powerful database application, rivaling ChessBase in most of the core functions at a fraction of the cost. In fact, there's a free "lite" version that you can download from the website www.exachess.com. If you're at all serious about chess database work, you'll want to buy the full version, which is still less than $100.

The Least You Need to Know

♦ The Internet is a tremendous resource for chess. Start with the resources listed here but don't be afraid to search the web yourself; new sites come online all the time.

♦ You can play chess against opponents all over the world by e-mail or in real time on the web.

♦ Handheld computer devices have already expanded opportunities for enjoying chess, and they will do so even more rapidly in the near future.

♦ Software packages that play chess, teach chess, and store chess information can help you improve your game and have fun at the same time.

Chapter 19

How Computers Play Chess

In This Chapter

- How computers "think" about chess
- How humans think about chess
- A bit of the history of computers in chess
- The ultimate man-versus-machine chess match
- What does it all mean?

How do computers "think?" How do they decide what moves to play? How did Deep Blue beat the World Chess Champion? And what does it mean for us humans? Let's explore these fascinating questions.

The Thinking Machine?

You may have heard that computers are at their best in simple, repetitive tasks involving a lot of elementary steps, such as recalculating a spreadsheet or searching a database. But chess isn't like that, right? Well, the answer depends on your perspective.

If you're a human being, you experience all kinds of thoughts and feelings during a chess game, and you think about things like pawn structure, weak squares, forks, pins, and the opposition.

But computers don't see chess that way. For us humans, chess is something to be figured out and understood. For computers (and their programmers), chess is a mathematical problem that can be solved, at least approximately, with massive, rapid calculations.

Let's look at an example of how a computer would find the best move and compare its "thinking process" with our own. Examine Diagram 1 and figure out how White can win. If you studied Chapter 8, it shouldn't take long to solve this problem. In fact, it's taken directly from Diagram 23 in the section on the "smothered mate" tactic, so you may even remember the exact sequence of moves: 1.Nf7+ Kg8 (if 1...Rxf7 2.Qxc8+ Rf8 3.Qxf8#) 2.Nh6+ Kh8 3.Qg8+ Rxg8 4.Nf7#.

Regardless of how you solved it, you relied on recognizing a pattern of the pieces on the board and associating that pattern with an idea. The ability to rapidly recognize such patterns is invaluable, and as you get better at chess you'll find yourself seeing more and more repeating patterns that will suggest moves and plans to investigate.

How would a computer deal with Diagram 1? Would it recognize the pattern and look up a solution plan (say, in the smothered mate file) in its memory? Nothing of the sort. Remember, computers like simple, mechanical operations, and recognizing patterns and implementing plans are complicated processes. Instead, the computer will simply list out every legal move White has in the position. Here they are: Qa2, Qb3, Qb4, Qa4, Qb5, Qa6, Qc5, Qc6, Qc7, Qxc8, Qd5, Qe6, Qf7, Qg8+, Qd4, Qe4, Qf4, Qg4, Qh4, Qd3, Qe2, Qf1, Qc3, Qc2, Qc1, Nf3, Ne4, Ne6, Nf7+, Nxh7, Nh3, f3, f4, g4, Kf1, Kg2, Kh2, and Kh1.

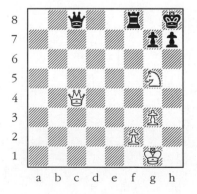

Diagram 1: White to play and win.

Did you realize that there are actually 38 legal moves for White? When you looked at the position, you probably only thought about a couple: Qxc8 to capture the queen; Qh4, Qe4, or Qd3 to threaten checkmate on h7; and (hopefully) Nf7+. Most of the others, after all, just lose the queen right away, or at best, leave White still down the exchange (rook for knight), so you were wise not to waste time thinking about them. There's no reason to think of any other move, and considering them all would slow you down. (Just reading through them takes a few seconds!) Computers, on the other hand, don't have ideas. But they do have speed: They can list out all the legal moves in a split second.

What happens next? Well, when you consider a move, you have to consider how your opponent might reply. The computer does the same, but again unlike a human, it simply looks at every legal response to every legal move. For example, the first move we listed for White was Qa2, which would bring up the position in Diagram 2.

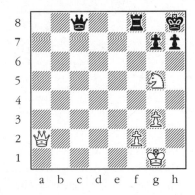

Diagram 2: White plays 1.Qa2.

To that, Black has the replies ...Qc7,...Qc6,...Qc5,..., well we won't list them all out again; the total number is 30 (for those of you keeping score at home), and the best one is 1...Qc1+ followed by 2...Qxg5 winning White's knight (and stopping the smothered mate threat). Now for each of White's 38 first moves, Black has about 30 replies to consider, so after one move by each player there are about 38×30 = 1,140 positions that could result. For each of those positions, the computer must repeat the process again, considering each of White's legal moves, all of Black's replies to each, and so on. In order for a computer to "see" the position after White's fourth move (Nf7# in the solution to the problem), a computer considering each of 30 possibilities on average per turn would wind up analyzing 30^7 = 21,870,000,000 future positions that could potentially occur. (That is, 30 moves for White times 30 moves for Black times 30 moves for White seven times up to 4.Nf7#.)

When it finally reaches the position that actually ends in checkmate, the program can make a note that 4.Nf7# was the best move in the position right before that one—nothing is better than giving mate—shown in Diagram 3.

Now a sort of backtracking process happens. Because 3...Rxg8 was Black's only legal move, the program knows that 3.Qg8+ was the best move in Diagram 4. Likewise, because Black had no alternative to 2...Kh8 a move earlier, 2.Nh6+ must have been the best move in Diagram 5, again because it leads by force to checkmate.

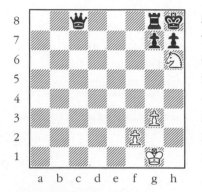

Diagram 3: Position after 3...Rxg8, before 4.Nf7#.

Diagram 4: Position after 2...Kh8, before 3.Qg8+.

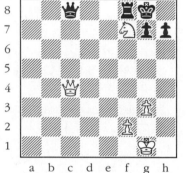

Diagram 5: Position after 1...Kg8, before 2.Nh6+.

Finally, by comparing the backtracked consequences of the alternatives at move 1 (including the side variation starting with 1...Rxf7), the program can conclude with certainty that 1.Nf7+ is the best move in the starting position. If you were unfortunate enough to have Black in this position against your favorite chess program, it would waste no time in playing 1.Nf7+ (and it would probably helpfully inform you that checkmate was inevitable).

Note how different this was from the human approach. If you noticed the smothered-mate theme you immediately saw 1.Nf7+ and then only needed to investigate two variations, totaling perhaps 12 to 15 possible future positions, a minuscule fraction of all the legal possibilities.

Now try the position in Diagram 6. A computer would find the answer before you could blink, because the winning combination is actually two moves shorter than that in Diagram 1. Here's a clue: Look for a smothered mate. The position doesn't look much like Diagram 1 at all, does it? But it uses the same tactic, and in a broad sense the pattern is similar. Note how Black's king is surrounded by his own pieces. They are defending him, but also hemming him in (together with White's e6-pawn). If White could safely give check with a knight it would be mate. Where can White give check with the knight? Not on d6, because the bishop controls that square. What about g7? No, the queen is on that square. But what if the queen could move off that square …?

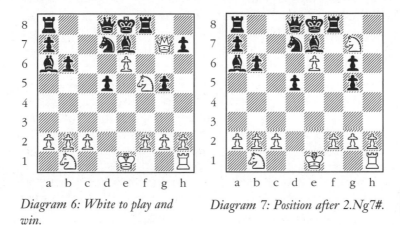

Diagram 6: White to play and win.

Diagram 7: Position after 2.Ng7#.

The solution is 1.Qg6+! hxg6 (1...Rf7 2 Qxf7#) 2.Ng7# (see Diagram 7), combining a clearance sacrifice with the smothered mate. But even though it was a shorter solution than Diagram 1, and therefore, easier for the computer, because it had to search far fewer positions to find the right move, it was probably harder for you to find, because it didn't quite "look like" any smothered mate you've seen. Plus, you had to combine two different tactics. As long as the computer has time to churn through all the possibilities, it will get the solution. But you can't use that method, so your solving ability will depend in part on your ability to recognize patterns and form the appropriate plans in response.

We saw that a simple four-move combination included over 21 billion possible outcomes. It turns out that computers don't really examine every single one of them. They use a mathematical technique called *alpha-beta pruning* to cut back on the number of alternatives examined, and they use heuristics, or rules of thumb, that tell them what kinds of moves to try first.

Chess Talk

Alpha-beta pruning is a mathematical technique for enabling computers to cut down on the number of moves they must consider. The basic idea is that if the computer finds one way to refute a possible move, it can eliminate that move from its search, rather than continuing to find more ways to refute it.

For example, computers are often programmed to use the heuristic of looking first at checks and captures on the theory that these moves might be part of a forcing combination to win material or checkmate. (By the way, you should use the same heuristic!) And thanks to alpha-beta pruning, once they've discovered one refutation for a move (that is, one line of play that shows why a move is worse than its alternatives), they don't need to waste time finding more refutations.

Chess Lore

Before there were computers, there were people who claimed to have built machines that played chess. A notorious case is the Turk, a fake chess-playing machine created by Wolfgang von Kempelen, which was first displayed in 1796. It was a large desk with a chessboard on top and a life-sized mannequin seated behind it. (The mannequin wore a turban and was supposed to be from Arabia, hence the name "The Turk.") When you played against it, the mannequin would move the pieces. It would often win its games, and people were amazed! But of course it wasn't a real machine. Inside the chest (but not the mannequin) was a small human chess player who made the moves.

The "machine" had a clever system of cabinets that gave it the illusion of being empty inside. It fooled people for a long time, but by 1820 several authors had deduced the trick.

But even with these time-saving measures, positions where a computer can calculate out to checkmate are rare. Because in most positions there are no moves that force an immediate win, how does the computer decide what move to play? The search operates in just the same way, but instead of marking each position as a win, loss, or draw, the computer "evaluates" the position: It assigns each position in the search a numeric score representing how favorable (or unfavorable) the computer's algorithm says that position is for the side to move. Then the backtracking procedure can find the variation likely to lead to the "best" (as measured by the evaluation formula) position a few moves down the road, even if it is not actually a checkmate.

In fact, this process is not unique to computers. We humans do something similar when we seek positions that give us as big an advantage as possible. We try to win material, gain space, increase the mobility of our pieces, develop an advantage in force near the king, create passed pawns, give our opponent weak squares, and so on. The only difference is that whereas we make a judgment, the computer performs a mathematical calculation.

Chess Lore _____

Why do you suppose computer scientists began programming machines to play chess in the first place? Were they already chess players who simply jumped at a chance to bring their hobby into their work? Well, that might have been true for a few of them, but beyond that these scientists considered that computers are tools for solving problems, and they recognized games like chess provide a good way to study problem-solving techniques.

The act of selecting a chess move has a lot in common with other tasks to which we might want to apply a computer—choosing the best way to invest our money, or selecting a route to navigate through city traffic. Answering these and countless other questions involves the same fundamental steps as chess thought by identifying possible alternative moves, calculating ahead the consequences for different choices, and evaluating the resulting situations. But for computer scientists, focusing on chess offers the added benefits of precise rules (that is, you know with certainty what choices are possible and which ones are illegal in any position) and an unambiguous measure of success (winning the game!). Real-life problems are often messier than that, which makes them a less convenient environment for developing problem-solving theory.

If you're a computer programmer who would like to learn more about chess programming, Paul Verhelst's web page (www.xs4all.nl/~verhelst/chess/programming.html) is a great source of links to all sorts of information and contacts on this topic.

How can a mathematical calculation take the place of a judgment? All these strategic elements, to some extent, can be quantified. The computer can add up the point values of each side's pieces (remember the chart in Chapter 5), it can measure how much space (that is, how many squares) each side controls, it can measure how many squares each piece can move to, and so on. Some factors are harder to measure. For example, king safety, a critical one, depends on the complex relationships between pawn structure, piece placement, which particular pieces are on the board, and so on. So it's difficult to reduce it to a single number. But some factors can be accounted for quite nicely by adjusting the values of the pieces; for example, a white rook might be worth 5 points normally, but 5.5 when it's on the seventh rank.

A numerical weight must be assigned to each factor to reflect its importance relative to each other factor. We know that, all else being equal, material is the most important factor, so it usually gets the highest number. The weights assigned to other factors are correspondingly lower. In the end, the weighted sum of all the factors yields a single number, and this number is the computer's evaluation of the position! In the very early days of computer chess, programmers decided to normalize their evaluations so that the material value of one pawn is the standard unit of measure. Doing so makes computer evaluations line up nicely with the traditional material point chart from Chapter 5. Thus, a typical computer evaluation might rate a position as +1.78, which means that the program thinks White has an advantage worth about 1.78 pawns.

You might have noticed a problem with this numerical approach to evaluating chess positions. Suppose that a computer playing White reached the position of Diagram 6 in its analysis but it didn't have time to search further. It would have to apply an evaluation function like the one just discussed to rate White's prospects. Because Black has an extra rook and minor piece, the score will probably be heavily in Black's favor, since material considerations will outweigh the fact that White's pawn, knight, and queen are temporarily well-placed near Black's king. After all, if White couldn't give mate in two moves, he would probably lose. An experienced human might "smell a rat" in this position, and figure that because his king is in such danger he shouldn't aim for this position (with Black), because even if he can't see it, there might be checkmate somewhere. Or he might figure that if he's going to go for this position, he had better look extra hard to make sure there isn't a checkmate somewhere. But the computer lacks these kinds of intuitive hunches. If it stops searching here, and applies its evaluation function, then it would be making a big mistake, because further search would reveal that in fact White is winning. This kind of mistake is called the horizon effect.

Virtually all chess programs use the basic algorithm outlined so far to decide which moves to make, though some implement it better than others, and each has its own special evaluation function. Sophisticated programs can extend their search deeper in cases like Diagram 6, but the basic weakness still remains. They will see every tactic, especially involving checkmate and material gain or loss, only up to the depth they can search in the time allotted. Everything beyond is invisible.

What About Artificial Intelligence?

You may have heard about something called *artificial intelligence*. And you've almost certainly heard about the best chess computer in the world, Deep Blue. Certainly Deep Blue is an example of a computer that plays chess well! Did Deep Blue use artificial intelligence? And does that mean it was "thinking"?

The definition of artificial intelligence (also known as AI) is a complicated subject. Even among experts there is no clear agreement on what it is! But basically, AI refers to any method a computer uses to solve a problem that seems to require intelligence to solve. (You can see how a definition like this would be open to interpretation!) If a computer is using methods to solve a problem other than executing an algorithm that reaches a solution directly, you could say that computer is using AI. (So for example, your calculator is not using AI, because to add two numbers, it executes an algorithm that directly leads to the solution.)

Deep Blue did use some AI methods. One of them is the alpha-beta pruning method I mentioned in the previous section. Another is called *machine learning*. The basic idea behind machine learning is to get the computer to run a calculation, and then compare the result of that calculation to an outside source already known to be correct. The computer then runs another program to analyze the similarities and differences between the result of its calculations and the validated results from the outside source. Then the computer runs yet another program to adjust how it performs its calculation, so that the next time it gets closer to the known, correct answer.

Chess Talk _____

Artificial intelligence (also known as AI) refers to any method a computer uses to solve a problem that requires intelligence to solve. Even among computer science experts, there is a lot of debate about exactly what counts as AI!

Chess Talk _____

Machine learning is a technique that enables computers to "learn" through experience. The basic idea is to create a program that allows the computer to compare the result of its calculation with the result of an external, correct calculation, and then to adjust how it makes future calculations on the basis of that comparison.

The people who programmed Deep Blue used machine learning at some points when building its evaluation function. They did this by comparing how Deep Blue evaluated positions with how grandmasters evaluated positions. When Deep Blue made errors in its evaluation compared to the grandmaster evaluation, Deep Blue adjusted its evaluation function to get closer to the grandmaster's judgment. However, most of the adjustment to Deep Blue's evaluation function was done "manually," by the programmers, and not by Deep Blue.

Deep Blue also used a third technique that one could call AI. A lot of effort went into developing a "selective search" technique. The basic idea here is that if the computer identifies a variation where each side's responses seem to be forced for a certain number of moves, it will follow that variation out to the end. In this way Deep Blue emulated something that humans do by focusing on the relevant moves. Alpha-beta pruning allows it to eliminate certain moves; heuristics allow it to examine certain moves first; and selective search allows it to examine certain combinations beyond what would otherwise be the limit of how many moves it could look ahead.

So is Deep Blue an example of AI? It did employ AI techniques, and those techniques did help it defeat Kasparov. But it's also true that much of the "horsepower" it had came from the brute-force methods I described in the last section by calculating millions and millions of moves each second, and applying the same mathematical calculation to each move. Because that's not anything like how humans play chess, it violates many scientists' sense of what constitutes AI. In the end, although AI gave it the extra push needed to win, Deep Blue still fundamentally relied much more on traditional, "calculator-like" techniques.

How is it possible for a computer to do something that seems to require human intelligence, yet not really be a good example of AI? We could probably keep a whole room full of philosophers busy with that question! But the basic answer is simple: There's more than one way to skin a cat. Humans play chess in a very nonalgorithmic way. (Compare that to how we add numbers. When we do it right, we're basically just executing an algorithm the same way a calculator does.) But it turns out that chess can also be approached by using (mainly) brute force and algorithms, which is how virtually all computers play chess, including Deep Blue.

One more thing is worth keeping in mind. AI only refers to a set of problem-solving techniques. It doesn't say anything about being conscious or having feelings. No matter how your computer plays chess, it's no more aware of playing chess than your calculator is of adding numbers, or your oven is of cooking food.

Will the Computer Overtake Us?

There are two basic ways to make a computer play better chess. Speed it up so it can see more possibilities, or give it more knowledge so it can evaluate the resulting positions better. Both of these techniques have been used to make computers stronger and stronger. Eventually, computers will get stronger than humans. Humans just can't get that much smarter, whereas computers can keep getting faster and can get better programs. Inevitably, they will surpass us. But for now the best human chess players are still as good as the best computers, and we can still do things they can't!

Chess Lore _____

A common misconception is the belief that in order to build and program a computer that plays chess well, you have to be a good chess player yourself. The misconception is based on the idea that chess-playing programs think the same way humans do. In fact, the programs rely heavily on their number-crunching power for their ability.

You need to know something about chess to program the evaluation function. However, it turns out that a grandmaster level of understanding is not necessary. For programming a computer to play chess, a solid understanding of the game such as you received in Parts 2 and 3 of this book is more than enough.

The success of various computer scientists shows the truth of this. For example, Belle's principal creator, Ken Thompson, is an average amateur chess player who almost never competes in tournaments. And what about the Deep Blue scientific team? Three members (Gerry Brody, Joe Hoane, and C. J. Tan) didn't even play chess before joining the project. The super-speedy Deep Blue chess processors were created by Feng-Hsiung Hsu, an amateur player. The best chess player on the team is Murray Campbell, a software specialist, who in his best days played at the level of national master, but even that is far below grandmaster level, and he hasn't played in tournaments for several years.

In May 1997, then–world chess champion Garry Kasparov played the world's strongest computer, Deep Blue. Kasparov was counting on the strength of his judgment and planning skills to overcome the brute force of the computer. He lost that match. Yet, if he had tried less hard to take advantage of the weaknesses of the computer, he might have won. Many people thought Kasparov lost because he wasn't smart enough. Ironically, he may have been too smart for his own good.

Man versus Machine

The first digital computer was switched on over 50 years ago in Philadelphia. Since then, scientists have been fascinated with the idea of computers playing chess. Especially within the artificial intelligence community, the game was adopted as a model arena for studying human thought. The pioneers of computer science, including Alan Turing, Claude Shannon, and Herbert Simon, were also pioneers of computer chess. In the 1950s and 1960s, enthusiasm was high for programming the machine to play the same way humans did (that is, using AI). However, the results of these efforts were poor. By the 1970s, the brute-force approach (of exhaustively considering all possible moves and countermoves as far out as possible), discussed earlier in this chapter, became the dominant paradigm. By 1983 the AT&T research project Belle was ready to become the first computer system to earn the master title from the U.S. Chess Federation.

This achievement was soon surpassed by Deep Thought, developed by a group of graduate students at Carnegie Mellon University, which sustained a rating in the grandmaster range during 1988 and 1989.

Clearly superior to all its (silicon) competitors, Deep Thought was invited to play a two-game match against Garry Kasparov in New York in late 1989. It was crushed. But its developers were not dispirited because IBM's research department had just agreed to hire them to work on its next-generation successor, eventually named Deep Blue (in part to reflect the corporate color of its sponsor).

Belle, Deep Thought, and Deep Blue share a key property. They all rely on microprocessor chips that are custom designed and built to work only on chess problems. By making the processes of generating legal moves, evaluating positions, and even managing the tree of possible variations part of the computer's hardware instead of its software, Deep Blue can now examine as many as 200 million future positions in just one second. With about 150 seconds to think about each move during a game played under regulation tournament conditions, it can "see" as many as 30 billion positions in the course of calculating a move. The numbers defy comprehension. When you consider how relatively few positions a human player—even a grandmaster—considers, it's a testimony to the enormous power of judgment and intuition that we don't get crushed every time! A little intelligent pattern matching can negate a brute force examination of *billions* of positions.

Kasparov played an earlier version of Deep Blue in February 1996 in a six-game match held in Philadelphia. Kasparov defeated the machine 4–2 and pocketed $400,000 for his efforts, but the victory was not easy.

The position in Diagram 8 arose in the first game. Kasparov, as Black, has given up a pawn and let his pawn structure be shattered (he has three pawn islands, all containing only isolated pawns) in return for an attack against Deep Blue's king, which looks dangerously undefended by its wayward army. A human opponent would never have allowed such a position as White, out of fear of Kasparov's attack or uncertainty about whether he had accurately calculated a defense. But Deep Blue doesn't worry about such things. Like all computers, it is unemotional and excels at short-term defense, where seeing every possibility for the opponent and calculating them out is a vital skill. The game concludes 31.g3 Nd3 32.Rc7 Re8 33.Nd6 Re1+ 34.Kh2 Nxf2 35.Nxf7+ Kg7 36.Ng5+ Kh6 37.Rxh7+. Kasparov resigns, because even though he is threatening ...Rh1#, after 37...Kg6 38.Qg8+ Kf5 39.Nxf3 his attack will be over, his king exposed in the middle of the board, and his army three pawns behind.

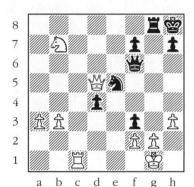

Diagram 8: White to move (Deep Blue–Kasparov, Philadelphia, Game 1, 1996).

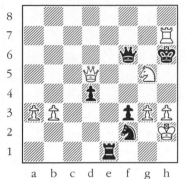

Diagram 9: Black resigns after 37.Rxh7+.

This shocking result was reported by the media around the world. For the first time ever, a world champion had lost to a computer in a regulation game. But Kasparov learned from his mistakes and came back to win a long strategic struggle in the second game and to draw the third and fourth encounters. Kasparov then won the last two games to blaze ahead to a convincing 4–2 victory. Yet the dramatic loss in the first game, followed by the come-from-behind surge by Kasparov, generated an incredible excitement. A rematch was quickly organized with an even larger prize of $700,000 if Kasparov won. (Kasparov would get $400,000 if he lost, equal to the winning prize for the 1996 match.) Meanwhile, the IBM scientists went back to the laboratory.

Kasparov met Deep Blue again in New York in May 1997. Kasparov won the first game in fine style. The critical position is shown in Diagram 10.

In this complicated position, the computer has made a poor evaluation. It saw a chance to attack White's position by playing 28...f5 29.exf5 e4. But Kasparov understands that he can afford to sacrifice material by playing 30.f4! Bxe2 (Black cannot afford to expose his king by opening the g-file with 30...Bxf4 31.gxf4) 31.fxg5 (see Diagram 11).

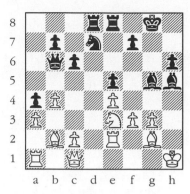

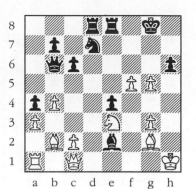

Diagram 10: Black to move
(Kasparov–Deep Blue, New York,
Game 1, 1997).

Diagram 11: Black to move, but
White has fantastic compensation
for the exchange.

Black has a material advantage—a quantifiable factor, well-suited to a computer's evaluation function. But his king is exposed, and White's dark-squared bishop is a monster. These are the sort of fuzzy, pattern-based considerations that a computer program is apt to misjudge. In any case, this is a hard position for even the best humans to assess, let alone a computer. But Kasparov quickly proves he has a tremendous advantage. Deep Blue plays 31...Ne5 (not 31...hxg5?? 32.Nc4! attacking the queen and threatening 33.Qxg5+), and Kasparov plays 32.g6. Now Kasparov has two connected passed pawns, and he exploits this advantage mercilessly: 32...Bf3 33.Bc3! Qb5 34.Qf1! Qxf1+ 35.Rxf1 h5 36.Kg1 Kf8 37.Bh3! b5 38.Kf2 Kg7 39.g4! Kh6 40.Rg1 hxg4 41.Bxg4 Bxg4 42.Nxg4+ Nxg4 43.Rxg4 Rd5 44.f6 Rd1 45.g7 (see Diagram 12).

The computer gives up here, because it realizes it is going to lose at least a rook to stop White from making a queen.

Kasparov ran into trouble in the second game, however. Part of his trademark style is to play active, aggressive chess with Black, but it seems that Kasparov was afraid that this would play too much into Deep Blue's strengths. So in game two, Kasparov chose to play a very passive opening with Black. Clearly, he was betting that he would gain more by playing against Deep Blue's weakness than he would lose by playing away from his own strength. This was a fatal miscalculation. The critical position is shown in Diagram 13.

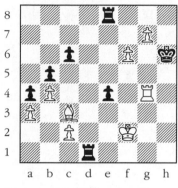

Diagram 12: Black resigned because White is going to make a queen.

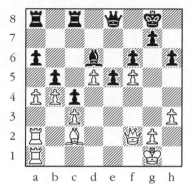

Diagram 13: White to move (Deep Blue–Kasparov, New York, Game 2, 1997).

Deep Blue has played very well and has completely outplayed Kasparov. Black's position is very passive. But Kasparov is banking on a tricky resource. He knows that computers typically love material, so he is inviting Deep Blue to play what looks like a very strong move: 36.Qb6. The point of this move is to attack both Black's bishop and his queenside pawns. But Kasparov has prepared a clever response: 36...Qe7! (sacrificing a pawn) 37.axb5 Rab8! (sacrificing a second pawn) 38.Qxa6 e4! (see Diagram 14).

Although Black is down two pawns, he is getting a lot of counterplay on the dark squares. Still, White can defend this position and hold on to its extra pawns. And Kasparov saw that; you might say he not only saw it, he was counting on it! He wanted the computer to make the classic mistake of trading a large and safe positional advantage for a murky material advantage. The apparent defensibility of White's position was part of what convinced Kasparov that Deep Blue would indeed go for 36.Qb6.

But this computer is too clever! Deep Blue rejects this position based on its evaluation function. It chooses instead to play 36.axb5 axb5 37.Be4! (see Diagram 15).

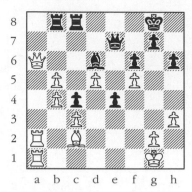

Diagram 14: White to move (a possible position from Deep Blue–Kasparov, New York, Game 2, 1997).

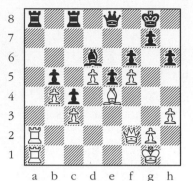

Diagram 15: White has played 36.axb5 axb5 37.Be4!.

White correctly maintains the grip on the position. For a top human grandmaster, this would be a routine decision. But for a computer to reject material gain for this kind of positional advantage was amazing. The crowd literally gasped when it saw what happened, and Kasparov's face fell. Although it turns out that Kasparov missed a miraculous drawing resource on the very last move, he was completely outplayed by Deep Blue, and he lost only eight moves later.

Deep Blue played a terrific game. But it needs to be emphasized that Kasparov made the first mistake by playing positions that go against his own style. This is a very basic mistake when playing anyone, including a computer. Kasparov was visibly upset at making this mistake and clearly intimidated by the ability Deep Blue demonstrated.

Unfortunately, Kasparov showed his emotion by indirectly accusing IBM of cheating by somehow "overriding" the computer from going after the pawns. The most unfortunate thing about this transparently ridiculous accusation is that Kasparov seems to have really believed it. This may have influenced what happened next.

Three more games produced three hard-fought draws. And that left Game 6 as the deciding contest. Once again, Kasparov had Black. And once again, he employed a dubious opening strategy. This time, the strategy he chose was not just suspect: It was outright bad! Kasparov played a line that is known to be very strong for White because of a piece sacrifice. Kasparov seems to have convinced himself that Deep Blue would not play this sacrifice because it would not "like" being down material. This was a catastrophic miscalculation. Deep Blue did exactly what its opening database told it to do and sacrificed the piece. Not only did Kasparov have an objectively very bad position, he was manifestly in no emotional state to play it, and Deep Blue won easily.

Chess Lore _____

Here is the complete score of Game 6 between Kasparov and Deep Blue. Take out your chess set and see how the machine beat the world chess champion! 1.e4 c6 2.d4 d5 3.Nc3 dxe4 4.Nxe4 Nd7 5.Ng5 Ngf6 6.Bd3 e6 7.N1f3 h6?? (This is a well-known error. Black should develop with 7...Bd6.) 8.Nxe6! Qe7 9.O-O fxe6 (not 9...Qxe6?? 10.Re1!) 10.Bg6+ Kd8 11.Bf4 (Grandmaster practice has shown that White's attack is overwhelming here.) 11...b5 12.a4 Bb7 13.Re1 Nd5 14.Bg3 Kc8 15.axb5 cxb5 16.Qd3 Bc6 17.Bf5! exf5 18.Rxe7 Bxe7 19.c4 and Kasparov resigns. Even though Kasparov still has a material advantage, White's attack will quickly win more material.

Garry Kasparov continues to play chess actively, and although he lost the World Championship in 2000 (see Chapter 16), he is still the highest rated player in the world. Deep Blue, on the other hand, has "retired"; IBM is putting its resources to other uses, and it has no plans to bring Deep Blue back. Other computers have gotten very good, but as yet none has attained the level of Deep Blue.

There have been other high-profile man-versus-machine exhibition matches since 1997, although none of them have attracted the massive attention garnered by the 1997 Kasparov–Deep Blue duel. In 2002, world champion Vladimir Kramnik played to a 4–4 tie against a program named Deep Fritz. And in early 2003, Kasparov was ready to try his once more against a computer, this time called Deep Junior. (The fashion in naming these top programs shows the impact of Deep Blue's achievement!) That match was also tied, by the score of 3–3. It ended controversially when, in the decisive final game, Kasparov accepted a draw in a position where he stood better. Some people saw in this further evidence of Kasparov's supposed "problem" with the psychology of playing against computers.

What Does The Rise of Computers Mean for Us?

People were amazed when Deep Blue beat Kasparov, as it showed that a computer could defeat the best human in the world in a game that was supposed to be the pinnacle of human intelligence. The matches of the past several years have now shown that an ordinary PC (not a computer specifically built only to play chess, such as Deep Blue) can play competitively against the best grandmasters. Unfortunately, in my view, many people focus on the wrong aspect of the rise of computers in chess. The truly interesting story is not what it means for human intelligence, but what it means for chess.

The ability of computers to play chess with the best grandmasters is extremely impressive. But it doesn't give us any reason to think about computers differently. Computers are still machines. They don't feel, they don't have any conscious awareness, and they don't even "think" in the way humans do. They do the same things they have always done. One of the things they do is play chess. Deep Blue played better than any machine ever had before, but it still played basically the same way that machines have always played. Kasparov lost because Deep Blue played a little bit faster and a little bit smarter than any machine had done before. (Plus Kasparov did not play very well compared to some of his previous matches.) The IBM team deserves tremendous credit for their accomplishment; but in the final analysis, they built a better machine, not a different one.

Now PCs are playing at the same level as the best grandmasters because commercial chess software programs have gotten very good, and because the power of the PC has multiplied over the past decade. The increasing ability of the software and hardware is an impressive testament to human ingenuity. But once again, there is nothing radically different about the way these computers are playing chess; they are still "crunching numbers" rather than "playing a game."

On the other hand, the rise of computers should cause us to think differently about the game of chess. For over 1,500 years, skill at chess has been seen as a sign of intelligence. ("The ultimate test of cerebral fitness," as the popular song "One Night in Bangkok" from the musical *Chess* put it—see Chapter 1.) But the rise of computers shows us that you don't necessarily need human intelligence to beat the smartest humans at chess! What other tasks will we learn can be done as well or better than humans in ways other than through human intelligence? And what will experience show us are the things that humans are uniquely good at?

Actually, right now and for a few short years, chess is in a class by itself. Think about almost anything in the world, and either machines or humans are clearly better at it. Machines are better at lifting heavy objects, but humans are better at throwing a touchdown pass. Machines are better at complicated mathematical calculations, but humans are better at writing poetry. And that's natural, because we can't build a machine that works like a human does.

But chess is an amazing exception. At this brief moment in history, even though computers and humans play chess entirely differently, the best computers and the best humans find themselves at almost exactly at the same level. It won't last. Eventually, computers will get faster and smarter, and they will be better at chess than humans. But surely we should celebrate this unique moment in history! I literally can't think of a single other activity where machines and humans are equally proficient, even as they operate in entirely different ways. Can you?

In the end, though, computers are tools just as all machines are tools. We can use them however we want to. I think we should use them to enhance our enjoyment of the game of chess. Computers can be opponents whenever we want. They can store more information, and make that information easier to access, than anyone could possibly have imagined just a few years ago. They can connect us with an opponent half a world away. They can help explain to the beginner chess player what is happening in a game between grandmasters. And who knows how many other ways this amazing machine can help us enjoy chess?

What does it all mean? It means whatever we want it to mean. I think we should want it to mean that the fun is just beginning!

The Least You Need to Know

- Computers exhaustively search through all future moves and countermoves to decide what to do in any situation.

- Humans rely less on search but more on pattern recognition, judgment, and planning to make decisions.

- The best computers and the best humans play chess entirely differently, yet for the moment they play equally well.

- Deep Blue has not played since it defeated Garry Kasparov in May 1997.

- Over the last few years, everyday PCs running commercially available software have tied matches against the world's best computers.

- Computers have a tremendous capability to enhance our enjoyment of the game of chess. This may be the true significance of the rise of computers.

Chapter 20

How to Beat the !?%@&?›!# Computer

In This Chapter

◆ Avoiding the computer's strengths

◆ Taking advantage of the computer's weaknesses

◆ Compensating for human frailties

Now that computers play chess—and play chess well—you need never be without someone (or at least something) to play chess with. Your computer is always ready to play whenever you are, it will record the moves for you, and it's never rude. In some ways, it's the perfect opponent.

I think it's great that computers can play chess, although I don't recommend that you play only them. Computers and humans play chess differently, so you can't experience the full range of possibilities of chess unless you play against both. Still, they're so convenient that for many of us they're a godsend, enabling us to play our favorite game when otherwise we wouldn't be able to find an opponent.

There's just one problem. Those darn machines sometimes play too well! I think the most common question I hear from people is whether I can beat computers. When I tell them yes, they often ask another question: "How can I beat my computer?" This chapter gives you some tips for beating your silicon opponent.

There's No Magic Bullet

First, the bad news: There's no foolproof method. The computer is playing chess, and you're playing chess. Whoever plays better will win, and that means you're going to have to play better than the computer to win. In other words, the best way to beat your computer is to improve your game. And because some computers play a very good game, it's not always going to be possible to improve your game enough.

On the other hand, that might not be such bad news after all. What fun would playing your computer be if you beat it by doing some trick? You might as well turn the thing off! So the tips I'm going to explain to you aren't meant to replace what you've learned in the rest of the book; they're meant to supplement it. You can't beat the machine by magic. But you can think about the tactics and strategies you've learned, and apply them intelligently in the knowledge that you're playing a machine. The machine has certain strengths, but it also has certain weaknesses. Its most important weakness is that it does not learn and adapt the way you can. If you keep the tips in mind, I'll explain how to apply them where they seem relevant. You'll definitely improve your results against the computer.

> **Patrick's Pointers**
>
> Bobby Fischer once said that the best kind of psychological warfare is playing good moves. He was talking about playing other people (and he was right!), but it's especially true when playing against the computer.

The Computer's Strengths

A computer has two advantages over humans:

- Because the computer is a machine, it never gets tired, careless, cocky, or upset. It always plays its 100 percent best game.

- Because the computer "sees" so many positions—and does so perfectly—its tactical ability is formidable.

"The Chess Machine"

From the period 1914 to 1924, José Capablanca lost only one game in all the tournaments he played in. He played so steadily and without mistakes that he got the nickname "the chess machine." But that was nothing compared to real chess machines! No human, no matter how steady or how consistent, can match the 100-percent performance that a computer makes every single time.

But that doesn't mean you shouldn't try. One of the things the computer does is challenge you to play more consistently. Because it will pounce on any careless errors you make, if you want to beat it you have to eliminate those errors the best you can.

This means two things. First, you have to be as objective as possible. You can't make a move that's too ambitious—say, a move that tries to win a position you should be trying to draw—because if you do, the computer will just pounce on you. Of course this is always true, but the difference is that against a human, sometimes you can bluff your opponent by your attitude. A human might be intimidated by the confident way you make a move or by the fact that you've beaten him before. Not a computer! One way that computers challenge you to become better players is that they will never be bluffed by an attitude, so the only way to beat them is by playing your best chess.

The second thing is that you shouldn't play when you're tired, hungry, or distracted. Once again, this is also true for human opponents, but sometimes when playing a human the same circumstances have an equal effect on both players. For example, if you and your friend play until dawn, both of you will probably play worse, and so fatigue may not have a big overall effect on the outcome of the games. But try doing that against a computer, and I guarantee you'll see a big difference!

> **Patrick's Pointers**
>
> When I play my computer, I adopt the "midnight rule": No playing after midnight! Learn your own physical and emotional limitations, and respect them. You can't expect to do as well as you'd like against a computer if you play when you're hungry, tired, or distracted, and you won't learn as much from those games either.

20/20 Vision

If you read Chapter 19, you know that there's a *big* difference between how many moves the computer considers, and how many we humans do. The computer examines more than a million times more moves! But not only that, it also never gets confused, or has trouble "seeing" the position. When reading the earlier chapters, if you've been trying to follow some of the positions without playing them out on a chess set, or without looking at every diagram, you've probably experienced some difficulty in remembering where all the pieces are. That's completely normal. Even grandmasters often have trouble following a game without playing it out on a set; it's just part of the way we humans are built. The computer has no such problem. However, it does have a limit as to how many moves ahead it can see in any position, as you know from Chapter 19. (Where that limit exists—the "horizon"—varies depending upon the program and what machine it's running on.) But within the bounds of what it can "see," the computer never gets confused, never forgets which pieces are where or whose turn it is.

The bottom line? The computer will see near-term tactics perfectly, no matter how hidden they are. Once again, the computer challenges you to play better because when playing the computer, it becomes much more important to spot all the tactics in a position. But if you want to beat the computer, my advice is to avoid positions that are "confusing" as much as possible. Steer for positions that can be played according to strategy; stay away from positions that are purely tactical.

Diagrams 1 and 2 are taken from two of my own games against computers. Diagram 1 shows the kind of position you should be very careful about playing. Both kings are potentially exposed, although Black's is in more danger than White's. To compensate for his exposed king, Black has a material advantage. To further add to the confusion, the pieces are scattered all over the board! Whatever is the correct evaluation, it's impossible for either side to play this position well without seeing a lot of tactics.

Chess Lore

Some of the examples of anti-computer play in this chapter come from my own games in the Harvard Cup Human Versus Computer Chess Challenge, a man-versus-machine tournament that was held each year from 1989 to 1995. In the Harvard Cup, a team of American grandmasters faced a team of computer systems (hardware/software combinations) in a match format, with each human playing each machine, and each side getting 25 minutes to play each game. (Regulation tournament play is slower; computers tend to do better the less time each side gets.) In 1989, the computers scored 9 percent of the possible points, but by 1995 they were up to 35 percent. The best computer performance in the Cup was by David Kittinger's program WChess, which scored +4 =2 running on a Pentium-based PC in 1994. (I know how tough it was: It beat me!) The most successful grandmaster in the history of the Cup is Joel Benjamin, who had three first-place finishes and a cumulative score of 17/20 in three appearances from 1993 to 1995.

As it happens, this position comes from an opening I've studied deeply, and I'm convinced that Black stands well. I'd be happy to play Black against any human in the world. But the computer is so good in these "crazy" positions that even though Black has an advantage, I should have been wary about going into this position against the computer. In fact, I soon missed a tactic and lost the game.

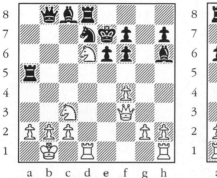

Diagram 1: White to move
(WChess–Wolff, Harvard Cup,
1994).

Diagram 2: Black to move
(Wolff–Zarkov X, Harvard Cup,
1994).

Blunders _____

There's a danger that if you always avoid positions the computer plays well, you won't get better at playing those positions. Don't be a slave to the thrill of beating your computer. Play different openings and different types of positions so you can develop all your skills, and keep the tips in mind for when you want to take out your frustration.

Diagram 2, by contrast, shows a much "quieter" position. I'd say that White has a small but sure advantage because of his better pawn structure. White's advantage in Diagram 2 is certainly less than Black's advantage in Diagram 1, but against the computer, in a position where tactics are less important, your chances of winning are better because the computer can't exploit its biggest strengths. I won the position in Diagram 2 very easily.

The Computer's Weaknesses

The computer is dumb.

What I mean is that it doesn't really "think" the way you or I think. It can't learn, it can't make a judgment call, it can't make plans. Instead, it always plays according to the *evaluation function* that's been programmed into it. Such a function tends to make two characteristic mistakes that you can take advantage of.

Greed Is Bad

If you've read the rest of this book, you know that material is very important, yet it can sometimes be outweighed by other factors. One of the hardest judgments to make is to decide when a strategic advantage outweighs a material advantage. Still, there are some cases that are pretty clear to everyone but computers. Because the computer follows an evaluation function that measures everything in terms of pawns, for the computer one more pawn is always good. Most of the time that's true, but sometimes it's obviously not. Diagrams 3–5 show one of my favorite examples of this.

Diagram 3: Black to move (Wolff–Socrates, Harvard Cup, 1993).

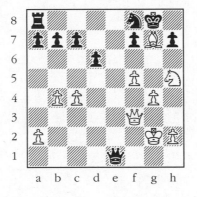

It's been a heck of a battle. Earlier in the game, I sacrificed a pawn for good compensation, and then launched an attack that would have succeeded had I played correctly. But I made some mistakes, and the computer outplayed me. Now the computer has a winning position if it plays correctly.

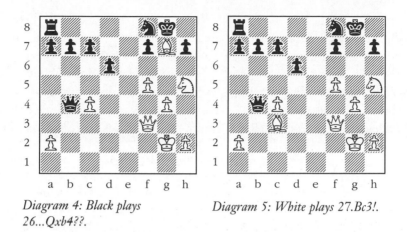

Diagram 4: Black plays 26...Qxb4??.

Diagram 5: White plays 27.Bc3!.

It's not obvious how Black should play, but you can understand what two moves Black should consider if you think the position through. Black has a material advantage, but his king is still exposed and his knight and rook are not active. Black needs to activate his pieces and defend his king. He'd also like to exchange pieces if he could, and he'd like to coordinate with the queen on e1 to cause problems for White's king, which is also exposed. Put all of that together, and two moves to consider are 26...Re8, to activate the rook and threaten 27...Re2+ or 27...Qe2+; and 26...Nd7, to activate the knight (and if 27.Qxb7 then 27...Re8). It would take a lot more thinking to decide which move is better, but at least you can see that 26...Re8 and 26...Nd7 are two of the best moves to consider.

> ### Patrick's Pointers
>
> Another way the computer's greed gets it into trouble is that it will take pawns with its queen even if doing so gets the queen trapped, so long as it doesn't see the queen being taken right away. Therefore, one strategy is to dangle a "poisoned pawn" in front of the computer's queen. But be careful! A computer can be very resourceful in rescuing the queen once it's apparently trapped.

Instead, the computer played an incredibly awful move. It played 26...Qxb4?? (see Diagram 4). What does this pawn have to do with Black's exposed king? Nothing. Common sense says that even if you don't see the problem with taking another pawn, it's a dumb idea: Black doesn't need another pawn, Black needs to take care of the king! But the computer doesn't have "common sense." According to its evaluation function, one more pawn increases its advantage by one point, and if it doesn't see the danger to its king then it will take the pawn every time.

In fact, after 27.Bc3! (see Diagram 5), White attacks the queen and sets up a deadly check on f6 for the knight. That the check is deadly isn't obvious, and the proof that White is now winning goes many moves deep. What's obvious—to everyone except the computer—is that Black shouldn't even allow the possibility. After 27...Qxc4 28.Nf6+ Kh8 29.Qe3!, my attack was in full swing, and I soon won.

Patrick's Pointers

Long-range plans tend to be more important in closed positions, whereas tactics tend to be more important in open positions. One good idea is to keep the position closed as long as you can, prepare to mount an attack on one side of the board, and refrain from opening the position up until the last moment. The computer often won't recognize that an attack is coming and will shift its pieces back and forth to no purpose.

Aimless Wandering

The computer has a function for evaluating positions, but it has no way to come up with a plan. As Chapter 19 explains, the way it chooses a move is to play whatever move leads to the position it assigns the highest value to. It's never really "aiming" for any kind of position at all, it's just playing whatever move happens to get the biggest number according to its evaluation function. I've already said that in one way this gives the computer an advantage: Because it looks at every single move in every position it considers, it doesn't overlook anything; so when one move makes a big difference—such as a tactic that wins material—it's sure to see it. But this aimlessness can also be a big disadvantage, because the computer can't form an idea of what position it ought to aim for several moves down the line. Garry Kasparov was able to exploit this weakness in the sixth and final game of his first match against Deep Blue in Philadelphia, February 1996. Deep Blue could have tied the match by winning this game, but instead Kasparov crushed it. Let's see how (see Diagram 6).

White has a comfortable advantage because of his extra space and superior pieces, whereas Black's position is solid and not too bad. But here Deep Blue started playing far below the level of a strong grandmaster: 11...Nh5? 12.Re1 Nf4 13.Bb1 Bd6 14.g3! Ng6 (see Diagram 7).

Diagram 6: Black to move
(Kasparov–Deep Blue,
Philadelphia, Game 6, 1996).

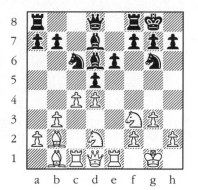

Diagram 7: Position after
14...Ng6.

White has improved the position of his rook (putting it on an open file) and his bishop (getting it out of the way of his other pieces while keeping it on its strong diagonal). Black has misplaced the knight (notice how it is "controlled" by the pawn on g3—see the section on the knight in Chapter 10 for more details) and the bishop (which is also frustrated by the strong pawn on g3).

Kasparov increased his advantage with some very strong moves: 15.Ne5! Rc8 16.Nxd7! Qxd7 17.Nf3 Bb4 18.Re3 Rfd8 (see Diagram 8). It might seem counter-intuitive for White to exchange his knight for Black's "bad" bishop, but this is where the genius of the World Champion comes to bear. Kasparov understood that it was more important for him to clear space for his own pieces and to weaken Black on the light squares.

Now Kasparov did two very smart things. He gained space on both the kingside and the queenside, and he closed the position up: 19.h4! Nge7 20.a3! Ba5 21.b4! Bc7 22.c5! (see Diagram 9).

Look what a strong grip White has on the position! He can expand on either side of the board at his leisure. A human would never have allowed such a passive position. But a computer—even such a strong computer as this original Deep Blue—just doesn't recognize the looming danger. With no immediate tactical problem within the horizon, a computer has no reason to believe anything is wrong. A human grandmaster would have opened the position up by playing ...dxc4 at some point, in order to ensure counterplay. The computer can't make such distinctions between positions, and so it doesn't realize how badly it stands.

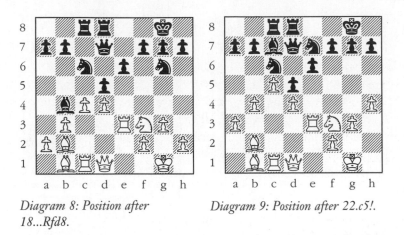

Diagram 8: Position after 18...Rfd8.

Diagram 9: Position after 22.c5!.

Deep Blue did nothing to impede White's progress over the next several moves: 22...Re8 23.Qd3! g6 24.Re2 Nf5 25.Bc3 h5 26.b5! Nce7 27.Bd2 Kg7 28.a4 Ra8 29.a5 (see Diagram 10).

Black's position has gotten steadily worse. White is taking more and more space, and he is driving Black's pieces backward. Also, he has positioned his pieces to aim more directly at Black's king. Why hasn't Deep Blue stopped this? Well, partly because it had a bad position to start with and it was facing a chess genius. But part of the problem is that Deep Blue just doesn't "get it." Its evaluation function is not sophisticated enough to make all the subtle tradeoffs necessary to handle a closed position dominated by strategic maneuvers. The proof is in its next decision, one that no grandmaster would have ever, ever made: 29...a6? 30.b6 Bb8?? (see Diagram 11).

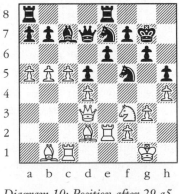

Diagram 10: Position after 29.a5.

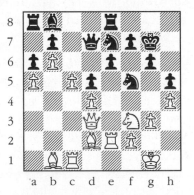

Diagram 11: Position after 30...Bb8??.

Take a look at Black's bishop and queen's rook, and then take another look at Black's last three moves. The bishop has no good square to move to and is trapping the rook. Black is practically down a rook! Suddenly White has a simple winning plan: focus all his energy on keeping the bishop on the terrible b8 square. Following this strategy, any attack is certain to succeed, because Black will never be able to use the rook. This simple strategic insight can overcome all the computer's deadly calculating power, because if the strategy is applied correctly none of the calculations can ever work without the use of that rook.

Kasparov's play was a model execution of this strategy: 31.Bc2 Nc6 32.Ba4! (this keeps Black locked up) 32...Re7 33.Bc3 Ne5? (this tactic only helps White, because it guarantees that the bishop will never again see the light of day) 34.dxe5 Qxa4 35.Nd4! Nxd4 36.Qxd4 (see Diagram 12).

> **CAUTION**
>
> **Blunders**
>
> Don't try so hard to play against the computer's weaknesses that you play bad moves, or play positions you don't like to play! Play to your strengths first, and to your opponent's weaknesses second. And this is just as true when you play humans as it is when you play computers.

Now if Black exchanges queens, White will win by playing c5-c6 and breaking through on the queenside (all the while keeping that bishop on the b8 square!). So Black retreated the queen, but this simply allowed White to shift the attack to the king: 36...Qd7 37.Bd2! Re8 38.Bg5! Rc8 39.Bf6+ Kh7 40.c6! (see Diagram 13).

Losing a pawn doesn't matter, what matters is breaking into Black's position while keeping that bishop under lock. If Black plays 40...Rxc6, then 41.Rec2! takes control of the c-file and infiltrates. So instead Deep Blue played 40...bxc6, but then resigned after 41.Qc5 Kh6 42.Rb2 Qb7 43.Rb4 (see Diagram 14).

Black can barely move anything! Finally, the concrete realization of White's advantage is close enough at hand that the computer could see what had been obvious to Kasparov for over a dozen moves: that Black could not defend. White's simple winning plan is to prepare g3-g4, expose the Black king, and attack. All the while, White keeps that bishop locked into b8, keeping Black's army cut off from defense. Whether one calculates 10 variations or 10 billion, none of the tactics in this position is ever going work for Black.

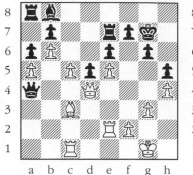

Diagram 12: Position after 36.Qxd4.

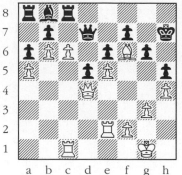

Diagram 13: Position after 40.c6!.

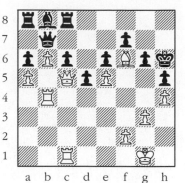

Diagram 14: Position after 43.Rb4, where Black resigned.

I can't say it strongly enough: If you want to play against the computer's weakness, aim for positions that are primarily strategic, rather than tactical. This is your advantage. Where strategy matters more than tactics, humans have the edge. And strategy tends to matter more than tactics primarily in closed positions.

Just be careful, though, not to fall into the trap Kasparov made for himself in his rematch against Deep Blue! You can only play against the computer's weaknesses when you play positions that are your strength. Play good moves. Play positions that you like to play. Only try to play against the computer's weaknesses after playing to your strengths.

The Least You Need to Know

♦ Be very careful when playing positions that are primarily tactical, and avoid them when possible.

♦ Be aware of your own physical and emotional limitations, and respect them.

♦ Aim for positions that are primarily strategic.

♦ Computers are terrible at playing closed positions because these require long-term planning; in closed positions, the computer tends to play aimlessly.

♦ The computer tends to be greedy and underestimate the danger to its queen or king, so try to use that to your advantage.

♦ Play to your strengths before playing against the computer's weaknesses.

♦ Don't be afraid to play positions the computer plays well. You can use the computer to train your own ability to play such positions better!

Chapter 21

It's Not Just a Game

In This Chapter

◆ Why many teachers are excited about chess

◆ Chess collectibles

◆ A few brain teasers

◆ A selection of inspiring or thought-provoking quotes

The whole point of chess is to *play* it, right? Well, yes and no. I hope that the previous chapters have given you some inkling of why, to a great many people, chess will always seem much more than "just a game."

You may have first picked up *The Complete Idiot's Guide to Chess* because you wanted to learn how to play chess better. I hope I've helped you do that. But my goal has also been to make this book as truly *complete* a resource as possible on everything about chess.

This final chapter covers some of the far corners of chess. Here it's not so much about playing chess as it is about appreciating the game in every possible way!

Can Chess Make You Smart?

One stereotype is that chess players are all "brains" and that only super-intellectuals can play it well. I hope this book has succeeded in puncturing that myth. But maybe there is some truth in *reversing* the cliché? You don't have to be a genius to play chess—but maybe playing chess can make you more of a genius! Many educators are finding that to be exactly the case.

In the mid-1970s, a teacher named Michael Sherman was working at Vaux Junior High, an inner-city school in Philadelphia. Many of his students came from low-income, fatherless homes. One thing that Sherman did was to start a chess team, the Bad Bishops. In a story that sounds like it was written in Hollywood, Sherman's so-called problem kids built up their chess program to the point where they traveled to San Clemente, California, for the 1977 National Scholastics tournament, and they won! The Bad Bishops would win the national title again in 1980 under teacher/coach Jeffrey Chesin. (I played two team members of The Bad Bishops myself in 1981 at a national scholastic chess tournament.)

However, the most remarkable thing about this story is not the Bad Bishops' *Bad News Bears*–style success in chess competitions. Sherman and Chesin also observed a remarkable improvement in the classroom performance of students who participated in the chess club. Attention spans and ability to concentrate improved while disruptive behavior declined.

When you think about it, it only makes sense. Chess is exercise for the mind. If lifting weights will develop your muscles, won't moving chess variations around in your head develop your brain? Chess trains critical thinking and problem solving. It rewards concentration and teaches that decisions have consequences.

The game also built up the self-confidence of Vaux's students, most of whom were not accustomed to thinking of themselves as excelling in "intellectual" activities. At the same time, chess teaches self-reliance; there are no excuses, no one but yourself to blame if you lose. Chess rewards realistic self-criticism and dedicated efforts to improve on your weaknesses. Is it any wonder that kids who practiced these life skills for the sake of chess saw payoff in other parts of their lives?

Teachers all over the country were quick to note what was happening at Vaux and a few other trailblazing schools. Research studies soon followed, to try to nail down the benefits of teaching chess to kids. For example, IBM sponsored a two-year study of the effects of chess in the District Nine schools in the Bronx, New York. In reading tests, students who joined chess clubs were found to outperform a control group who did not join chess clubs. Other studies have suggested that chess may improve performance in classroom math.

Chess also has been shown to increase school attendance, simply because chess is fun and kids who have had a taste of it want to be around to get more. Plus, it's an activity that can be played indoors or out, where girls and boys can compete together on equal footing, and which does not require special facilities or expensive equipment! As a result, more and more schools today have active, thriving chess clubs. The USCF's national scholastic championship tournaments attract thousands of kids from all over the country. More kids are playing chess today than ever before. If you are an educator who wants to learn about chess in schools, or needs help starting a chess club in your school, turn back to Chapter 17 where the section "Chess Competition for Children" will point you toward the resources you need.

> **Patrick's Pointers**
>
> The United State Chess Federation offers "A Guide to Scholastic Chess," a free booklet for teachers and school administrators on how to set up and run a scholastic chess club. You can order a copy from the USCF website or just download the guide itself at http://www.uschess.org/scholastic/sc-guide2.html

> **Patrick's Pointers**
>
> Although I no longer play chess professionally, I have visited schools from time to time to play chess with the kids there. Usually there is a teacher or parent who has volunteered his or her own time to create a program for the kids. Every time I've gone it's been a pleasure to see how the kids have enjoyed it. If you are involved in your local school and you think you might enjoy creating such a program, I encourage you to do it!

Collectibles

Plenty of iconic "stuff" is sure to accrue around something as established and popular as the game of chess. (For that matter, plenty of chess stuff has piled up around my own house over the years!) There seems to be something deep inside many people that makes them want to collect and preserve everything from old books, to the autographs and correspondence of famous players, to mementoes from past World Championship matches, to every other imaginable chess-theme collectible.

If that sounds like you, you might want to check out Chess Collectors International (CCI). This organization puts together shows and seminars throughout the world. Attendees can hear lectures, participate in workshops, and purchase collectibles either directly or at auction. Membership information for CCI is available at its website, www.chesscollectors.com.

Probably the two most popular chess collectibles are chess sets and chess-theme stamps.

All the Pieces

Chapter 1 contained a little bit about the mysterious origins of chess. Although no one is absolutely certain where the game began, there's no doubt that it moved across the ancient world, carried along by travelers through the Mideast, Asia, and eventually Europe. Chess sets acquired a similarly rich history, as local variations in the form of the pieces arose wherever chess was played.

Broadly speaking, there are two kinds of chess sets: practical playing sets and decorative sets.

Sets designed for actually playing chess tend to be simple in form. The standard design for modern chess sets is the so-called Staunton pattern. Staunton sets feature the familiar castle tower for the rook, horse's head for the knight, bishop's miter for the bishop, and king and queen crowned with a cross and a coronet, respectively. Howard Staunton, one of the strongest players of the "romantic era" in chess history (see Chapter 16), lent his name to the basic design in 1849. It quickly became popular and has remained so to this day. All modern grandmaster tournaments use some form of Staunton pieces.

Ornate decorative sets, on the other hand, are created primarily as works of art. After all, every chess piece is basically a miniature sculpture. Although they could still be used for playing an occasional game, these sets are not ideal for that. They tend to be more fragile and, moreover, they don't always make it easy to remember which piece is which.

Old chess sets tell stories. As long as people have been playing the game, there have been pieces carved in the image of local rulers or religious figures. Military campaigns have inspired commemorative chess sets, with real-life officers immortalized in the form of chess pieces. On the other hand, Muslim prohibition against carving images in the likeness of living creatures produced simpler, less decorative, more abstract piece designs during chess's Arabic period in the seventh century.

Cantonese ivory chess pieces, late eighteenth century.

Aside from their form, the material from which pieces are fashioned is apt to indicate something about their place and date of creation. Artisans have employed wood, stone, ivory, bone, paper, metal, glass, resins, plastics, and just about every other malleable material to create chess pieces. Prisoners have been known to mold chess sets out of their bread rations!

One of the best collection of chess sets in the United States can be found in the Fine Arts and Special Collections Department of the John G. White Collection of Chess. It is housed at the Main Library, 125 Superior Ave., Cleveland, Ohio.

Stamp Acts

The first chess-theme stamp was issued in Bulgaria in 1947. The occasion was the Balkan Games, a multi-sport international competition at which chess was one of the events. After that, it became quite common for chess-loving countries to issue stamps commemorating important chess matches and tournaments, famous players, or even particular chess positions.

A good online catalog of chess stamps can be found at www.tri.org.au/chess/catalogue.html. Beyond that, there are lots of individual philatelists (stamp collectors) who have put their collections and commentary online. It appears that the Internet suits stamp collecting as well as it does chess!

Chess Lore _____

What do Andorra, Brazil, Bulgaria, Cuba, Dahomey, Djibouti, Dominica, Ecuador, Egypt, Faroe Islands, France, Great Britain, Hungary, Iceland, Iran, Israel, Mali, Monaco, Netherlands, Niger, Rumania, Russia, San Marino, Surinam, Sweden, Tunisia, Tuvalu, United Arab Emirates, Wallis and Futuna, Yemen, and Yugoslavia all have in common? They've all issued chess-theme postage stamps—and this list is probably incomplete. Conspicuously absent, however, is the United States. Despite occasional lobbying efforts by American philatelists (stamp collectors), the U.S. Postal Service has never released a chess stamp.

Jon Edwards, a chess master and one of the strongest correspondence chess players in the United States, has a web page (www.queensac.com) that includes a presentation of his chess stamp collection. You'll find other interesting things to read there as well! I've heard that former World Champion Anatoly Karpov owns one of the most complete chess stamp collections. However, as far as I know his catalog isn't on the web.

One final source that you can go to for information about chess philately is the Chess On Stamps Study Unit. Join this organization and receive its quarterly publication, *Chesstamp Review*, by writing to COSSU president Ray Alexis, 608 Emery Street, Longmont, Colorado, 80501, or e-mail, chessstuff911459@aol.com.

The first chess stamp,
Bulgaria 1947.

... And Have You Seen This One?

As I've mentioned several times, one of the best ways to practice tactics is to solve the chess problems that you'll find in countless books, newspaper columns, and websites like www.wolffchess.com. As far as improving your play is concerned, the value of problems depends a lot on how realistic the positions are. But there are other chess problems of a sort that really have nothing to do with practical chess, and no value for improving your game—but they can still be fun!

For example, take a crack at this one. (1) Your task is to compose a game where, on each turn, Black's move mirrors whatever White just did. For example, if White begins 1 f4, Black must reply 1...f5. If White ever plays, say, Na3, Black's response must be ...Na6, etc. Now here's the problem: From the normal starting position, construct a game so that White checkmates Black on the fourth move.

If you're like 99% of players who are confronted with this challenge, your first thought will be 1 e4 e5 2 Bc4 Bc5 3 Qh5 Qh4, only to notice that this won't work because the d8 square is vacant and 4 Qxf7+ is not mate. So—back to the drawing board! (Unless you give up, in which case you can find the solutions to all of these puzzles in Appendix C, as usual.)

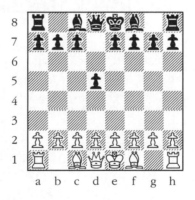

White to move.

(2) At least this looks more like normal chess. All four knights have been exchanged somehow and Black has come out a tempo ahead because his d-pawn is already advanced. But wait; that's thinking too much like a real chess player! To solve this puzzle you have to think *backward*. How did this situation arise? From the normal starting position, see if you can compose a little game that reaches this position. Remember that absurd moves are fine, so long as they're legal!

Who thinks up this stuff, anyway? Sam Loyd (1841–1911), for one. Loyd was one of the most colorful and imaginative figures in the history of chess. A magician, ventriloquist, and composer of all manners of puzzle, he invented the board game Parcheesi. Another of Loyd's creations that is still popular today was something he called the "14-15 puzzle." It consists of fifteen tiles, plus one empty spot, arranged four-by-four in a little tray. By successively sliding tiles into the blank spot, the solver must gradually rearrange the set into the proper order.

The 14-15 puzzle.

Loyd offered, and then answered, the challenge of composing the shortest possible game to end in stalemate. He found a way to do it in just ten moves! 1 e3 a5 2 Qh5 Ra6 3 Qxa5 h5 4 Qxc7 Rah6 5 h4 f6 6 Qxd7+ Kf7 7 Qxb7 Qd3 8 Qxb8 Qh7 9 Qxc8 Kg6 10 Qe6

Stalemate!

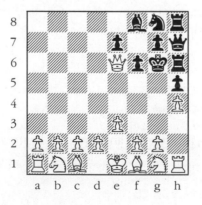

To engineer stalemate in just ten moves seems so incredible, I doubt you will be able to beat Loyd's record. But feel free to try.

Another Loyd problem (3) stipulates that White will begin a game with the moves 1 f3, 2 Kf2, 3 Kg3 and 4 Kh4. Your task—how does Black play to deliver mate on the fourth move?

A different sort of problem utilizes the geometry of the chess board and pieces to issue a challenge such as this (4): arrange eight queens on an otherwise empty board so that none of the queens attacks another.

Finally, try your hand at the so-called knight's tour (5). Start with an empty board. Put a knight on any square. Now try to find a path of successive moves for the knight so that it visits every square once and only once. That is, in exactly 63 moves the knight must cover the 63 squares besides the one where it started. Bonus points if you can explain why it would be impossible to create a knight's tour on the 62 square board you'd create by sawing off the a1 and h8 squares. Double bonus for finding a Re-Entrant Knight's Tour, where the sixty-fourth move returns the knight to the same square where it began.

The Wisdom of Chess

For as long as people have been playing chess, they've been talking about it, too. I've decided to close with a selection of wisdom and opinion from famous chess masters (and a few others). I've arranged the quotes topically. I can't say I agree with all of them, but because chess is a battle of ideas, that alone wouldn't be fitting grounds for disqualifying a good turn of phrase. Some of these "chess proverbs" are instructive; some are amusing; some just inspire you to think about them more—kind of like chess itself.

- ◆ What is chess?

    Chess is a fight. —Emanuel Lasker

    Chess is the art which expresses the science of logic. —Mikhail Botvinnik

    Chess is life. —Bobby Fischer

    Chess is everything—art, science and sport. —Anatoly Karpov

    Chess is life in miniature. Chess is struggle, chess is battles. —Gary Kasparov

    Chess is a fighting game which is purely intellectual and excludes chance. —Richard Reti

Chess is in its essence a game, in its form an art, and in its execution a science. —Baron Tassilo

Chess is a sea in which a gnat may drink and an elephant may bathe. —Hindu proverb

Chess is a test of wills. —Paul Keres

Chess is a beautiful mistress. —Bent Larsen

◆ Chess and life

The game of chess is not merely an idle amusement; several very valuable qualities of the mind are to be acquired and strengthened by it, so as to become habits ready on all occasions; for life is a kind of chess. —Benjamin Franklin

Chess is so inspiring that I do not believe a good player is capable of having an evil thought during the game. —Wilhelm Steinitz

Many have become Chess Masters, no one has become the Master of Chess. —Siegbert Tarrasch

Chess, like love, like music, has the power to make people happy. —Siegbert Tarrasch

It has been said that man is distinguished from animal in that he buys more books than he can read. I should like to suggest that the inclusion of a few chess books would help to make the distinction unmistakable. —Edward Lasker

The chessboard is the world, the pieces are the phenomena of the Universe, the rules of the game are what we call the laws of Nature and the player on the other side is hidden from us. —Thomas Huxley

◆ Some tips on chess strategy

When you see a good move, look for a better one. —Emanuel Lasker

The hardest game to win is a won game. —Emanuel Lasker

Before the endgame, the Gods have placed the middle game. —Siegbert Tarrasch

In order to improve your game, you must study the endgame before everything else, for whereas the endings can be studied and mastered by themselves, the middle game and the opening must be studied in relation to the endgame. —Jose Raul Capablanca

It is always better to sacrifice your opponent's men. —Savielly Tartakower

The tactician must know what to do whenever something needs doing; the strategist must know what to do when nothing needs doing. —Savielly Tartakower

The winner of the game is the player who makes the next-to-last mistake. —Savielly Tartakower

Some part of a mistake is always correct. —Savielly Tartakower

Play the opening like a book, the middle game like a magician, and the endgame like a machine. —Rudolph Spielmann

It is not a move, even the best move that you must seek, but a realizable plan. —Eugene Znosko-Borovsky

Good positions don't win games, good moves do. —Gerald Abrahams

The Pin is mightier than the sword. —Fred Reinfeld

Strategy requires thought; tactics require observation. —Max Euwe

One bad move nullifies forty good ones. —I. A. Horowitz

The most powerful weapon in Chess is to have the next move. —David Bronstein

I began to succeed in decisive games, perhaps because I realized a very simple truth: not only was I worried, but also my opponent. —Mikhail Tal

In blitz, the knight is stronger than the bishop. —Vlastimil Hort

You need not play well—just help your opponent to play badly. —Genrikh Chepukaitis

The most important feature of the chess position is the activity of the pieces. This is absolutely fundamental in all phases of the game: opening, middlegame and especially endgame. The primary constraint on a piece's activity is the pawn structure. —Michael Stean

Half the variations which are calculated in a tournament game turn out to be completely superfluous. Unfortunately, no one knows in advance which half. —Jan Timman

Modern chess is too much concerned with things like pawn structure. Forget it! Checkmate ends the game. —Nigel Short

If your opponent offers you a draw, try to work out why he thinks he's worse off. —Nigel Short

◆ On Famous Chess Players

Chess was Capablanca's mother tongue. —Richard Reti

Alekhine is a poet who creates a work of art out of something that would hardly inspire another man to send home a picture post card. —Max Euwe

Look at Garry Kasparov. After he loses, invariably he wins the next game. He just kills the next guy. That's something that we have to learn to be able to do. —Maurice Ashley

Not all artists may be chess players, but all chess players are artists. —Marcel Duchamp

Every chess master was once a beginner. —Irving Chernev

The Least You Need to Know

◆ Chess is becoming more and more popular in schools because many kids enjoy it and there is some evidence it has beneficial effects for students.

◆ Some people collect chess sets, stamps with chess themes, and other objects connected with chess.

◆ You may enjoy solving puzzles and brainteasers that use chess as their theme that have nothing to do with improving your chess game.

◆ Chess has been both the subject and source of wisdom and wit for many years.

Your Chess Rolodex

This appendix lists alphabetically the names and essential contact information (telephone numbers, e-mail addresses, websites, or street addresses) for all of the organizations mentioned in this book.

Aficionado, Inc.
315 Richardson Drive
Mill Valley, CA 94941
1-800-465-9301
415-888-2033 (international)
415-888-2103 (fax)
www.chess.com

The American Chess
School
140 School Street
Bradford, PA 16701
814-368-8009
www.amchess.org

American Postal Chess
Tournaments
PO Box 305
Western Springs, IL
60558-0305
630-663-0688
630-663-0689 (fax)
http://correspondencechess.
com

Atlanta Chess Center
3155 E. Ponce de Leon
Avenue
Scottdale, GA 30079
404-377-4400

Bookup Corp.
2763 Kensington Place
West
Columbus, OH 43202-
2355
1-800-949-5445
614-263-7219
614-262-9788 (fax)
www.bookup.com

Boylston Chess Club
240 Elm Street, Suite B9
Somerville, MA 02144
617-629-3933
http://world.std.com/
~boylston

British Chess Magazine
44 Baker Street
London W1U 7RT
England
44 20 7486 8222
44 20 7486 3355 (fax)
bcmchess@compuserve.com
www.bcmchess.co.uk

Cadogan Books plc
3rd Floor
27-29 Berwick Street
London W1V 3RF
United Kingdom
44 171 287 6555
44 171 734 1733 (fax)
am@cadogan.co.uk (e-mail)

Canadian Correspondence
Chess Association
39 Deguire #312
Montréal, Québec
Canada H4N 1P2
514-745-0987
http://correspondencechess.
com/ccca

Chess & Bridge Ltd.
The London Chess Center
369 Euston Road
London NW1 3AR
England
44 20 7388 2404
44 20 7388 2407 (fax)
www.chess.co.uk

Chess & Bridge, Inc. (USA
address)
2363 Oak Tree Lane
West Palm Beach, FL 33409
1-888-243-7706

ChessBase USA
PO Box 609
Ardmore, TN 38449
1-800-524-3527
256-423-8345 (fax)
www.chessbaseusa.com
www.chessbase.com

Chessco
PO Box 3037
Davenport, IA 52802-0005
1-800-397-7117
319-323-7117
319-323-0511 (fax)
www.chessco.com
tpi@chessco.com (e-mail)

Chess Collectors International
c/o Floyd Sarisohn
PO Box 166
Commack, NY 11725
631-543-1330
631-543-7901 (fax)
www.chesscollectors.com

Chess Combination, Inc.
(U.S. distributor for *New In
Chess* magazine)
2423 Noble Station
Bridgeport, CT 06608-0423
1-800-354-4083
302-380-1703 (fax)

Chess Digest, Inc.
Box 609
Ardmore, TN 38449
1-800-524-3527 (orders)
256-423-8345 (fax)
1-800-524-3525 (customer
service)
www.chessdigest.com

Chess Emporium
10801 N. 32nd Street, Suite 6
Phoenix, AZ 85032
602-482-4867
602-494-6025 (fax)
www.chessemporium.com

Chess Federation of Canada
2212 Gladwin Crescent, Unit
E-1
Ottawa, Ontario K1B 5N1
Canada
613-733-2844
613-733-5209 (fax)
www.chess.ca

Chess Forum
219 Thompson Street
New York, NY 10012
212-475-2369
212-475-3905 (fax)
www.chessforum.com

The Chess House
PO Box 705
Lynden, WA 98264
1-800-348-4749
360-354-6815
360-354-6765 (fax)
www.thechesshouse.com

Chess Informant
PO Box 739
11001 Beograd
Francuska 31
Yugoslavia
www.sahovski.com
sales@sahovski.co.yu (e-mail)

Chess-in-the-Schools
520 Eighth Avenue, Floor 2
New York, NY 10018
212-643-0225
2112-564-3083 (fax)
www.chessintheschools.org

Chess Life
c/o U.S. Chess Federation

Chess Monthly
c/o Chess & Bridge, Inc.

Chess On Stamps Study Unit
c/o Ray Alexis, President
608 Emery Street
Longmont, CO 80501
chessstuff911459@aol.com
(email)

Chess Palace
4336 Katella Avenue
Los Alamitos, CA 90720-3564
562-598-5099
www.chesspalace.com

Chrysalis Books (Batsford)
The Chrysalis Building
Bramley Road
London
W10 6SP
United Kingdom
020 7314 1469
020 7314 1594 (fax)

Correspondence Chess
League of America
c/o Volker Jeschonnek,
President
PO Box 257
Cairo, OH 45820-0257
www.chessbymail.com

David McKay Co., Inc.
c/o Random House, Inc.

Dover Publications, Inc.
31 East Second Street
Mineola, NY 11501
Fax: 516-742-6953
www.doverpublications.com

Europe Echecs
4B2 Rue Roussillon
25000 Besançon
France
33 381 41 01 26
33 381 51 71 64 (fax)
abo@europe-echecs.com
(e-mail)
www.europe-echecs.com

Féderation Internationale des
échecs (FIDE)
PO Box 166, CH-1000
Lausanne 4
Switzerland
41-213103900
41-213103905 (fax)
www.fide.com

Franklin Mercantile Chess
Club
2012 Walnut Street
Philadelphia, PA 19123
215-496-9686

Interchess BV
(publisher of *New In Chess*)
PO Box 1093
1810 KB Alkmaar
The Netherlands
1-800-354-4083
31-725127137
31-725158234 (fax)
www.newinchess.com

International Computer Chess
Association
c/o David Levy
5 Akenside Road
London NW3 5BS
England
info@icga.org (e-mail)
www.dcs.qmw.ac.uk/~icca

International Correspondence
Chess Federation
www.iccf.com

Marshall Chess Club
23 West 10th Street
New York, NY 10011
212-477-3716
www.marshallchessclub.org

Mechanics Institute Chess
Club
57 Post Street, 4th fl.
San Francisco, CA 94104
415-421-2258
www.chessclub.org

National Scholastic Chess
Foundation
171 East Post Road, Suite 206
White Plains, NY 10601
914-683-5322
nscf@nscfchess.org (e-mail)
www.nscfchess.org

New In Chess
c/o Interchess BV
c/o Chess Combination, Inc.
in the U.S.

Oxford University Press
198 Madison Avenue
New York, NY 10016
212-726-6000
www.oup.co.uk

Random House, Inc.
1540 Broadway
New York, NY 10036
1-800-733-3000
212-782-9000
212-302-7985 (fax)
www.randomhouse.com

Rochester Chess Center
221 Norris Drive
Rochester, NY 14610
1-800-662-4377
716-442-2430 (fax)
www.chessset.com

Russell Enterprises, Inc.
PO Box 30
Milford, CT 06460
www.chesscafe.com

U.S. Chess Center
1501 M Street NW
Washington, DC 20005
202-857-4922
www.chessctr.org

U.S. Chess Federation
(USCF)
3054 NYS Route 9W
New Windsor, NY 12553
845-562-8350
845-561-2437 (fax)
www.uschess.org

Village Chess Shop Ltd.
230 Thompson Street
New York, NY 10012
212-475-9580
212-982-7471 (fax)
www.chess-shop.com

Wilshire Book Company
12015 Sherman Road
North Hollywood, CA 91605
818-765-8579
818-765-2922 (fax)
www.mpowers.com

World & U.S. Chess Hall of
Fame & Sidney Samole
Museum
13755 SW 119th Avenue
Miami, FL 33186
786-242- 4255
http://www.uschesshalloffame.
com/

Your Move Chess & Games
832 N. Broadway
N. Massapequa, NY 11758
1-800-645-4710
www.icdchess.com

Appendix B

Other Chess Notations

Throughout this book I've used a form of algebraic notation to describe chess moves. In this appendix, I explain the other major system for describing chess moves, called descriptive notation. Descriptive notation is no longer commonly used, but many older books and magazines still in print use it, and if you want to be able to read them, you have to know it.

First, you should be aware that there are also variants of algebraic notation in use. Each language has its own names for the chess pieces, so if, for example, you encounter a French chess publication, you will see the symbols R (roi/king), D (dame/queen), T (tour/rook), F (fou/bishop), and C (cavalier/knight). This can be confusing, although you'd be surprised how quickly you can figure out which letter stands for which piece. Fortunately, more and more publications use a language-independent *figurine algebraic* notation. In this system, the pieces are referred to by the same pictorial symbols used in chess diagrams.

You should also keep in mind that some versions of algebraic notation leave out the "x" for capture moves and the "+" for checking moves, and sometimes when one pawn captures another only the files are listed (for example, instead of cxd4 you might see cd4 or even just cd). No information is lost by compacting the notation in these ways, but because it does get a bit more confusing, you don't see these variants as frequently as the standard notation I've been using. Finally, there are two minor variations to keep in mind. First, the letters "e.p." are sometimes put after an *en passant* pawn capture. Second, sometimes a win for White, draw, or win for Black is indicated by "1-0", "½-½", and "0-1" respectively.

Now to descriptive notation. Actually, "descriptive" is a misnomer; in my opinion, this old-fashioned system is less descriptive and more confusing than algebraic (unless you grew up with it). Chess notation is a case in which the United States has caught up with the rest of the world, most of which has been using algebraic notation for decades. (The metric system might take a bit longer!)

In descriptive notation, the pieces are referred to just as in algebraic, except the pawns are explicitly named "P," and in very old books "Kt" is sometimes used instead of "N" for the knight. But the similarity between the two notations ends there. For one thing, each square on the board has two different names, not just one as in algebraic. Each square is named by putting its file in front of its rank (as in algebraic notation), but in descriptive notation each file and rank is named both from White's point of view and Black's point of view. Furthermore, the files are referred to according to the piece that stood on them at the beginning of the game: K for king, Q for queen, KB for king bishop (the bishop on the king's side of the board), QB for queen bishop, KN for king knight, QN for queen knight, KR for king rook, and QR for queen rook.

Diagram 1 shows the names of the files and ranks from each player's perspective. (Note that if no ambiguity is introduced, the K or Q can be omitted from before the B, N, or R in the name of a square or a piece.) A move consists of a piece name, followed by a hyphen, followed by a square name; a capture consists of the capturing piece name, an x, and the captured piece name. If this all seems cumbersome compared to algebraic, that's because it is. You don't even want to know how they did it in the nineteenth century before this "simplified" system was invented!

Diagram 1: The names of the ranks and files from each player's perspective in descriptive notation.

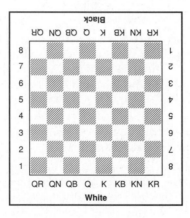

You'll probably understand descriptive notation better if you play through a brief game in it: 1.P-Q4 N-KB3 2.P-QB4 P-K4 3.PxP N-N5 4.B-B4 B-N5+ (+ for checks, sometimes "ch") 5.N-Q2 N-QB3 6.N-B3 (not N-KB3, because the knight at Q2 is pinned and cannot move) Q-K2 7.P-QR3 KNxKP! (the punctuation marks are the same) 8.PxB?? N-Q6 mate (no # in descriptive). In algebraic that game went: 1.d4 Nf6 2.c4 e5 3.dxe5 Ng4 4.Bf4 Bb4+ 5.Nd2 Nc6 6.Nf3 Qe7 7.a3 Ngxe5! 8.axb4?? Nd3#.

If you've read Chapter 3 and this appendix, you know how to read and write chess moves in all the major chess notations. The whole world of chess is open to you now! Don't worry too much about descriptive notation: You're better off sticking to algebraic anyway! If you've got a book or magazine in descriptive that you want to read, take another look at this appendix and go over the sample game above. With a little practice, you'll have no trouble understanding whatever you want to read.

Answers to Exercises

Answers to Exercises from Chapter 1

Jeopardy Questions:

- ◆ Chess for $100: Who was Humphrey Bogart?
- ◆ Chess for $200: What is castling?
- ◆ Chess for $300: What is a grandmaster?
- ◆ Chess for $400: What is en passant?
- ◆ Chess for $500: Who is Boris Spassky?

Answers to Exercises from Chapter 2

Exercise 1: The pawn on f5 may capture the bishop on e6, which is written "1.fxe6". The pawn on e2 may move to e3 or e4, which are written "1.e3" and "1.e4", respectively. The pawn on a4 may capture the pawn on b5, which is written "1.axb5". What about the pawn on c3? I played a little trick on you! This pawn may not move, because if it moved, the bishop on a5 would put the white king into check. You can *never* play a move that would put yourself into check.

Exercise 2: The knight on b7 has no moves. The knight on f6 can move to d7, e8, g8, h7, or h5, which are written "1...Nd7", "1...Ne8", "1...Ng8", "1...Nh7", and "1...Nh5", respectively. Or the knight may capture either of the pawns on d5 or g4, which are written "1...Nxd5" and "1...Nxg4" respectively. But the knight cannot move to e4, because his own pawn blocks him.

Exercise 3: The bishop on f8 cannot move. The bishop on e6 can move to g8, f7, f5, d7, c8, d5, or c4, which are written "1...Bg8", "1...Bf7", "1...Bf5", "1...Bd7", "1...Bc8", "1...Bd5", and "1...Bc4", respectively. The bishop can also capture the pawn on g4 or the queen on b3, and these are written "1...Bxg4" and "1...Bxb3" respectively.

Exercise 4: This was another tricky question! White's king is in check from the black rook, so White must remove the check. The only way to do that by moving the rook is to capture the rook on e6, so this is the only move White can make with the rook. This move is written "1.Rxe6+". The "+" sign indicates that the move is check, as is explained in Chapter 3.

Exercise 5: The black queen can move to a2, b3, c4, e6, c6, e4, e5, f5, c5, b5, d4, d3, d6, d7, or d8. These moves are written "1...Qa2", "1...Qb3", "1...Qc4", "1...Qe6", "1...Qc6", "1...Qe4", "1...Qe5", "1...Qf5", "1...Qc5", "1...Qb5", "1...Qd4", "1...Qd3", "1...Qd6", "1...Qd7", and "1...Qd8", respectively. Black can also capture the pawn on f3, the rook on a5, or the queen on d2. These moves are written "1...Qxf3", "1...Qxa5", and "1...Qxd2+" respectively. Again, as explained in Chapter 3, the "+" indicates check.

Exercise 6: The white king can capture the queen on d5, but it can't capture the pawn on e5, because this pawn is protected by the queen, and if White made this move it would put his own king in check. The white king can move to e3 or f5, which are written "1.Ke3" and "1.Kf5" respectively, or it can capture the queen on d5, which is written "1.Kxd5".

Exercise 7: It must be Black's turn, because his king is in check. Black's legal moves are to move his king to e8 or g8, or to capture the bishop with his knight. These moves are written, respectively, 1...Ke8; 1...Kg8; 1...Nxc5.

Exercise 8: Black has exactly twenty legal moves. He can move either pawn one or two squares forward, he may move his queen's knight (the knight on b8) to a6 or c6, or he may move his king's knight (the knight on g8) to f6 or h6. These moves are written, respectively, 1...a6; 1...a5; 1...b6; 1...b5; 1...c6; 1...c5; 1...d6; 1...d5; 1...e6; 1...e5; 1...f6; 1...f5; 1...g6; 1...g5; 1...h6; 1...h5; 1...Na6; 1...Nc6; 1...Nf6; 1...Nh6.

Exercise 9: White has eight legal moves with a pawn. These moves are written, respectively, 1.a3; 1.a4; 1.c4; 1.d5; 1.dxe5; 1.g3; 1.g4; 1.h4. White has six legal moves with his king's bishop (the bishop on b3). These are 1. Ba4; 1.Bc2; 1.Bc4; 1.Bd5; 1.Be6; 1.Bxf7+. White has no legal moves with his queen's bishop (the bishop on c1), because it is blocked by the pawn on b2 and the knight on d2.

Exercise 10: Black can make three legal moves with his king's knight: 1...Nf6, 1...Ne7, or 1...Nh6; notice that the second move is not written "1...Nge7" because there is no need to distinguish the knight on g8 from the knight on c6. Black cannot move his queen's knight, because if he does so his king will be in check. (The knight is *pinned* to the king; you will learn more about the pin in Chapter 6.) Black can make two legal moves with his queen's rook (the rook on a8): 1...Rb8 or 1...Ra7. Black cannot move his king's rook (the rook on h8), because it is blocked by the knight on g8 and the pawn on h7.

Exercise 11: Black is in check, therefore he must eliminate the check. There are only two moves that do this: 1...Qc8 or 1...Qxg8. The best move is 1...Qxg8. After 1...Qc8 2.Rxc8 is checkmate. However, after 1...Qxg8 although White can capture the queen with 2.Nxg8, the game will be a draw, because there is no way to checkmate the king with only a knight and king. (See Chapter 3 for more about when the game is a draw.)

Exercise 12: White has one legal move with his king: 1.Ka5. (All other king moves put White into check.) White has six legal moves with his knight: 1.Nc6+; 1.Nd5; 1.Nf5; 1.Ng6; 1.Ng8; 1.Nc8. White has nine legal moves with his rook: 1.Rg8+; 1.Rg6; 1.Rg5; 1.Rg4; 1.Rg3; 1.Rg2; 1.Rg1; 1.Rf7; 1.Rh7. After 1.Rg8+, we have the position in Exercise 11.

However, the best move is 1.Nc6+ Qxc6+ (1...Ka8 allows 2.Ra7 checkmate, and 1...Kc8 allows 2.Rc7 checkmate) 2.Kxc6, and White can force checkmate with rook and king. See Chapter 4 for more about how White can win this position.

Answers to Exercises from Chapter 3

Exercise 1: Yes, he can. Black has just moved the pawn two squares, so White can respond by capturing *en passant* on the very next move. Were you thrown off by the fact that White is in check? But capturing the pawn *en passant* removes the check, so it is okay.

Exercise 2: The only way for White to promote the pawn to a queen on this move is to capture the rook giving check to his king, and the move is written, "1.cxd8=Q#". Notice the "#" is there because when White plays this move, Black is in checkmate! White can't play 1.c8=Q, because his king is in check and that must be dealt with.

Exercise 3: White castling queenside is written, "1.O-O-O". Black cannot castle queenside on the next move, because the black king must pass through the d8 square to do so, and this square is controlled by the white rook on d1. By the way, notice that White could castle queenside even though the black bishop on g7 was attacking his rook on a1. There is no rule against castling if your rook is attacked! (If you got confused on this exercise, you should go back and review the castling rules in this chapter.)

Exercise 4: Black can play 1...Qg4+!, when White's only possible response is 2.Kh1. Black then plays 2...Qf3!+, but not 2...Qe4+?, because after 3.f3 Qxf3+ 4.Rxf3 the checks stop. The game could continue: 3.Kg1 Qg4+ 4.Kh1 Qf3+ 5.Kg1 Qg4+ and so on forever until the game is declared a draw.

Exercise 5: White can play 1.Rg3+! Kh7 (or 1...Kh8) 2.Rh4#.

Exercise 6: Black is not in stalemate because he has one possible move, 1...h3. And if White is alert enough to see that 2.Nc7# is checkmate, then he'll win the game!

Exercise 7: White can't castle queenside, because then his king would pass through check on d1. But White can castle kingside, which is written: 1.O-O. Notice that he can castle kingside even though the rook on h1 is attacked.

Exercise 8: This position should not be declared a draw! Without the black pawn on h3, there would be no legal way to construct a checkmate. But with the pawn, there is a way. In fact, this position is actually winning for White: 1.Ng4! h2 (the only legal move) 2.Nf2 checkmate. White forces the pawn to take the h2 square from Black, and then White delivers checkmate with the knight. This is a good pattern to remember.

Exercise 9: Black should play 1...h2! when White must allow Black to be stalemated (e.g., 2.Ne4), or else Black will move the king to g1 and then promote the pawn safely (e.g., 2.Kg3?? Kg1 and 3...h1=Q). If Black plays 1...Kh2, then he loses after 2.Ng4+! Kh1 3.Kf1! h2 4.Nf2#.

Exercise 10: Yes, if White plays 1.g4, Black can play 1...hxg3+ *en passant*. Kasparov did not push the pawn, precisely because he did not want Black to be able to capture *en passant* in this position. But as you will see in a later exercise, in this case he made the wrong decision.

Exercise 11: Black should play 1...c1=R!, when he can easily win White's last pawn and force checkmate. (See Chapter 4 to see how to force checkmate with the rook.) Black should not play 1...c1=Q?? because then White will be in stalemate and the game will be drawn. Black also should not promote to a knight or a bishop, because then he will not be able to force checkmate. Even though Exercises 8 and 9 illustrate positions where the knight and king can give checkmate against a pawn and king, that is a very rare case. Here, if Black made a knight or bishop, White would draw very easily.

Exercise 12: Black can't castle on either side because he is in check. If Black blocks the check with either his knight or his bishop, he will be in big trouble. (Do you see why? If not, you might want to ask yourself the same question after you read Chapters 5 and 6.) So Black will have to move his king either to f8 or d8, which will make it difficult for Black to get his king to a good square. Black should have castled earlier!

Answers to Exercises from Chapter 4

Exercise 1: White plays 1.Qf7! Black has no other move than 1...Kc8, and then White has several ways to give checkmate: 2.Qc7#, 2.Qe8#, 2.Qf8#, and 2.Qg8#. But White should *not* play 1.Qe6?, because then Black is in stalemate. (Give yourself credit also for 1.Qe2! which forces checkmate after 1...Kc8 2.Qe8#.)

Exercise 2: White plays 1.Ra1! Black has to play 1...Kc8, and then White plays 2.Ra8#.

Exercise 3: b4 and a6.

Exercise 4: White should push the pawn so that he can promote it to either a rook or (better) a queen. Then White will be able to deliver checkmate. There are two ways to carry the plan out. The simplest is 1.b6 Kd8 (Black brings the king over to try to stop the pawn from reaching the edge of the board...) 2.b7 (but Black doesn't get there in time!) and White will promote the pawn on the next move. Another way is to play 1.Kc7, which prevents the black king from going to d8 or d7. The way is then clear for White to push the pawn to b8, make it a queen, and win the game.

Exercise 5: Black wins with 1...Kg6!, threatening checkmate with 2...Qf7, 2...Qe8, or 2...Qd8. White has no good defense. But see Exercise 6 for White's best try!

Exercise 6: Black should play 1...Kxf6 2.Kh8 Qg7#. Black should *not* play 1...Qxf6?? as then White would be stalemated.

Exercise 7: White plays 1.Re7! Kh5 2.Rh7#.

Exercise 8: After 1...c1=R 2.Kb2, here's how I did it: 2...Rc5 3.Ka2 Rb5 (there's nothing wrong with 3...Rc3 and 4...Rxa3 except that it takes longer) 4.Ka1 Kb3 (NOT 4...Kxa3?? and it's stalemate!) 5.Kb1 (5.a4 Rd5 and 6...Rd1#) 5...Rc5! (quickest) 6.a4 (6.Ka1 Rc1#) 6...Kxa4 7.Kb2 Kb4 8.Ka2 Rc2+ 9.Kb1 Kb3 10.Ka1 Rc1#.

Answers to Exercises from Chapter 5

Exercise 1: The knight on d4 attacks the pawns on b5 and e6, and the knight on c6. The pawns are each protected: The pawn on b5 is protected by the pawn on a6, and the pawn on e6 is protected by the pawn on f7. So White should not capture either of the pawns. But the knight on c6 is only defended once, by the bishop on b7, while it is attacked twice: by the bishop on f3 as well as the knight on d4. White can win a knight by playing 1.Nxc6+ Bxc6 2.Bxc6. Just as good is 1.Bxc6 Bxc6 2.Nxc6+, which wins a knight for a bishop. In either case, White gains a large material advantage.

Exercise 2: No. If White plays 1.Rxb7??, Black will play 1...Bxb7 and win a whole rook for a measly pawn! And if White plays 1.dxc5, Black wins the pawn back right away with 1...Bxc3+.

Exercise 3: White attacks the pawn on e6 with his queen, and the pawn on h6 with his bishop on d2. White should not capture either of them because they are both protected. The pawn on e6 is protected by the pawn on f7, and the pawn on h6 is protected by the pawn on g7 and the rook on h8.

Exercise 4: Yes. Both moves win a pawn. White attacks the pawn on d4 three times, and Black defends it only twice, so he can capture it. The game might continue: 1.Nfxd4 Nxd4 2.Qxd4 Qxd4 3.Nxd4, and White has won a pawn. 1.Qxd4??, however, is a very bad move because it loses the queen after 1...Nxd4.

Exercise 5: Black should play 1...Qxg5!, which wins a bishop for nothing.

Exercise 6: Black should capture the knight on c4, and not the one on e6. The white rook protects each of the knights once, but Black attacks the white knight on c4 with two rooks (notice the power of doubled rooks), so he wins a knight by 1...Rxc4 2.Rxc4 Rxc4.

Exercise 7: No: 1...Nxc3 2.Rxc3 Rxc3 3.Kxc3 is a series of equal trades, as is 1...Rxc3 2.Rxc3 Nxc3 3.Kxc3.

Exercise 8: After 1.dxc6 Rxc6 material will be equal. But that does not mean White should not play 1.dxc6!, because it is still the best move. In the diagrammed position, White has a material disadvantage: Black has a knight for White's pawn. White must grab the chance to even the situation with 1.dxc6.

Exercise 9: White can play three captures: 1.Bxf6, 1.Nxc6, and 1.Nxe6. None of them gives White a material advantage:

After 1.Bxf6 Bxf6, White has made an even trade. (Maybe Black has gained a tiny material advantage, because he now has a bishop for a knight.)

After 1.Nxc6 bxc6, White has made an even trade.

After 1.Nxe6? Bxe6, White has lost a knight for a pawn.

Exercise 10: White can play three captures: 1.axb5, 1.dxe5, and 1.Bxf7+. None of them gives White a material advantage:

After 1.axb5 axb5, White has made an even trade.

After 1.dxe5 dxe5, White has made an even trade.

After 1.Bxf7+? Kxf7, White has lost a bishop for a pawn.

Exercise 11: White should capture the rook on b6. After 1.Bxb6 Bxb6, White has won a rook for a bishop. (Capturing the knight on f6 is at best only an even trade.)

Exercise 12: No. The white queen is more valuable than either the black knight or the black rook. Because both of these pieces are protected, White should capture neither of them.

Exercise 13: Yes. After 1.Rxd7 Bxd7 2.Rxd7, White wins a knight and a bishop for a rook. According to the chart of the relative value of the pieces, a knight and a bishop together are worth a little more than 6, while a rook is only worth 5.

Exercise 14: No. After 1.Rxd7 Bxd7 2.Rxd7, now that the king is on c8, Black can play 2...Kxd7, when White has lost two rooks for only a knight and a bishop. (Make sure you understand the difference between this exercise and Exercise 13.)

Exercise 15: No. In particular, notice that 1...Be5?? 2.Bxe5 is a disaster, because Black loses a bishop for nothing, and also 1...Kg7? 2.Bxf6+ Kxf6 loses a rook for a bishop.

Exercise 16: No. Black still should not defend the rook, for the same reason as in Exercise 15. Black still cannot block the attack by moving a piece to e5, because even though he has one more piece which attacks this square (the knight on g6), White also has one more piece that attacks this square (the knight on f3), so they even out. (For example: 1...Be5?? 2.Nxe5 Nxe5 3.Bxe5.) Nor should Black capture the knight on f3, because it is defended by the pawn on g2: 1...Rxf3? 2.gxf3, and White wins a rook for a knight.

Exercise 17: Yes. Black can attack White's queen with 1...Nf4, when White should meet the threat to the queen rather than capture the rook, that is, 2.Bxf6?? Nxe2+ and Black wins a queen for a rook.

Exercise 18: The white knight attacks both the queen and the rook at the same time. This is called a "fork," which you will learn about in Chapter 6. Because both pieces are attacked at the same time, Black cannot move both of them to safety in the next turn. The best move is for Black to play 1...Bxe4, capturing the piece that attacks both the queen and the rook, and so removing the threat to them both. After 2.Qxe4 material is even.

Exercise 19: The white bishop attacks the rook, but the rook cannot move because if it did, that would expose the king to check, which is not allowed. This is called a "pin," which you will learn about in Chapter 6. The best move is 1...Nxe4, and after 2.Rxe4 material is even.

Exercise 20: No. The rook cannot move because that would expose the king to check, and there is no other way for him to defend against the threat.

Exercise 21: He can play 1...Ne4, which only loses a pawn after 2.Bxe4 dxe4 3.Rxe4. But losing a pawn is better than losing a rook for a bishop, so 1...Ne4 is the best move.

Exercise 22: After 1...Ne4, White has a better move than to capture the knight: He can play 2.f3! This move attacks the knight with a pawn, so Black should move the knight. But then White will capture the rook for the bishop. (Here's an extra question for you to solve on your own. Did you consider that after 1...Ne4 2.f3, Black could play 2...Rg3, to pin the pawn to the bishop? After 3.fxe4 Rxd3, Black "saves" the knight, by capturing the bishop on d3. But White can win the knight in several ways, two of which are 3.Bb1 and 3.Kh2. Can you see why?)

Exercise 23: White should play 1.fxe3 to keep material even, because the knight on e3 attacked the rook. If White played 1.cxd5? or 1.Bxd5?, Black would play 1...Nxd1+ 2.Rxd1; if White played 1.Rxd5?, Black would play 1...Nxd5 2.Bxd5 (or 2.cxd5), in either case with the advantage of the exchange.

Exercise 24: No. After 1.Rxe8+ Rxe8 (or 1...Nxe8), if 2.Qxe8+? Nxe8 3.Rxe8+ Kg7, Black has a queen for a rook and knight, a material advantage for Black.

Exercise 25: Yes. After 1.Rxe8+ Rxe8 (or 1...Nxe8) 2.Rxe8+ Nxe8 3.Qxe8+, White has won a knight for nothing. Because the rooks are in front of the queen, White captures with less valuable material first, and so is left with the more valuable piece (the queen) in the end.

Exercise 26: No. Now that Black's queen is on c6 instead of c7, the rook is protected one more time. After 1.Rxe8+ Rxe8 2.Rxe8+ Qxe8 3.Qxe8+ Nxe8 material is still even.

Exercise 27: Black should play either 1...Qc5 or 1...Qd8, to move the queen out of the attack and defend the bishop at the same time. (Not 1...Qxd5, because after 2.Bxd5 Bxd5 White would have a queen for two minor pieces; not 1...Bb4, because after 2.Bxb4 White would win material; and not 1...Bc5, because after 2.Bxa5 Bxd4 3.Ne7+! Kh8 4.Rxd4 White is ahead a minor piece.) Then after 2.Nxe7+ Qxe7 material is still even.

Exercise 28: Black should play 1...Bxc1 2.Rxc1 b6 (to protect the knight), after which Black will be ahead a rook for a bishop.

Exercise 29: Black should still play 1...Bxc1 2.Rxc1 b6. However, now after 3.b4! White will win the knight, as Black cannot move it without putting his own king in check. After White plays 4.bxc5, White will be ahead in material—two pieces for a rook.

Exercise 30: White cannot move the queen, as it will be captured on any square it moves to. White could block the attack with 1.Ne5, but then Black wins the exchange with 1...Nxe1 2.Rxe1, and on top of that can attack two pieces at the same time with 2...f6. And it does no good to block the attack with 1.Nf6+ or 1.Bf6, because Black can capture either piece with a pawn, winning material. But White can save the queen by counterattacking: 1.Nh6+! Now if 1...Kh8, 2.Nxf7+ Kg8 3.Nh6+ Kh8 4.Nf7+ is perpetual check. But if (after 1.Nh6+) 1...Bxh6, then 2.Bxh6! threatens checkmate on g7, gaining time to move the rook on e1 out of the attack by the knight.

Answers to Exercises from Chapter 6

Exercise 1: White plays 1.f5!, which threatens to capture Black's pawn on e6. If Black plays 1...exf5 or 1...exd5, White plays 2.e6.

Exercise 2: White should be worried, because his knight is pinned to his king, and if White defends the knight, Black will attack it again by playing 1...e6. Therefore, White will lose the knight.

Exercise 3: White should play 1.Rf1!, which pins the queen to the king. But notice that 1.O-O is illegal, because the queen controls the f1 square, which the white king would have to pass through.

Exercise 4: White cannot win the queen! White cannot play 1.Rf1+ because his own king is in check, and he cannot play 1.O-O+ because it is not allowed to castle when you are in check. White's best move is to play 1.g3, which attacks the bishop on h4 and also threatens 1.Rf1+ or 1.O-O+. Therefore, 1.g3 wins the bishop because Black has to respond to the threat to the queen instead of to the threat to the bishop.

Exercise 5: White should win. If Black plays 1...h1=Q, White skewers the king and queen by playing 2.a8=Q+, and then he wins the endgame with an extra queen. Other-wise, White can stop Black from queening after he makes a queen, and should win.

Exercise 6: White should play 1.d4+!, which attacks both the rook and the king by discovered check, and so wins the rook.

Exercise 7: White's threat is to play 2.Qf3, attacking the knight again, and winning it. Black has no defense, because he cannot move the queen out of the pin without losing the knight.

Exercise 8: No, for two reasons. First, Black can move the queen out of the pin because the knight is protected by the pawn on g7. Second, Black can play 1...h6 to attack the bishop. If White plays 2.Bxf6, Black plays 2...Qxf6; if White plays 2.Bh4, Black can block the pin by playing 2...g5.

Exercise 9: If Black plays 28...Rxe6, White plays 29.Rc8! which pins the queen to the king and wins material. In fact, Black resigned after 28.Nxe6! and I won the tournament.

Exercise 10: White should play 1.Nc5+!! Kb8 2.Na6#!

Exercise 11: Black should play 1...Nxe4!, which uncovers an attack against the queen. If White captures the knight with 2.Qxe4, Black pins the queen with 2...Re8.

Exercise 12: White plays 1.Qxa7+!! Kxa7 (if 1...Kc7, then 2.bxc8=Q+ gives double check, and White skewers the king and queen so that after 2...Kxc8 3.Qxe7 White is up a whole queen) 2.bxc8=N+!! and after 3.Nxe7 he should win.

Exercise 13: White's threat is to play Nd6, checkmate! Because the e-pawn is pinned, Black cannot capture the knight. Clearly 1...Ngf6?? would be a terrible blunder, as White then plays 2.Nd6#. (But not 2.Nxf6+ Nxf6, which is just an even exchange of knights.)

Exercise 14: After 1...Qg1+!! 2.Kxg1 Nxe2+ captures the bishop and forks king and queen. After 3...Nxc3, Black is a piece ahead and has a winning position.

Exercise 15: White combines the pin with the discovered attack, plus a mating pattern: 1.Be7!! Nxe7 (1...Qxg4 2.Rxd8#; notice that both 1...Qxe7 and 1...Qxd1 are illegal because of the pin!) 2.Rxd7 Rxd7 3.Nc3 and White has a winning material advantage.

Exercise 16: White won by combining the pin with the skewer with 1.Rd8!! Qxd8 2.Qh8+ Kf7 3.Qxd8. Note that 1.Qh8+ Kf7 doesn't work, because the king protects the queen on e8.

Exercise 17: White wins with 1.Rxf8+!! Kxf8 2.Ng6#. Remember always to look at a double check when you see it! (And notice that 1.Rd7+ does not win, because 1...Nxc4 attacks the White queen, so that 2.Rxd8 Nxd2 3.Rxd2 maintains material equality. Also, 1.Rxb7+ Nxc4 accomplishes nothing for White.)

Exercise 18: White combined the pin and the double-attack with 1.Rd8!! Rxd8 (White threatened both 2.Rxh8 and 2.Rb7#, and 1...Ra7 is met by 2.Rxa7 Rxd8 [2...Kxa7 3.Rxh8] 3.c7+) 2.c7+ and 3.cxd8=Q+ with a winning material advantage and a mating attack to boot.

Exercise 19: Black continues 2...Ng3+!! 3.Kxg3 (3.Kg1 Rh1#) 3...f4#. A beautiful use of discovered check!

Exercise 20: White played 1.Bf3!! exf3 (the queen has no safe square to move to, and there is no effective counterattack) 2.exf3+ and the pawn captured the queen on the next move. A nice use of discovered check!

Exercise 21: Black won with 1...Nh4!, threatening 2...Qg2#. White has nothing better than either 2.Qf3 Nxf3+ 3.Nxf3, or 2.gxh4 Qxc3, in either case losing the queen for a knight.

Answers to Exercises from Chapter 7

Exercise 1: White wins material by playing 1.Nxe5!, and if 1...dxe5 then 2.Nxc5. But White should not play 1.Nxc5, with the idea that if 1...dxc5 then 2.Nxe5, because after 1.Nxc5 Black has the "in between" move 1...Nxf3+!, and after 2.gxf3 dxc5 material is still even.

Exercise 2: Fischer played 27...Bxa4!, and Spassky resigned. Fischer's point was that after 28.Qxa4 Qxe4, he has the double attack of ...Qxe1+ and ...Qxg2#, to which Spassky would have had no defense (and 29.Qe8+ Kh7 does not solve White's problem).

Exercise 3: No, it would be a very *bad* idea! After 1.Rd1?? Re1+! Black wins material by combining deflection with the x-ray. If 2.Rxe1 Qxd6, Black wins queen for rook, and if 2.Kh2 Rxd1, Black wins a whole rook.

Exercise 4: If White could get the queen on g3 to g7, it would be checkmate. And there is a way to do it: 1.Rxh7+! and then 2.Qg7#. But notice that the clearance sacrifice does not work with 1.Rg8+?? because after 1...Rxg8 Black defends the g7 square!

Exercise 5: No, 1.Bxe7 is just an even trade after 1...R8xe7. But it would be a terrible blunder for Black to reply 1...R5xe7?? because then 2.Rxe7 would win a whole rook. Notice also that the "in between" move 1...Rxe2?? would also be a disaster: After 2.Rxe2 White defends the bishop!

Exercise 6: The killer move is 1.d5!, deflecting the rook from the defense of the queen. If the rook moves, White captures the queen, and if 1...Qxa3, then White does not immediately recapture the queen, but plays the killer "in between" move 2.dxe6+ Kxe6 3.Rxa3, winning a whole rook for only a pawn.

Exercise 7: The fact that Black's king and queen are lined up along the open diagonal should be a red flag that White would like to get his bishop to f3. The best way to do that is to play 1.Nxd4!, capturing a pawn, attacking the queen, and threatening to play 2.Bf3 pinning and winning the queen.

Exercise 8: I played 43...Rxb2! and after 44.Rxb2 I won the rook back with 44...Qc1+ and 45...Qxb2. The one extra pawn was enough to win the game.

Exercise 9: I played 59...Rxh3! to divert the queen away from the pin. If 60.Qxh3 fxg5, Black comes out a knight ahead. And neither of White's checks hurt Black: After 60.Qd7+ Kf8 or 60.Qg6+ Ke7, White has no follow-up. (Always make sure the checks aren't dangerous when you calculate some way to win material.)

Exercise 10: White plays 1.Qe2! Qxe2 (if Black plays 1...cxd3?? White plays 2.Qxe7; if Black moves the queen, White plays 2.Bxc4) 2.Bxe2, recapturing the queen and moving the bishop out of harm's way.

Exercise 11: White could play 3.Rxd4!! Rxd4 (3...Rxg3 4.Rxd8 Kxd8 5.Kxg3) 4.Nf5+ and 5.Nxd4. A nice way to combine attacking the defender (the rook defending the f5 square) with the fork. Kasparov drew the game, but had he found this tactic he would have played 1.g4, which would have given him tremendous chances of winning.

Exercise 12: 1.Ne6+!! fxe6 (if the king moves, White captures the queen on f6; the queen can't capture the knight because it is pinned) 2.Rc7+! followed by Qxf6. Not only does White win the queen, he also has a mating attack.

Exercise 13: 1.Rb8!! threatens 2.Qg7# and leaves Black with no good defense: If 1...Qxb8 then 2.Nxf7#, and if 1...Rxb8 then 2.Qg7#.

Exercise 14: 1...Bc3+! wins the queen no matter what piece White puts on d2 (2.Bd2 or 2.Rd2 Qxd5; 2.Qd2 Bxd2+ and then 3...Qxh1+ just for good measure).

Exercise 15: 1.Qxe5! picked off the knight, because 1...Qxe5 is met by 2.Rd8+ Ke7 3.Re8#.

Exercise 16: 1.Rg8+!! Kxg8 (1...Rxg8 2.Qxc1 is a winning material advantage for White) 2.Qg3+ Kf8 (2...Kh8 3.Qg7#) 3.Qg7+ Ke8 4.Qg8#.

Exercise 17: 1...Rh1+!! 2.Kxh1 (2.Kg2 Rxh5) 2...Nxg3+ and 3...Nxh5.

Exercise 18: Black wins material with 1...Rxd2! 2.Qxd2 (2.Rxe7 Rxd1+ and 3...Bxe7; 2.Bxd2 Qxa7) 2...Rxd2 (2...Qxa7? 3.Qxd8+! Bxd8 4.Bxd2) 3.Rxe7 Rd1+! (3...Bxe7 4.Bxd2) 4.Kh2 Bxe7 and Black is up a rook. Note that 1...Rxa7 does not win material: 2.Rxd8+! Qxd8 3.Qxd8+ Bxd8 4.Bxa7.

Exercise 19: White won with 1.Re7!! (Not 1.Rd6?? Bxd6 2.Qxd5+ Kf8) 1...Qxe7 (if 1...Bxe7 or 1...Nxe7 then 2.Qf7#) 2.Qxd5+ and checkmate next move.

Exercise 20: 1.Rh8! Qxh8 (1...Qc8+ 2.Rxc8; 1...h6 2. Rxh6#; otherwise White plays Rxh7#) 2.g4#.

Answers to Exercises from Chapter 8

Exercise 1: I played 44.Bb7! and Black resigned. Moving the bishop off the d5 square threatens 45.Rd8#, and moving the bishop to b7 prevents both rooks from defending against the threat, because the rook on b6 is now blocked from moving to b8, and 44...Ra8 is met by 45.Bxa8.

Exercise 2: After 22.Bxe6+!, Black resigned. There is nothing better than 22...dxe6, after which 23.Rf8# is checkmate.

Exercise 3: If White plays 26.Nxd1, then 26...e1=Q# is checkmate. If White plays 26.Rxd1, Black wins with the beautiful move, 26...Qxc3!!. The point of this move is to threaten 27...e1=Q, and also to deflect the white queen away from the defense of the rook on d1, so that if 27.Qxc3, then 27...exd1=Q+ mates next move. In fact, White has nothing better than either 27.Qb1 or 27.Rf1, both of which allow Black to capture the rook with check, gaining a decisive material advantage.

Exercise 4: If 1.Qxh5, then 1...Nf2# is checkmate. If 1.Qg3, then Black wins with 1...Qxh2+! 2.Qxh2 Nf2#. In fact, White is lost in the position in the diagram, even though he is ahead a whole bishop!

Exercise 5: If it's Black's turn to move, then 1...Qh3! wins, because Black threatens 2...Qg2# and White has no defense. If it's White's turn to move, he should play 1.Nd2!, which threatens to capture the bishop (so that 1...Qh3?? 2.Nxf3 would be a disaster for Black). Black must move the bishop away, and then if Black brings the queen to h3 later to threaten checkmate again, White will have two defenses—either moving a pawn to block the diagonal (the pawn on f2 to f3 or the pawn on e3 to e4) and so cut off the bishop's control of the g2 square—or playing Qf1 to defend the g2 square directly. By the way, 1.e4? with the idea of meeting 1...Qh3 with 2.Ne3 does not work, because then 2...Ng4! forces checkmate.

Exercise 6: White's idea was to march his king to h6 and play Qg7 checkmate. Incredibly, Black has no good defense. In the game, Black played (after 33.Kf4) 33...Bc8, and after 34.Kg5 he resigned. Black cannot stop the king from going to h6 by playing 34...Kh7, because after 35.Rxf7+ Rxf7 36.Qxf7+ Kh8 37.Kh6, Black will be checkmated. Please note that it's very rare to be able to use the king so aggressively when there are so many pieces on the board! This is an exceptional position.

Exercise 7: I played 14.Bxh6!, which wins a pawn, because if Black plays 14...gxh6, then after 15.Qd3! White threatens both 16.Qxc4 and 16.Qg3+ followed by 17.Qg7#. Playing 14.Qd3 right away doesn't work because after 14...Nd6, 15.Qg3 is not check, and Black can just capture the knight on f5; 14.Bxh6 exposes the black king to an important check.

Exercise 8: 1.Ng5!! Qxg6 2.Qxh7+!! Qxh7 3.Nf7#.

Exercise 9: 1...Ne5! attacks the bishop on d3 and also threatens 2...Qf3+ 3.Kg1 Bh3. White cannot defend against both threats.

Exercise 10: 1...Qxg3+!! (tamer moves don't work, for example, 1...Rd5 2.cxd5 Qxg3+ [or 2...Bxg3+ 3.Kg1] 3.Kh1 Qh3+ 4.Rh2!) 2.Kxg3 Rg5+!! 3.Kh3 (the only legal move) 3...Rf3#.

Exercise 11: White wins with 1.Ne6!! fxe6 (or else Black loses the queen) 2.Qh5+ g6 3.Qxg6#. This is a kind of "smothered mate" with the queen. Note that 1.Qh5 makes no headway against 1...g6!

Exercise 12: White plays 2.Rxe8!! Rxe8 3.Qg4+ Bg7 (or 3...Kh8 4.Bxf6+ Bg7 5.Qxg7#) 4.Bxf6 followed by 5.Qxg7#. Notice how the attack worked: First White exposed the Black king (1.Nh6+ gxh6), then White eliminated a crucial defender of the f6 and g7 squares (2.Rxe8 Rxe8), and then White forced checkmate with the queen and bishop using the f6 and g7 squares (3.Qg4+ and 4.Bxf6).

Exercise 13: 1.Qc7+!! Nxc7 2.Nb6+! axb6 (or 2...Kb8 3.Rd8#) 3.Rd8#.

Exercise 14: 1.Qxf8+!! Kxf8 2.Bh6+ Kg8 3.Re8#.

Exercise 15: 1.Qa4+!! (not 1.b4 Qa3+! and Black gains time with the check to defend) 1...Qxa4 2.Nc7+ Kf8 3.Rxd8+ Qe8 4.Rxe8#.

Answers to Exercises from Chapter 9

Exercise 1: Black has played better. White's first move does little to control the center, and weakens the kingside. (If White wants to fianchetto his king's bishop, 1.g3 is a much better move.) Black's move, on the other hand, is superb. It fights for control of the center, and it helps develop his pieces. If White plays 2.f3??, he does nothing to develop his pieces, and little to fight for the center. But its worst feature is that because it weakens the diagonal e1-h4 which leads to the king, Black can give checkmate with 2...Qh4#. This is called the "Fool's Mate," and it is the fastest possible checkmate.

Exercise 2: It would be an excellent move; 1...d5 not only fights for control of the center, and helps to develop the queenside pieces, it does all that with gain of time, because it attacks the bishop on c4. Notice that the pawn on d5 is adequately protected, because the queen on d8 protects d5. One of the advantages of pushing the d-pawn is that doing so increases the scope of the queen along the d-file.

Exercise 3: Black's second move allows White to exchange the less valuable c-pawn for the more valuable d-pawn. White's extra center pawn will give him better control of the center than Black. Black's third move exposes the queen to attack, and allows White to develop a piece with gain of time by playing 4.Nc3.

Exercise 4: This is a good position for Black to fianchetto the king's bishop. Because White's d-pawn has pushed forward to d5, and because Black has pawns on d6 and c5, the bishop will have very good control of the diagonal, and it will be strongly placed there. Notice how the bishop's control of the diagonal will go right through the center and reach White's queenside!

Exercise 5: White should castle queenside. Castling kingside would be a very bad idea, because White's king would be exposed there. Not only does it lack some protection by its pawns, it would be especially susceptible to attack because Black already has the open h-file which leads right to the king's position.

Exercise 6: It is a bad move. Although White makes two attacks at the same time (4.Qxc5 and 4.Qxf7#), Black defends both easily with 3...e6 (the pawn blocks the bishop's control of the f7 square, and the bishop on f8 defends the pawn on c5). Black defends both threats by making a very useful developing move that he would want to make anyway. Meanwhile, White's queen is exposed and out of play. Black will soon play ...Nf6 and gain time to develop his knight to the center while attacking the queen. Always be very suspicious of double-attacks that bring the queen out too early in the opening!

Exercise 7: Black threatens to capture the pawn on e4, and White must respond to that threat. White's best moves are 3.exd5 (meeting the threat with gain of time), 3.e5 (gaining space), 3.Nc3 (defending the pawn with a knight, while keeping the diagonal open for the bishop on c1), and 3.Nd2 (defending the pawn with a knight, while ensuring that if Black tries to pin the knight with 3...Bb4, White can break the pin with 4.c3). It is less good to defend the pawn with the bishop or with the queen, because Black will capture the pawn and then play ...Nf6, gaining time to develop. (This is an example of the principle, "Develop knights before bishops.") Also not good is 3.Bb5+, as after 3...c6 White must retreat the bishop and so must defend the e4 pawn with the bishop. Finally, while 3.f3 has a worthy idea behind it (recapture a center pawn with a wing pawn), it fails tactically: 3...dxe4 4.fxe4 Qh4+ and 5...Qxe4. This is an example of how dangerous it is to move your f-pawn too early in the opening!

Exercise 8: The bad move is 3...Be7?, which allows White to gain a huge advantage in the center with 4.e4. Both 3...Bb4 and 3...d5 are good moves, as they not only develop in the center, but they also hinder White from playing 4.e4. Notice that after 3...d5, if White plays 4.cxd5 then Black can recapture with 4...exd5, keeping a strong pawn in the center. This is a huge improvement over Exercise 3, where Black was not able to keep his strong pawn in the center, and where he lost time by moving his pieces several times in the opening.

Exercise 9: The problem with each move is that it is too passive. Moving first gives White the initiative, but this will evaporate if he does not develop his pieces as aggressively as is reasonably possible. Moving the bishop to b5 or c4 places the bishop on an active square; on b5 it harasses Black's knight, while on c4 it controls a central diagonal. On e2 the bishop does not contribute to the fight for the center, so this move does not put any pressure on Black's game. Moving the bishop to d3 is even worse. At least on e2, White can continue his development normally. But on d3, the bishop blocks the d-pawn from moving forward, hindering White's future development.

Exercise 10: The big drawback of 5...exd4? is that it opens the e-file. White continues 6.Re1! and Black's knight is in trouble. If 6...d5 then 7.Nxd4! threatens both 8.Nxc6 bxc6 9.Bxc6+ and 10.Bxa8, and 8.f3, attacking the pinned knight. If 6...f5 then 7.Nxd4 threatens both 8.f3 and 8.Nxf5. Black might try (after 6...f5 7.Nxd4) 7...Nxd4 8.Qxd4 Be7, but after 9.Qxg7 White has restored material equality and has a raging attack against Black's king. The moral is to be very careful about opening files against your king in the opening, especially when playing Black!

Answers to Exercises from Chapter 10

Exercise 1: White should aim for a position where he has a knight against Black's bad bishop. That is why I played 22.Bxf5! Qxf5 23.Nxc6! Bxc6. Black's bishop is terribly restricted by its own pawns; not only the pawns on d5 and e6, but even the pawn on g6 restricts it, because the bishop has no hope of becoming more active by playing ...Be8 and ...Bg6 or ...Bh5. White has a very large advantage in the position, and I won by maneuvering the knight to the kingside and attacking Black's king.

Exercise 2: The knight goes to h1 in order to go to g3, and then to either f5 or h5. But moving the knight has another advantage: It enables the queen to shift to h2, where together with the rook (and the knight once it completes its journey), it will put great pressure on Black's kingside. The game continued: 17...f6 18.Qh2 h6 19.Ng3 Kh7 20.Be2 Rg8 21.Kf2! (the king is perfectly safe on this square in this position, and moving it off the first rank allows the rook on a1 to move over to the kingside to join the attack), and White won by virtue of his attack against the black king.

Exercise 3: The correct move is 15...f6, which blunts the diagonal b2-g7 leading straight to the king. Notice that this move follows the rule of putting pawns on the opposite color of the one bishop Black has. (Black puts the pawns on black squares because he has the white-squared bishop.) Doing so would accentuate the power of his own bishop, and lessen the power of White's "extra" bishop. The move he played was 15...f5?, which makes it impossible to block this diagonal with a pawn. After 16.f4 Nc6 17.Bc4+ Kh8 18.Bb2 Qe7 19.Rae1 Rf6 20.exf5 Qf8, White had already won back one pawn and his attack was stronger than ever. In fact, Morphy won this game very nicely with 21.Re8!! Qxe8 22.Qxf6! Qe7 (22...gxf6 23.Bxf6#) 23.Qxg7+!! Qxg7 24.f6. I urge you to study this position and understand why Black must lose material here.

Exercise 4: Black has good play after 17...Rdc8! which attacks the knight on c3, and in general puts great pressure on White's queenside. Notice how the two bishops put pressure on the b2 and a2 pawns. It is very common for the two bishops to give enough compensation for a pawn in such a position. White decided not to defend the pawn by playing 18.Rfc1 (18.Rac1 loses the a-pawn after 18...Bxc3 19.bxc3 Qxa2) because he did not like his position after 18...Rc7 followed by doubling rooks on the c-file. But even after he gave back the pawn, White's a-pawn remained weak, and Black won the game by attacking on the queenside.

Exercise 5: White should attack Black at his weakest point: The f7 pawn. One way to do this is to play 1.h5 and 2.g6. (Also possible is to play 1.Qf3 before pushing the kingside pawns, and still another idea is to play 1.Rh3 with the intention of playing 2.Rf3 and then push the kingside pawns.) Notice how much more active White's bishop is than Black's bishop!

Exercise 6: White should play 1.Bh6! to exchange off the fianchettoed bishop. In fact, whenever you want to attack a king that stands behind a fianchettoed bishop, it is usually a good idea to exchange off that bishop: It is a valuable defensive piece, and once it is removed the king is much more exposed. In this position, the move has the additional virtue of enabling the queen to move closer to Black's king with decisive effect; for example 1...Bxh6 2.Qxh6 and the threat of checkmate is devastating. If Black allows White to capture the bishop and then give check with the queen on h6, once again the queen's power will overwhelm Black.

Exercise 7: Black should play 1...Red8! to seize control of the open d-file, and then once he has taken control of the d-file, he should put one (or both) rooks on the second rank by playing ...Rd2. Black has an enormous advantage in the endgame.

Exercise 8: White has a large advantage because of his greater control of the center, and because his knight and queen are so much better than their black counterparts. There are many ways to exploit these advantages, but the best way is 1.e5! fxe5 2.fxe5 dxe5 (Black must not allow this pawn to get to e6, or it will become much too powerful). 3.Qxe5, and the threats of 4.Nxc7 and (much more important) 4.Ne7+ are very difficult for Black to meet. The following variation is especially instructive: 4...Qg7 5.Ne7+! Kf8? (5...Kh8 6.Qxc7 is better, but still winning for White) 6.Qd5! (threatening not only 7.Qxa8+ but also 7.Qd8+! which mates on the back rank) 6...Re8 (the only rook move to defend both threats) 7.Nxg6+!! Qxg6 8.Rxe8+ and White wins material, because Black cannot recapture the rook: 8...Kxe8 9.Qd8#.

Exercise 9: The idea is to continue 3.Nf3! and 4.Ne5! when the knight is a powerhouse on e5. If Black captures the knight with his bishop, he gives up the bishop pair, and trades off his more powerful bishop to do so. (The dark-squared bishop is more powerful because most of Black's pawns are on light squares.) After 1.e5 Be7 as played in the game, White's pieces (particularly his knight) were very passive, and this led to his downfall.

Exercise 10: White has the advantage because he has the two bishops well placed in an open position. One possible plan to neutralize this advantage is to exchange a pair of bishops by playing 1...Nd7 and 2...Bf6. For example: 1...Nd7 2.Qc2 h6 (White threatened 3.Bxh7+ and 4.Bxh7+) 3.Rad1 Qc7 (not 3...Bf6? 4.Bxf6! and if 4...Qxf6 or 4...Nxf6 then 5.Bh7+!) followed by 4...Bf6. White still has the advantage, but once Black exchanges his passive bishop for White's powerhouse bishop, he will be closer to an equal game.

Exercise 11: In contrast to Exercise 10, here White's bishops are passive, while Black's pieces (including his queen and his bishop) are active. In addition, although White has an extra pawn, it is doubled and isolated. (See Chapter 11 for more about doubled and isolated pawns.) So Black has a very good game. The obvious move is 1...Qxc5, and this is enough to give Black an advantage. But Anand found an even stronger way to play: 1...Qe5!, threatening 2...Nd4. After 2.Qa4 (attacking the knight on c6) 2...Rad8! 3.Be1 Nd4!, Black had a fantastic initiative, and soon won.

Exercise 12: Black played 1...Rd8!, with the tactical justification that 2.Rxb5?? Rd1+ 3.Bf1 Bh3 forces 4.Nd2 Rxa1, when Black is winning. With the rook on the open file, Black quickly built up a dominating position and won the game.

Exercise 13: White has a winning advantage. Black's queen is so passive that Black is practically playing without it. Meanwhile, Black has no active play elsewhere—notice how the bishop on e3 and the pawn on d4 restricts Black's bishop and his rooks. White's light-squared bishop is a monster. So long as White is careful not to allow Black's queen to get out, he has a winning plan of attacking the king. The game continued 1...h6 2.a6! f5 3.Bh3! Rf8 4.a7+ Kc8 5.Qb1! (forcing the g-pawn to advance, giving White the f4 square for his bishop) 5...g4 6.Bf1 Kd7 7.Bd3 Ke6 8.Bf4 Rf7 9.Qc2 Bf8 10.Qe2+ and Black resigned because it will be mate shortly. See how horrible the queen was on a8. You can't play without your most powerful piece like that!

Exercise 14: White should play 1.Nh4! and maneuver this knight to f5. White should follow this up with moving the rook on a3 to the kingside (either Rg3 or Rh3), and then bringing the queen into play via g4 or h5. The passive Black bishop will be more of a target than a defensive piece, and the knight on f5 will be a powerhouse. The attack should be decisive. For example: 1.Nh4! Qf7 2.Nf5 Kh8 3.Rh3 Rg8 4.R1e3! (this threatens 5.Rxh7+! and 6.Rh3+) 4...Bf8 5.Rh5! followed by 6.Reh3, with a devastating attack. This is a good example of how an advantage in having more active pieces (the White knight versus the black bishop, and also the White rooks versus the Black rooks) can lead to an opportunity to attack the opponent's weakest point (in this case the king, because the knight on f5 looks straight at the kingside).

Exercise 15: Black can play 1...Bd8! followed by 2...Ba5 or 2...Bb6, activating the bishop by getting it outside the e5 and d6 pawns. Black would be no worse in the resulting position.

Answers to Exercises from Chapter 11

Exercise 1: If it's Black's turn, he should play 1...h4! to attack the g3 pawn. In fact, White must lose a pawn after this move; he can't protect g3 enough times (Don't overlook that the black queen on c7 also attacks it!), and after 2.gxh4 (2.g4 fxg4 3.hxg4 Rxg4) 2...Rxh4 3.Rh1 Rgh8 Black wins the h-pawn. If it's White's turn, he should play 1.h4! to stop this move.

Exercise 2: White can create a pawn duo and increase his control of the center with 10.f4.

Exercise 3: After 27...Nxd5 28.exd5, White can create an extremely strong pawn duo next move with 29.c5. White should attack Black's weakened queenside and advance his pawns. The strong pawns and pair of bishops will completely dominate Black's position. (In particular Black's bishop on f8 will remain very passive.) By advancing the pawns and threatening to promote one of them, Black will be forced to lose material. Black will try to attack White's king, but he will not have enough material in that part of the board for his attack to succeed. This is a *very* complicated position, so don't worry if this explanation leaves you unconvinced. Study the continuation of the game at your leisure, and see if you can understand why White won. Notice in particular the strength of the pawn duo: (after 27...Nxd5 28.exd5) 28...Qg6 29.c5 e4 30.Be2 Re5 31.Qd7 Rg5 32.Rg1 e3 33.d6 Rg3 34.Qxb7 Qe6 (Black threatens 35...Rxh3+!) 35.Kh2!. (But now Black must lose material, because amazingly after 35...Qe5 36.Qxa8, Black doesn't have a good discovered check!) Black resigned.

Exercise 4: The doubled pawns are nothing to be concerned about. Although moving the pawn from f2 to e3 does create another pawn island, all of White's pawns are well protected so it is not too much of a drawback. On the plus side, the pawn controls the center better on e3 than on f2, and most importantly, White gains the useful f-file for his rook. In fact, Black decided to play 20...Qe6 21.Qxe6 fxe6, doubling his own pawns to neutralize the open f-file by putting his own rook there.

Exercise 5: Here the doubled pawns are a serious weakness. Not only does the pawn on f6 block the fianchettoed bishop's diagonal, even more seriously the d6 pawn is isolated and very weak. Kasparov drew this position, but only after suffering for many moves.

Exercise 6: Black should play 1...c3!, after which White is much worse. For example, after 2.bxc3 Qxc3 3.Rfc1 (to protect the c-pawn) 3...Nf4! 4.gxf4 Rxd2 White's pawns are a shambles, and Black's pieces are much more active than White's.

Exercise 7: White played the very strong move 21.Rd1! when the game continued 21...Bxc5 22.Bxc5 Qe5 23.Bxf8 Kxf8 24.Rd4! and White had a large advantage. Black's d-pawn is isolated and weak, and Black has no threats against White's position. (Notice how useful it is for White to exchange several pairs of pieces when playing against the isolated pawn: The exchange of pieces has neutralized any hope Black would have of causing trouble to White's king, but White has kept enough pieces to put pressure on Black's d-pawn.) White won a long game.

Exercise 8: White wins with 1.a5!. This move stops Black from making a passed pawn on the queenside, because if the b-pawn moves White can capture it (*en passant* if necessary) and his passed pawn will be further advanced than Black's. Black cannot use the king to capture the pawn, because then White will make a passed pawn on the kingside and win, for example 1...Kc5 2.f4 Kb5 3.g5 Kxa5 4.h6 and White queens before Black. So Black must keep his king near the kingside, but then White will distract the king by making a passed pawn on the kingside and then win on the queenside. Here is one sample line to illustrate how this might happen: 1...Ke5 2.Ke3 Ke6 3.f4 Kd5 4.g5 fxg5 5.fxg5 Ke5 6.h6 gxh6 7.gxh6 Kf6 8.Kd4 Kg6 9.Kc5 Kxh6 10.Kb6 Kg6 11.Kxb7 Kf6 12.Kxa6 Ke6 13.Kb7 followed by a6-a7-a8=Q and wins.

Exercise 9: White should play 1.fxe5. Remember that as a general rule, you should capture toward the center. Here there are three specific reasons why this capture is correct: (1) It opens the f-file, activating the rook on f1. (2) It opens the c1-h6 diagonal, activating the bishop on c1. (3) It maintains the pawn on d4, which keeps the knight on c5 passive. Kasparov in fact played 1.fxe5! and won without trouble. Had White captured 1.dxe5, Black could have gotten counterplay with 1...Nc5!.

Exercise 10: White has a pawn structure advantage, because he has four pawns to Black's three on the kingside, while Black's extra pawn on the queenside is doubled. But this advantage is currently limited, because Black's h-pawn restrains White's g- and h-pawns. (See "When One Pawn Holds Two" in Chapter 11.) If White plays g2-g4 and allows ...hxg3, White will have split pawns on the kingside, and in particular the h-pawn will be isolated and weak. But if White can play g2-g4 without allowing ...hxg3+, White will have a powerful pawn duo on f4 and g4, and will be able to establish an even more powerful pawn duo via f4-f5 on e5 and f5.

Exercise 11: White to move should play 1.c5!, threatening both 2.cxd6 and 2.c6, in both cases undermining Black's pawns. Black to move should play 1...b6, stopping c4-c5.

Exercise 12: Black should play 1...f4!. This move undoubles Black's pawns and it attacks White's pawn on e3. In addition, it activates Black's bishop on c8. White is faced with a difficult choice. If he plays 2.exf4 Nxf4, Black suddenly has very active pieces close to White's king (the knight on f4, the bishops on c7 and c8, the rook on e8). If White defends the e3 pawn, e.g. with 2.Qd3, then after 2...fxe3 3.fxe3 Qe7 4.Nd1, Black has the better pawn structure and more active pieces, plus the two bishops to boot.

Exercise 13: It may appear at first to be a bad move, because it allows Black to exchange off his weak, doubled pawn on c5. But in fact it is a very good move, because it accomplishes three things: (1) It takes control of the weak c5 square (see Chapter 13 for more about weak squares), which allows White to post his knight strongly on c5. (2) It exposes the a-pawn as a weakness on the open a-file. (3) It weakens the d-pawn, by undermining the c5 pawn that defends it. The game continued 1.b4 Nf5 2.Ne5 Bxe5 3.fxe5 cxb4 4.axb4 Qxe4 5.Rxe4, and White quickly had an overwhelming position. It is not always a good idea to exchange a doubled pawn, but in the right situation it can be a powerful idea if executed well.

Exercise 14: White should play 1.h5! followed by 2.hxg6. This opens the h-file against the king, which will enable White to bring his queen and rook into the attack, with deadly force. Play might continue: 1.h5! b5 2.hxg6 hxg6 3.Bh6! with a winning attack. By the way, this position is taken from the Dragon Variation of the Sicilian Defense (see Chapter 9). Black can avoid this fate if he plays the opening better than this, but still this is a good illustration of the dangers he faces when White employs this strategy.

Exercise 15: White should play 1.cxd4. This capture is correct because (1) it captures towards the center; and (2) other captures leave White with three pawn islands, instead of two. (Remember, all things being equal, the fewer pawn islands the better!) The game continued 1.Nxd4?! Bd7! 2.Nb3?! (better was 2.Nxc6 Bxc6 3.Bxc6 bxc6, but Black is better here as his pieces are more active) 2...Qc7 3.Nc5 Be8 and Black was better because of his better pawn structure.

Answers to Exercises from Chapter 12

Exercise 1: Always be on the alert for a tactic. Black wins a pawn by 10...Nxd4! 11.Nxd4 Qh4+.

Exercise 2: The two moves are 7.e5 and 7.d5, but 7.e5 is less effective, because after 7...dxe5 8.dxe5 Qxd1+ 9.Bxd1 Nd7 (9...Bxf3 10.Bxf3 Nxe5 doesn't win a pawn because of 11.Bxb7) 10.Bf4 Bb4 all of Black's pieces are active, and White's e5-pawn is weak. I played 7.d5! exd5 8.exd5. Now Black didn't want to retreat the knight to e7 or b8 (notice that after 8...Ne7 Black wouldn't be threatening to capture the d5-pawn; notice also that 8...Ne5? is a mistake because 9.Nxe5 wins a pawn), so he played 8...Bxf3 9.Bxf3 Ne5 10.Be2 Be7 11.O-O O-O, but I had the advantage because of my two bishops and more space. By pushing my d-pawn instead of my e-pawn, I kept Black's dark-squared bishop constrained and avoided the exchange of queens. Also, the pawn on d5 is supported by the queen, which makes it harder for Black to attack than the e5-pawn would have been after 7.e5.

Exercise 3: Count squares and it's clear that White has more space. In particular, the strong pawn on d5 gives him more space on the queenside, so that's where he should attack. A very good move here is 14.b4!, as Reshevsky played. This move gains more space on the queenside, and it also prepares the pawn push c4-c5 (after White controls the c5 square enough times so that this move doesn't lose a pawn, of course), which will put even more pressure on Black's queenside and center.

Exercise 4: White has more space. One of the advantages of the isolated center pawn is that it usually gives the side who has it more space than the opponent. With more space, you can attack. One of the most important reasons you should not trade too many pieces when you have the isolated center pawn is the same reason you should not trade too many pieces when you have an advantage in space: The more pieces you keep, the more effective your attack will be.

Exercise 5: Black's space advantage is on the kingside, so he should find a way to attack there if he can. I found a way to press my attack and also gain more space: 17...g5! 18.Nge2 Ng4! Because White's knight has been driven back, White has less space; because Black's pawn and knight have advanced on the kingside, Black has more space. Now Black's attack in the center and the kingside more than compensates for the sacrificed pawn. (Part of Black's compensation comes from the fact that the d3 square is weak, and Black has the possibility of maneuvering the king's knight to that square with ...Ne5-d3.) In fact, White quickly lost after 19.b3 Qe5! 20.g3? (20.Ng3 was forced) 20...Qf5, and the threat of 21...Ne5-f3 with a winning attack forced White to play 21.Nxe4 Qxe4 22.f3, but after 22...Qxe3+! 23.Qxe3 Nxe3 24.Bxe3 Nc2 I won easily with the material advantage I gained from the knight fork.

Exercise 6: The space count is roughly equal, although Black is threatening to gain more space on the queenside by playing ...a6 and ...c5. My move 14.c4? was terrible because after 14...b4! my bishop on d3 had become a very bad piece, and Black threatened to gain a huge amount of space on the queenside by playing ...c5. I couldn't play 15.c5, because after 15...Nxc5 16.Qxb4 Nxd3 17.Qxe7 Rxe7 18.Rxd3 Ba6! Black wins material. I tried to get tricky with 15.a3, hoping for 15...a5, when I planned to play 16.axb4 axb4 17.c5 Nxc5 18.Qxb4 Nxd3 19.Qxe7 Rxe7 20.Rxd3 and if 20...Ba6 then 21.Ra3! pins the bishop to the rook on a8. But Gurevich was too smart for that, and he played 15...c5!. Now if 16.axb4 cxb4 17.c5 Nxc5 18.Qxb4 Nxd3 19.Qxe7 Rxe7 20.Rxd3 Ba6 there is no pin along the a-file, so Black wins material again. I had to let Black gain lots of space on the queenside, and he won a nice game.

Exercise 7: Fischer overlooked that Black could play 13...f5!, gaining space on the kingside. (Not 14.exf6?? because of 14...Qxf4+.) Fischer won the game, but in Fischer's opinion, the space that Black gained on the kingside gave him about equal chances in this position.

Exercise 8: The game continued: 9.cxd6 (Fischer says that White should give back the pawn in order to complete his development and castle, and he suggests that the best way to do this is 9.Nf3 Bg4 10.Be2, although I think that after 10...dxe5 Black is better.) 9...exd6 10.Ne4 (Fischer quotes Grandmaster William Lombardy as saying that 10.Nf3 would have been "more realistic," although after 10...Bg4 Fischer still likes his position. Notice that after 10.exd6 Nxd6, Black will play ...Re8 next move, pinning the bishop on e3 to the king. White will not be able to castle, and Black will have a huge attack against the king for only one pawn.) 10...Bf5! (Black continues to develop with gain of time. Notice that 10...dxe5? 11.Qxd8 Nxd8 12.Bc5 loses the rook for bishop.) 11.Ng3 (Fischer thinks that 11.Nxd6 Nxd6 12.Qxd6 Qxd6 13.exd6 is a better chance for White, but he concedes that after 13...Nb4! Black will get back the pawns and maintain an attack.) 11...Be6 12.Nf3 Qc7 and because White could still not afford to open the e-file and the fianchettoed bishop's diagonal with 13.exd6, Black regained the pawn next move with 13...dxe5, and also kept his attack. This is a complicated and difficult position, and I don't expect you to be able to see everything, even if you study it for some time. The most important thing for you to understand from this exercise is when the center opened up, and White was far behind Black in development, Black's active pieces were able to exploit White's weaknesses and his exposed king. Those advantages were worth more for Black than the one or two extra pawns were worth to White. If you want to push your pawns to gain space, you must be certain that your opponent can't open the center and use his developed pieces to attack your undeveloped position!

Exercise 9: Black gains space and strikes at White's strong e4 pawn by playing 1...d5!. White must either allow Black to capture on e4, which will weaken his pawn structure and also weaken his dark squares, or he must capture on d5, which will surrender control of much of the center to Black. Two sample lines:

(a) 2.Qe1 dxe4 3.Rxd8+ Qxd8 4.fxe4 e5 and Black has equal space and better pawns.

(b) 2.exd5 Nxd5 3.Nxd5 Rxd5 4.Qe1 Rxd1+ 5.Qxd1 e5, and Black has at least as good a pawn structure as White, and controls more space. Notice how Black's game improves once he exchanges off White's strong center pawn on e4.

Exercise 10: White has more space, as a space count shows, so 14...Nd5! is an excellent move to trade pieces. Because White's queen is attacked, the knight can't be captured. The game continued 15.Qd2 Nxc3 16.Bxc3 Bxc3 17.Rxc3 Nf6 18.f3 Qc7 19.e4 b5 20.Rdc1 Rc8 21.Ne3 Qa5 and chances were equal, because Black had solved his problem of a space disadvantage.

Exercise 11: White played 1.f5! Bd7 2.g4!, taking a terrific amount of space on the kingside. Notice that although his light-squared bishop is very bad, Black's light-squared bishop is even worse! Meanwhile, White's grip in the center prevents Black from getting counterplay there, so White can focus on attacking on the kingside, where his extra space gives him a large advantage. After 2...Ne8 3.Ng3 Qd8 4.g5! Bc8 6.h4 f6 7.Qh5! White's attack was in full swing, and he soon won.

Exercise 12: Kramnik played 1.g4! h6 2.h4! Bc8 3.g5 hxg5 4.hxg5 Nfd7 5.f4! Ng6 6.Nf3, and White had a large advantage because of his space advantage and more active pieces. A very important thing to note is that the plan beginning with 1.g4 was only possible because Black's pieces did not have active squares to go to when they were attacked, and so they had to retreat. For example, when White played 3.g5, Black had to retreat his knight to d7 and couldn't go to e4 or d5, and when White played 5.f4, Black had to retreat his knight to g6, and couldn't go to c4, d3, f3, or g4. If you are going to push your pawns forward to take more space, be sure that your opponent can't move his pieces forward to more active squares!

Exercise 13: Black should play 1...d5! so that 2.g5 can be met by 2...hxg5 3.hxg5 Nxe4, and 2.exd5 can be met by 2...Nxd5. Always look to meet an attempt to gain space by a counter-thrust in the center!

Exercise 14: Black should play 1...c5! so that 2.e4 can be met by 2...cxd4! 3.Nxd4 Bb7. By exchanging the c-pawn for the d-pawn, Black has neutralized White's space advantage.

Exercise 15: 1...c5 is less effective because after 2.d5! White's space advantage has increased, not decreased. Striking with ...c7-c5 against this pawn formation can be effective in positions where the dark-squared bishop is fianchettoed on g7, because it increased the power of the bishop along that diagonal. (For example, see Exercise 4 in Chapter 9.) But here Black's bishop is in no position to operate along that diagonal, and so Black simply loses space for nothing. Much better is 1...Ne4! to exchange knights. After 2.Qc2 Nxc3 3.Qxc3, now Black can play 3...c5 much more effectively, because White's queen no longer supports d4-d5 in response. Grandmaster practice has shown this position to be roughly equal.

Answers to Exercises from Chapter 13

Exercise 1: White can play 1.Bg5! and then 2.Bxf6. The bishop can't control d5 directly, but it can contribute by exchanging itself for Black's knight, which does control d5.

Exercise 2: White can play 1.Ng5! which exploits the weakened g5 square. White threatens 2.Bxf6 and 3.Qh7+ followed by 4.Qh8#, and Black has no defense. For ex-ample, 2...bxa4 3.Bxf6 axb3 (3...gxf6 4.Qh7+ Kf8 5.Qxf7# or 5.Qh8#; 3...Bxf6 4.Qh7+ Kf8 5.Qh8#) 4.Qh7+ Kf8 5.Qxg7# or 5.Qh8#. If Black's g6 pawn were on h7, however, then Black's attack on the queenside would win, because White would have no way to get to Black's king in time. For example, 1.Ng5 would be easily met by 1...h6!

Exercise 3: Botvinnik's idea was to exploit the weak d5 square by putting his bishop on it. The game continued 18.Be4! Rb8 19.Rad1 b6 20.h3 Ba6 21.Bd5 and White had a large advantage thanks to his space advantage and his super-strong bishop on d5.

Exercise 4: Black has very weak squares on f6 and h6, which White exploited by playing 25.Nh2! Nd4 26.Ng4. The game continued 26...Rd8 27.Nf6+ Kg7 28.Qe3! and Black couldn't play 28...Rxd6 29.cxd6 Qxd6?? because of 30.Ne8+ forking the king and queen. White soon won this game due to his excellent play.

Exercise 5: I overlooked the very strong move 26.Qc1! Bb5 (There's nothing better.) 27.Bxb5 axb5 28.Qh6!, and White had a winning attack because he threatens 29.Rxe4! and 30.Ng5, and there's no good defense. I soon lost.

Exercise 6: I played 27.Qg4! which threatens 28.Nxh6+, but more importantly threatens 28.Rd8! which deflects the queen away from the bishop, allowing Qxg7#. Bronstein defended against the second threat by playing 27...Rb1 (27...Kh7? 28.Rd8! Rxd8 29.Rxd8 still wins; the pin is not as important as the deflection), but after 28.Nxh6+ Kh7 29.Nf5 I quickly won because Black's king was so exposed.

Exercise 7: The correct move is 35...Qg3!, because after 36.Nxe6 Ra2! 37.Re2 (What else?) 37...Ra1+ Black wins. White would have to play something like 36.Ne2, but then 36...Qh2 is very strong. Instead, Lasker played 35...Qh2?, and after 36.Nxe6 Ra2 37.Re2 Ra1+ 38.Kf2, there was no checkmate because 38...Qg1+ 39.Kg3 is okay for White. Lasker played 38...fxe6, but after 39.Qg6! he lost a pawn, and eventually the game.

Exercise 8: I played 17...Bf8!, and after 18.Qe2 Bg7 not only were the squares around my king well defended, my bishop also had a strong post where it could attack White's isolated d-pawn.

Exercise 9: White must move the king, because any attempt to block the check loses material. (For example, 21.Nf3 Qxd2 22.Rxd2 Bxc3.) Let's look at each king move:

(a) 21.Kh3 Qd7+ 22.g4 h5 23.Qf4 hxg4+ gives Black a fearsome attack, because 24.Qxg4? loses material to 24...Re3+ 25.Kh4 Bf6+.

(b) 21.Kg1 Bxd4+! 22.Qxd4 Re1+! 23.Kf2 (23.Rxe1 Qxd4) 23...Qxd4 24.Rxd4 Rxa1 wins material, as Fischer points out.

(c) 21.Kf2 is a tough nut to crack, but Fischer gives the following beautiful variation: 21...Qd7! 22.Rac1 Qh3 (threatens 23...Qg2# as well as 23...Qxh2+) 23.Nf3 Bh6 24.Qd3 Be3+ 25.Qxe3 (25.Ke2 Qg2+ 26.Ke1 Qf2#) 25...Rxe3 26.Kxe3 (White still has a material advantage, but because of the weakness of his white squares it won't last.) 26...Re8+ 27.Kf2 Qf5! and Black pins and wins the knight on f3. Notice that White can't defend it by playing 28.Rd3 because the queen would capture the rook.

(d) 21.Kf1 is what Byrne played, but after 21...Qd7! he resigned. Fischer gives two variations to explain why:

(d1) 22.Qf2 Qh3+ 23.Kg1 Re1+!! 24.Rxe1 Bxd4 and Black will soon play ...Qg2#.

(d2) 22.N4b5 Qh3+ 23.Kg1 Bh6 and the check on e3 will be deadly.

This is a very difficult exercise, so don't worry if you had trouble finding all these moves. In fact, Robert Byrne said after the game that until he resigned, two grandmasters who were explaining (in a separate room) the game to spectators thought that Byrne was winning!

Exercise 10: Black can (and did) play 1...a4! 2.Nc1 (2.Nxc6 bxc6 3.Nd4 is strongly met by 3...Qb6! As 4.Nxe6?? Re8 5.Bf5 Ne4! loses material for White) 2...a3! 3.b3 Qa5. Black quickly got a strong attack thanks to the weakness of the b2 square. Indeed, Black already threatens 4...Qc3 with checkmate to follow!

Exercise 11: White to play should play 1.a6! to get his knight to c6, e.g. 1...Nc5 2.axb7 Rxb7 3.Nc6! with a large advantage. Black to play should play 1...a6 to prevent this move and maintain the c6 square. Although this weakens the b6 square, the knight already covers this square, so that weakness is less important.

Exercise 12: 1.Qa6!! (not 1.Nb5? a5 and there is no easy way in) 1...dxc6 2.Nb5! cxb5 3.c6! and checkmate.

Exercise 13: The a7 and a8 squares are weak. In addition, Black's king is blocked in by the queen and rook. White can exploit this with 1.Qa7! when Black has no way to prevent 2.Qa8# next move!

Exercise 14: 1.h5! followed by 2.Nh4 is very strong. The knight will come to f5 or g6, and the queen can come to g4.

Exercise 15: 1...Nb7! Followed by 2...Nc5 is very strong. The knight will come to d3, and Black can press his advantage on the queenside by playing ...a5 and ...b4.

Answers to Exercises from Chapter 14

Exercise 1: After 2...Kb6, White wins by playing 3.Kf6 Kxa6 4.h4! (But be careful. Don't play 4.Kg7?? g5! and suddenly Black wins because he makes a queen first with his f-pawn!) 4...Kb6 5.Kg7 Kc6 6.Kxh7 Kd6 7.Kxg6 Ke6 (to protect the f-pawn) 8.h5 and White advances and promotes the h-pawn. For example: 8...Ke7 9.Kg7! followed by h6-h7-h8=Q.

Exercise 2: Black's bishop prevents White's king from supporting the advance of the pawns. The solution is for White to remove the bishop: 1.Rxd5! Rxd5 2.Kc4 wins. For example: 2...Rd8 3.d5 Ka4 4.c6 Ka5 5.Kc5 Ka6 6.c7 Rc8 7.Kc6! and White wins by pushing his d-pawn. Notice that 1.Rxg5? Ka4 is not nearly as effective, as this allows Black to bring his king back into play to draw.

Exercise 3: White has a large advantage, because Black's bishop is bad, and because White's king is better centralized. In particular, Black's a-pawn and h-pawn are both weak. White wins by playing 1.Ne4+ Ke6 2.Nf6 (2.Nc5+ Ke7 3.Nxd7 Kxd7 4.Kd5! also wins, because by taking the opposition White is able to capture Black's pawns no matter how Black moves the king, for example 4...Ke7 5.Kc6-b6xa6, or 4...Kc7 5.Ke6-f6-g7xh7. But notice that 4.Ke5? Ke7! or 4.Kc5? Kc7! are drawn.) 2...Kf5 3.Nxh7 and White will play 4.Nf6 and 5.h7 and 6.h8=Q to win.

Exercise 4: Capablanca played the correct move: 23.Ke2! The king is in no danger because of the reduced material, and so it should be centralized. Capablanca won a very nice endgame, thanks largely to his powerful king position.

Exercise 5: White to move wins by 1.c6! (Not 1.b6? Nd4 2.b7 Nc6 blockading the pawns, and allowing Black to capture them with his king.) 1...Nd4 (or 1...Ne5 2.c7) 2.c7 and promotes to a queen. Black to move draws by 1...Nd4! (or 1...Ne5! 2.c6 Nc4! 3.c7 Nb6) 2.b6 (2.c6 Nxb5 captures the b-pawn and stops the c-pawn) 2...Nc6! and now that the pawns are blockaded, Black can bring the king over to capture the pawns.

Exercise 6: White to move wins most easily with 1.Kd6! Ke8 (or 1...Kc8 2.Ke7) 2.Kc7 Ke7 3.d5 and pushes the pawn to make a queen. White can also win with either 1.Ke6 or 1.Kc6. For example: 1.Kc6 Kc8 (1...Ke8 2.Kc7 Ke7 3.d5; 1...Ke7 2.d5 Kd8 3.Kd6! takes the opposition and wins) 2.d5 Kd8 3.Kd6! Kc8 (or 3...Ke8 4.Kc7) 4.Ke7 followed by pushing the d-pawn to make a queen. Notice that 1.Ke5? Ke7! and 1.Kc5? Kc7! both draw. Black to move only draws by taking the opposition with 1...Kd7!; one sample variation goes 2.Ke5 Ke7! 3.d5 Kd7 4.d6 Kd8! 5.Ke6 Ke8! and draws.

Exercise 7: After 55...Rxh3 56.Rxh3 Kxh3 57.Kf2 followed by 58.Be5, White blockades both pawns. The best Black can hope to do is to win the bishop for both pawns, but then with only a bishop left he can't win. (You should analyze the position to convince yourself that there is no way for Black to break White's blockade.) Browne saw this, and realized it would be a draw, so he tried to avoid exchanging rooks by playing 55...Kf5??, but then after 56.Rh6! he was threatened with 57.Rf6#. Black can only avoid checkmate by giving up his rook, for example 56...Re1+ 57.Bxe1 or 56...Rxh3+ 57.Rxh3. Browne played 56...g4, but after 57.hxg4+ he resigned, because 58.Rxh1 would be next, leaving him with a lost position.

Exercise 8: Black has a large advantage for two reasons: Black's pawn structure is much better than White's (one pawn island against three), and White's pieces are passive whereas Black's pieces are active. White's passed pawn is useless, because it can't be advanced. In fact, Black is about to win the pawn by playing the knight to a5, when White won't be able to defend it again. Capablanca won the b-pawn, and then won the game.

Exercise 9: By making this sacrifice, Black gains several things: (1) His king becomes very powerful. (2) He gets rid of White's only active piece. (3) He gets a powerful protected passed pawn on e4, and the potential for connected passed pawns by advancing his kingside pawn majority. (4) White's queenside pawn majority is useless, because Black's two pawns hold White's three, and because Black's knight and king attack the pawns. (5) White's rook is terribly passive. Black won by advancing his kingside pawns. White had no hope of blockading the pawns because Black's king and knight supported them so powerfully.

Exercise 10: White can't draw because he can't get his king into the corner. After 57.Kd2 Kb3! 58.Kc1 Black wins by simply advancing his a-pawn. Notice that Black's bishop serves double duty along its diagonal: It stops White's king from crossing b1 to get to a1, and it controls the h7 square, thereby stopping the pawn from promoting.

Exercise 11: The trick that my opponent missed is 41...Bh4!. Normally it would be insane to put the bishop on a square where it could be captured, but here the idea is that if 42.gxh4 then 42...g3! 43.hxg3 (or else 43...gxh2) 43...h2 makes a queen. Meanwhile the threat after 41...Bh4! is 42...Bxg3! 43.hxg3 h2 and wins. White had to play 42.e4 Bxg3 43.Bg1, but after 43...Bxf4 I won the bishop by playing 44...g3 45.hxg3 Bxg3 and 46...h2, and then I soon won the game.

Exercise 12: Black's plan is to capture White's kingside pawns and then win on the queenside. It turns out that Black has to use his protected passed pawn as a decoy, but then he can win both of White's remaining queenside pawns, so he wins. The game might go as follows: 4.gxh5+ (4.g5 h4 wins because Black can blockade White's connected passed pawns, but White can't stop both of Black's passed pawns) 4...Kxh5 5.Kd3 Kg4 6.Ke4 b3! 7.Kd3 Kxf4 8.Kc3 Ke3 9.Kxb3 Kd3 10.Kb2 Kxc4 11.Kc2 (11.Ka3 Kc3 12.Ka2 Kb4 wins one a-pawn anyway) 11...Kb4 12.Kd3 Kb3 13.Kd2 Kxa4 14.Kc3 Kb5 and Black wins with the two pawns. The winning plan is to push the c-pawn, and then when White tries to make Black stalemate him, Black forces White's king to move by pushing his a-pawn. For example: 15.Kb3 c4+ 16.Kc3 Kc5 17.Kc2 Kb4 18.Kb2 c3+ 19.Kc2 Kc4 20.Kc1 Kb3 21.Kb1 c2+ 22.Kc1 a4! (This is the difference of having the extra pawn!) 23.Kd2 Kb2 and Black makes a queen and wins. (Notice again the key role played by the opposition!)

Exercise 13: White holds the draw if he blockades all of Black's pawns. With 1...Kc4, Black is trying to penetrate with his king to b1, so he can win White's bishop. White must stop the king from penetrating, so White plays 2.Ke3! Kb3 3.Kd2! (White must stop the king from getting to the d3 square, and then stop the king from getting to the c2 square.) If Black tries to advance the d-pawn, White makes sure his king covers the key d4 square when the Black king covers it: 1...Kc4 2.Ke3 d5 3.Bh8. If Black brings the king back to e6, White stops the king from penetrating to f5 and g4 (where it might threaten the g3 pawn) as follows: 1...Kc4 2.Ke3 Kd5 3.Bh8 Ke6 4.Kf4. Black has no way to break the blockade, so White draws.

Exercise 14: No, Black wins this position. The difference is that Black has another passed pawn (and White's passed pawn is securely blockaded). Black begins the same way as in the last position: 1...Kc4 2.Ke3 Kb3 3.Kd2, but now Black plays 3...h4! and White's king is overloaded. White must stop the h-pawn, but then he must let Black's king penetrate. The game could continue 4.Ke3 Kc2 5.Kf4 Kb1 6.Bh8 a1=Q 7.Bxa1 Kxa1 8.Kg4 d5 9.Kxh4 d4 10.Kg4 d3 11.Kf3 Kb1 followed by 12...Kc2, 13...d2 and 14...d1=Q.

Exercise 15: Black draws by 1...Kc6! (not 1...a4?? 2.bxa4+ Kxa4 3.Kc4 Kxa3 4.Kxc5 and White wins with Kd5-e5-xf5, or 1...Kb6?? 2.Kc4 Kc6 3.a4! Kd6 4.Kb5 and White wins a crucial tempo over the main line; for 1...Ka6 2.Kc4 Kb6, see the variation "a") 2.Kc4 and now there are two moves.

(a) 2...Kb6 3.Kd5! (3.a4 Kc6 gains the opposition and White cannot break through; 3.b4?? cxb4 4.axb4 a4! 5.b5 a3! 6.Kb3 Kxb5 7.Kxa3 Kc4 and Black wins!) 3...Kb5 4.Kd6! (4.Ke5 a4! 5.bxa4+ Kxa4 and because Black's c-pawn is so fast, White must play 6.Kd5 Kb5 7.a4+ Kb4 8.a5 c4 9.a6 c3 10.a7 c2 11.a8=Q c1=Q and White has winning chances, but the queen endgame is not clear. Queen endgames like this one are rarely clear!) 4...c4 (not 4...a4?? 5.bxa4+, or 4...Kb6?? 5.a4) 5.bxc4+ Kxc4 6.Ke5 Kb3 7.Kxf5 Kxa3 8.Kg5 Kb3 9.f5 a4 10.f6 a3 11.f7 a2 12.f8=Q a1=Q and because White wins Black's h-pawn, this endgame is known to be winning for White. White's plan is to try to exchange queens while advancing and promoting the pawn. Black's plan is to try to give perpetual check. These endgames have been analyzed by computers, and probably only computers can play them without making tons of mistakes!

(b) 2...Kd6! 3.Kb5 (again, 3.a4 Kc6 is drawn after 4.Kc3 Kd5 5.Kd3 Kd6! 6.Kc4 Kc6) 3...Kd5 4.Kxa5 Ke4 5.a4 (not 5.b4?? c4! 6.b5 [6.Ka4 c3 7.Kb3 Kd3] 6...c3 7.b6 c2 8.b7 c1=Q 9.b8=Q Qxa3+ and 10...Qb3+, winning for Black) 5...Kxf4 6.Kb6 Kg3 7.a5 f4 8.a6 f3 9.a7 f2 10.a8=Q f1=Q and Black is not worse.

It's amazing how complicated chess can be with just kings and pawns, isn't it?

Exercise 16: There are two key variations after 1...g4.

(a) The game continued 2.Nxg4 Kh3 3.Kb3 Kg2 4.Ne5 (4.Kxb4 Kxf3 5. Ne5+ Kg2 gives White no chances to win) 4...Kxh2 5.Kxb4 g5 6. Kc3 Kg3 7.Kd2 g4! 8.fxg4 (8.Nxg4 Kxf3) 8...f3 9. Nxf3 (9. g5?? f2; 9.Ke1 Kf4) 9...Kxg4 and the game was called a draw.

(b) 2.fxg4 g5!! 3.Kb3 f3 and White has two choices. He can capture on b4 and make a draw by stalemate. Or he can play 4.Ne4 Kxg4 5.Kxb4 when Black can force a draw with 5...Kh3.

Exercise 17: White wins with 1.Rb5! Black can make no headway without advancing the pawn, but if he advances the pawn, the king will not be able to defend it: 1...g3 2.Rb3! g2 3.Rg3 followed by capturing the pawn. So Black must wait, while White brings the king around to capture the pawn.

Exercise 18: No, the game is drawn. Black must be careful to use his king to shepherd the pawn forward, while keeping the White king away. The game could continue: 1.Kc6 g3 2.Kd5 (2.Ra4 g2 doesn't help White at all) 2...Kf4! (Not 2...g2?? 3.Rg8! or 2...Kg4? 3.Ke4! g2 4.Rg8+ Kh3 5.Kf3 and White catches the pawn) 3.Kd4 g2 4.Rg8 Kf3 5.Kd3 Kf2 6.Rf8+ Ke1 7.Rg8 Kf2 and White will have to give up the rook for the pawn.

Exercise 19: White should play 1.Rd7! taking the seventh rank. Black has a very difficult game after this move. If Black defends the pawn with 1...Rb8, then White keeps the rook on the seventh rank, and both Black's king and rook are very passive. But if Black keeps the rook active, for example, with 1...Re6 2.Rxb7 a6, then Black loses a pawn for nothing. White should probably win the endgame in either case.

Exercise 20: After 1.Rd7, Black should play 1...Re6! Now after 2.Rxb7 Ra6! Black counter-attacks White's a-pawn, and restores material equality with active play. White can try to keep some pressure by playing 2.b5!? Rb6 3.a4 a6! 4.Rd5 axb5 5.axb5, when White's rook is more active than Black's, but here Black has relatively active pieces, and is only slightly worse. Always, always, *always* look for ways to keep your rook active in rook endgames, whether you're attacking or defending!

Answers to Puzzles from Chapter 21

Puzzle 1: 1.c4 c5 2.Qa4 Qa5 3.Qc6! Qc3 4.Qxc8 checkmate. By the way, notice that 1.c3 doesn't work: 1...c6 2.Qa4 Qa5 3.Qxc6 Qxc3 and now 4.Qxc8+ is not checkmate because Black can play 4...Qxc8.

Puzzle 2: 1.Nf3 Nf6 2.Ne5 Nc6 3.Nxc6 dxc6 4.Nc3 Nd5 5.Nxd5 cxd5 is one way to reach the position. The trick is that Black's d-pawn has gotten to d5 by making two captures!

Puzzle 3: 1.f3 e5 (1...e6 also works) 2.Kf2 Qf6 3.Kg3 Qxf3+ 4.Kh4 Be7 does it.

Puzzle 4: There are, in fact, 92 solutions to the so-called Eight Queens Problem. Here is one of them.

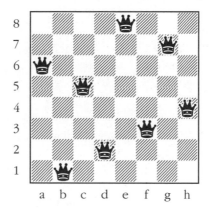

Do you notice how many of the queens sit a knight's hop apart from one another? This is because a knight's hop is the most efficient (closest together) way two queens can share space on the board without attacking each other.

The Eight Queens Problem is a favorite programming assignment in introductory computer science courses. In fact, you can observe a computer algorithm as it works out a solution by visiting the website www.iol.ie/~jmchugh/csc302/more/queens. This also illustrates a basic difference between how computers and humans play chess (see Chapter 19). The computer relies on brute-force calculation to place its queens. Most humans figure out that the queens should probably be a knight's hop away from each other, and use that insight to cut down the number of solutions to consider.

Puzzle 5: If it surprised you that there are ninety-two solutions to the Eight Queens Problem, you won't believe how many ways there are to solve the Knight's Tour! Here is one of them.

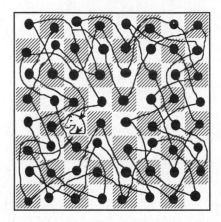

It turns out that the Knight's Tour has all sorts of implications that make it interesting to mathematicians. Many thesis papers have been devoted to examining an aspect of this problem. The website www.borderschess.org/KnightTour.htm is a nice entrée to the topic, if this is your cup of tea.

For all that, the mathematicians still can't even tell us for certain how many solutions exist. The number is enormous, however—perhaps 20 digits long. Of course, there are not as many solutions to the more restrictive re-entrant tours. Only about 122 *million* of those solutions exist.

Glossary

alpha beta pruning A mathematical technique that allows the computer to cut down on the number of moves it must consider when it calculates the possibilities in a chess position.

backward pawn Loosely speaking, a pawn in a pawn chain (in the strict sense of "pawn chain") that protects another pawn in the chain. Strictly speaking, such a pawn that cannot be protected by another pawn, and that has no chance of safely advancing in the near future.

bad bishop A bishop whose mobility is restricted by its own pawns.

black-squared bishop The bishop that moves along the black squares. Each player starts the game with one black-squared bishop.

capture The act of moving one of your pieces to a square occupied by one of your opponent's pieces, thereby removing your opponent's piece from the board. Once a piece is captured, it is gone for the rest of the game.

castling A special move of the king. Under certain circumstances, the king can move two squares to the left or right toward one of the rooks, and then place that rook on the square immediately next to it on the opposite side. See Chapter 3 for details on this move.

check Refers to when the king is attacked. When the opponent threatens to capture the king on his next move, the king is "in check."

checkmate Refers to when the king is attacked, and there is no way to prevent it from being captured in the next turn. Checkmate ends the game; the player whose king is checkmated loses, and the player who checkmates the other king wins.

clearance sacrifice To sacrifice a piece in order to vacate the square it was standing on.

closed Refers to when the center is filled with pawns that block one another. When the game is closed, there are few open files in the center.

deflection Refers to when one piece is forced to move away from a square where it is needed for some reason. When this happens, the piece is "deflected" from the square.

develop To move a piece (except for a pawn or the king) off its original square onto another square in the opening.

discovered check A check that results because one piece moves, and the piece that was behind it gives check.

double check Refers to when the king is put in check by two pieces at once.

draw The chess term for a tie. When the game is a draw, neither player wins.

en passant A French phrase that means "in passing." It refers to a special pawn capture, where one pawn captures another that has advanced two squares to land on the square immediately to its left or right. On the very next turn, and only on the very next turn, the pawn may capture the enemy pawn as though it had advanced only one square.

exchange As a verb, a synonym for *trade*. As a noun, it refers to the material advantage of a rook versus a minor pieces. To be "up the exchange," for example, is to have a rook in return for the opponent having a bishop or knight.

file A vertical row of squares. The chessboard has eight files.

fork When one piece attacks two or more of the opponent's pieces at the same time, it is called a fork.

forward pawn The most advanced pawn in a pawn chain (in the strict sense of "pawn chain").

friend or foe A convenient way to distinguish between one of your pieces and one of your opponent's pieces. Naturally, a friend is one of your pieces, and a foe is one of your opponent's pieces.

good bishop A bishop whose mobility is not restricted by its own pawns.

grandmaster The highest title one can earn as a chess player. It is awarded by FIDE, the world chess federation.

in between An "in between" move is one that can be played between two moves you thought had to be played consecutively. An "in between" move is often a check or a threat to capture some piece.

insufficient material Refers to when neither side can possibly put the other king into checkmate. When there is insufficient material, the game is automatically a draw.

luft German word for "air." To "make luft" is to advance one of the pawns in front of the castled king in order to relieve the weak back rank.

open Refers to when the center has no pawns that block one another. When the game is open, there are lots of open files in the center.

open file A file that is either completely or relatively cleared of pawns and pieces, so that if a rook were posted on the file it would control all or most of the squares along it.

opening repertoire The set of opening sequences one has prepared in advance in order to reach a middlegame one is comfortable playing.

opposite-colored bishops   Refers to when you have one bishop and your opponent has one bishop, and each bishop moves on different colored squares (for example, your bishop moves on the white squares and your opponent's bishop moves on the black squares).

outside passed pawn   A passed pawn that is away from most of the other pawns and that is not a center pawn.

passed pawn   A pawn that can no longer be captured or blocked by another pawn so long as no pawn changes files by capturing.

pawn chain   Loosely speaking, any group of pawns of the same color on squares that touch each other; strictly speaking, a group of pawns of the same color on squares that touch each other diagonally. In the strict sense, the pawn is a "chain" because each pawn protects another and is protected, except for the base (which is not protected by a pawn) and the forward pawn (which doesn't protect any pawn).

pawn duo   Two pawns of the same color on the same rank and on adjacent files.

pawn structure   Any configuration of pawns of the same color.

perpetual check   Refers to when one side can put the other king into check forever. If one player announces he will give perpetual check, and there is no way for the other player to escape from the checks, the game is a draw.

pin   When a piece is on a square between a friend and a foe, and moving the piece would open a line that exposes the friend to capture by the foe, that piece is "pinned" to its friend. A "pin" refers to such a situation.

protected passed pawn   A passed pawn that is protected by another pawn.

rank   A horizontal row of squares. The chessboard has eight ranks.

resign   To concede defeat.

sacrifice   To voluntarily give up material for some reason.

skewer   An attack where a long-range piece (rook, bishop or queen) threatens two or more opposing pieces along a single line.

smothered mate   Refers to when the knight gives check, and it's checkmate because the king is surrounded by its own pieces and so has nowhere to move.

stalemate   Refers to when the player whose turn it is to move has no legal move, and his king is not in check. When the position is stalemate for either player, the game is a draw.

tactic   A move or sequence of moves played to achieve some goal, such as the win of material or checkmate.

trade   To capture one of the opponent's pieces and allow the opponent to recapture some material in return. For example, to trade knights is to capture one of the opponent's knights and allow the opponent to capture a knight in return.

weak back rank   When your king is on the rank that is closest to you, and a check by the opponent's rook or queen along that rank would be checkmate, you have a weak back rank.

weak square   A square that one player can control but the other can't. It's not really correct to call a square "weak" unless it's also important, so whether a square is weak is a judgment call.

white-squared bishop   The bishop that moves along the white squares. Each player starts the game with one white-squared bishop.

X-ray   Refers to when a piece exerts control by "following" a foe along a diagonal, rank or file.

zugzwang   Name for the situation when it would be a disadvantage for either player to have it be his turn to move.

zwischenzug   German word that is sometimes used in chess parlance to mean "in between" move.

Index

G

H

I-J

N

X–Y–Z